AF361556

ITALIAN FUTURISM AND THE FIRST WORLD WAR

ITALIAN FUTURISM AND THE FIRST WORLD WAR

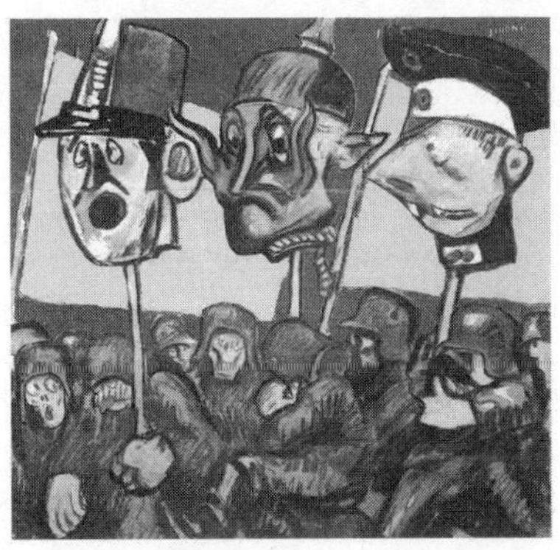

SELENA DALY

UNIVERSITY OF TORONTO PRESS
Toronto   Buffalo   London

ISBN 978-1-4426-4906-4

∞ Printed on acid-free, 100% post-consumer recycled paper with vegetable-based inks.

Toronto Italian Studies

___

Library and Archives Canada Cataloguing in Publication

Daly, Selena, author
Italian futurism and the First World War / Selena Daly.

(Toronto Italian studies)
Includes bibliographical references and index.
ISBN 978-1-4426-4906-4 (cloth)

1. Futurism (Literary movement)—Italy. 2. World War, 1914–1918—Literature and the war. 3. World War, 1914–1918—Italy. 4. Authors, Italian—20th century—Biography.
I. Title. II. Series: Toronto Italian studies

PQ4053.F87D34 2016   850.9'114   C2016-902988-3

___

University of Toronto Press acknowledges the financial assistance of the Irish Research Council "New Foundations" Scheme towards the publication of this book.

University of Toronto Press acknowledges the financial assistance to its publishing program of the Canada Council for the Arts and the Ontario Arts Council, an agency of the Government of Ontario.

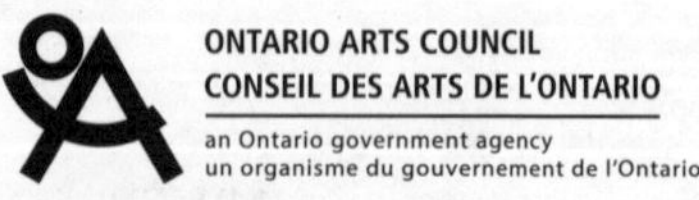

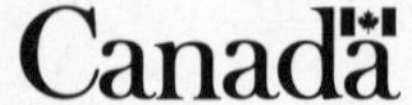

Contents

Figures

Acknowledgments

This book has been conceived, researched, and written in three different countries on two continents. Thus there are many people to whom thanks are due.

Heartfelt thanks to Professors Claudio Fogu and Jon Snyder of the Department of French and Italian at the University of California, Santa Barbara, for their support and the provision of such a conducive environment in which to bring the manuscript to completion.

The research was carried out in several archives in Italy and the United States, and I would like to thank all those whom I encountered for their help in the process. In particular, I am grateful to Maria Chiara Berni, director of the archive at the Fondazione Primo Conti in Fiesole; Camillo Zadra, director of the Museo Storico Italiano della Guerra in Rovereto; Caterina Tomasi of the Fondazione Museo Storico del Trentino in Trento; the staff of the Beinecke Rare Book and Manuscript Library at Yale University in Connecticut; Sarah Sherman of the Getty Research Institute in Los Angeles; and the Special Collections team in the Getty Research Institute, particularly Sally McKay, head of Special Collections Services, who facilitated access to Marinetti's very inaccessible *libroni*. I am especially indebted to Federico Zanoner, archivist at the Archivio del '900, Museo d'arte moderna e contemporanea di Trento e Rovereto in Rovereto, for his support, help, and friendship over the past number of years. *Grazie mille di tutto.*

This book would not have been possible without the financial assistance of a number of different institutions. I would like to thank the Irish Research Council, whose two-year postdoctoral fellowship (2012–14) at the School of History, University College Dublin, enabled me to work on the book with minimal interruption. The Irish Research Council also awarded me a New Foundations grant to defray the costs of publication. In 2015, I was a Fulbright Scholar at the University of California, Santa Barbara, and I would like to offer my sincere thanks to the Fulbright Commission of Ireland. Funding from the Royal Irish Academy and the Getty Foundation in Los Angeles allowed me to undertake archival research in Italy and California. I am most grateful to both institutions.

Richard Ratzlaff, my editor at University of Toronto Press, has been a joy to work with, offering prompt advice and encouragement throughout the process. I would also like to acknowledge the late Ron Schoeffel for his early support of this book. In addition, thanks are due to managing editor Anne Laughlin, copy editor Angela Wingfield, indexer Judy Dunlop, and everyone at University of Toronto Press.

I am grateful to the many colleagues with whom I have discussed aspects of this book at conferences and meetings around the world. In particular, I would like to thank Dr Günter Berghaus, who read the entire manuscript and provided invaluable insights and corrections. I would also like to thank the two anonymous reviewers of University of Toronto Press for their helpful comments and suggestions, and the reader of the Manuscript Review Committee for thorough consideration of the book. Any errors are, of course, my own.

I thank Dr David Kerr of the School of History at University College Dublin, my postdoctoral mentor as I worked on this project, for his belief in it and his constant encouragement. His feedback was always incisive and has ensured that this is a more polished book than it would otherwise have been. I have happy memories of our perambulatory meetings around Belfield in all weathers, discussing matters, both academic and non.

Thank you to my friends for offering both interest in the book and distraction from it. For their constant and unwavering support, whatever the physical distance, I thank my sister, Erika, and my parents, Anne and Leslie. And lastly, thanks to my husband, Andrea, for his enthusiasm and patience in learning about Futurism and for his ability to always make me laugh.

ITALIAN FUTURISM AND THE FIRST WORLD WAR

Introduction

The Pope, like a piece of stinking black manure, dangles precariously from an aeroplane high up over the Adriatic Sea. Below, Austrian soldiers stand with their cannons pointed at the Italian poet-aviator in the cockpit, horrified at the fate that has befallen their spiritual leader, who has been kidnapped from the Vatican. The pilot flies towards Trieste, followed by the masses of the Austrian army, while Italian troops take advantage of the distraction to march towards Vienna. The Austrian soldiers fire howitzers into the night sky in their desperate search for the pontiff. Soon the Italian pilot tires of the game and decides to cut the Pope's chains, letting him drop into the Adriatic to become the emperor of the fish.[1]

So concludes Filippo Tommaso Marinetti's *roman politique en vers libres* (political novel in free verse), *Le monoplan du pape* (The Pope's aeroplane, written in 1911 and published the following year) that described an imagined war between Italy and the Austro-Hungarian Empire. When the First World War broke out two years later, and Marinetti was campaigning for Italy to end its neutrality and join the conflict on the side of the Entente powers, he had the book translated into Italian and republished "scopo propaganda" (for propaganda purposes), and renamed it a "romanzo profetico in versi liberi" (prophetic novel in free verse).[2] He boasted that he had accurately predicted the war, and indeed some of the aspects of *Le monoplan du pape* did come to pass. The descriptions of the destruction that warfare wrought on the landscape, and the unfolding of battles in the mountains, where the Austrians held the highest peaks, reflected elements of the fighting on the Italian front during the Great War. The novel was ultimately, though, a fantasy of twentieth-century warfare, and the detached aerial perspective was far removed from the realities of trench combat in the Alps and on the

Carso plateau. This book sets out to examine the imaginings, realities, and myths of the experiences of Marinetti and the other Italian Futurists during the First World War.

War had been a central component of Futurism's imaginary since Marinetti, a prominent poet and journalist, had launched the movement in February 1909 by publishing the founding manifesto on the front page of *Le Figaro* in Paris. He famously declared that war was the "sola igiene del mondo" (sole hygiene of the world)[3] and believed that this "cleansing war" would initiate a revolution in Italy's stagnant cultural life by breaking all links with the past. In 1911 he spoke of the Futurists' "attesa febbrile della guerra" (feverish waiting for war),[4] and later that year he finally had his first taste of war when he travelled to Libya to work as a war correspondent after Italy's invasion of Tripoli.[5] In October 1912 Marinetti was once more close to the action, as a journalist covering the Battle of Adrianople, part of the First Balkan War between Bulgaria, Serbia, Greece, and the Ottoman Empire.[6] This experience inspired the experimental novel *Zang Tumb Tumb*, which demonstrated Marinetti's most important literary innovation, *parole in libertà* (words in freedom), which consisted of the liberation of the word from the constraints of syntax, grammar, and punctuation.[7]

As is evident from the plot of *Le monoplan du pape*, Marinetti never disguised his hostility towards Austria-Hungary. Even before the establishment of Futurism, he had been an enthusiastic irredentist, arguing for Italy's claim on the cities of Trento and Trieste and their surrounding areas, which were Italian speaking but part of the Austro-Hungarian Empire. He held the first *serata futurista* (Futurist evening) in Trieste in 1910, and he included pan-Italianism as one of the key tenets of the Futurist political manifestos of 1911 and 1913.[8] Thus, when the war broke out with Germany and Austria-Hungary on the one side and England, France, and Russia on the other, there could be no doubt as to where the allegiances of the Futurists lay. Although Italy had been defensively linked to Germany and Austria-Hungary through the Triple Alliance since 1882, because the latter was the aggressor against Serbia on this occasion, Italy was not obliged to enter the war alongside the Central powers. Thus, on 3 August 1914, Italy declared its neutrality in the conflict, a status it maintained for almost ten months. Having secured promises of Italian territorial gains in the secret Treaty of London of April 1915, on 24 May 1915 Italy entered the Great War on the side of the Entente.[9]

* * *

The years 1915–16 have always been considered a watershed in the development of Futurism. The painters Carlo Carrà[10] and Gino Severini[11] began to distance themselves from Marinetti's sphere of influence, and two other leading figures died in the war: Umberto Boccioni,[12] the movement's most famous painter, and Antonio Sant'Elia,[13] the founder of Futurist architecture. In the earliest art-historical studies of the movement, these events were deemed to have heralded the demise of Marinetti's avant-garde phenomenon and to mark the conclusion of Futurism's "heroic period" of 1909–15. In 1965 Maurizio Calvesi wrote that "il futurismo si spegne nel suo slancio migliore" (Futurism is extinguished at its best) as a result of Carrà's conversion to metaphysical painting and the deaths of Boccioni and Sant'Elia.[14] Marianne W. Martin's foundational study, *Futurist Art and Theory* (1968), also concluded in 1915, arguing that the deaths of Boccioni and Sant'Elia had brought the Futurists' "final joint venture to a tragically heroic end."[15]

Although today the idea that Futurism ended in 1915–16 is untenable, the presentation of the First World War as a dramatic conclusion to the movement's first phase has persisted in Futurist criticism.[16] The war has been blamed for "destroy[ing] their movement by realizing their ideals."[17] In a similar vein, Walter L. Adamson has stated that with the outbreak of the war "Futurism's original myth has, arguably, been realized. The war is no longer a mythic projection into the future but a present reality [...] If the founding myth has been realized, the rationale for the movement no longer exists."[18] Statements such as these have obscured the need for a thorough analysis of the experiences of the Futurists during the First World War and of the changes wrought on the movement during these years. The changes that the movement underwent during the war years are still often attributed solely to the changes in the group's protagonists.[19]

In this book I will argue that the change in Futurism did not come about as a reactive response to these events but occurred as part of a strategy adopted by Marinetti in 1915 to revitalize a movement whose avant-garde provocations were becoming less effective. He deliberately set out to broaden the movement's reach and used the Futurists' status as soldiers and war veterans to achieve this aim, at the expense of some of its literary and artistic ideology.

The fact that 1916 has been treated as the end point of the movement's first phase has bisected the Great War period, and thus the years 1914–18 have not been considered as a discrete unit worthy of comprehensive, independent study. Since the 1980s a number of studies of

Futurist political engagement have been produced, and the years of the Great War feature therein.[20] However, the period is treated in a cursory fashion, with the focus generally on the ten months of the Futurists' involvement in Italy's interventionist campaign (August 1914–May 1915) and on the foundation of the Partito Politico Futurista (Futurist Political Party) in late 1918, thus almost entirely overlooking Italy's years at war.

Prior to the war Marinetti had declared that the Futurists would approach any future conflict "danzando e cantando" (dancing and singing).[21] That the Futurists considered war as celebratory and to be enjoyed is a well-worn trope in Futurist scholarship. In 1968, in his introduction to Marinetti's writings, Luciano De Maria wrote that "per Marinetti la guerra, se da una parte è legge profonda della vita, dall'altra nella sua manifestazione concreta, è festa" (for Marinetti, if the war, on the one hand, is a profound law of life, on the other, in its concrete manifestation it is a celebration),[22] and two years later, Mario Isnenghi used the phrase *guerra-festa* (war-celebration) to describe Marinetti's war experience, as portrayed in his 1921 semi-fictional memoir *L'alcòva d'acciaio* (The steel alcove).[23] Günter Berghaus and Marja Härmänmaa have both focused on Marinetti's representation of war "as a ludic, festive occasion, a gymnastic exercise beneficial to the health of a population"[24] and as an improvised "artistic game."[25] There is a need, however, to clearly distinguish between post-war representations of the First World War (such as those in *L'alcòva d'acciaio*), which did often conform to a concept of guerra-festa, and contemporary portrayals of the unfolding war, both by Marinetti and by other Futurists in the pages of journals such as *L'Italia Futurista* (1916–18), which revealed views of the conflict that were realistic, brutal, and often lacking in any kind of celebratory tone. It is also necessary to look beyond Futurist representations of war and to examine to what extent guerra-festa can be said to actually reflect the experiences of Futurists who served in the Italian Army.

It has been important to place Futurist war-time activities within their historical context and to examine how they were received by the media and the general public at the time. Thus, the approach adopted in this book is primarily that of cultural history, rather than visual or literary analysis.[26] This approach is reflected in the dominant sources used in the following chapters. Newspaper reports are frequently used (particularly in chapters 1 and 3 and in the epilogue) in order to understand the way in which the perception of both Futurism and the Futurists changed as the war progressed. Futurist testimonies are often unreliable sources of evidence, and thus contemporary media sources are employed in order to counteract some of the myths that the Futurists propagated about their own pursuits during the war. This fact notwithstanding, when used carefully, Futurist sources are extremely valuable to a study of this kind, and the reader will find that extensive use has been made of letters written by Futurists (particularly in chapters 2 and 4), many of which are published here for the first time, or for the first time in English.[27] As John Horne has observed, letters provide a "means of exploring representations of combat and of mapping both public and private responses to the disparity between anticipated modes of battle and the realities of trench warfare."[28] These letters offer new perspectives, insights, and detail about Futurist combat experiences, cultural activities, and group dynamics during the war years.

A recurring theme throughout the book is the tension between the demands of Futurism as an artistic and literary movement and the need for Marinetti's new vision of Futurism to respond to the requirements of a society at war. Marinetti's fixation on his military service with the Italian Army caused friction within the Futurist ranks, so that during the war he was often pulled between the competing poles of art and politics. Readers will note that there is a strong focus on the Futurist leader and his actions in this book. The role of Marinetti in the development of Futurism is a topic that has fascinated scholars almost since the inception of Futurism as an academic field of study. While Enrico Crispolti has always argued against a "Marinetti-centric" approach to Futurism,[29] Calvesi and De Maria have insisted on his importance, with Calvesi even claiming that it was possible to state that "senza Marinetti il futurismo, anche in pittura, non sarebbe esistito" (without Marinetti, futurism, even in painting, would not have existed).[30] While it is true, as Adamson points out, that there was more multiplicity in the later war years and the post-war period than in the heroic phase,[31] my research for this book has repeatedly confirmed the central place of Marinetti in the movement and the extent to which it suffered when he was not fully engaged with it. Nonetheless, the book does also shed light on the attitudes and actions of many other key Futurists, including Boccioni, Fortunato Depero,[32] and Mario Carli.[33] In addition, it has been my intention, wherever possible, to broaden the focus to include lesser-known Futurists, whose names have been largely overlooked, for example Giuseppe Steiner[34] and Angelo Rognoni,[35] among many others.[36]

This book offers a reconstruction of the Futurist movement in the First World War period, encompassing Futurist activity from demonstrations to theatre, from military service to propaganda. The book adheres to a strict chronology of the war, beginning in August 1914 and ending in November 1918, which provides the scope to explore the neglected aspects of Futurism during the war years and to deliver new insights into the period. The book is divided into four chapters and progresses broadly in chronological order. Chapters 1 and 3 focus on Futurist activity on the home front in the cities and towns of Italy, while chapters 2 and 4 unfold at the front lines, in the military barracks, and in the trenches. Chapter 1 deals with the interventionist months (August 1914 to May 1915), while the second chapter focuses on Futurist military experiences. Chapter 3 focuses primarily on the period of May 1915 to January 1917, and the final chapter picks up in January 1917 and concludes in November 1918.

Chapter 1 examines the Futurists' role in the ten months of the interventionist crisis, which has often been identified as marking the full politicization of Marinetti's movement, and seeks to demonstrate how, on the contrary, Futurism remained a resolutely cultural and artistic phenomenon at this stage. The chapter provides a re-evaluation of the established narrative of this period, with the Futurists' self-presentation as decisive and influential actors in this period being challenged, and argues that they were far less important than they themselves, and previous scholarship, have claimed.

Chapter 2 considers Futurist combat and military experiences, broadening the horizon beyond the few short months of combat that Marinetti, Boccioni, and others saw with the Battaglione Lombardo di Volontari Ciclisti e Automobilisti (Lombard Battalion of Volunteer Cyclists and Motorists) in autumn 1915. Primarily using war-time letters, this chapter reconstructs the lived experiences of Futurist soldiers and officers, examining their daily lives, attitudes to military discipline, and relationships with other soldiers. This analysis uncovers a hitherto unacknowledged diversity and complexity of Futurist military experiences, while also revealing some of the similarities in the treatment that they received because of their status as avant-garde intellectuals. Particular attention is paid in this chapter to the role played by Futurism for these men, arguing that the social network and ideological framework provided by Marinetti's movement aided the Futurists in successfully coping with the physical and psychological difficulties of life on the front lines.

The third chapter of the book examines the cultural and literary activities of Futurism on the home front during the war years, addressing the impact of the war, and specifically of Marinetti's military service, on the development of the movement. The chapter asserts that the 1915–18 period is characterized by the phenomenon of *futurismo moderato* (moderate Futurism), a term coined by Marinetti in a manifesto of December 1915. This strategy entailed the adoption of a less antagonistic attitude towards the general public and a sacrifice of certain aspects of the Futurist avant-garde program in order to appeal to as broad a section of society as possible, particularly the soldier and officer populations.

The final chapter of the book shifts once more to the front lines and considers the Futurists' promotion of the war among soldiers and officers at the front in 1917 and 1918. The chapter considers both the Futurists' formal involvement with the Italian Army's propaganda service and also their non-state-sanctioned Futurist propaganda targeted at soldiers. The former consisted of Marinetti's activities as a propagandist and the publication of the Futurist trench newspaper *Il Montello*, while the latter comprised the founding of the journal *Roma Futurista* and of the Futurist Political Party, both in 1918. These activities continued the approach of futurismo moderato, modifying the Futurist message in order to appeal to these new military audiences. The epilogue considers the brief lifespan of the Futurist Political Party from November 1918 to January 1920, as Marinetti sought to balance the competing demands of artistic and political Futurism.

1 Futurist Non-belligerence: The Failure of Futurist Interventionism

The Myth of Futurist Interventionism

The interventionism crisis began with Italy's declaration of neutrality on 3 August 1914 and ended when Italy entered the war on the side of the Allies on 24 May 1915. This ten-month period is one of undeniable importance to Italy, not only in the context of the subsequent three years of war but also for the country's political development in the post-war years and under Fascism. The interventionist crisis established the framework for the intellectual and political divisions that would remain in place in Italy for the following thirty years.[1]

It was a time of intense politicization, in which it was imperative for every political party and cultural group to adopt a clear position with regard to Italy's neutrality or risk being pushed to the sidelines. Italy witnessed an unprecedented level of rhetorical violence during this period. As Antonio Gibelli has observed, "cominciava a farsi strada l'idea che contro i recalcitranti non vi fosse altro linguaggio che quello della violenza" (the idea started to take hold that the only language that could be used against the recalcitrants was the language of violence).[2] At first glance, it appears entirely logical that the Futurists were at the forefront of the interventionist campaign, as generations of Futurist scholars have claimed. After all, the movement was built on a rhetoric of violence and had been glorifying war since 1909. Thus, Futurist ideology was seemingly perfectly coherent with the increasingly belligerent mood of late 1914 and early 1915.

In reality, however, the Futurists, led by Marinetti, failed to mould themselves as a decisive force during the interventionist struggle, and they were consistently overshadowed by other figures, principally

Benito Mussolini, Gabriele D'Annunzio, and Cesare Battisti.[3] Futurist interventionism was far less influential and effective than both the Futurists themselves and previous Futurist scholarship have acknowledged. Scholars of Futurism have characterized the contribution of the Futurists as "indubitabilmente di rilievo" (of undoubtable significance).[4] Emilio Gentile has claimed that the Futurists "divennero uno dei fattori più attivi dell'interventismo" (became one of the most active factors in interventionism).[5] In actual fact, the Futurists were far from being protagonists of the interventionist struggle. Initially Marinetti was extremely reluctant to adopt a firm line in the face of Italy's declaration of neutrality in August 1914. During the entire ten-month campaign the Futurists organized only four independent demonstrations (two in Milan in September 1914, and two in Rome in December of the same year), none of which had any meaningful impact on the unfolding political and societal crisis.

The significance of the Futurists' activity during the interventionist crisis has consistently been overstated in Futurist scholarship. By enriching the interventionist campaign with effective slogans and images, their role has been defined as decisive.[6] Accounts of Futurist interventionism often focus on the performative aspect of their demonstrations in September and December 1914. This perceived theatricality consisted of Futurists burning Austrian flags and causing disturbances in public places, and of Francesco Cangiullo[7] wearing the red, white, and green "anti-neutralist" suit that had been designed by Giacomo Balla[8] earlier that year.[9] The difference between the style of action of the Futurists and that of other interventionist groups has been highlighted by Claudia Salaris, who wrote that "l'azione futurista in questo campo presenta connotazioni tutte proprie e molto vivaci, che nulla hanno in comune con l'interventismo retorico degli altri nazionalisti. [...] I futuristi portano nell'azione politica interventista il loro spirito bizzarro e quella mistica un po' sportiva e per nulla convenzionale del 'passo di corsa.'" (Futurist action in this area was characterized by a unique vibrancy that had nothing in common with the rhetorical interventionism of other nationalists. [...] The Futurists introduced into interventionist politics their bizarre spirit and the almost sportsmanlike and unconventional mystique of their 'parade.')[10]

A recently published anthology of Futurist writings declared that "the Futurists were the smallest [interventionist] group numerically, but the most inventive in creating a politics of theatricality that could resonate through the contemporary media."[11] While Futurist activity did receive some media attention, their exploits did not resonate in the way they would have hoped; rather, for the most part, the tone of press reports alternated between derision and light-hearted mockery. Although their methods were certainly inventive and creative on a couple of isolated occasions, this approach in no way characterized the entirety of their activity during the period.

From 1915 onwards, their politically engaged activity consisted of individual Futurists attending and taking part in interventionist demonstrations to campaign in favour of Italy's entry into the war. Their activities at these events were generic, principally because in most cases they were demonstrating alongside other pro-intervention groups in which the Futurists "were not the key figures nor the dominant force [...], and hence could not impose their style of combat on their allies."[12] Their rhetoric was similarly underwhelming; no national Futurist publication existed at this time in which they could air their views, and while they did issue some political manifestos, the impact of these was limited and found resonance primarily among groups of students. The alliance between Marinetti's followers, who had their base in Milan, and the Florentine Futurists of the magazine *Lacerba*, which had already been compromised in the spring of 1914 owing to differences over aesthetic matters, was further ruptured because of the two groups' differing approaches to the interventionist crisis. Giovanni Papini and Ardengo Soffici, the editors of *Lacerba*, were intensely critical of Marinetti's lack of action during this crucial period. Far from being a decisive force in the campaign waged against Italian neutrality, Futurism began to collapse during this period because it was *insufficiently* political and belligerent. Its members increasingly retreated into artistic activity and primarily engaged in the promotion of Futurism as a cultural, rather than a political, phenomenon. The importance of Futurist activity to the interventionist campaign has been consistently exaggerated, leading to a misrepresentation of their actions during the period, which I will address over the following pages.

Before proceeding, it is necessary to consider how and why this misleading account of Futurist interventionist activities has endured in scholarship for so long. In their discussion of myths in modern Italian political history, Ernesto Galli della Loggia and Luciano Cafagna have noted the "remarkable extent to which the standpoints of political actors and the interpretations of historians have overlapped."[13] This observation could equally be applied to the accounts of Futurist involvement in the interventionist crisis. The dominant narrative of Futurist interventionism is the version of events that was constructed by the Futurists themselves in various manifestos from as early as November 1915,[14] which aimed to establish the Futurists as the principal agitators in favour of Italian intervention into the First World War, as a way of shoring up support for the movement and proving its continued vitality and relevance. Scholarly discussion of the Futurist involvement in interventionism tends to align itself with this "mythic" construction of events, which accepts the Futurists' own propaganda that they were among the most active and influential forces pressing for Italy's entry into the war.[15] In discussions of Futurist interventionism, the reader is invariably provided with accounts of the same events (the September and December 1914 demonstrations) without any contextualizing framework, implicitly suggesting that these events were particularly significant and worthy of mention.[16] When attention is given to the impact of Futurist interventionist activities, they are generally described as "spettacolarmente efficaci" (spectacularly effective),[17] with no evidence offered to support such a claim.[18] In his discussion of the construction of myth and public memory, John Foot has observed that "with time, in some cases, the myth substitutes reality, becoming the guiding force around which a certain story is told and transmitted. In these cases, the myth has become history – it has taken on a life of its own, ready to be reproduced in various forms of literary and visual media."[19]

Such is the case of Futurist interventionism. Thus a consideration of the impact, efficacy, and influence of Futurist interventionist activities on the political landscape is long overdue.

Futurist Reaction to the Outbreak of the War

Much of the initial reaction of the Futurists to the outbreak of hostilities in Europe was what would have been expected of them. They were enthusiastic at the prospect of war but impatient at the Italian government's inaction. As early as 17 July 1914, even before the official declaration of hostilities on a European scale, Balla enthusiastically wrote to Marinetti: "siamo veramente MOVIMENTO FUTURISTA GUERRISMO tua lettera eccita di più nostro desiderio igiene guerra – […] Vogliamo Trieste Trento / Stati Uniti d'Europa" (we are really the WARLIKE FUTURIST MOVEMENT your letter arouses even more our desire for hygienic war – […] We want Trieste Trent / United States of Europe).[20]

Corrado Govoni's[21] reaction was similarly bellicose and impatient. Also writing to Marinetti in August 1914, he wondered:

> Ma perché non si mobilita?
>> Che cosa si aspetta?
>> Tutti sanno qui che l'Austria ammassa truppe e truppe ai confini. Aspettiamo forse di essere aggrediti dalla nostra fu alleata per la stupida soddisfazione di proclamare la nostra bestiale lealtà sulla faccia sghignazzante del mondo dei forti e dei coraggiosi?

> (Why don't we mobilize?
>> What are we waiting for?
>> Everyone here knows that Austria is amassing hordes of troops at the borders. Are we waiting perhaps to be attacked by our former ally just for the stupid satisfaction of being able to proclaim our beastly loyalty to the sneering faces of the world's strong and courageous?)[22]

Papini complained to Carlo Carrà around the same time, writing: "Cosa faccia questo porco governo non si capisce bene. Siamo tutti d'accordo che bisogna andare addosso all'Austria ma non si vede ancora quale sia la decisione di Roma. Speriamo bene." (It's not clear what this damn government is doing. We are all agreed that we must attack Austria but it is not yet clear what Rome's decision is. Let's hope for the best.)[23] Pro-France sympathies are also evident in Futurist letters of August 1914; for example, Soffici wrote that "l'idea che quella orribile merda tedesca può dilagare sulla Francia e insudiciarla e appestarla mi mette fuori di me, e vorrei in questo momento esser ministro per tirare questa vile (almeno finora) Italia dalla parte dei nostri maestri ed amici." (The idea that that horrible German shit can spread all over France and soil and infect her makes me mad, and right now I'd like to be a minister to pull this cowardly (at least for now) Italy onto the side of our masters and friends.)[24]

However, enthusiasm was not the only reaction that the war elicited from the Futurists, and the very different personalities, regional origins, and financial backgrounds of those associated with the movement had a strong impact on their responses to the outbreak of war. Fortunato Depero, an Austrian citizen stranded in Trentino at the start of hostilities, and Gino Severini who was in a financially precarious position, are two striking examples of reactions diverging from typically Futurist positions.

When war broke out between Austria and Serbia in July 1914, Depero found himself in his home town of Rovereto, in Italian-speaking Austria-Hungary, unable to depart for Italy. Almost immediately he tried to desert, and made his way to the Italian border, where he was arrested: "per fortuna non mi perquisirono perché in tasca tenevo una lettera dove dicevo che sarei scappato e avrei raggiunto la fidanzata" (luckily they didn't search me because in my pocket I had a letter that said I was planning to escape and join my fiancée).[25] At the end of July he was called to present himself for a military inspection for the Austrian army, and as an Italian-speaking irredentist he was terrified at the prospect of being called up to fight for the enemy. After three days of smoking and drinking excessively, and not eating, he presented himself at the inspection "più morto che vivo" (more dead than alive) and was declared unfit for war, which he considered a "miracolo – incredibile – avvenimento imprevisto e sbalordiente" (miracle – incredible – an unexpected and astounding event).[26] Nonetheless, Depero was unable to leave Austria for Rome and had to endure an anxious wait to see if he would be granted a passport.[27] He wrote to his fiancée, Rosetta Amadori, at the beginning of August of his plans for them to travel to America in 1915, stating that "il *futurismo* si dimentica – altre preoccupazioni politiche subentrarono" (we must forget about *futurism* – other political concerns have replaced it).[28] Although Depero would become an official member of the Futurist inner circle just a few months later,[29] in the face of war his Futurist convictions revealed themselves to be rather weak, with pragmatism winning out over aesthetic principles.

The response of Severini to the war was also pragmatic, as demonstrated by a comparison of two letters he sent in August 1914 – one to Marinetti on 6 August and one to Carrà on 10 August. From Montepulciano in Tuscany he wrote to Marinetti that "Mi dispiace moltissimo di essere così isolato dal mondo e nell'impossibilità di raggiungere i grandi centri dove si vive in questo momento la vita più febbrile e intensa. Consideratemi moralmente vicino a voi per le attitudini che gli avvenimenti suggeriranno o imporranno." (I'm really sorry to be so isolated from the world and that it is impossible for me to reach the large cities where one can experience this moment of such frenzied and intense life. Consider me morally close to all of you with regard to the attitudes that these events will suggest and impose.)[30]

It would appear, though, that Severini was merely telling Marinetti what he likely wanted to hear. In his letter to Carrà a few days later he expressed rather different sentiments, writing: "Figurati se muoio di rabbia di essere obbligato a vivere lontano da Parigi o da un centro importante" (You're crazy if you think I'm dying of rage at being obliged to live far away from Paris or another important centre).[31] In spite of this disingenuousness, his pro-war feelings were not in doubt, and he felt Italy should take advantage of the moment to attack Austria. Nonetheless, Severini's priorities remained artistic rather than political. He complained that the war meant he would not be paid by those who owed him money[32] and that the war "mi chiude ogni possibilità di aiuto dalla Francia" (closes off every possibility of my getting help from France).[33] He had also been planning to send a manifesto to Marinetti but decided that it was pointless because of "gli ultimi avvenimenti europei che ti assorbiranno e che ti faranno schizzar chi sa dove" (the most recent European events that will absorb you and make you run off who knows where).[34]

Severini was right to fear that the outbreak of war might cause Marinetti to depart from Italy. Upon the declaration of Italy's neutrality, Marinetti's first instinct was to find another way to actively participate in Europe's war. Thus, on 6 August, he attended a meeting in Milan, which had the aim of "formare un corpo di volontari per recarsi a combattere in favore della Francia" (forming a volunteer corps to travel to fight for France).[35] Trade unionists and members of the Socialist and Republican parties had been invited to attend, but the group was prevented from gathering by police because demonstrations threatening to Italy's neutrality had been banned by Prime Minister Antonio Salandra. Following "battibecchi vivacissimi" (very lively spats), the crowd moved to Piazza del Duomo, where Marinetti spoke to around a hundred people in favour of fighting for France, before police intervened and broke it up.[36] The demonstration was reported by the newspapers *Il Secolo* and *Il Piccolo Giornale d'Italia*. Among those who saw the articles was Giuseppe Ungaretti, who wrote to Marinetti on 9 August, stating: "Dai giornali abbiamo saputo che si organizza una legione di volontari in favore della Francia. In diversi abbiamo lavorato allo stesso scopo qui a Pisa e a Livorno. Siamo ai suoi ordini perché la cosa riesca." (We learned from the newspapers that a legion of pro-France volunteers is being organized. Several of us have worked towards the same goal here in Pisa and in Livorno. We are at your service so that the thing succeeds.)[37] However, according to Marinetti, the newspaper reports "hanno svisato completamente la dimostrazione da noi organizzata" (completely twisted the demonstration that we organized).[38] Marinetti was reported as having cried "Bisogna andare a Vienna e a Berlino!"

(We must go to Vienna and to Berlin!), but he repeatedly declared in letters to friends that this had not been the case.[39] He claimed that the demonstration "non aveva altro scopo che di far conoscere al governo l'opinione di Milano. Gridammo solamente *Viva la Francia!* E nessuno di noi gridò *a Vienna* o *a Berlino!*" (had the sole aim of making the government aware of the opinion of Milan. We only shouted *Long live France!* And none of us shouted *To Vienna* or *To Berlin!*).[40] His intention was to "far sapere al Governo che Milano è nettamente favorevole a una preparazione cauta ma energica contro l'Austria" (make the Government aware that Milan is definitely in favour of cautious but energetic preparation against Austria).[41] The press, it would appear, however, desired a less cautious and more provocative response from the Futurist leader than he was willing to provide.

An examination of the first six weeks of Italian neutrality shows that Marinetti, despite having preached for five years about the glories of war, was plagued by uncertainty over an appropriate Futurist response to the crisis. Following the ill-fated August demonstration Marinetti told Cangiullo, "Bisogna prepararsi in silenzio al *momento divino* in cui ci *sarà possibile batterci contro l'Austria*" (We have to prepare ourselves in silence for the *divine moment* in which it will *be possible for us to fight against Austria*).[42] Not having experienced success with a visible, public demonstration, he told Cangiullo that "bisogna fare una propaganda spicciola verbale […], dappertutto, approfittando ognuno della propria influenza" (we must employ a simple verbal style of propaganda […], everywhere, with everyone taking advantage of his own influence).[43] At this stage, far from wishing to violently erupt as a pro-interventionism force, as Futurist scholarship has claimed, Marinetti was advocating a program of quiet and individual propaganda. He wrote on 19 August that "in materia teatrale, tutto è sospeso, nulla si può prevedere, e perciò poco si prepara" (in the area of theatre, everything is postponed, it is impossible to predict anything, so we are preparing very little).[44] Marinetti's cautious attitude frustrated Papini, who complained of his lack of action, declaring in a letter, "Almeno un manifesto anti-tedesco, perdio!" (At least an anti-German manifesto, for God's sake!)[45] And to Marinetti in September he wrote, "Non credo che un manifesto – mandato privatamente agli indirizzi che possiedi – sarebbe sequestrato" (I don't think that a manifesto – sent privately to the addresses in your possession – could be confiscated).[46]

Certainly part of the reason for Marinetti's relative inaction was due to the fact that his preferred course of action would have been to depart for the war immediately, with either the Italian or the French Army. He wrote to Soffici that he was waiting "ansiosamente che l'Italia bon gré mal gré vi partecipi, cosa poco probabile, per offrirmi come volontario o come semplice proiettile da introdurre in un grandissimo cannone a lunghissima portata" (anxiously for Italy to participate, willingly or not, which is not very likely, to offer myself as a volunteer or as an ordinary bullet to be placed into an enormous, long-range cannon).[47] Throughout the month of August, Marinetti's departure for France remained a real possibility. He wrote to Luciano Folgore[48] on 25 August that "noi aspettiamo qui ansiosamente la possibilità di batterci. Se questa sfumerà, partirò per Parigi." (We are anxiously waiting here for the chance to fight. If that doesn't happen, I will leave for Paris.)[49] By the end of the month, however, Marinetti had decided not to depart for France, a move that Francesco Balilla Pratella[50] considered "logicissimo" (entirely logical).[51] Instead, on 27 August, Marinetti enrolled in the Lombard Battalion of Volunteer Cyclists and Motorists, along with Luigi Russolo,[52] and two days later purchased two bicycles for them in Milan.[53] Enrolling in the battalion was one of the few decisive actions taken by Marinetti during the initial weeks of Italian neutrality. As we will see, throughout the war there would be a tension between Marinetti's fervent desire to fight and his need to position Futurism as an effective cultural force in support of the war effort.

Demonstrations, Arrests, and Manifestos

Marinetti eventually shook himself out of his inertia, and the Futurist interventionist campaign began in earnest on 15 September 1914.[54] As the site of his first demonstration he chose the opening night of a production of Giacomo Puccini's opera *La Fanciulla del West* at the Dal Verme theatre in Milan. At the end of the first act Marinetti and Armando Mazza[55] unfurled Italian flags from one of the upper galleries, shouting "Down with Austria," while Umberto Boccioni ripped up an Austrian flag and threw the pieces into the auditorium below.[56] They were swiftly ejected from the theatre. Marinetti organized a second, follow-up demonstration the next night in the centre of Milan at the Galleria Vittorio Emanuele II, an upmarket shopping arcade. A group of ten Futurists, led by Marinetti and Boccioni, waved Italian flags and ordered a café orchestra to play the Italian national anthem. They overturned some tables and continued on through the arcade. When it seemed that they were not receiving enough attention, they pulled Austrian flags out of their underpants and burned them, shouting anti-Austrian slogans. The police intervened almost immediately. In reality, the incident was not so much a demonstration as a minor scuffle between the police and the Futurists who resisted arrest. The entire event lasted less than an hour. Marinetti, Boccioni, and Ugo Piatti,[57] along with seven others, were arrested and detained in San Vittore prison for six days.[58] The length of their incarceration was due to attempts by the authorities to charge them with the serious crime of having committed hostile acts towards a friendly, foreign state and for burning a foreign flag. Eventually the first charge was dropped, and although the second was upheld, it required intervention from the Austrian government in order to be pursued further in the courts.[59]

As Marinetti would repeat adamantly at every opportunity for the next decade and more, the Futurists were the first interventionists. These two demonstrations in Milan were indeed the first two pro-intervention and anti-Austrian events held during Italian neutality.[60] In his inimitable self-promoting style, Marinetti sought to exaggerate the importance of these two events, but the reality was rather more muted. The account of the prefect in Milan is certainly a more reliable source of the details about the Futurists' exploits. The official report stated that the two demonstrations were a fact that "per se stesso meriterebbe neppure di essere riferito" (in itself does not even deserve to be mentioned).[61] With regard to the Futurist interruption of Puccini's opera, the prefect recorded that the audience barely noticed what was happening. In order to highlight the irrelevance of the event, he also pointed out that even newspapers that would have been happy to report on an anti-Austrian demonstration barely mentioned the Futurists' actions. This was certainly a reference to the Milanese *Corriere della Sera*, which was staunchly pro-intervention.[62] Their review of the performance of *La Fanciulla del West* declared it to have been a complete success, and only at the end of the review did it devote one paragraph to the Futurists, briefly describing their actions, without identifying them by name, and it ended by saying that after they had been removed from the theatre, "il resto della serata trascorse in tranquillità perfetta" (the rest of the evening continued in perfect calm).[63] While it has been argued that the Futurists "chose the occasion of a prime event in the Italian cultural calendar to publicise their ideas,"[64] it has been almost entirely forgotten that the demonstration did not have the desired effect and in fact received very little publicity at all.

The demonstration on the following day in the arcade received a little more attention but still largely passed under the radar. *La Sera*, a

Milanese newspaper, reported that the crowd in the arcade "nella sua apatia tranquilla non arriva neppure ad indignarsi" (in their calm apathy cannot even manage to be indignant).[65] The day after the demonstration the *Corriere della Sera* published a short account of it on the local-news pages. According to that report, the onlookers followed the event with curiosity but did not take part: "L'intervento della polizia provocò tra i dimostranti qualche piccolo tafferuglio durante il quale fu rovesciato qualche tavolo e andò rotto qualche vetro" (the involvement of the police caused a few small brawls between the demonstrators, during which a couple of tables were overturned and some windows were broken).[66] For such a fervently interventionist newspaper as *Corriere della Sera* to report on the first anti-Austrian demonstration in such downbeat terms indicates both the true scale of the events and the newspaper's unwillingness to be aligned with the Futurists' antics. On 18 September the newspaper reported the names and occupations of the ten men arrested in the "small demonstration" and noted that some, including Marinetti, were also accused of violently resisting arrest, resulting in injuries to three policemen. According to the official police report, "[il] pubblico che affollava in quell'ora la galleria mostrò subito la più viva e sentita disapprovazione per quegli energumeni che non poterono vociare che brevissimi istanti perché intervennero subito funzionari ed agenti" (the public who filled the galleria at that time loudly expressed their disapproval of those brutes who could only shout out very briefly before the employees and police immediately intervened).[67] It is also important to highlight that, apart from the initial report on the demonstration in the Dal Verme theatre, all the articles discussing the demonstration in the arcade were published in the "Corriere Milanese" section of the *Corriere della Sera* newspaper, which was only printed in Milan.

Outside Milan these September demonstrations were either not reported at all or not taken seriously by the press. Small reports appeared in the Milan-based newspapers *Il Secolo* and *La Sera*,[68] and a slightly longer report in the Venetian newspaper *L'Adriatico*, which noted that the crowd in the arcade appeared, "piuttostoché ostile, indifferente" (rather than hostile, indifferent) to the Futurists.[69] In fact, it was the Futurists' imprisonment for six days that garnered more interest from the press around Italy than did the demonstration, mainly because the authorities' response seemed excessive considering the small scale of the Futurists' actions. On 22 September the Turin-based daily *La Stampa* mentioned the Futurists for the first time when it reported that they had been released from prison after their demonstration the previous week.[70] Other publications used the Futurists' incarceration as material for their humorous pieces. A short article in *Il Piccolo Giornale D'Italia* (Rome) appeared under the light-hearted headline "Marinetti in gattabuia" (Marinetti in the slammer), while *Il Successo* (Genoa) featured a cartoon of the Futurists in prison with the caption "Come tutto questo è passatista!" (This is all so passé!).[71]

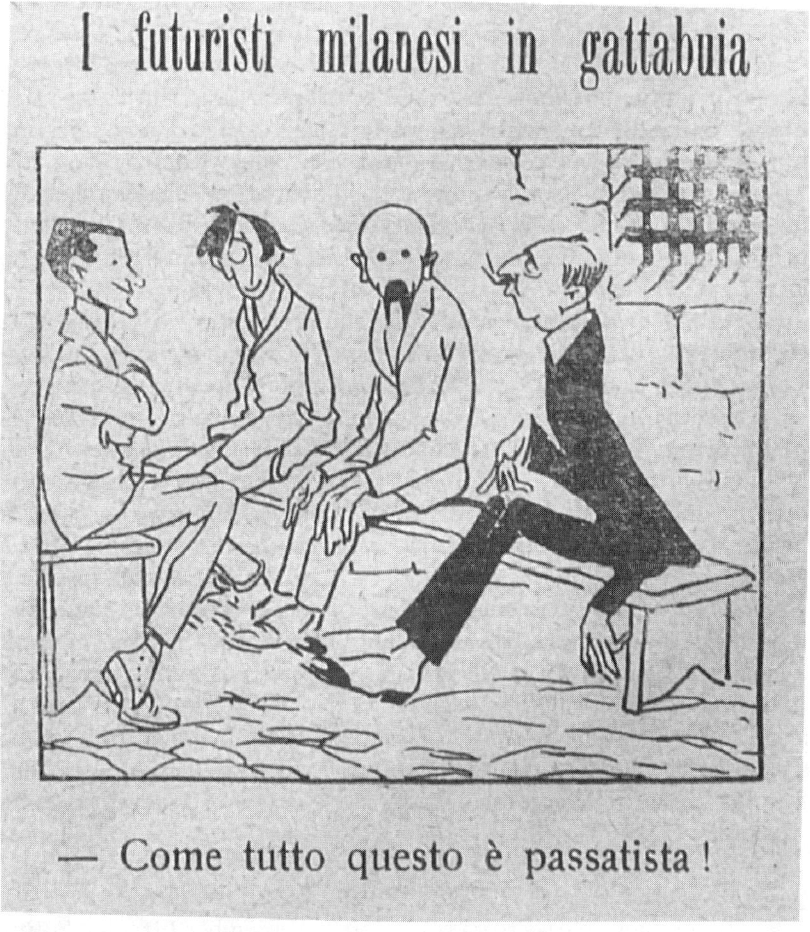

Figure 1.1. "I futuristi milanesi in gattabuia" (The Milanese Futurists in the slammer), *Il Successo* (Genoa), 27 September 1914. Courtesy of Biblioteca Nazionale Centrale di Roma.

The humorous newspaper *Il Centesimino* (Milan) went even further in its mockery of the Futurists. It featured the story on its front page with the sarcastic headline "L'Italia rompe la neutralità – Marinetti a capo delle sue truppe assalta la Galleria – Sconfitto dal gen. Cosentino – 8 Futuristi prigionieri di guerra – L'ingresso dei prigionieri a S. Vittore." (Italy breaks its neutrality – Marinetti leads his troops in an assault on the Galleria – Defeated by Gen. Cosentino – 8 Futurist prisoners of war – The prisoners enter San Vittore.)[72] In the article the newspaper included the "official report from the Futurists," which read "Pif – paf. Bum zum. Tiritic, abbasso l'Austria. Fuoco. Musica. Palle di sterco. Viva l'Italia. Patapumicic. Pom, pam, pum, pom, pem. Titnitiritir!" (Pif – paf. Bum zum. Tiritic, down with Austria. Fire. Music. Balls of manure. Long live Italy. Patapumicic. Pom, pam, pum, pom, pem. Titnitiritir!) It also featured indecipherable squiggles, which purported to be drawings of the episode by "Boccioni," with sarcastic captions such as "La Galleria presa in assalto, oppure un gatto in una cesta di carbone" (The Galleria under assault, or a cat in a basket of coal).[73]

According to Boccioni, in arresting the Futurists and imprisoning them for six days, the police "volevano premere su noi per il futurismo e per il terrore che si ripetessero le dimostrazioni" (wanted to put pressure on us because of Futurism and fear that the demonstrations would be repeated).[74] The police's tactics appeared to achieve the desired result. Following the release of the Futurists from prison, their interventionist activity stuttered to a halt once more. They had been planning a *serata* in Montecatini in late September that "sarà da noi trasformata in una violenta dimostrazione antineutrale" (will be transformed by us into a violent anti-neutralist demonstration).[75] However, Marinetti cancelled it because "la nostra condizione di libertà provvisoria vieta ai futuristi e al futurismo italiano qualsiasi manifestazione di Teatro e di Piazza" (the nature of our provisional release from prison forbids the Futurists and Italian Futurism from any demonstration in theatres or in public spaces),[76] a prohibition that Marinetti took very seriously, at least until December 1914.[77] He commented in early November that, although he was preparing many activities, he was "personalmente legato e imbavagliato dalla libertà provvisoria" (personally bound and gagged by [his] provisional release).[78]

Following their release from prison on 21 September 1914, the Futurists issued a visual manifesto entitled "Sintesi futurista della guerra" (Futurist synthesis of war), backdated to 20 September. Documentary evidence suggests that the manifesto was likely written a number of weeks later, towards the end of October.[79]

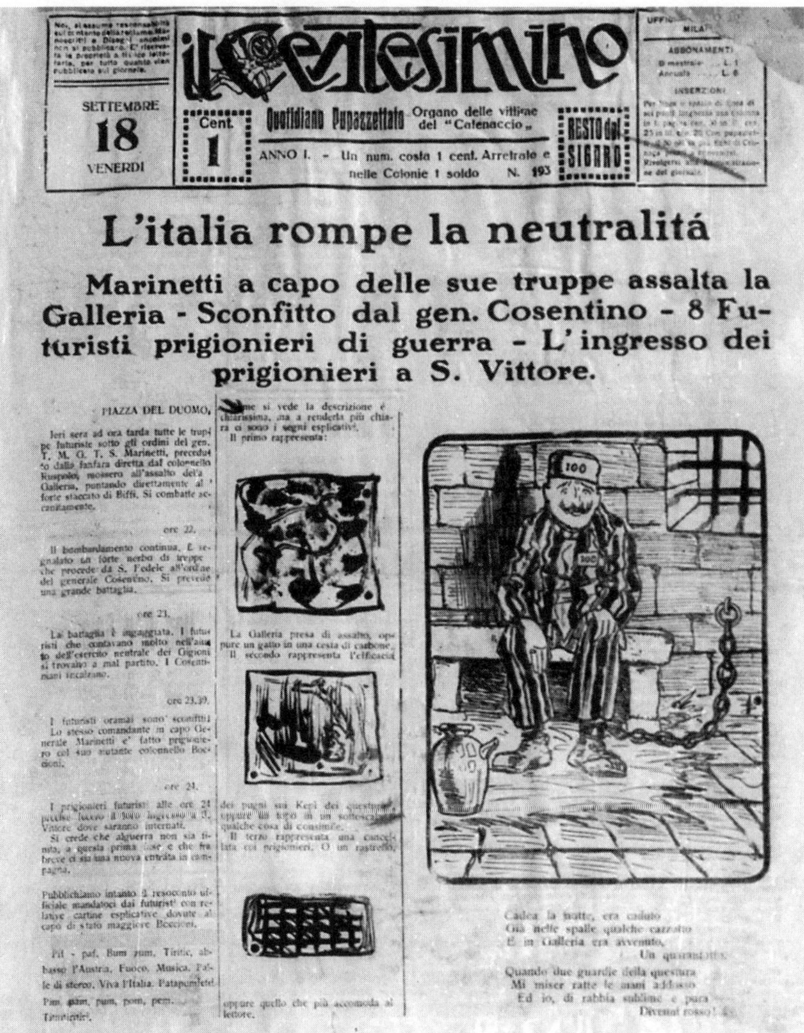

Figure 1.2. "L'Italia rompe la neutralità" (Italy breaks its neutrality), *Il Centesimino* (Milan), 18 September 1914. Detail of Libroni, 1904–44, Papers of Filippo Tommaso Marinetti and Benedetta Cappa Marinetti. Courtesy of Getty Research Institute, Los Angeles (accession no. 920092).

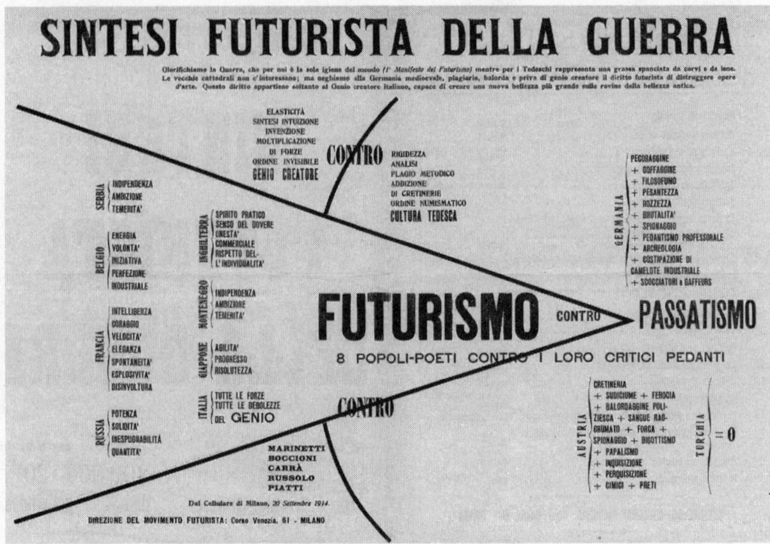

Figure 1.3. Filippo Tommaso Marinetti, Umberto Boccioni, Carlo Carrà, Luigi Russolo, and Ugo Piatti, *Sintesi futurista della guerra* (Futurist synthesis of the war), dated 20 September 1914. Courtesy of Archivio del '900, Museo d'arte moderna e contemporanea di Trento e Rovereto, Rovereto.

Backdating the manifesto allowed the Futurists to pretend that it had been written during their incarceration. It also tied the manifesto to the German destruction of Reims Cathedral that had occurred on that date, and the manifesto constituted the Futurists' response to that atrocity. The destruction of Reims Cathedral was a problematic event for the Futurists. In the first manifesto of 1909 Marinetti had declared his desire to destroy libraries, museums, and all repositories of passéist art. Now, at Louvain and Reims, their hated adversaries had put these Futurist ideas into practice, and the Futurists were compelled to respond. The manifesto reads: "Le vecchie cattedrali non c'interessano; ma neghiamo alla Germania medioevale, plagiaria, balorda e priva di genio creatore il diritto futurista di distruggere opere d'arte" (Old cathedrals don't interest us; but we deny medieval, plagiarist, foolish, talentless Germany the Futurist right to destroy works of art). The manifesto was widely distributed; it claimed a print run of 300,000 (although Marinetti estimated a much lower figure of 20,000) and was apparently well received by students.[80] Another famous piece of Futurist ephemera was

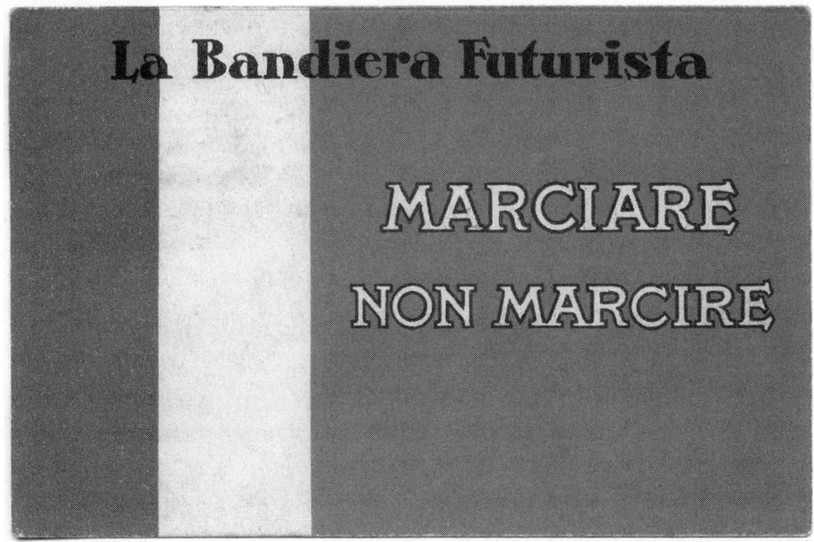

Figure 1.4. "La bandiera futurista" (The Futurist flag) postcard, 1914. Courtesy of Fondazione Echaurren Salaris, Rome.

also launched around the end of 1914: the postcard of "La bandiera futurista" (The Futurist flag), in which the Futurist red invaded the pacifist white and green, and which featured the slogan "Marciare non marcire" (March, don't rot).[81]

The next Futurist demonstrations took place in Rome in December 1914, when Marinetti and other Futurists invaded the lecture halls of professors whom they deemed to be neutralist and pro-German. On 10 December the Futurists went to La Sapienza University, entered a lecture hall, stood on the desk, broke a bottle of water and a glass, and shouted anti-Austrian slogans. They were quickly ejected from the building but returned the following day. The nature of the second demonstration was similar to that of the previous day, with the creative addition of Cangiullo unbuttoning his overcoat to unveil Balla's anti-neutralist suit.[82] Students, some of whom had been forewarned, began throwing punches, as well as apples, potatoes, and even an electric light bulb at their professor. These demonstrations in Rome received a slightly more positive response than did the Milanese events. However, considering that they were designed as Futurism's first interventionist act in the capital, planned to gain maximum exposure, Marinetti and his allies must have felt a great sense of disappointment at the relative lack of interest and attention they received.[83] Newspaper reports indicate that their actions were not taken particularly seriously but rather provided some colour to accounts of interventionist activities, with no mention being made of any of the speeches or ideas presented.[84] Even the Futurist Mario Carli was not convinced by Marinetti's style of interventionist action. He was supposed to go to La Sapienza University "per fare una chiassata" (to make a racket), but he pretended to have forgotten, because he deemed such actions to be *"minchionarie!"* (*damn pointless!*).[85] Although many Futurist scholars have praised the performative and eccentric aspect of Futurist interventionism, they have failed to acknowledge that the Futurists were a marginal and ineffective group, who had very limited influence over general public opinion with regard to the war.

There is also a notable tendency in Futurist criticism to claim that the interventionist crisis in Italy marked a decisive turn by the Futurists away from artistic pursuits in favour of political engagement. It has been argued that during this ten-month period "l'intero movimento futurista si trasforma in un'avanguardia antiaustriaca e interventista" (the entire Futurist movement transforms into an anti-Austrian and interventionist avant-garde)[86] and that "si verifica la piena politicizzazione del futurismo" (the complete politicization of Futurism occurs).[87] Although Marinetti's first instinct in August 1914 was to involve Futurism in the unfolding political crisis, this attitude by no means characterized the entire ten-month period of interventionism, and the complete politicization of Futurism certainly did not take place. Upon the outbreak of the war Marinetti suspended artistic activity but did not replace it with any meaningful political engagement. During the interventionist period Futurism still identified itself completely as an artistic movement and did not envisage a transformation into a political entity in any way. Indeed, in an interview of 11 December 1914, when Marinetti was asked whether he had plans to become involved in political life, he stated explicitly that "il nostro è certamente un movimento d'arte e di artisti. Non possiamo però fare astrazione dal fattore politico, che regola in gran parte l'attività umana" (ours is certainly a movement of art and artists. We cannot, however, abstract ourselves from political realities that, to a large extent, govern human activities).[88] Marinetti said that he expected soon to organize "una vera azione politica" (some real political action) by running for election, but that this would only happen after the war.[89] It is revealing that in the midst of the interventionist crisis Futurism steadfastly continued to identify itself as a cultural movement, with politics relegated to the stance of a mere sideshow.

Towards the end of 1914 Marinetti realized that Italy's neutrality was likely to last longer than he had anticipated. He called it a "terribile momento d'indecisione e sospensione" (terrible moment of indecision and waiting)[90] and wrote to Severini: "io non posso restare inerte. Facciamo continuamente delle dimostrazioni antiaustriache ma ciò non mi basta. L'inazione mi ucciderebbe. Bisogna dunque riprendere il lavoro artistico." (I cannot remain inert. We continually hold anti-Austrian demonstrations but this is not enough for me. Inaction would kill me. Thus, we must resume our artistic work.)[91] He expressed similar sentiments to Pratella, stating the need to restart artistic activities and assuring him of their victory "malgrado le immense e continue difficoltà" (despite the immense and continued difficulties).[92] Thus, in November 1914, he organized the launch of Folgore's collection of poetry *Ponti sull'Oceano* and sent Antonio Sant'Elia's architecture manifesto to the printers.[93] At the same time, he launched the manifesto "In quest'anno futurista (In this Futurist year)," his first of the interventionist period.

Although this manifesto would be followed shortly by the Rome demonstrations in December 1914, part of its purpose was to indicate the new direction soon to be adopted by Futurist interventionism, which leaned more towards artistic, rather than political, engagement. The manifesto, addressed to the students of Italy, declared that **"la guerra attuale è il più bel poema futurista apparso finora" (the current war is the most beautiful Futurist poem that has appeared up to now)**,[94] and Marinetti stated that the Futurists had always considered "la Guerra come unica ispirazione dell'arte, unica morale purificatrice, unico lievito della pasta umana" (war as the only inspiration for art, the only purifying morality, the only yeast of the human dough).[95] Declarations such as these can be interpreted as a justification for the turn that Futurism was about to take. By presenting the war as the motivating force behind their art, the Futurists could claim that any artistic activities were also legitimate political and interventionist endeavours. After the first forays into political engagement in September and December 1914, from 1915 onwards participation in interventionist demonstrations became an individual activity undertaken by members of the movement but not under the banner of Futurism. The attention of the movement as a whole was redirected towards art, which was rather disingenuously paraded as a significant element of the interventionist crisis. Balla began a series of paintings inspired by the interventionist demonstrations, while Boccioni published a collage, *Carica di cavalleria*, in a special issue of *La Grande Illustrazione*, in aid of the Belgian refugees. Carrà meanwhile collected a series of twelve war-themed drawings in *Guerrapittura*, published in a small print run in spring 1915.[96]

Becoming aware of the seriousness of the war and predicting its longevity, Marinetti realized the need for Futurism to become "l'espressione plastica di quest'ora futurista" (the plastic expression of this Futurist hour).[97] However, while he was keen to relaunch Futurism as an artistic movement, he also showed evidence of a changing view with regard to Futurist iconoclasm. In the first signs of a new, more inclusive version of Futurism, Marinetti wrote to Severini that he was aiming for an "espressione ampia, non limitata a un piccolo cerchio di intenditori; [...] una espressione talmente forte e sintetica da colpire l'immaginazione e l'occhio di tutti o quasi tutti i lettori intelligenti" (broad expression, not limited to a small circle of experts; [...] an expression so strong and synthetic that it will strike the imagination and the eyes of all, or almost all, intelligent readers).[98] Anticipating Severini's possible objections, he clarified that he did not view such an approach as a "prostituzione del dinamismo plastico" (prostitution of plastic dynamism), although he acknowledged that the proposed new direction for Futurism would probably result in "quadri o [...] schizzi meno astratti, un po' troppo realistici e in certo modo una specie di post-impressionismo avanzato [... e forse anche] un nuovo dinamismo plastico guerresco" (fewer abstract paintings or [...] sketches, [work that is] a bit more realistic or in a certain way a kind of advanced post-impressionism [... and maybe also] a new warlike plastic dynamism).[99] Such a weakening of Futurism's dogmatic avant-garde approach would become more evident following Italy's entry into the war and as the conflict progressed, with Marinetti showing himself to be increasingly willing to compromise Futurism's key messages in order to keep the movement alive and relevant.

The Futurists scaled back their political activities in 1915, and although they continued to engage in interventionist events, none had the Futurist flavour that had been present in the September and December 1914 demonstrations. It is difficult to trace, with any accuracy, the extent of their interventionist activity in 1915, as the Futurists were keen to exaggerate both the frequency of their participation in demonstrations and their own importance at them. Cangiullo recalled in his memoir that the interventionist demonstrations in Rome were "sempre più frequenti ed imponenti" (ever more frequent and more impressive) and that he, Marinetti, and Depero were arrested "immancabilmente ogni domenica" (without fail every Sunday).[100] Similarly, in a letter of spring 1915, Marinetti boasted to Severini in Paris that "noi organizziamo e conduciamo ogni sera delle dimostrazioni interventiste" (we organize and lead interventionist demonstrations every evening).[101] Pratella claimed that Marinetti had been at the head of over thirty interventionist demonstrations in December 1914, although the veracity of this claim is hard to prove.[102]

In early 1915 Marinetti continued to exercise some caution regarding the organization of Futurist events, owing to fears of censorship by the authorities. One strategy was to recast artistic events as political ones, as part of the effort to exaggerate their role in the interventionist struggle. In January 1915 he held a small talk and poetry reading in Rome on the poet Folgore, whose *Ponti sull'Oceano* had just been published. Marinetti had specified to Folgore that "la Conferenza-Declamazione sarà naturalmente privata e per inviti. Così non potrà essere vietata" (the talk-reading will of course be private and for invited guests. That way it cannot be prohibited).[103] The one traceable newspaper mention reported that Marinetti had given a speech on the war and that "il pubblico acclamò senza darsi alle sfrenate dimostrazioni che generalmente accolgono le geniali manifestazioni futuriste" (the audience applauded without yielding to the wild demonstrations that usually greet the brilliant Futurist events).[104] The phraseology of this caption and its recasting of the poetic event in a political light suggest that the photograph and caption were provided by Marinetti himself. Similarly, in his chronicle of Futurist war-related activites, Pratella wrote that in December 1914 Marinetti "tiene discorsi interventisti a Faenza e Ravenna" (makes interventionist speeches in Faenza and Ravenna).[105] In reality, neither of these events was political in nature. The event in Ravenna, in fact held on 7 January 1915, was a performance of Futurist theatre.[106] The event in Faenza was also wholly artistic; it took place on 6 January, and Marinetti travelled there with Folgore and Paolo Buzzi[107] to open a small Futurist exhibition by the local painter Giovanni (Giannetto) Malmerendi,[108] rather than for interventionist purposes.[109]

Marinetti's speech at the opening of the exhibition appears to have been well received: the critic from *Il Socialista* criticized the audiences of bigger cities who had caused commotion at previous Futurist gatherings, advising instead that one should "ascoltare, sentire colla serenità ed obbiettività di chi vuol imparare e giudicare" (listen calmly and objectively in order to be able to learn and judge),[110] and wrote that Marinetti entertained the crowd. The only point at which, apparently, the audience was not appreciative of Marinetti was when he began to praise the war, with the *Socialista* critic stating that "se non ci fosse stata, la conferenza appariva più bella" (if that had not happened, the conference would have been better).[111] Similarly *Il Piccolo* noted that Marinetti's affirmations of war as the "hygiene of the world" provoked "battibecchi e interruzioni" (quarrels and interruptions), and sarcastically wrote that, before finishing, "Marinetti formulò il voto simpaticissimo che presto ci si andasse tutti quanti a fare ammazzare, il quale voto gli fu dal numeroso uditorio gentilmente contraccambiato con rinunzia in suo favore ai diritti di precedenza" (Marinetti made the charming vow that we should all soon go off and get killed which was kindly reciprocated by the large audience, but they insisted that Marinetti should go first).[112]

Smaller episodes of Futurist interventionist action, in which Marinetti was not directly involved, were also recorded around the country. In December 1914, at the Teatro Turreno in Perugia, some young Futurists (Alberto Presenzini-Mattòli[113] and Giannino Mariotti[114]) interrupted a neutralist demonstration and were subsequently beaten and injured.[115] In the same month Cangiullo was arrested along with two other Futurists for distributing Futurist postcards and shouting anti-Austrian slogans.[116] In Piazza, Sicily, another group of aspiring young Futurists had six thousand flyers printed with slogans such as "W il Futurismo" (Long Live Futurism) and "W la Guerra" (Long Live the War), which they distributed among a crowd of soldiers and onlookers, to a mixed response.[117]

In addition, some Futurists took part in the many interventionist demonstrations happening in the capital. The Futurists were noticed at these demonstrations, and their presence drew comment, but they had little influence on how the events unfolded.[118] At only one event did Marinetti even succeed in separating himself from the crowd to deliver a speech. It is clear also, both from Futurist testimony and from newspaper reports, that on more than one occasion they provoked the authorities into arresting them in order to provide evidence of their fervently interventionist and active stance. Cangiullo described one instance when he and Depero thought themselves to have been "definitivamente sconfitti" (definitively defeated) in not having been arrested at a demonstration, until they remembered the Futurist propagandist postcards in their pockets. They promptly attached them to their hats and distributed them to others in the crowd. They did so "per sparare l'ultima cartuccia, ormai ogni cosa noi facessimo era un buco nell'acqua" (as a last resort, by this stage anything we did was in vain), and they continued their Futurist propaganda sadly, their voices hoarse, until they were finally arrested, which made them rejoice.[119]

In February 1915 Marinetti, Cangiullo, Balla, Guglielmo Jannelli,[120] and Auro d'Alba[121] were all arrested at a demonstration organized to coincide with the reopening of the Italian parliament at Montecitorio.[122] Although the demonstration, and Marinetti's participation in it, was reported in national newspapers, the Futurists' role in the event was very marginal.[123] The demonstration was begun by some Nationalists who joined hundreds of people outside Montecitorio, shouting "Long live Italy! Long live the Army! Long live the war!" The police pushed the demonstrators back, out of Piazza Montecitorio, at which they began booing and shouting. One newspaper noted that Marinetti and his comrades were "i più accesi" (the most passionate) in the confrontation with the carabinieri, which resulted in their arrest, much to the delight of the Futurists.[124] More than a month later the Futurists took part in another demonstration, this time in Milan on 31 March, in Piazza del Duomo. The demonstration was led by Mussolini, and Peppino Garibaldi (a grandson of the famous general and who had volunteered to fight in France) featured prominently. According to Futurist rhetoric, Marinetti was also present and influential, although *La Stampa* merely reported that towards the end of the rally "il futurista Marinetti pronuncia brevi parole" (the Futurist Marinetti spoke briefly).[125] The account of Cangiullo is characteristically more excitable: he described onlookers throwing anything that was German or Austrian from their balcony windows, while Marinetti and Mussolini addressed the crowd from the steps of the duomo until two o'clock in the morning.[126] In Milan in April, along with a group of pro-intervention Socialists, Marinetti interrupted a performance of a Viennese operetta at the Teatro Fossati, demanding that Italian music be performed instead. According to a report in *Il Secolo*, "il pubblico in buona parte si associò ai dimostranti" (a good part of the audience joined in with the demonstrators), and once the curtain had dropped, "l'orchestra a richiesta dei dimostranti suonò gli inni patriottici, tra grande entusiasmo" (at the request of the demonstrators the orchestra played patriotic songs to great enthusiasm).[127] One of the demonstrators was injured in the commotion, and the actors in the company tried to justify themselves, stating that they had believed the operetta to be Italian. While condemning the violence of the Futurist demonstrators, *Il Secolo* highlighted the greed of directors who made minor changes to operas and plays in order to trick their audiences into believing that they were not watching Austrian works.

The final pro-intervention demonstration in which the Futurists were involved occurred in Rome on 11 April. Marinetti's involvement was slightly more high profile than it had been at previous events, and he succeeding in being arrested along with Mussolini. There had been an interventionist demonstration planned for Piazza della Pilotta, and a neutralist one planned for Piazza dell'Esedra, both in the centre of the city. Both demonstrations were banned by the authorities, and Piazza della Pilotta was blocked to prevent protesters gathering. Mussolini, who had arrived in the capital by train that morning, was to be the star of the demonstration. After being turned away from Piazza della Pilotta, the interventionists made their way towards the Trevi Fountain, where Marinetti and Mussolini together led the procession.[128] Newspaper estimates reported a crowd of between four and five thousand people, though it was noted that most of these were curious onlookers, rather than committed interventionists, who joined in on the spur of the moment. At the Trevi Fountain Mussolini was prevented from delivering his prepared speech, so they moved on again to nearby Piazza Barberini, where he was arrested when he once more attempted to address the crowd. The interventionists damaged a shop window, causing the police to intervene and charge on horseback into the piazza. In a letter to Folgore, Marinetti recounted the "feroce cazzottatura" (terrible punch-up), describing how he was alone but wanted to make the police retreat. He received "una legnata alla testa e un colpo di chiave sotto l'occhio. Un po' di sangue ma nulla di grave" (a blow to the head with a stick, and was hit under my eye with a key. A bit of blood but nothing serious).[129] Marinetti's involvement was described in less heroic terms by one newspaper: "si era, come al solito, cacciato in mezzo ai dimostranti, e fu arrestato poco dopo il Mussolini in piazza Barberini." (as usual, he threw himself into the middle of the demonstrators and was arrested shortly after Mussolini in Piazza Barberini.)[130] This comment makes clear that Marinetti was well known for provoking the authorities, and it is also telling that he was arrested soon after Mussolini. As Mussolini was one of the most well-known agitators for intervention on a national scale, Marinetti attempted to attach himself to Mussolini's name and persona in order to attract maximum attention at the demonstration.

In reports of the April demonstration at Piazza Trevi, however, neither Marinetti nor Mussolini was taken very seriously. A humorous rhyming poem entitled "Comizi, dimostrazioni, arresti," which appeared in *Due Soldi*, poked fun at the supposed closeness between Marinetti and Mussolini.[131] The first verses went as follows:

Marinetti e Mussolini
Si trovarono vicini
Cosicchè furono stretti
Mussolini e Marinetti.

Presi insieme poveretti
Marilini e Mussoletti
da tre quattro questurini
Mulinetti e Mussilini.

Li chiamarono cretini
Malimetti e Mulissini
loro disser: – Sozzi! inetti!
Malignini e Mumoletti.

(Marinetti and Mussolini
found themselves beside each other
And so they became close
Mussolini and Marinetti.

Arrested together, poor things
Marilini and Mussoletti
by three or four policemen
Mulinetti and Mussilini.

They called them cretins
Malimetti and Mulissini
they said: – Filth! Incompetents!
Malignini and Mumoletti.)

A cartoon in *L'Illustrazione Italiana* featured Mussolini confiding to Marinetti that "A proposito di intervento non abbiamo potuto constatare che quello delle guardie e dei carabinieri" (when it comes to

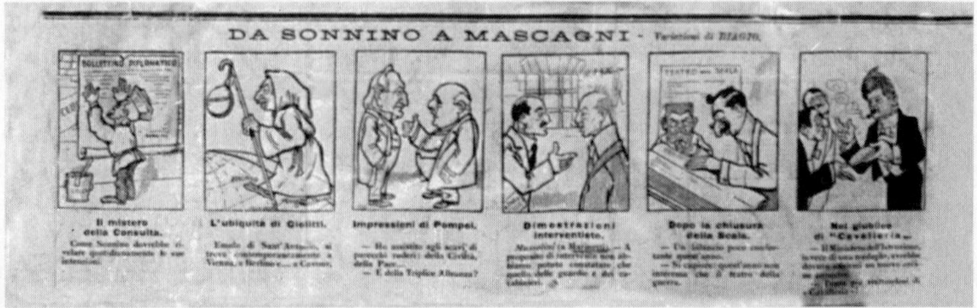

Figure 1.5 (fourth panel from left). Biagio, "Dimostrazioni interventiste" (Interventionist demonstrations), *L'Illustrazione Italiana* (Milan), 19 April 1915. Detail of Libroni, 1904–44, Papers of Filippo Tommaso Marinetti and Benedetta Cappa Marinetti. Courtesy of Getty Research Institute, Los Angeles (accession no. 920092).

intervention, we haven't been able to establish any except that of the police and the carabinieri).[132]

A more serious assessment of Marinetti and Mussolini appeared in *La Voce del Popolo* of Brescia, which worried that the fate of Italy might rest in the hands of a reported alcoholic (Mussolini) and a comedian (Marinetti).[133]

Although they were certainly acquainted with one another at this time, there is a divide between critics about the extent of the interaction and the nature of the relationship between the two men during the interventionist period. On the one hand, it has frequently been reported that "nelle giornate della furia interventista si stringono amicizie e alleanze decisive per il futuro del movimento" (in the days of interventionist fervour they established a friendship and an alliance that would be decisive for the future of the movement).[134] Berghaus stated that they "staged together an anti-neutralist demonstration" in Rome and that they "organized an interventionist demonstration in Milan,"[135] but I have found no evidence of Marinetti having been involved in the organization of these events. On the other hand, scholars such as Crispolti and De Felice have argued that contact between the two men at this stage did not go beyond "il ritrovarsi su un medesimo fronte, e tuttavia con motivazioni diverse" (finding themselves at the same battle lines, and nevertheless with different motivations),[136] and that "veri e propri rapporti non ve ne erano stati e si era trattato di un generico incontro tra interventisti impegnati nelle stesse agitazioni" (there was no real relationship and that there was only a generic meeting between interventionists engaged in the same struggle).[137]

The latter views are, I believe, correct. The contention that Mussolini and Marinetti were closely linked during the interventionist crisis was, once again, largely a myth constructed by Marinetti both in 1915 and in the post-war years. Mussolini was a well-known figure, and his desertion of socialism in order to campaign for Italy's entry into the war had earned him notoriety all over the peninsula.[138] Thus it was in Marinetti's interest to appropriate Mussolini as a Futurist in order to mask the reality regarding just how minor a role Futurism itself was playing in the interventionist campaign. The first example of this happened in December 1914, in the interview that appeared in *Il Piccolo Giornale d'Italia*. Marinetti declared that "in questo momento le nostre file ingrossano sempre più e la nostra legione è oramai divenuta, per effetto ed la conseguenza del tragico conflitto, un folto numeroso esercito, che si allarga e si stende per tutta l'Europa" (at the moment our ranks continue to grow and our legion, as an effect and a consequence of the tragic conflict, has become a great numerous army, which stretches and extends all over Europe).[139] At this, the interviewer – who was fellow Futurist Jannelli – expressed surprise, asking, "Tanto cresciuto è il numero degli aderenti e degli iscritti alle vostre idee?" (Has the number of adherents and subscribers to your ideas really grown that much?) If a fellow Futurist was taken aback, it is fair to conclude that Marinetti was exaggerating for the sake of appearances. Marinetti replied evasively (which is also revealing), "Qualunque aumento di cifre, non basterebbe a dimostrare con esattezza e precisione, la larga penetrazione compiuta nella coscienza del pubblico dalle nostre idee" (Whatever the increase in numbers, it would not be enough to accurately and precisely show the huge penetration of our ideas into the public consciousness).[140] The example Marinetti used to demonstrate the widespread penetration of Futurist ideas was Mussolini, to which Jannelli replied "con viva meraviglia" (with profound surprise), "Mussolini si è convertito al futurismo?" (Has Mussolini converted to Futurism?) Marinetti replied that Mussolini's "azione recente, il suo atteggiamento, la sua ribellione dimostrano chiaramente la sua coscienza di futurista" (recent actions, his attitude and his rebellion clearly demonstrate his Futurist consciousness),[141] which was Marinetti's enigmatic way of admitting that Mussolini had not, in fact, joined the Futurist ranks. Mussolini never joined the movement, and clearly explained in a letter to Cangiullo in February 1915 the position of his newspaper *Il Popolo d'Italia* vis-à-vis Futurism:

Noi abbiamo delle simpatie per il futurismo e ne comprendiamo l'intima essenza e la magnifica forza, ma perché dobbiamo trasportare sul nostro giornale una polemica che noi non abbiamo provocato e che non ci può interessare se non in linea accademica. Tutti i nostri sforzi tendono oggi all'azione e a null'altro – non escludiamo che domani si possa anche fare del futurismo e della polemica, su di esso, ma oggi abbiamo di più urgenti cose da fare. ·

(We sympathize with Futurism and we understand its intimate essence and its magnificent strength, but why should we introduce into our newspaper a debate that we did not start and that holds only an academic interest for us. All of our efforts are directed these days towards action and nothing else – we do not exclude the possibility that in the future we may also address Futurism and the debates surrounding it, but today we have more urgent things to do.)[142]

The Split with *Lacerba*

Since January 1913 Soffici and Papini had been editing the avant-garde journal *Lacerba* in Florence, which oscillated between sympathy and hostility towards Marinetti and Futurism. From March 1913 to March 1914 the Milanese and Florentine groups were closely aligned. *Lacerba* became a de facto Futurist journal, which published numerous manifestos by Marinetti, Russolo, Boccioni, and others. However, in the spring of 1914 Papini launched an attack on Boccioni, resulting in a series of combative articles.[143] This polemic was an indication of the many differences that still existed between the two groups regarding the conception of art, the organization of the movement, and attitudes towards newcomers and towards industrial modernity.[144] Thus, when the war broke out in August 1914, the relationship between Marinetti in Milan and Papini and Soffici in Florence was already strained.[145]

One of Marinetti's very first actions following the outbreak of hostilities in August 1914 was to write to Soffici, expressing his views on the war and offering advice on the editorial direction of the journal. Marinetti counselled that "la prossima *Lacerba* dovrebbe essere ferocemente antiaustriaca" (the next issue of *Lacerba* should be fiercely anti-Austrian) and that Soffici should "far sì che questo numero non contenga assolutamente nulla di italianamente scettico e pessimista" (ensure that this issue contains absolutely nothing in the Italian style of scepticism or pessimism).[146] In the following days Marinetti travelled to Florence "per trasformare, con Soffici, *Lacerba* in giornale politico coll'unico scopo di preparare l'atmosfera italiana alla guerra contro l'Austria" (to transform *Lacerba*, with Soffici, into a political newspaper, whose sole aim is to prepare the Italian atmosphere for war against Austria).[147] While Marinetti undoubtedly considered his intervention to have been both decisive and successful, the views of Papini and Soffici were rather different. On 7 August Papini had received a letter from his publisher, Attilio Vallecchi, suggesting that *Lacerba* should devote itself to issues of the moment.[148] This was likely to have been far more influential on *Lacerba*'s subsequent turn than Marinetti's words would be, although Marinetti's supporters were not of the same opinion.[149] Soffici made it clear in a letter to Aldo Palazzeschi that the political turn of *Lacerba* was down to Papini alone,[150] and a few months later he wrote to Marinetti, explicitly declaring that "*Lacerba* diventa per mia volontà e per quella degli amici di Firenze, *politica*" (*Lacerba* has become, because of my wishes and those of my Florentine friends, *political*).[151]

Although the editors of *Lacerba* had resented Marinetti's interference before the war,[152] following Italy's declaration of neutrality Papini and Soffici realized that by uniting their efforts with those of the Milanese Futurists they were likely to achieve more than they would by acting separately. Thus, they were open to a collaboration. Papini wrote to Carrà:

> Io e Soffici riteniamo che il momento è decisivo per tutta la nostra civiltà e che bisogna lasciar l'arte per un po' di tempo. Bisogna montare un po' questi vigliacchi italiani. Ci s'aspettava che i futuristi, i quali hanno colto tutte le occasioni per affermarsi, avrebbero fatto qualche manifestazione in questi momenti. Perché tanto silenzio? Cosa fa Marinetti? [...] Noi facciamo la parte nostra in "Lacerba" e si sarebbe disposti anche a far di più se appoggiati.

> (Soffici and I firmly believe that this is the decisive moment for our entire society and that we must leave art to one side for a little while. We must excite these Italian cowards. We expected the Futurists, who have taken advantage of every opportunity to prove themselves, would have held some demonstrations at this time. Why all this silence? What is Marinetti doing? [...] We are doing our part in "Lacerba" and we would be willing to do more if we were supported.)[153]

Papini and Soffici were not the only ones who expressed surprise at Marinetti's initial inaction in support of intervention. At the end of August 1914 Pratella, a loyal follower of Marinetti, praised *Lacerba* as "una rivista politica, cosa assolutamente indispensabile" (an absolutely essential political journal) but stated that even this was insufficient. He complained that "avanguardia vuol dire *sul culmine*, nello *spazio* e nel *tempo* oggi il *Futurismo* non è *sul culmine*" (avant-garde means being *at the summit*; today, in *space* and *time, Futurism* is not *at the summit*).[154]

A comparison of the interventionist actions of the *marinettiani* and the *lacerbiani* in the first six weeks of the war shows a stark contrast. The date of 15 September marked the Futurists' first demonstration in Milan (not counting the pro-France demonstration Marinetti attended in August that had been organized in conjunction with other groups). By the same date *Lacerba* had already published three issues discussing the benefits of intervention and the dangers of neutrality. Claudia Salaris has called *Lacerba* "la palestra interventista per molti intellettuali" (the interventionist gymnasium for many intellectuals),[155] and the Milanese Futurists had no official publication that could compete with *Lacerba*, which had a print run of at least eight thousand per issue.[156] In the 1 September issue of *Lacerba*, Marinetti's final contribution appeared: an extract from *Le monoplan du pape*, entitled "Il massacro dei sottomarini" (The massacre of the submarines), which had been first published in French in 1912. The poem featured a plane bombing submarines, and Marinetti stated that it was "oggi un esplicito programma italiano" (today an explicit program for Italy).[157] Soffici, however, was contemptuous of this as a contribution towards the interventionist cause, telling Carrà, "I versi di Marinetti scritti 3 anni fa non credo siano un atto tale da contare e da portare un elemento efficace nella lotta che tutti dobbiamo intraprendere contro la vigliaccheria del nostro governo e del nostro popolo" (I don't think a poem written by Marinetti 3 years ago is an act worthy of being taken into account as an effective element of the struggle that we must all undertake against the cowardice of our government and our fellow Italians).[158]

The acrimonious final rupture between Marinetti and the *lacerbiani* occurred in December 1914, heralded by Papini and Soffici's article "Lacerba, il Futurismo e Lacerba." The split was due to both artistic differences, which had been brewing since February 1914, and political ones, which had developed since the outbreak of the war. Analysing the letters exchanged in the months preceding this final parting of ways, it is not artistic matters but political ones that dominate the discussions. This suggests that Papini and Soffici would have been willing to overlook their artistic differences with Marinetti if he had engaged more actively with them regarding intervention. However, their frustration about Marinetti's handling of the intervention crisis made them realize that a definitive split was their only option. The interaction between the *lacerbiani* and the *marinettiani* also reveals just how ineffective were the interventionist activities of Marinetti and his followers, especially in the first months of the war, and belies the statement made by Caroline Tisdall and Angelo Bozzolla that "to some extent, the Interventionist period [...] masked the growing lack of cohesion within the group."[159]

On 17 September Papini wrote to Marinetti from Tuscany, criticizing the latter's lack of interventionist action:

Quest'inazione futurista fa cattivissima impressione. A Roma socialisti e nazionalisti hanno saputo fare un po' di rumore – e voi altri a Milano niente. E a Milano avrebbe più importanza che a Roma. Il futurismo ha nel suo programma l'adorazione della guerra e ora che la guerra c'è – e quale guerra! – tu stai zitto e fermo? [...] Bada che si tratta di un momento importantissimo e se il F. è assente c'è il caso che la guerra ammazzi anche lui [...] Ma dovresti far qualcosa a Milano – altrimenti non sei più Marinetti!

(This Futurist inaction is making a terrible impression. In Rome the Socialists and the Nationalists have managed to make a bit of noise – and nothing from you lot in Milan. And it would be more important in Milan than in Rome. Part of Futurism's program is the worship of war and now that we have a war – and what a war! – you stay silent and immobile? [...] Be aware that this is an incredibly important moment and if F[uturism] is absent, there is a chance that the war will kill it as well [...] But you should do something in Milan – otherwise you're not Marinetti any more!)[160]

Papini's exhortation to Marinetti to organize something in Milan was written after the small demonstrations on 15 and 16 September. Papini's ignorance of the Milanese events of the preceding days highlights just how little resonance they had had in other locations around Italy. Even following the diffusion of news about the arrests of Marinetti and Boccioni, the *lacerbiani* were dismissive of the impact of these actions, and of Marinetti's management of Futurism since the outbreak of the war. In a letter to Carrà at the end of September, Soffici expressed his disappointment and the sense of isolation felt by *Lacerba* during the previous two months, writing that the *marinettiani* "non hanno fatto altro che emmerder il mondo con fanfare guerresche non hanno avuto il fegato di mandarci una riga che esprimesse una *idea*. Il futurismo si è eclissato dal mondo dell'intelligenza quando avrebbe dovuto mostrarsi" (have not done anything except piss everyone off with warlike pomp; they have not had the guts to send us even a line that expresses an *idea*. Futurism has disappeared from the intelligentsia when it should be making itself heard).[161] He was particularly dismissive of "le dimostrazioncelle con le bandierine" (the little demonstrations with those little flags), which irritated him more than silence, and he said that they proved "la nostra *fondamentale* divergenza dallo spirito futurista" (our *fundamental* divergence from the Futurist spirit).[162] Soffici continued that Marinetti had submitted "uno scrittarello" (a little scribble) to be published in *Lacerba*, which was "un semplice stelloncino di cronaca per render conto al mondo che Marinetti Boccioni e gli altri sono stati arrestati (per insulti alle guardie!) trattenuti e rilasciati!" (a simple short news article to tell the world that Marinetti and Boccioni and the others were arrested (for insulting the police!), detained and released!). He stated:

> Dovremmo pubblicar tutti questi fatterelli in prima pagina, quando si tratta dei destini del mondo, della nostra civiltà? Semplicemente Marinetti e gli altri mirano alla réclame. Ma questa volta non l'avranno. *Lo stelloncino non uscirà*. E non uscirà più nulla che abbia lo scopo di lusingare la *vanità* dei nostri compagni. È un pezzo che in *Lacerba* non si è fatto che il servizio della vanità. Ogni scritto che vi è apparso (scritti futuristi ufficiali) aveva una mira di *plastonnage* personale […] Ora basta.

> (Are we supposed to publish all these unimportant events on the front page, when the future of the world and our society is at stake? Marinetti and the others just want publicity. But they won't get it this time. *The short article will not be published*. And we will not publish anything else that aims to flatter the vanity of our associates. For a while now, *Lacerba* has only been in the service of vanity. Every piece of writing (official Futurist writing) that has appeared in it aimed at personal *plastonnage* […] Now, enough.)[163]

It is not known how Marinetti reacted to this refusal to publish his account of the demonstrations and his arrest, but there are indications from those loyal to Marinetti (viz. Pratella and Balla) that by October 1914 the relationship was very much on its last legs.[164] The article "Lacerba, il Futurismo e Lacerba" of 1 December 1914 by Soffici and Papini discussed their differences with their Milanese counterparts, and for the first time they publicly referenced Marinetti's response to the interventionist crisis as one of the motivating factors behind their split. They stated that since *Lacerba* had transformed into a "giornale di propaganda politica in senso nettamente futurista, non abbiamo più sentito, e, diciamolo, con molto stupore, i nostri amici [futuristi] accanto a noi" (newspaper of political propaganda in the strictly Futurist sense, we have not heard a word – and we say this with the greatest surprise – from our [Futurist] friends nearby).[165] In commenting on this article, Salaris wrote that Papini and Soffici accused Marinetti "di essersi impegnato poco nell'interventismo (!)" (of having engaged little with interventionism (!) [*sic*]).[166] And yet, in spite of Salaris's incredulity, objectively the Futurists had achieved very little during the first four months of Italy's neutrality. In the words of Soffici and Papini: "Le manifestazioni futuriste in favore dell'intervento italiano, che avevamo invocato ed aspettavamo numerose e impetuose, sono state rade e insignificanti e hanno culminato nella piccola dimostrazione milanese e nell'inopportuno e vacuo manifesto di Balla sul vestito neutrale." (The Futurist demonstrations in favour of Italian intervention, that we had prayed for and that we expected to be numerous and violent, were rare and insignificant and culminated in a small demonstration in Milan and in the inappropriate and vacuous manifesto by Balla on the neutral suit.)[167]

Lacerba's criticisms of Futurist interventionism continued into 1915. In the famous "Futurismo vs Marinettismo" article of February 1915, while there were no explicit references to the war, the editors' objections to Futurist interventionism were made clear in the list of characteristic tendencies of the two strands.[168] The characteristics "raffinatezza [e] rarità" (subtlety [and] rarity) were associated with "Futurismo" (*Lacerba*) while "goliardismo propagandista [...e] pubblicolatria, neofitismo" (juvenile, crowd-pleasing propaganda, [...] amateurism) were associated with the *marinettiani*.[169] *Lacerba*'s most blatant condemnation of the actions of Futurism during Italy's neutrality came in April 1915, in a sarcastic article by Soffici, under the pseudonym Elettrone Rotativi (Rotating Electron), entitled "Adampetonismo" (Adam's Fart Doctrine), a parody of the Milanese Futurists. In the section "Politics" he wrote that "in tempo di pace l'Adampetonismo proclama entusiasticamente la guerra. In tempo di guerra, manifesta" (in times of peace Adampetonism enthusiastically professes war. In times of war, it demonstrates), instead of employing other means to put pressure on the government, such as writing, unpicking the arguments of pacifists, persuading intelligent people, or influencing public opinion.[170] He identified six steps that constituted the "adampetonista's" mode of interventionism:

1   Bruciare una bandierina di foglio gialla e nera.
2   Camminare in una via centrale con nella destra il vessillo nazionale e nella sinistra una bandierina di foglio gialla e nera capovolta.
3   Scrivere su cartoline tricolori con per motto un calembour d'occasione.
4   Urlare nei tumulti abbasso! e evviva!
5   Uscire con un vestito tricolore.
6   Schiaffeggiare una guardia per farsi portare in questura per tre ore.

(1   Burning a little paper yellow-and-black flag.
2   Walking in a city-centre road with a national flag in your right hand and a little upside-down yellow-and-black flag in your left.
3   Writing puns on tricolour postcards.
4   Shouting "down with!" and "long live!" during demonstrations.
5   Wearing a tricolour suit.
6   Hitting a guard so you can get taken to prison for three hours.)[171]

He accused Marinetti of desiring only popularity, notoriety, and flattery and of considering "la réclame come la principale conferma del proprio genio" (publicity as the principal confirmation of his genius).[172]

Futurism in Crisis: Periodicals and Theatre

In the wake of the split with *Lacerba*, Marinetti and Milanese Futurism were left in a vulnerable position as they had no official Futurist newspaper in which to air their views on a national scale. Marinetti wrote to Folgore in November 1914 that "probabilmente faremo presto un *giornale nostro, veramente futurista*" (probably we will soon launch *our own, truly Futurist, newspaper*).[173] No such publication was forthcoming, however, and again, in March 1915, Marinetti wrote that he had the intention of "fondare prestissimo un giornale assolutamente futurista" (establishing very soon an absolutely Futurist newspaper).[174] Plans for this journal were apparently underway, but then, in May, Remo Chiti[175] wrote to Carli that "il giornale non uscirà più per la data fissata; prima perchè Marinetti è ammalato; poi perchè si aspettano le decisioni italiane" (the newspaper won't come out on the arranged date; first because Marinetti is ill; and second because we are waiting for the Italian decisions).[176] Such a Futurist magazine, run under the explicit direction of Marinetti and his closest associates, did not come about until June 1916, when *L'Italia Futurista* was launched. In the absence of a dedicated Futurist newspaper, edited by the movement's protagonists, Marinetti attempted to intervene in a number of other publications, all with unsuccessful results. He first set his sights on *Gli Avvenimenti*, an illustrated weekly newspaper launched on 3 January 1915 and edited by Umberto Notari, with whom Marinetti had had close contact for many years. It had a fiercely pro-intervention stance and an initial print run of fifty thousand copies. Marinetti, ever the opportunist, saw a chance to hijack Notari's publication and to mould it as the Futurist mouthpiece, and indeed the newspaper's third issue, published on 17 January 1915, featured a full page devoted to Futurism. In a letter to Folgore, Marinetti was keen to point out that Futurism would continue to feature prominently, writing, "Altre pagine simili seguiranno, sulle Parole in libertà, gli'Intonarumori, il Dinamismo plastico, con fotografie di tutti i principali futuristi e con quadri e clichés di parole in libertà" (other similar pages will follow, on Words in freedom, the Noise-tuner machines, Plastic dynamism, with photographs of all the leading Futurists and with paintings and pictures of words in freedom).[177] Given that this letter was written at the height of the interventionist crisis, Futurism's lack of political engagement can be seen in the intention to use their visibility in *Gli Avvenimenti* for the promotion of Futurism's artistic, rather than political, messages. On 21 February 1915 extracts of Futurist "synthetic theatre" were published, and although Pratella, Boccioni, and Mario Sironi[178] were regular contributors to *Gli Avvenimenti*, they were not identified as Futurists, and their contributions did not reference Futurism.[179] The Futurists were associated exclusively with the artistic and literary concerns in the pages of the newspaper, with no mentions being made of their interventionist pursuits. Marinetti and his associates, it would appear, desired more space in the newspaper in which to air their ideas, which prompted the following response from the editor, Notari:

Il giornale nostro non è un giornale di battaglia; non un giornale di tecnica letteraria; se così fosse, le cose vostre, piene di spirito e di originalità passerebbero tutte. *Gli Avvenimenti* è, semplicemente, un giornale, per cui mi occorrono, tenuto calcolo anche della sua giovinezza, mille precauzioni e cento ipocrisie.

Ho spiegato a Marinetti queste e altre ragioni per cui al futurismo e ai futuristi non posso consacrare tutto quello spazio che essi desiderano e meritano. Un po' alla volta.

Credo, anzi, che questa tattica sarà più giovevole al movimento, di qualsiasi altra.

(Our newspaper is not a polemical newspaper; or a newspaper about literary technique; if it were, your contributions, full of wit and originality, would all be published. *Gli Avvenimenti* is, simply, a newspaper, so therefore, taking account of its youth too, I must take a thousand precautions and engage in a hundred hypocrises.

I explained this to Marinetti along with other reasons why I cannot dedicate to Futurism and the Futurists all the space that they want and deserve. Little by little.

I believe, actually, that this tactic will be more useful to the movement than any other.)[180]

While Marinetti was courting Notari in Milan, Cangiullo was entering into close contact with Ferdinando Russo, editor of the weekly magazine *Vela Latina*, in Naples. In March, Cangiullo wrote to Pratella requesting an article for the newspaper, stating that "Marinetti lo à approvato [...] è importantissimo un giornale futurista o semi – qui a Napoli!" (Marinetti has approved it [...] having a Futurist newspaper – or semi-Futurist – here in Naples is extremely important!).[181] Such a declaration was rather premature, however, as the newspaper could not be described as Futurist at this stage. Only from October 1915 would Russo grant Cangiullo two "Futurist pages" per issue to highlight the movement's activities and achievements.

The only periodical during the interventionist period that can be regarded as truly Futurist (in the *marinettiano* sense of the term) was *La Balza*. It was based in Messina in Sicily and was edited by three young Futurists – Jannelli, Luciano Nicastro,[182] and Vann'Antò (pseudonym of Giovanni Antonio Di Giacomo).[183] It ran for only three issues – 10 April, 27 April, and 12 May – in the weeks immediately preceding Italy's entry into the war. From the planning stages, the young men looked to older, more established Futurists for advice on the magazine's direction, with Pratella being the main source of guidance. The young Sicilians did not envisage their newspaper becoming the major vehicle for spreading knowledge of Futurist activities all over Italy, as their initial vision was firmly based in the Sicilian context. Pratella, clearly aware of

Futurism's difficult position in not having an official publication, told the young editors that "il vostro giornale invece deve contenere carat-teri *sconfinanti*, così da concorrere al primato: cioè da poter diventare in breve tempo l'organo ufficiale del futurismo italiano" (your newspaper must have a *boundless* nature, to be able to fight for the top spot: that is, to be able soon to become the official organ of Italian Futurism).[184] Pratella also praised the format and price of the journal and informed Jannelli of exactly what Futurism needed –an official publication with up-to-date news of Futurist theatre performances and publications: "Dire insomma tutto ciò che non *vogliono dire* gli altri giornali, quando si tratta di cose *futuriste riuscite* ed *accolte bene dal pubblico*" (So, you must say everything that the other newspapers *don't want to say*, when it comes to *Futurist affairs that have been well received by the public*).[185] Pra-tella enlisted Marinetti to provide these details of Futurist activity and informed Jannelli that everyone in Milan was enthusiastically awaiting *La Balza*'s first issue.[186]

The newspaper's first issue received an enthusiastic response from Marinetti and Balla,[187] and Marinetti proposed that they change the name to *La Balza Futurista* from its second issue, a sure sign of approval. Pratella (as well as Marinetti and Balla) continued to offer advice and concerned himself with the promotion of the magazine around Italy.[188] After the journal's demise Nicastro noted in a letter to Pratella that "La Balza riceveva molta luce da voi e che anzi ogni numero per me diventava vivente solo dopo la vostra lettera di approvazione, d'incoraggiamento, di consigli" (La Balza received a lot of attention from you and every issue only came alive for me after your letter of approval, full of encouragement and advice).[189] The magazine featured contributions from all the protagonists of the movement, and also pub-lished manifestos and examples of synthetic theatre. Perhaps if it had been able to continue publishing after Italy's entry into the war, *La Balza Futurista* would have become the official publication of the Futur-ist movement, which was so urgently required. It was not to be; the publication of all weekly and biweekly newspapers was prohibited by the authorities in Messina in May 1915, and Jannelli and Vann'Antò soon departed for the front.[190] The fact that Futurism, in May 1915, was reduced to relying on a newspaper produced in the peripheral town of Messina as its official publication is an indication of just how marginal a phenomenon Futurism had become during the interventionist crisis.

The extent to which Futurism during the interventionist crisis was still overwhelmingly, almost exclusively, only an artistic movement is demonstrated by the first synthetic-theatre tour, which took place between February and March 1915 in nine northern Italian cities. It has been suggested by some critics that synthetic theatre was an important weapon in the Futurist interventionist arsenal. According to Salaris, it assumed "una funzione centrale nella battaglia politica a favore della guerra. Politica e spettacolo si compenetrano" (a central function in the political battle in favour of the war. Politics and theatre merge),[191] and she argued elsewhere that Marinetti used this new genre of theatre "subito come veicolo di propaganda politica" (immediately as a vehicle for political propaganda).[192] Similarly, Giusi Baldissone has argued that "il teatro futurista è legato all'ideologia, e il gesto improvvisato e provocatorio è finalizzato a quella" (Futurist theatre is linked to ideology, and the improvised and provocative gesture is aimed at that).[193] Such assertions are true if one reads only the manifesto of Futurist synthetic theatre, launched early in 1915. The manifesto, which bears two dates (11 January and 18 February 1915), began in the following way: "Aspettando la nostra grande guerra tanto invocata, noi futuristi alterniamo la nostra violentissima azione anti-neutrale nelle piazze e nelle Università, colla nostra azione artistica sulla sensibilità italiana, che vogliamo preparare alla grande ora del massimo Pericolo." (Waiting for the great war for which we have prayed so long, we Futurists alternate our violent anti-neutralist action in the squares and in the universities with our artistic action focused on the Italian consciousness, which we want to prepare for the great hour of maximum Danger.)[194] In a clear defence of their lack of an official publication, the authors, Marinetti, Emilio Settimelli,[195] and Bruno Corra,[196] stated that it was impossible to influence public opinion through publications because only 10 per cent of the population read magazines and newspapers, while 90 per cent attended the theatre. Thus, they concluded: "**non si possa oggi influenzare guerrescamente l'anima italiana, se non mediante il teatro**" (**it is not possible to influence the Italian spirit in favour of the war, except through theatre**).[197] The remainder of the long manifesto was concerned exclusively with the artistic aspects of the new genre, and no further references to the current political situation were made. While the inventors of Futurist synthetic theatre may have intended it to assume a political function, as Salaris suggested, this did not come to pass during the 1915 tour in the midst of Italian neutrality.

The tour, which began in Ancona on 1 February, was completely removed from any political action or engagement. In his exaggerated chronicle of interventionist activity Pratella stated that the performances were "precedute da discorsi interventisti" (preceded by interventionist speeches), but there is no evidence that this was the case.[198] Although Marinetti frequently appeared on stage at the performances to address the audience, in none of the numerous reviews is there any mention of a political tenor or interventionist slant to his speeches.[199] Rather, in his addresses to the audiences, he merely asked them to reserve their rotten vegetables and other projectiles for him at the end of the performance, instead of pelting the actors (who were not actually Futurists),[200] or he spoke about the innovations of the new theatrical genre.[201] In addition, the performances had no charitable dimension, for example in aid of the Belgian refugees.[202] It is possible that Marinetti, in spite of the alleged political intention outlined in the manifesto, was wary of censure from the authorities should the performances turn into interventionist demonstrations. As has been mentioned above, in September 1914 he had cancelled the planned *serata* in Montecatini because the Futurists were denied the right of assembly. A theatre critic wondered on 5 February 1915 whether "il *fenomeno* è tramontato" (the sun has set on the *phenomenon*).[203] Another referred to the whole tour as a "combriccola futurista" (Futurist gathering). It was a "combriccola ormai in piena putrefazione, e molto, ma molto passatista [...] L'unica cosa che le si può fare, è recitarle le preghiere dei morti" (gathering by now in complete decay, and very, I mean very, passéist [...] The only thing that can be done to it is to give it the last rites).[204] It is possible that such comments heralding the death of Futurism pushed Marinetti to increase his visibility at interventionist demonstrations in the subsequent months in an effort to prove to his detractors that the movement was still a vital force in Italian life.

A curious contradiction in the political intent of the synthetic-theatre manifesto was the statement that "**il teatro futurista** saprà esaltare i suoi spettatori, cioè far loro dimenticare la monotonia della vita quotidiana, scaraventandoli attraverso **un labirinto di sensazioni improntate alla più esasperata originalità e combinate in modi imprevedibili**" (**Futurist theatre** will know how to excite its audiences, that is how to make them forget the monotony of their daily lives, flinging them into **a labyrinth of sensations inspired by the most exasperating originality and combined in unpredictable ways**).[205] This escapist function of the synthetic theatre was at odds with the manifesto's professed desire for political engagement but was completely in keeping with the dominant mood of the first tour. Even a magazine with Futurist sympathies, in reporting on the manifesto and the Venetian performance, highlighted the genre's escapist function, while ignoring any possible political element.[206] The only reference made to the interventionist crisis in any of the reviews was by the Bergamasque critic who noted that Marinetti had arrived in the city, having just been released after his arrest during an interventionist demonstration in Rome. It is very clear, however, that the critic considered Marinetti's interventionist antics and the theatre tour to be utterly separate activities, as he began the review by highlighting its escapist function, stating that "in tempi grigi si può essere grati a quelle persone di buona volontà che hanno studiato di far trascorrere un'ora di irrefrenabile ilarità al pubblico pagante" (in sad times we must be grateful to those men of good will who help a paying audience pass an hour in irrepressible hilarity).[207] An examination of the *sintesi* performed reveals that there was no political content whatsoever. All twelve pieces that were performed during the tour were devoid of political references, although some were theatrically innovative creations.[208]

On the whole, the reception of the tour was negative. Although the first performance in Ancona received a positive response, the subsequent performances in Bologna, Padua, Venice, Verona, Bergamo, Genoa, Savona, and San Remo[209] were marred by half-empty theatres and rowdy groups who often made it almost impossible to hear the actors perform.[210] Chiti recalled having seven or eight rotten oranges thrown at him and lots of boos.[211] One reviewer of the performance in Verona remarked that the evening had resulted in "per i fruttivendoli ottimi affari" (excellent business for the greengrocers).[212] Unsurprisingly, Marinetti's view of the tour's success was much more positive as he reported "folle enormi, molte centinaia di giovani simpatizzanti ed entusiasti" (enormous crowds, many hundreds of sympathetic and enthusiastic young people).[213] While the *teatro sintetico* was undoubtedly a significant evolution of Futurist theatre in artistic terms and succeeded in opening "una piccola breccia nella munita cittadella del 'teatro tradizionale'" (a small breach of the fortified citadel of 'traditional theatre'),[214] it had no relevance for the interventionist struggle. It was only during the second and third tours in 1916 and 1917, which contained new material, that the genre assumed a political dimension and played a role in supporting morale on the home front.

Interventionist fervour took off in Italy in late April and May 1915, the so-called "radiant days of May." While Gabriele D'Annunzio, Marinetti's great rival, was addressing enormous audiences all over Italy and urging them to support Italy's intervention into the war, Marinetti was nowhere to be seen.[215] With Italian mobilization imminent, Marinetti had presented himself in early May for formal enlistment but was declared unfit for duty owing to a hernia.[216] In an interview in early 1916, Marinetti recalled how "ad ogni costo volevo fare il soldato" (I wanted to be a soldier at any cost),[217] and so he underwent an operation, followed by another for an attack of phlebitis. Thus, during the days of "radiant May" he found himself recuperating rather than demonstrating. Just as his desire to fight had prevented him from taking decisive action in August 1914, his belligerence also prevented him from leading his Futurist followers in the most significant period of the interventionist crisis. It is rather fitting then that when Italy finally entered the war on 24 May 1915, Marinetti was at home in bed. He recalled that "la folla milanese volle che mi affacciassi al balcone della mia casa. Alcuni amici mi alzarono in trionfo e si gridò a me la notizia esplosiva 'Marinetti, la guerra è scoppiata!'" (the Milanese crowd wanted me to come out onto the balcony of my house. Some of my friends lifted me up in triumph, and the crowd called out the explosive news: 'Marinetti, the war has broken out!')[218]

2 Futurism at the Front: Futurist Military and Combat Experiences

The Lombard Battalion of Volunteer Cyclists and Motorists

Six hundred soldiers on bicycles cycle past the Castello Sforzesco in Milan, down Via Dante and towards Piazza della Scala, bound for Peschiera on the shores of Lake Garda near the Italian front lines. It is 21 July 1915, and they are the Battaglione Lombardo dei Volontari Ciclisti e Automobilisti (Lombard Battalion of Volunteer Cyclists and Motorists), the only volunteer corps officially recognized by the Italian Army's high command during the war.[1] On that July day, fresh from a short period of training at Gallarate, just outside the city,[2] the volunteers were greeted with "entusiastiche manifestazioni cittadine" (enthusiastic civic displays).[3] Crowds thronged the route, blocking the tramways; they filled balconies and hung out of trees, the spectators applauded, and the women handed out flags, flowers, sweets, and cigarettes.[4] Three aeroplanes took off from Malpensa airport, following the parade of cyclists, and unfurled tricolour banners adorned with good-luck messages that had been signed by the pilots.[5] Among those six hundred cyclists were six Futurists – Marinetti, Boccioni, Russolo, Sant'Elia, Sironi, and Piatti.[6]

It is unsurprising that the Futurists regarded the Lombard Battalion of Volunteer Cyclists as a good home for their bellicose aspirations. A recruitment advertisement for the battalion evoked the role of volunteers in the Risorgimento, reminding men that "[la] difesa della Patria!" (the defence of the homeland!) was a citizen's most sacred duty.[7] In August 1914 Marinetti described it as a "corpo predisposto alle avanscoperte pericolose e alle audacie più futuriste" (corps predisposed to dangerous reconnaissance and to the most Futurist acts of courage).[8] The battalion was a "fucina di patriottismo, […] il crogiuolo della

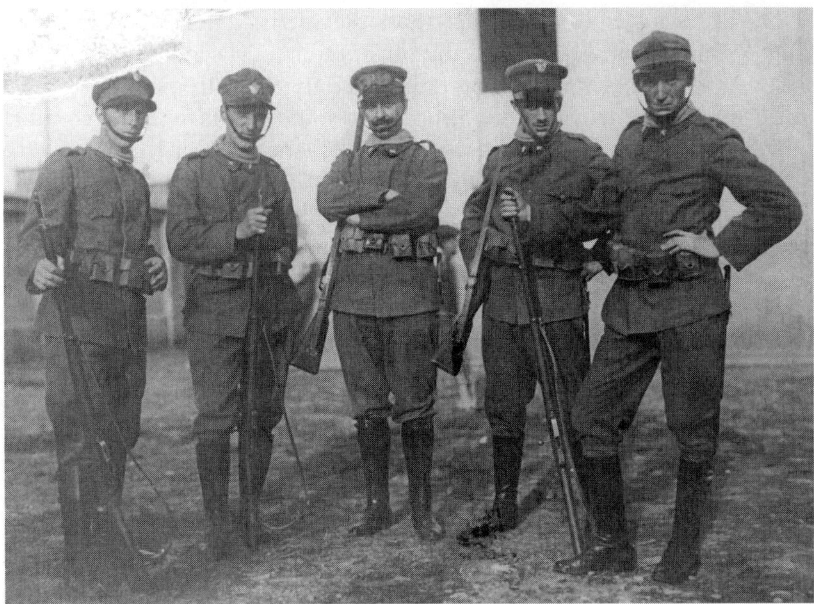

Figure 2.1. Futurist members of the Lombard Battalion of Volunteer Cyclists and Motorists, 1915. Left to right: Boccioni, Piatti, Marinetti, Sironi, Sant'Elia. Courtesy of Museo d'arte moderna e contemporanea di Trento e Rovereto, Archivio del '900, Fondo Angelini.

passione irredentistica" (forge of patriotism, [...] the crucible of irredentist passion),[9] and Marinetti recalled that its ranks contained

> studenti, monarchici, operai rivoluzionari, avvocati ligi all'ordine, notai anarchici perseguitati, massoni e clericali, poveri e milionari, pittori e poeti tradizionali, avanguardie, semifuturisti e futuristi, [che] si erano già incontrati in piazza del Duomo e in Galleria, quasi ogni sera, durante l'inverno e la primavera, per cazzottare e mettere in fuga i neutralisti dell'*Avanti*.

> (students, monarchists, revolutionary workers, law-abiding lawyers, persecuted anarchist notaries, Freemasons and clericalists, poor and millionaires, traditional painters and poets, avant-gardists, Futurists and semi-Futurists, [who] had already met in the Piazza del Duomo and in the Galleria, almost every evening, during the winter and spring, to punch and chase away the neutralists of *Avanti* [the newspaper of the Socialist Party].[10]

The Futurists were in high spirits as they arrived at Peschiera, where they remained until the beginning of September. Marinetti was initially invigorated by his new routine; he enjoyed the "sole tropicale" (tropical sun), swimming in the River Mincio and Lake Garda, and the comfort of the straw mattresses in the dormitory. His days consisted of

> violentissima sveglia di tromba lacerante alle 4: bicicletta da pulire, esercitazioni: ripetere 4 o 5 volte un assalto in ordine sparso per prendere una collina dove non troviamo … austriaci! Poi si ritorna pedalando al ritmo delle canzoni militari. Si riprende energia malgrado il sole e il diluvio di sudore. L'energia non manca.

> violent wake-up call with ear-splitting trumpet at 4 a.m.: bicycle to clean, drills: repeat 4 or 5 times a disorderly assault to capture a hill where we don't find … Austrians! Then we return pedalling to the rhythm of military songs. We get our energy back despite the sun and bucketloads of sweat. Energy is not lacking.[11]

Boccioni was similarly enthusiastic: "aspettiamo ansiosamente la Gioia immensa di batterci per la nostra grande e forte Italia!" (We anxiously await the immense Joy to fight for our great and strong Italy!)[12] The battalion organized a celebration on 20 September to commemorate the conquest of Rome in 1870, which had marked the end of the process of Italian unification. Marinetti was nominated president and judge of the sporting competition, which included a slow bicycle race under "enemy fire" (consisting of figs, tomatoes, and other vegetables) as well as other games such as tug of war, long jump, swimming, and, of course, cycling races.[13] Tasked with guarding a fort on an island in the lake at nights, Marinetti enjoyed declaiming his words-in-freedom poem "Bombardamento di Adrianopoli" and had fellow soldiers play Pratella's "Inno di Guerra" on the piano.[14] Despite having to sleep outside in a tent, Boccioni wrote that "l'entusiasmo è moltiplicato […] Io non lavoro non penso, faccio una vita rude e fisica che mi inebria!" (my enthusiasm has multiplied […] I'm not working, I don't think, I'm living a rough and physical life that intoxicates me!)[15] and informed Pratella that he was "in eccellenti condizioni di spirito e fisicamente sopporto tutto come non mi aspettavo" (in excellent spirits and physically I am tolerating everything much better than I expected).[16]

In early September the Volunteer Cyclists discovered that they were to be transformed into an Alpine battalion, leaving their bicycles behind to engage in mountain combat on foot.[17] By this stage Marinetti had begun to tire of the military routine and particularly disliked the mountains, which he described as "stupidissime professorali e pedanti" (stupid, professorial and pedantic). "Non le amo. Ma bisogna vincersi" (I don't love them. But I must get over it), he continued.[18] Marinetti also wrote of his desire to fight "per non morire d'impazienza" (so I don't die of impatience).[19] Eventually, on 14 October, the Futurists had their first taste of military engagement when Marinetti, Boccioni, and Sant'Elia were sent on a reconnaissance mission four kilometres from the Italian line into Austrian-held territory, where they succeeded in taking an Austrian trench that had been abandoned. In typically telegraphic style Boccioni wrote of his "allegria uscita reticolati gioia festa" (happiness exit barbed wire joy celebration),[20] while Marinetti enjoyed the "piacere fisico totale VEDERE una pattuglia nemica (GUSTARLA) che fugge sgusciando da una trincea" (total physical pleasure of SEEING an enemy patrol (TASTING IT) that flees wriggling out of a trench).[21] This trench was taken without firing a single shot, but a week later the Futurists received their first experience of battle when they were involved with the regular Alpine troops in the capture of the Austrian position at Dosso Casina. It was the volunteers' task to draw attention to themselves so that the Alpine soldiers could approach the enemy from the other side. Realizing they were surrounded on two sides, the Austrians retreated and abandoned their position.[22] At Dosso Casina the Futurists found themselves in real danger, under a hail of shrapnel for six days, waiting for entire nights in their trenches in the pitch black with their bayonets raised, hearing the Austrians draw closer but forbidden from shooting so as not to reveal their positions.[23]

In spite of the hunger, exhaustion, and intense cold to which they were subjected during this period, once Marinetti and Boccioni were engaged in action, their good humour remained undimmed. If anything, their admiration for war as the supreme embodiment of the Futurist spirit increased. Boccioni called war "una cosa bella, meravigliosa, terribile!" (something beautiful, marvellous, terrible!)[24] and was pleased to have finally seen some action. The experience was also a realization of Marinetti's long-held dreams: "Tutti i tramonti sanguinosi della mia adolescenza (nostalgia di battaglie) sono soddisfatti" (All the bloody sunsets of my adolescence (longing for battles) have been satisfied).[25] Marinetti considered the assault on Dosso Casina to represent "futurismo assoluto" (absolute Futurism),[26] an expression he used numerous times in letters to friends and newspapers following the successful capture of the Austrian position.[27] Although its members expected to return to the front after a short period of rest, the battalion received news in early November that it was to be disbanded. It departed from Lake Garda on 1 December and arrived in Milan six days later.

The exploits of the Futurists with the Lombard Battalion of Volunteer Cyclists have long been used by scholars as a compelling shorthand for Futurist combat experiences of the First World War, an embodiment of the "guerra festa" position discussed in the introduction herein.[28] The fact that so many Futurists fought together in a single battalion (and all except Russolo in the same platoon) has provided an attractive collective experience to observe, which largely corresponded to the Futurists' anticipated response to the war. The judgment of Enrico Crispolti is typical; he concluded his account of the Volunteer Cyclists and its disbandment by writing, "L'avventura bellica di gruppo dei futuristi è finita. Gli impegni militari si rinnoveranno singoli e disparati, e per alcuni con esito fatale." (The Futurists' collective war adventure is over. They will take up military engagements again separately and disparately, for some with fatal consequences).[29]

As this chapter will demonstrate, Futurist military and combat experiences were more prolonged, and the reactions to combat more varied, than the scholarly focus on the Lombard Battalion of Volunteer Cyclists has allowed. Over fifty Futurists served in the Italian Army during the First World War.[30] Some were territorial soldiers who never saw the front lines, such as Pratella. Most, however, saw active combat: some, like Depero, for only a few weeks, while others, like Luciano Nicastro, fought almost continuously for the duration of the war. Some Futurists served in "elite" battalions such as the Alpini and the Arditi, but the majority of combatant Futurists served in regular battalions, including the infantry, the anti-aerial division, the engineers' corps, and the artillery. They served as private soldiers, second lieutenants, lieutenants, and even captains.

Combat Motivation

On the whole, combatant Futurists were motivated by patriotism, nationalism, and irredentism in their desire to fight, like many other young, middle-class volunteers who considered the war to be the "fourth war of independence" and as the culmination of the Risorgimento.[31] For a number of Futurists, this desire to do their military duty was intensified by a desire to serve as private soldiers instead of officers.

Beginning service with the Volunteer Cyclists, Boccioni insisted upon the pleasure that he felt to be fighting, not as an officer but as a private soldier – "umile cooperatore all'opera grandiosa" (humble collaborator in this magnificent endeavour).[32] In December 1915 Nicastro wrote of his impending departure to Messina to be informed of his regiment, and appeared particularly proud of his decision to enlist as a private soldier "come protesta a certe vigliaccherie!" (as a protest against certain acts of cowardice!).[33] In March 1917 Paolo Orano,[34] having difficulty with his application to become an officer, was willing to accept a position in the infantry so that he could immediately go to the front once his training was over.[35] Of course, given the educated status of the Futurists, not all were content to serve as private soldiers. After their time with the Volunteer Cyclists, both Marinetti and Boccioni served as officers. Cangiullo regretted that he could not enlist as an officer because one of his brothers had already availed himself of this opportunity.[36] Prior to the war Remo Chiti went to great lengths to avoid passing the medical examination and being enlisted in the army: "avevo due pipe grumose che fumavo contemporaneamente alternandole con sigari e sigarette; [...] sono stato una notte intera colla pipa accesa in bocca, mezzo ubriaco, con una sete indiavolata, senza dormire e senza del resto potermi addormentare." (I had two lumpy pipes that I smoked simultaneously, alternating them with cigars and cigarettes; I spent the whole night with the lit pipe in my mouth, half drunk, with a monstrous thirst, without sleeping and without being able to go to sleep.)[37] Once Italy's entry into the war was imminent, however, he was enthusiastic at the prospect of his military service, hoping that he would not fail the medical again.[38] In these expressions of patriotism and enthusiasm the Futurists' reactions were no different from those of young reserve officers, most of whom had also been interventionists.

A disproportionate number of combatant Futurists were volunteers. Of the over four million men who served at the Italian front during the war, only eight thousand were volunteers, mostly bourgeois, ideologically motivated irredentists, like the Futurists.[39] In addition to those Futurists from Italy who served with the Volunteer Cyclists, Athos Casarini,[40] a Futurist who had emigrated to New York in 1909, returned to Italy from America in 1915 to enlist voluntarily. There were also three Futurists who were Austrian citizens, from Trentino, who volunteered for the Italian Army: Fortunato Depero, Ennio Valentinelli (also known by the pseudonym Acciaio),[41] and Umberto Maganzini (also known as Trilluci).[42] In total, 687 men from Trentino volunteered and served in the Italian forces. The bravery of this decision should not be underestimated. As Austrian citizens, by volunteering to fight for the Italian Army, these men left behind their families; any goods or property they owned in Austria would be confiscated; and as deserters of their own nation they would likely be executed for treason, if captured.[43] This was "una scelta estrema, […] che deve necessariamente poggiare su motivazioni salde e radicate" (an extreme choice, […] that had to be based on firm and deeply rooted motivations), stemming from their belief in the necessity of liberating the unredeemed territories.[44]

Depero escaped over the border to Italy in August 1914, while Valentinelli did not leave Austria until the spring of the following year, just before Italy entered the war. He managed to leave Rovereto on 8 April 1915, using a false passport,[45] and his first destination upon arrival in Italy was the headquarters of the Commissione dell'Emigrazione Trentina in Milan, where he also received lodging.[46] On 1 June he enrolled as a volunteer soldier in the Italian Army and began active service. By 16 July 1915 Depero was also in the "zona di Guerra" and beginning active combat.[47] Owing to health problems he would remain only a few weeks at the front,[48] but during this short time uppermost in his mind was his belief in irredentism, which had clearly spurred him to volunteer for combat. He wrote of his joy at being able to "finalmente marciare su suolo nostro da redimere – puoi immaginare per noi trentini che sogno" (finally march on our land to be redeemed – you can imagine what a dream it is for we *trentini*), and he highlighted his enthusiasm at being able to "marciare contro austriaa [*sic*] odiatissima per liberare le nostre famiglie" (march against most-hated austriaa [*sic*] to liberate our families).[49]

Emilio Gentile has stated that "l'adesione dei futuristi alla guerra fu totale e disciplinata" (the adherence of the Futurists to the war was total and disciplined).[50] While this statement is largely accurate, within this swell of enthusiasm it is necessary to acknowledge that the decision to serve was not always solely driven by ideology and patriotism. Valentinelli was also motivated by more practical concerns. In April 1915 he was a twenty-one-year-old university student and a refugee from an enemy nation, with no documents, no source of income or employment, and no contacts in Italy.[51] He told the Refugee Committee in December 1915 that "non ò nessun parente in Italia, essendo stata internata la mia famiglia in Austria; dove non l'ò mai potuto sapere" (I have no relatives in Italy, since my family has been interned in Austria; I have never been able to find out where).[52] Volunteering for the Italian

Army was surely, at least in part, an economic decision as well as a patriotic one.[53]

Mario Carli's decision to volunteer was motivated by his "ardente desiderio di azione" (ardent desire for action)[54] and his desire to "cessare di essere un disoccupato e per rendermi utile al mio paese" (stop being unemployed and to make myself useful to my country).[55] Carli's father was suspicious of his motives, assuming that his Futurist companions had influenced his son's decision to enlist. Mario was at pains to reassure him that

> non so chi avrebbe potuto influire su questa decisione, essendo i miei stessi amici (Settimelli, Corradini, Chiti) esentati da ogni obbligo di leva. È stato un vero e proprio bisogno che io ho soddisfatto, un bisogno fisico e morale, sia di uscire da una situazione così malsicura com'era la mia, sia di fare qualche cosa di positivo per la mia patria.

> (I don't know who could have influenced this decision, seeing as my own friends (Settimelli, Corradini, Chiti) are exempt from military service. It was a real need that I satisfied, a physical and moral need, both to leave a situation as unstable as mine was, and to do something positive for my country.)[56]

Alongside this patriotic view of his own participation in the war, in the same letter Carli revealed a certain pragmatism and a concern that "in avvenire, nella mia carriera pubblica, qualunque essa sia, mi potrebbe essere rinfacciata la mia astensione come una vigliaccheria" (in the future, in my public career, whatever it may be, my abstention could be held against me as cowardice). He also admitted to considering the possibility of remaining in the army beyond the end of the war because "potrebbe darsi che per un anno o due o tre lo stipendio di ufficiale non fosse completamente incomodo: un impiego come un altro, un appoggio sicuro che mi permetterebbe di continuare tranquillamente la via che mi sono tracciata" (it may be that an officer's salary for one or two or three years would not be entirely unwelcome: a job like any other, a secure post that would allow me to calmly continue the path I have laid out).[57]

Within the Futurist ranks in 1915 there were also cases of those who were unwilling to volunteer for the war. While the pro-war sentiments of Carrà and Govoni were not in doubt, neither had a desire to engage prematurely in combat. Carrà decided to stay at home until he was

obliged by the government to enlist, preferring to stay in Milan to look
for a studio space.[58] Govoni considered his duties "verso la mia piccola patria (la famiglia) ben più pressanti che verso quell'altra grande"
(towards my little homeland (my family) much more pressing than
those towards the larger one).[59]

Life in the Trenches: Hardships, Discipline, Bombardments

For those who did volunteer or were enlisted in the Italian Army, conditions on the Italian front lines, particularly in the early months of Italy's
intervention, were brutal. The 300-kilometre-long front snaked through
Alpine peaks of between 1,000 and 3,000 metres, which were held by
Austrian forces, and then through the barren, limestone Carso plateau
towards the sea. Despite delaying its intervention for ten months, the
Italian Army suffered from a lack of equipment and arms as it began
to fight in the summer of 1915.[60] As the distribution of vehicles had
been delayed, the Second Army crossed the Austrian border with just
one automobile, and in May 1915 the entire army possessed only two
hundred heavy field howitzers and three hundred machine guns.[61] The
lack of appropriate equipment extended to soldiers' uniforms and basic
essentials, a particular problem for troops fighting in Alpine regions.
Rations were also woefully insufficient. At the outset of the war, combatants received a minimum daily ration of 3,900 calories (rising to 4,100 for
Alpine troops),[62] but by late 1917 the ration had been reduced to just 3,067
calories.[63] The war in the mountains saw more soldiers die as a result of
natural factors than of the direct effects of combat and artillery fire.[64]

When Italy entered the war, the trenches constructed by the soldiers
were shallow and offered little protection to the men. General Luigi
Cadorna, chief of staff of the Italian Army until the rout of Caporetto in
October 1917, was also against constructing robuster trenches in concrete, as the German Army did, for fear that the soldiers would become
too comfortable in them.[65] As the war progressed, however, the complexity of the trench system developed; of no little importance was the
fact that they were now deep enough to protect men while they were
standing, although mud could still turn them into *"zuppe nere"* (*black
soup*).[66] In the winter of 1917–18 Marinetti himself was in charge of a
bombardiers' unit that had been transformed into a unit of "zappatori"
(diggers) to construct trenches.[67]

Combatant Futurists at the front lines were subjected to all these
hardships during their military service. The months spent with the
Volunteer Cyclists were particularly challenging because the battalion

was entirely unprepared for mountain combat, and they had to walk for days in thick fog in temperatures of minus fifteen degrees Celsius, wearing only light summer uniforms.[68] During autumn 1915 Marinetti made frequent requests to his secretaries, Nina and Marietta Angelini, for various items including old shoes, toothpaste, woollen socks, a fur gilet, and jumpers.[69] He recalled after his return to Milan that he and his fellow soldiers were "senza guanti, senza passamontagna, colla mantellina soltanto, niente vino, niente alcool, niente caffè, una pagnotta per quattro uomini, una scatola di carne per tre, tutte le Siberie nelle ossa" (without gloves, without balaclavas, with just a light cape, no wine, no alcohol, no coffee, one loaf of bread between four men, one tin of meat between three, all of Siberia in our bones).[70] Boccioni also highlighted the problems caused by deficiencies in equipment, writing that he spent nights sleeping outside without blankets "con le gambe d'un amico tra le gambe e abbracciati per battere meno i denti. Eravamo giunti ad un punto tale che io tendevo l'orecchio sperando un contrattacco nemico e così potermi riscaldare" (with a friend's legs between mine and hugging each other so our teeth would chatter less. We were at the stage where I stuck my ear out, hoping for an enemy counter-attack just to warm myself up).[71] For Boccioni, the experience of being under fire for seven days was "nulla in confronto alle orribili sofferenze causate dal freddo, dalla fame e dalle marce prolungate fino a venti ore" (nothing in comparison to the horrible suffering caused by the cold, hunger, and prolonged marches of up to twenty hours).[72] Marinetti claimed that the conditions of the Volunteer Cyclists were far inferior to those of any other creature. Huddled on a rock, two metres square, he reflected: "Gli alpini hanno dei magnifici baraccamenti, ben riscaldati dagli aliti: i lupi e gli orsi hanno delle grotte profonde […] noi, invece, viviamo la vita tragica dei cani idrofobi inseguiti a fucilate e dei lebbrosi medioevali!" (The Alpine soldiers have magnificent barracks, heated by their breath: wolves and bears have deep caves […] we, on the other hand, live the tragic lives of rabid dogs hunted with rifles and of medieval lepers!)[73]

The Volunteer Cyclists were not the only ones who had to grapple with such conditions. Cold, exhaustion, and lack of sleep were the norm for soldiers and officers all over the front lines, and the Futurists in their midst were no exception. Vann'Antò recalled that sleep was impossible, "protetto dal lenzuolo freddo del chiarore lunare" (protected with the cold sheet of the moon's glimmer).[74] The letters of Luciano Nicastro to his mother, begun during the great retreat of autumn 1917, were filled with accounts of his physical suffering: "Come le foglie la nostra pena si trascina, senza sole, nel fango, con la pioggia; col vento, si va: ogni ordine è una fatica a cui si resiste per volontà nostra." (Like the leaves, our pain drags itself along, without sun, in the mud, with the rain; with the wind, we go; every order is a strain that we tolerate with our will.)[75] While his sense of duty was strong, he wrote bitterly of his exhaustion, his bloody feet after marches of 150 kilometres, "il bivacco eterno delle notti fredde, il sonno via" (the eternal camping in cold nights, no sleep).[76] As well as the cold, the life in the trenches entailed other sources of discomfort, including disease, insects, rats, and lice. Giuseppe Steiner recalled an outbreak of malaria at the front, and Valentinelli was treated for dysentery at one stage.[77] Boccioni incredulously commented that when one was waiting to fight, war consisted of nothing more than "insetti + noia" (insects + boredom).[78] In his poem "La gioia" (Joy), Steiner captured a typical scene from the front, writing: "Domani se viene buon sole / massacro tutti i pidocchi che ho!" (Tomorrow if it's sunny / I'll kill all my lice!)[79] Marinetti's particular torment in 1917 was rats. He complained to Pratella of "molte granate e topi con passi da elefante. Si dorme poco!" (lots of grenades and rats with elephant's feet. I don't sleep much!)[80] and devoted an entire drawing to a representation of his rat-infested living quarters at the front.

The Futurists experienced particular difficulties with military hierarchy and discipline. The Battalion of Volunteer Cyclists was disbanded in December 1915 ostensibly because a group of soldiers on bicycles was not fit for combat in mountain regions, but there were also suggestions that issues with discipline had played a role in the decision. *La Gazzetta dello Sport* journalist Renzo Codara acknowledged that some would regard the step as the result of "una decisa antipatia per i Corpi Volontari da parte degli alti gradi dell'esercito" (a decided dislike of the Volunteer Corps on the part of the higher ranks of the army), although he did not personally share that opinion.[81] One former Volunteer Cyclist claimed that the battalion was disbanded because its members were disorderly and unpopular with the army command.[82] Marinetti himself confirmed their rowdiness when he recounted an evening in which the entire battalion got drunk, played a trick on its sergeant, and was subsequently punished. Marinetti also received individual censure for his rule breaking. He was given three days in prison in Peschiera for having swum beyond the designated area in the lake. On another occasion his enthusiastic and loud declamation of "Bombardamento di Adrianopoli" while under fire by the Austrians was not well received by his lieutenant, and he was ordered to be quiet.[83] Marinetti commented that the commanding sergeant of their battalion "esigeva giustamente, ma senza ottenerla, una disciplina

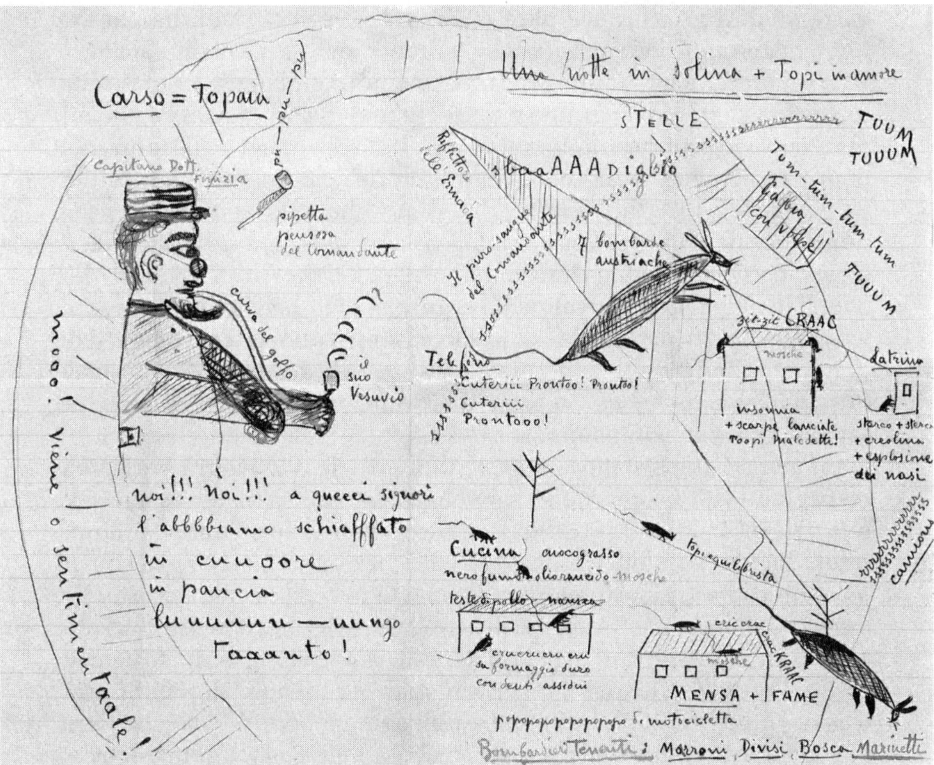

Figure 2.2. Filippo Tommaso Marinetti, *Carso = Topaia: Una notte in dolina + Topi in amore* (Karst = Rats' nest: A night in a sinkhole + Rats in love), ca. 1917. © Artists' Rights Society, New York / SIAE, Rome, 2015. Courtesy of Getty Research Institute, Los Angeles (accession no. 870379).

assoluta, che noi volevamo invece relativa" (rightly demanded, but did not receive, absolute discipline, which we wanted to be relative), and he acknowledged the very difficult task of commanding the "plotone degl'Intellettuali [...] poiché ne facevano parte i cervelli più alti e più bizzarri che mai siano stati assoggettati, insieme, alla disciplina militare" (Intellectuals' platoon [...] because in it were the brightest and strangest brains that had ever been subject, together, to military discipline).[84] Marinetti continued to have a bumpy relationship with military discipline even after his time with the Volunteer Cyclists. In a speech in July 1918 he proclaimed that "il deposito ci fa schifo!" (the barracks disgust us!). The phrase was subsequently published in the *Corriere mercantile* newspaper, which drew the ire of General Zavataro, who reproached him, calling the proclamation "cretinerie contrarie alla disciplina!" (stupidity contrary to discipline!),[85] and he was reminded that "quando si porta l'uniforme d'ufficiale si deve stare nelle forme nei limiti" (when you wear an officer's uniform, you have to stay within the lines).[86] In 1918 the "relative discipline" that Marinetti had desired when serving with the Volunteer Cyclists became a *"disciplina elastica"* (*elastic discipline*),[87] which he sought on behalf of the Arditi soldiers who had demanded special treatment because of their heightened exposure to danger.[88] Marinetti believed in reconciling the Arditi's love of freedom with the "disciplina necessaria ad un esercito che vuole vincere" (discipline necessary for an army that wants to win),[89] and had advocated on their behalf for special privileges.

On arrival at his station in Pieve di Cento in 1917, Carrà presented his captain with a copy of his 1915 volume *Guerrapittura*. It was not well received by his superior, who began to "prendermi di mira e a farmi tutti i dispetti possibili e immaginabili" (pick on me and to play every possible and imaginable prank on me).[90] On one occasion, upon arriving back at the barracks one hour late, Carrà was ordered to a chicken-coop-turned-prison for a period of five days, along with five men accused of theft. The other men were released the next day, but Carrà was required to complete the entire punishment period. When he complained to his friend Umberto Notari about the injustice of this experience, he was advised not to "prendere l'avventura tanto sul tragico" (take the adventure so seriously) and to consider it "una scena grandiosa per un quadro degno del tuo pennello" (impressive scene for a painting worthy of your brush).[91] Valentinelli also expressed frustration with his superiors, declaring it impossible for him to adapt and submit to the demands of "tanti borghesacci in uniforme" (many vile bourgeois in uniform). He also railed against "certi stupidi ufficiali che non sono mai stati al fronte [che] vengono qui a rimproverare perché manca un bottone perchè si va in cucina prima dell'ora del rancio, perché non si è presenti all'appello, perché si piscia su per le porte delle case borghesi ecc." (certain stupid officials who have never been to the front coming here to rebuke us because a button is missing or because you go to the kitchen before ration time, because you're not present at a roll-call, because you piss on the doors of bourgeois houses, etc.).[92]

While Marinetti's view of military hierarchy was unambiguous, his attitude towards the private soldiers whom he commanded was less clear. His feelings veered between contempt and admiration, and his war-time notebooks are filled with contradictory statements. On 18 December 1917 he declared: "Amo la mia razza. Mi sento fratello di queste anime spensierate troppo affettuose violente sensibilissime alla dolcezza di un sorriso amico, pronti a sventare l'inganno o la derisione." (I love my race. I feel like a brother to these carefree souls too affectionate violent, so receptive to the sweetness of a friend's smile, ready to thwart a trick or derision.)[93] A few weeks later he complained:

> Il fante s'infischia di tutto. Accende il fuoco nei fienili per riscaldarsi. Si corica fra le gambe dei muli. Si risveglia con una cacata enorme di vacca sulla pancia. Brucia tutto per scaldarsi. Non sa mai la strada. Dichiara d'essere arrivato il giorno precedente per non rispondere alle domande.

> (The infantryman doesn't care about anything. He lights a fire in a hayloft to warm himself. He lies down between the legs of mules. He wakes up with an enormous cowpat on his stomach. He burns everything to warm himself. He never knows the way. He pretends to have only arrived the previous day so as not to have to answer questions.)[94]

The Alpine soldiers, however, received nothing but praise from the Futurists, who regarded them as the fullest embodiment of Italian bravery.[95] Ugo Tommei[96] called the *alpino* "miracoloso," writing, "Quando a guerra finita si potrà spiegare bene con quali audacie e su quale terreno à combattuto l'italiano, non si vorrà credere a tanto sacrificio e strafottenza del pericolo" (When the war is over, and it will be possible to properly explain the courage and kind of terrain Italian soldiers fought on, people won't believe the sacrifice and disregard of danger).[97] Valentinelli expressed similar sentiments about the Alpini: "I soldati sono rozzi, ma buonissimi e coraggiosissimi. Ànno virtù militari straordinarie questi alpini bergamaschi e bresciani. Loro brontolano contro tutto, ma se viene un ordine qualunque, giusto o ingiusto, difficile o facile, loro ubbidiscono meravigliosamente." (The soldiers are rough, but full of goodness and courage. These Bergamasque and Brescian alpini have extraordinary military virtues. They complain about everything, but when an order comes, whether right or wrong, difficult or easy, they marvellously obey.)[98] Russolo, who was himself an Alpine soldier, was amazed at an alpino "forte, calmo, sapiente conoscitore della montagna" (strong, calm, wise expert of the mountains) who, in pitch-black night-time, could put his ear to a rock and state with certainty that there was no Austrian patrol on its way.[99]

It was a source of great pride to Marinetti that the Battalion of Volunteer Cyclists was transformed into an Alpine unit, and he emphasized this point at a speech made to other soldiers on 20 September 1915.[100] On that occasion Marinetti spoke for an hour and a half, "suscitando deliri di applausi" (causing delirious applause).[101] In this speech he was keen to downplay any suggestion that the Futurist soldiers regarded themselves as an elite group within the army and to counteract the perception that, as intellectuals, they would be unsuited to the demands of military life. Instead, Marinetti positioned himself alongside the Alpini, the men of action. He stressed the need for a well-trained body over a finely tuned mind, stating that "Bisogna […] che l'Italia sia sempre muscolarmente preparata a tutte le fatiche: occorrono nervi saldissimi, istinti sicuri e muscoli allenatissimi […] Si tributerà onore e gloria ad un italiano fortissimo e perfetto nel suo poderoso equilibrio fisico." (Italy must […] always be muscularly ready for all kinds of exertion: steady nerves, certain instincts and well-trained muscles are needed […] A strong Italian, perfect in his powerful physical balance will be bestowed with honour and glory.)[102] From the perspective of an active soldier, fighting alongside the Alpini, Marinetti rejoiced that finally "si trascureranno […] i mille eruditi italiani inchiodati dalla paralisi tra montagne di libri" (the thousands of erudite Italians nailed with paralysis among mountains of books will be neglected),[103] while those fighting in the real mountains of Italy will triumph.[104]

As the war drew on, Italy's preparedness gradually improved, resulting in a more efficient and sophisticated trench system and vast improvements in the supply of weapons, which by the middle of 1916 were being produced on an industrial scale.[105] Although in some ways it can be argued that alpine warfare was of a "seemingly primitive nature [… which] returned battle to the chivalrous age of war,"[106] the Italian experience of combat was profoundly influenced by technological advances. The Italian Army had artillery pieces, trench mortars, and machine guns at its disposal, as well as toxic gas.[107] Nonetheless, trench warfare on all fronts in the First World War was characterized by long periods of waiting during the day and intense, short-lived bursts of action at night during bombardments. This mode of engagement diverged significantly from Futurist imaginings and expectations of warfare. In an article of 1916 Settimelli admitted the Futurist naivety prior to the war: "Credevamo fosse fatta da tre quarti di baionetta e da un quarto di trincea. È invece fatta da tre quarti di trincea e da un quarto di baionetta." (We believed that it was made up of three-quarters bayonet and one-quarter trenches. It is actually made up of three-quarters trenches and one-quarter bayonet.)[108] Similar observations were made by Futurists at the front. Carli defined heroism as "tre quarti immobilità aspettante, e [...] un quarto vertigine travolgente" (three-quarters expectant immobility, and [...] one-quarter overwhelming dizziness).[109] In their first weeks with the Volunteer Cyclists, Marinetti and Boccioni had been particularly aggrieved at the lack of action they were experiencing. Marinetti expressed his impatience, writing in a letter: "Sono al *Fronte ... Fronte pensoso che aspetta*. Sotto cannoni italiani e davanti a cannoni austriaci *che non parlano*!!!!!" (I'm at the *Front ... thoughtful Front that's waiting*. Under Italian cannons and in front of Austrian ones *that don't speak*!!!!!)[110] Boccioni also complained about the lack of progress in battle: "Sono stato in trincea per ora silenziose [*sic*] come quelle dei tedeschi davanti a noi [...] Tutta la notte i fasci luminosi dei riflettori nostri percorrono il cielo creando delle visioni di notte guerresca bellissime. Tutto però tace. Quando avverrà l'avanzata?" (I've been in the trenches that are silent for the moment like the German ones opposite us [...] All night the bright beams of our reflectors sweep the sky creating beautiful night-time war visions. Everything is quiet though. When will the advance begin?)[111]

The interplay between long silence and the explosions of noise and bombardments was frequently evoked in the writings of combatant Futurists. Vann'Antò's experiences of the trenches were dominated by waiting rather than by fighting, and time began to lose all meaning for him:

Notte Silenzio – t-tttùuum (fucile nostro) ta-pum (austriaco) ta pum siii lenzio

Notte pressione manifredde sulle guance pullulio di spilli ai piedi proibito dormire – contate le ore ore ore impossibile 12 ore = 1 ora = 1 minuto [...] *Quando sarà giorno! quando sarà giorno!*

(**Night Silence** – t-tttùuum (our rifle) ta-pum (Austrian) ta pum siii lence

Night pressure coldhands on cheeks swarms of needles at our feet sleep forbidden – count the hours hours hours impossible 12 hours = 1 hour = 1 minute [...] *When will it be morning! when will it be morning!*)[112]

The moment of bombardment was also the subject of the free-word composition "Artiglieria in azione" by Acciaio (pseudonym of Ennio

Valentinelli). He begins by describing the dawn and the "lunghe trincee dormienti vedette allerte intirizzite lento snodarsi di fumo dalle cucine da campo odore di caffè" (long sleeping trenches look-outs alert numb with cold slow twisting smoke from camp kitchens smell of coffee).[113] The silence and peace of this scene are then suddenly shattered by a bombardment:

> rrr ombo (sordo) uuluuulato (lontano) "svÈglia'H!" crescendo crescendo **scarantantanarsi** [...] "sveglia! sveglia! sveglia!" scompiglio feroce teste braccia gambe fucili silenzio [...]
> **TAN NNN 305** scoppio boato metallico
> enorme macignifischi sviscerati scoppiettio di pietre strillanti polvere ghiaia zampillare di zolle umide di rugiada gavette lucide
> [...] TANNNN 4km di distanza ALLEGRO AGITATO scatenarsi 149.

> rrr umble (dull) hooowliiing (distant) "wAKe Up!" louder louder **hurling ourselves into our dens** [...] "wake up! wake up! wake up!" fierce confusion heads arms legs rifles silence [...]
> TAN NNN 305 explosion metallic roar
> Huge heavy whistling intense little explosion of screaming stones dust gravel
> gushing damp clumps of dew shiny mess tins
> [...] TANNNN 4 km away HAPPY AGITATED 149 unleashed.[114]

Valentinelli captures the "tirannia del rumore" (tyranny of noise), describing the "tonnellate di urli occhi chiusi timpani indolenziti" (tons of shouts closed eyes aching eardrums), before concluding, in a rather matter-of-fact way that it was ten-thirty and "ora del rancio" (time for rations).[115] It is a banal ending to such a violent episode and marks the soldier's return to the monotony of trench life, broken only by bombardments and the delivery of rations. The consequences of bombardments were also in evidence in the accounts of combatant Futurists. Luca Labozzetta's[116] "Trincea" includes images of "carne tritolata informe materia cerebrale sangue sangue sangue rosso vermiglio sangue rubino" (exploded minced brain matter blood blood blood red vermilion ruby blood).[117] Guizzidoro's[118] free-word composition is a particularly gruesome and visceral evocation of the realities of trench life: "[io sono] ritto su un mucchio di caduti i piedi a guazzo nel fango sanguinoso che trabocca dai ventri decomposti [...] Ho le mani gelate non più lana. Io vo scaldar le dita nelle budella fumide del primo che mi verrà tra i piedi." ([I am] upright on a pile of bodies splashing in the bloody mud that overflows from decomposing bowels [...] My hands are frozen no more wool. I warm my fingers in the steaming guts of the first one under my feet.)[119]

Modern methods of warfare did not have an impact on only the soldiers in the trenches. The landscape of the Italian mountain front was also subjected to a dramatic process of modernization and industrialization during the First World War. Overcoming his initial dislike of the mountains, Marinetti came to see them as "propizie alla creazione delle forze elettriche e di fiamme ubertose favorevoli alla velocità dei treni" (propitious to the creation of electric energy and fertile flames favourable to the speed of trains).[120] Very quickly whole villages were established in the mountains behind the front lines, comprising hospitals, warehouses, workshops, and kitchens. Hundreds of kilometres of roads and tunnels were constructed, as well as telegraph wires, railways, water pipes, and cable cars.[121] From 1916 onwards both the Italians and the Austrians employed mines, tunnelling under enemy trenches to explode mines below them. This approach constituted, for Marinetti, an early realization of his dreams of Futurist warfare. Marinetti wrote that war "dà la sua vera bellezza alle montagne, ai fiumi, ai boschi" (confers real beauty on the mountains, the rivers, the forests)[122] and declared that he loved the mountains of Trentino for the first time because "avevano finalmente riacquistato la loro anima essenziale che è l'artiglieria" (they had finally reacquired the essence of their soul, which is to be artillery).[123] Similarly, the purpose of the valleys was to reverberate with the sounds of cannons. Marinetti deemed nature to be incomplete without war and stated that it was war that endowed the mountainous landscape with a new purpose:

Le forme aggressive delle alte montagne hanno finalmente oggi ragione d'essere, tutte rivestite dalle fitte traiettorie, dai sibili e dai rombi curvi delle cannonate. I fiumi, trincee naturali, hanno oggi una vita logica. Interrompono la forza del nemico e vuotano i campi di battaglia alpestri di tutti i cadaveri che trascinano al mare.

(Today the aggressive shapes of the high mountains have a reason to exist, all covered by thick trajectories, by the curved hisses and roars of the cannons. The rivers, natural trenches, today have a logical life. They interrupt the strength of the enemy and empty the Alpine battlefields of the bodies that they drag to the sea.)[124]

Marinetti was particularly enthusiastic when describing the destruction that this accelerated industrialization had wrought on the mountain landscape. Whereas, in the past, the mountains had been gutted by winding tunnels, "oggi si decapitano con delle mine colossali" (today they are decapitated by colossal mines).[125] In this way the romantic sense of solitude typically associated with the Alpine environment could be destroyed: "si annullano le mulattiere pazienti e lunghissime a zig-zag con le linee rette volanti degli aeroplani" (the long and patient zig-zagging mule tracks are cancelled out by the flying straight lines of the aeroplanes).[126]

Marinetti transformed the Alpine landscape so that the experience of mountain combat would conform to Futurist visions of technologically enhanced and industrialized modernity. The man-made environment, transformed by war, surpassed the traditional religious and nostalgic associations of nature and landscape. Marinetti's intention was to "distruggere la vecchia poesia della distanza e delle solitudini selvagge" (destroy the poetry of distance, and of solitude in the wild), and he declared that "la nostra sensibilità futurista [...] non si commuove più davanti al cupo mistero d'una valle inesplorata, di una gola di monti" (our Futurist sensibility is no longer moved by the dark mystery of an unexplored valley or of a mountain gorge).[127] Marja Härmänmaa has argued that "in Marinetti's cosmology [...] Nature is characterized by aggressive and violent forces [...] Respect if not fear towards the forces of Nature seems to be a fundamental element in Marinetti's ideology."[128] While this judgment holds true for Marinetti's early Futurist works (including *Mafarka il futurista* and *Zang Tumb Tumb*), I would argue that after his first combat experiences in 1915 this attitude of respect is far less evident and has been replaced, for the most part, with a firm belief in Futurist and man-made superiority over the natural environment, encapsulated in his free-word drawing *Battaglia a 9 piani* (Nine-storey battle).

Battaglia a 9 piani shows a cross-section of the mountains with Lake Garda in the middle. One side is Austrian, the other is Italian. The drawing was published in January 1916 on the front page of the periodical *Vela Latina*.[129] John White has called *Battaglia a 9 piani* an example of Marinetti's "war reportage," writing that "Marinetti's dual authority as renowned modernist poet and eyewitness to a number of historically prestigious battles underwrites Italian Futurism's patriotic campaign to persuade fellow countrymen to abandon their neutralist stance."[130] However, given that the drawing was issued in a publication that was

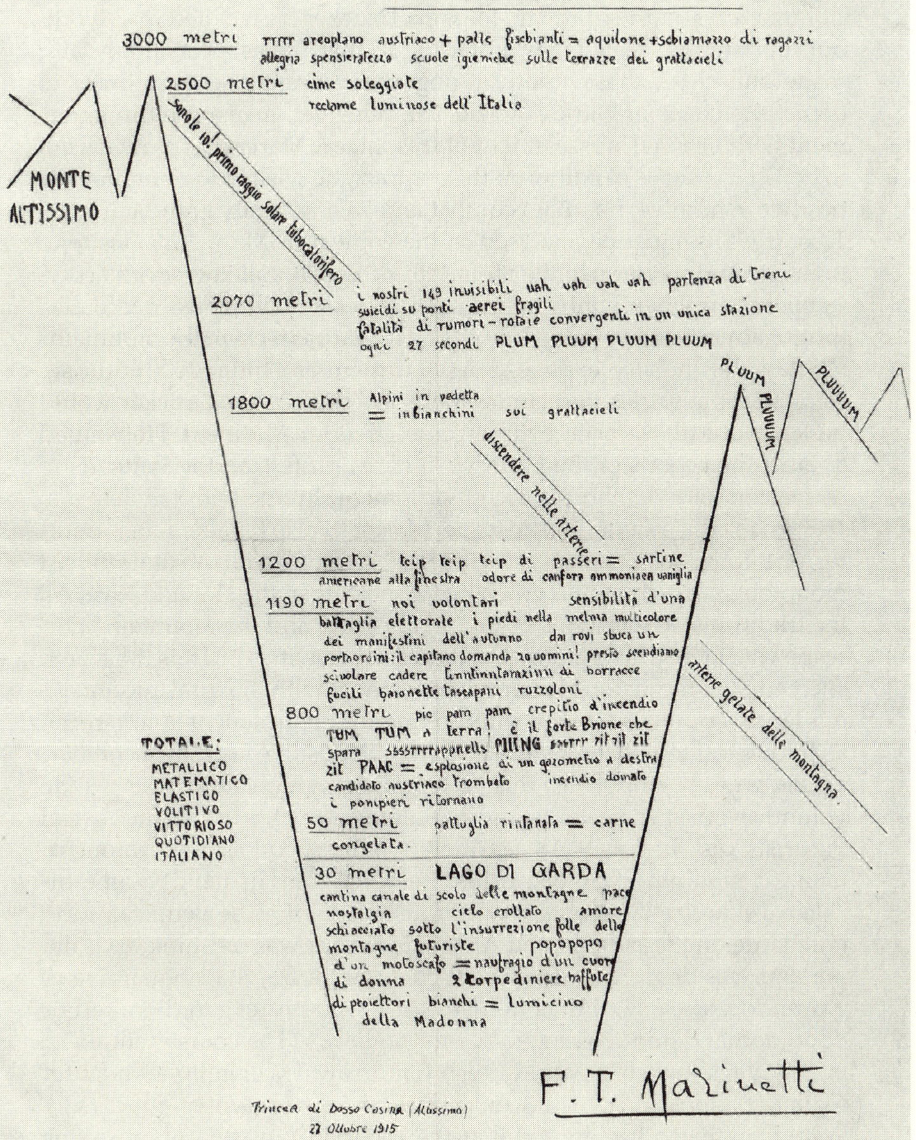

Figure 2.3. Filippo Tommaso Marinetti, *Battaglia a 9 piani* (Nine-storey battle), 1915. Courtesy of Museo d'arte moderna e contemporanea di Trento e Rovereto, Archivio del '900.

very closely aligned with Futurism, Marinetti was more likely preaching to the converted than reaching out to neutralists, as White suggests. Commenting on the drawing, Johanna Drucker has written that "without, apparently, seeing any paradox in this whatsoever, [Marinetti] made one of his most orderly typographic arrangements in order to depict the chaos of battle."[131] I do not, however, find myself in agreement with Drucker's assessment of this image. Marinetti's aim was not to depict the chaos of battle; on the contrary, he wished to underline the positive aspects of mountain combat and its essentially Futurist nature. This drawing must be analysed in the context of Marinetti's desire to urbanize and modernize the mountains: they are called *grattacieli* (skyscrapers), and their sunny peaks are the "réclame luminose dell'Italia" (bright advertising of Italy). Not only did Marinetti claim the mountains for Italy, but he also expressly defined them as "futuriste" (Futurist). Depicting the battles in the mountains as "chaotic," as Drucker would prefer, would have been counterproductive for Marinetti. He wanted to exalt the actions of the Futurist soldiers, professing the Futurists to be masters of this inhospitable environment. In line with his desire to "futur-ize" the mountain landscape, Marinetti also heralded the "insurrezione folle delle montagne futuriste" (crazy revolt of the Futurist mountains), which would crush peace, nostalgia, the sky, and love. All the traditional associations of mountaineering and the mountain landscape would be destroyed by the Futurists' activities.[132] Thus, Marinetti succeeded in reconciling his urban movement with the rural, mountainous landscape of Trentino by interpreting the environment in urban and technological terms and by underlining the positive aspects of combat.

One way of embracing this technologically enhanced war was to volunteer for specific units and battalions, which a small number of Futurists did. In July 1918 Marinetti's request to join the armoured-tank division was granted, to his great delight. His tank became his "alcova d'acciaio" (steel alcove), protecting him as he ventured forth into battle. In the same period Armando Mazza was finishing his training and was desperate to fight: "Il corso finirà fra una cinquantina di giorni. Io vorrei che finisse domani. Andrò in un regg.to di fanteria e dopo domanderò il passaggio nei mitraglieri." (The course will finish in fifty days. I wish it would finish tomorrow. I will go to an infantry regiment and then I will ask for a transfer to the machine-gunners.)[133] Walter Adamson has argued that the Futurists "insisted upon setting themselves apart in their 'futurist squads,' which were usually devoted to the most technologically exciting and ostensibly daring activities, such as the armoured-car division or the aviation unit,"[134] but in fact the Futurists who fought in these battalions were in the minority. Many veterans and serving members of the elite Arditi battalions joined the Futurist Political Party in autumn 1918, but most had no prior affiliation with the movement. Only four Futurists who were active during the war years served with the Arditi: Mario Carli, Jamar 14,[135] Cesare Cerati,[136] and Ottone Rosai.[137]

Futurist Emotions in War-Time

The Futurists, of course, did not escape the war unscathed. Marinetti calculated that more than 60 per cent of their members had been affected, between deaths, injuries, and mutilations.[138] Numerous Futurists were injured, including Cerati, Guizzi Doro, Steiner, and Nino Formoso.[139] Luigi Russolo suffered a severe head injury and underwent a long convalescence. Having already received a silver medal for his action on Altipiano d'Asiago, Antonio Sant'Elia was killed in action by a shot to the forehead from a machine gun in 1916. Other minor Futurists also lost their lives, including Athos Casarini, Luca Labozzetta, Ugo Tommei, and Ugo Cantucci.[140] Most famously, Boccioni died after falling off a horse during training in August 1916, which was a traumatic blow to the movement's morale.[141]

Marinetti was devastated by the loss of Boccioni, his closest friend. Paolo Buzzi reported in a letter to Pratella in August 1916 that "Marinetti è col cuore e col cervello spezzato; naturalmente non l'ho mai visto più alto e eretto e spavaldo contro l'agguato del destino. So il dolore della sua vasta anima" (Marinetti's heart and head are broken: of course I have never seen him taller more erect more arrogant against the ambush of destiny. I know the pain of his vast soul).[142] Emilio Gentile is correct in noting that "l'accettazione entusiastica della guerra non cedette alla delusione dei lunghi anni in trincea" (the enthusiastic acceptance of the war did not surrender to the disappointment of the long years in the trenches).[143] However, although the Futurists – Marinetti included – did not radically alter their beliefs about the war and its validity, they were in no way immune to the psychological and emotional pressures that combat entailed.[144] Statements such as those of Gentile feed into a trend in Futurist scholarship, which asserts the uniqueness of Marinetti's combat experiences and his distance from any so-called normal responses to the realities of war. Claudia Salaris claimed that "il Marinetti in divisa è senza dubbio un soldato *sui generis*" (Marinetti in uniform is without doubt a soldier *sui generis*),[145] and in a similar vein Mario Isenghi has argued that Marinetti essentially experienced a "guerra privata [...] meno lontana dalle sue personali esigenze e più vicina alle forme avventurose e libertarie" (a private war [...] less distant from his personal needs and closer to adventurous and libertarian forms).[146] However, such observations do not reflect the significant shift in tone that can be observed in the letters he wrote to his closest confidantes following Boccioni's death, once he had returned to the front in early 1917, which reveal a hitherto-absent negativity. Despite the difficult physical conditions, Marinetti's high spirits had seemed almost impenetrable during his time with the Volunteer Cyclists.[147] Although Marinetti was an officer from 1917, and thus enjoyed superior living conditions and a higher status within the army, his emotional state was much more fragile. Without the moral support of his Futurist friends that he had enjoyed with the Volunteer Cyclists, his nostalgia for home revealed itself in his letters.

Marinetti's letters to Cangiullo and Pratella, written in 1917 and 1918, reveal a side of his war experience that is rarely glimpsed in his notebooks and is entirely absent from his public writings, or indeed his letters from his time with the Volunteer Cyclists in 1915. His loneliness in the winter of 1916–17 is palpable. He appealed to Cangiullo: "Perché non mi scrivi? Aspetto di te una lunga lettera (con disegni caricature divine pazzie ecc.) che mi faccia *ridere*" (Why don't you write to me? I'm waiting for a long letter from you (with drawings divine crazy caricatures etc.) that will make me *laugh*).[148] On New Year's Eve 1916 he was depressed and dispirited: "In trincea. Piena di neve. Sacco a pelo nel mio ricovero profondo. Penso al genio giocondo del divino Grande Cangiullo che mi divertirebbe col suo spirito diabolico fresco esplosivo se fosse *qui con me*. Ti auguro salute e disinvoltura rosea nella dura lacerante vita." (In the trenches. Full of snow. Sleeping bag in my deep shelter. I'm thinking about the playful genius of the divine Great Cangiullo that would entertain me with his diabolical fresh explosive spirit if he were *here with me*. I wish you health and rosy carefreeness in this hard painful life.)[149]

Around the same time, Marinetti also admitted to Pasqualino Cangiullo (Francesco's younger brother)[150] that he had "pochi pensieri dolci" (few pleasant thoughts), and he appeared to have some doubts as to whether he would return from the war "in piedi con polmoni sani e muscoli pronti" (standing with healthy lungs and strong muscles).[151] Although attempting to keep his emotions in check, Marinetti could not disguise how much he missed Cangiullo's company: "Io *ho la pelle dura* [...] Ma sento acutamente la nostalgia dell'amico geniale forte e delizioso." (I *have a thick skin* [...] But I acutely long for my brilliant strong and wonderful friend.)[152] His low spirits persisted into 1918. In a letter to Pratella, Marinetti appeared to resent the burden of his military service, writing bitterly:

Ti sento spaventosamente e dolorosamente pessimista! Perché? Sei giovane sano forte. Sei uno dei più grandi e potenti ingegni del nostro tempo. Hai una meravigliosa bambina, una donna intelligente che ti vuol profondamente bene, una famiglia che ti circonda di calore morale, molti amici che ti amano, un pubblico vasto profondo ad ascoltarti. Vivi negli arabeschi e nelle ondate musicali del tuo genio, in casa tua, nella tua Romagna preferita! Questo non ti basta?!

   Ed io che spingo sempre più a velocità pazze la mia vita senza quiete né riposo!

(You seem frighteningly and painfully pessimistic! Why? You are young healthy strong. You are one of the greatest and most powerful talents of our time. You have a wonderful daughter, an intelligent woman who loves you deeply, a family that surrounds you with moral warmth, lots of friends who love you, a vast deep public that listens to you. You live in the musical arabesques and waves of your genius, at home, in your adored Romagna! Is that not enough for you?!

   And I who push my life ever forward at crazy speeds without peace or rest!)[153]

A month later, in an unusually frank letter to Marietta Angelini, Marinetti revealed the extent of his nostalgia for home and even jokingly acknowledged the surprisingly un-Futurist nature of his complaints:

Ogni sera penso a te e alle tue mani miracolose, davanti alla pessima minestra insipida che mi prepara il mio soldato – *cuoco*!!!!???
   Dove sono i *risotti* e i *minestroni* paradisiaci della Marietta? ...
   E quest'inverno che non finisce mai! Siamo sempre nel fango *gelato*.
   E la Castità atroce *assoluta* assoluta!
   Cosa ne dici della mia energia e della mia volontà eroica??

(Every evening I think about you and your miraculous hands, faced with the terrible bland soup that the soldier-*cook* (!!!!???) prepares for me.

> Where are Marietta's heavenly *risotti* and *soups*?...
> And this never-ending winter! We are always in the *frozen* mud.
> And atrocious *absolute* absolute Celibacy!
> What do you think of my energy and my heroic will??)[154]

These letters jar with the expected response of Marinetti to his combat experiences during the Great War. It is essential to remember, however, that these frank admissions were shared only with a very few trusted correspondents; in letters to others, Marinetti's tone was invariably upbeat, positive, and quintessentially Futurist in outlook. As Fabio Caffarena has noted in his study of Italian soldiers' war-time letters, there is no immediacy in them, and "gli scriventi confezionano, quand'anche involontariamente, l'immagine di sé che si vuol comunicare" (the writers package, even if involuntarily, the image of themselves that they wish to communicate),[155] which is true of Marinetti and his carefully managed, public self-image.

While the Futurists may not have questioned the central validity of Italy's war, many combatant Futurists did have mixed feelings about the impact of their military service on their artistic and literary pursuits. Boccioni was conscripted in July 1916, and he approached this experience with an attitude that was rather different from the one he had held in the previous year with the Volunteer Cyclists.[156] His first concern was for the financial well-being of his mother during his absence with the army, and thus, immediately prior to his departure for the front, he sought to recoup monies owed to him.[157] Boccioni's anxiety was also heightened by the fact that he had just begun a romantic relationship with noblewoman Vittoria Colonna, from whom he did not wish to be separated.[158] Although he tried to convince himself that once he would be in the barracks "con un po' di allegria tutto si accomoda" (with a bit of cheerfulness, everything will pan out), later in the same letter he revealed the extent of his dissatisfaction and trepidation: "Questa interruzione della mia vita (per lo meno artistica) mi mette terrore in certi momenti. Poi mi passa. Cominciava un bel periodo e [...] avevo davanti un periodo di calma. Coraggio e avanti!" (This interruption of my life (at least my artistic life) terrifies me at certain moments. Then it passes. A good period was starting for me and [...] I had a period of calm in front of me. Buck up and onwards!)[159]

Primo Conti[160] had similar concerns as he waited to be called up. He wrote of the "nodo complicato di promesse dentro di me: ricerche pittoriche da svolgere, un *romanzo* da finire, e il progetto di qualche mese di raccoglimento e di studio" (complicated knot of promises inside me: painting research to pursue, a *novel* to finish, and a plan for a few months of reflection and study), but he tried to reassure himself that "sento che in fondo la vita militare non potrà farmi che bene" (I feel that deep down military life can't but do me good).[161] Folgore also harboured negative thoughts about the wisdom of pursuing combat in favour of art. Francesco Meriano wrote to him that "capisco che lei ha ragione riguardo all'idea generale che specialmente in questo momento è meglio creare che combattere e meglio combattere idee che uomini" (I know that you are right about the general idea that especially in times such as these it is better to create than to fight and better to fight ideas than men).[162]

The Role of Futurism for Combatant Futurists

Despite these fears many Futurists were able to continue their creative pursuits while engaged in military service. In fact, it was a surprise to some of them that boredom could be an issue. After more than a year of active service, the reality of life in the trenches had sunk in for Valentinelli, and in one of his free-word compositions he referred to the "vastità di noia" (depth of boredom) and was overwhelmed by "inerzia capogiro stanchezza malessere noia stupidità" (inertia vertigo tiredness disquiet boredom stupidity).[163] In one of his poems Giuseppe Steiner recalled having "nulla da fare" (nothing to do) during the day in the trenches, so he shot and killed two squirrels that were playing in the snow. The poem's concluding lines were "Gli scoiattoli non vegnono più / ed io mi annoio." (The squirrels don't come any more / and I'm bored.)[164]

That both men expressed their boredom in literary compositions demonstrates the role that Futurism was able to play for them in supporting their psychological well-being at the front. After expressing his unhappiness at living "in solitudine in un angolo remoto del Lido di Venezia" (in solitude in a remote corner of the Venice Lido),[165] where he was stationed with an anti-aerial battery, Luciano Folgore dedicated himself to writing a long poem about his experiences between August 1917 and August 1918, entitled "Poema della Guardia," as a way to combat his boredom.[166]

Although they were unable to escape the realities of combat life, as intellectuals the Futurists did in some cases receive special treatment, primarily in the form of sharing meals with higher-ranking officers and being afforded some time to paint or write. During their service with the Volunteer Cyclists both Boccioni and Marinetti enjoyed a special status as minor celebrities within the ranks. Marinetti claimed that during his reconnaissance missions in 1915 he found many soldiers and lieutenants who "amano il Futurismo conoscono *tutti noi* e vogliono spiegazioni" (love Futurism, they know *all of us* and they want explanations).[167] While charged with guarding a fort on Lake Garda, a young Sardinian captain, Bellisai, invited Marinetti, Boccioni, and Sironi, to his room to discuss Futurist painting and architecture. According to Boccioni, "ovunque si vada Marinetti ed io siamo chiesti subito dagli ufficiali che c'invitano a pranzo e si riesce così a passare qualche serata" (everywhere Marinetti and I go we are immediately asked by officers to dine with them and so we manage to pass a few evenings like that).[168]

When he was in hospital recovering from an injury in summer 1917, Carrà encountered a doctor who asked whether he was related to the Futurist painter of the same name. When Carrà replied that he was that painter, the doctor informed the nurses that they should "avere per me riguardo" (have respect for me).[169] Thus, while recuperating, he was afforded materials and space to devote himself to his work. He described himself as "quasi felice" (almost happy) to be in hospital because "da qualche giorno posso lavorare [...] Era tanto tempo che non dipingevo. Erano 4 mesi e mi sembravano 4 secoli" (I've been able to work for the last few days [...] I had not painted for a long time. It had been 4 months but seemed liked 4 centuries).[170] By August of 1918, in convalescence with a serious injury to his hand, Carli was more than ready to redirect his energies towards Futurism, writing that "l'astinenza forzata per quasi tre anni da tutto ciò che non è guerra, ha immagazzinato in me delle riserve immense di energia costruttrice, che hanno bisogno di essere prontamente impiegate" (the enforced three-year abstinence from everything that isn't war has stored up in me immense reserves of constructive energy, that need to be used immediately).[171]

Pratella also received some preferential treatment, though more because of his status as a well-known composer than because of his role as a Futurist. Serving as a territorial soldier in Rimini, he was given a transfer to his home town of Lugo so that he could manage its school of music, of which he was director. He was given "molte ore libere per occuparmi della scuola, l'esonero da tutti i servizi di caserma e l'autorizzazione di sostare a leggere o a scrivere nell'ufficio di fureria" (lots of free time to deal with the school, exemption from all duties in the barracks, and the permission to stay in the orderly's office to read and write).[172] Pratella never went to the front, and throughout his military service he continued to write his column on music for *Gli Avvenimenti* in Milan and collaborated with *L'Eco della Cultura* in Naples. In spite of his comfortable and safe position, which gave him the possibility of visiting his family every weekend, Pratella complained of the tedium of life in the barracks, calling himself "[un] uccello che non canta in gabbia" ([a] bird who doesn't sing in his cage). He continued: "questa vita impossibile tediosa mi snerva e mi accascia gradualmente, raffina-tamente, giorno per giorno, senza tregua" (this impossible tedious life wears me down and I gradually become discouraged, nobly, day by day, with no break).[173]

Both Boccioni and Cangiullo wished to obtain maximum benefit from their particular artistic and literary talents while serving in the army. Initially Boccioni had wished to enter the engineers' corps as a draftsman, but he could not convince his superiors that "nella qualifica di *pittore* ci sta anche il *disegnatore*" (within the qualification of *painter* is also the *draftsman*).[174] Some weeks later, when he was introduced to his future commanding lieutenant, Boccioni tried to "dargli l'impressione di chi ero e mi promise agevolazioni" (give him an understanding of who I was and he promised me preferential treatment).[175] Just a few days after this encounter Boccioni was offered a position as a scribe in the offices, which he ultimately refused, preferring to "fare il mio dovere in batteria" (do my duty in the artillery).[176] This decision paid great dividends to Boccioni, who was highly regarded by his peers and superiors as a result. As an artist of some renown, he was given free time to write and study twice a week if he wished. He wrote to his friend Ferruccio Busoni:

I superiori [...] sono molto gentili con me e mi usano cortesie eccezionali, specialmente rivolte alla mia qualità d'artista. È una cosa che mi ha molto consolato. I primi [giorni] sono stati atroci [...] Mi si concede, tutto in via eccezionalissima, qualsiasi permesso e tutti hanno stima per me e grande rispetto. Ho giovato molto il mio nome che è qui più conosciuto di quello che potessi immaginare, e l'avere rifiutato di entrare in fureria come scrivano ... La mia dichiarazione di volere rimanere in batteria per fare tutto il mio dovere di soldato mi ha dato molta considerazione.

(My superiors [...] are very nice to me and are exceptionally polite, particularly about my artistic talents. It has given me great consolation. The first [days] were atrocious [...] I am granted, completely outside of normal rules, any permission and everyone has great respect and esteem for me. I have benefited a lot from my name, which is more known here than you could imagine, and to have refused to work in the office as a scribe … My declaration that I wished to stay in the artillery to do my soldierly duty has afforded me a lot of respect.)[177]

Upon arriving at Valmontone where he was based with other infantry soldiers, Cangiullo suffered from the isolation of military life and confessed to being "un po' depresso" (a bit depressed). He continued: "Non ti descrivo come passo i giorni! Ò perduto ogni cognizione di tempo, di luogo. Non so più dove, come e come'è che viva. Non ò più un'immagine! Non ò più una trovata!" (I won't describe how I pass my days! I have lost all perception of time, of place. I don't know where, how to live. I don't have any images! I don't have any good ideas any more!)[178] In a stroke of good fortune, however, his captain, Luigi Valazzi, had met Pratella before the war and had fond memories of him. Thus, to make life easier for himself, Cangiullo requested from Pratella a letter of recommendation, stating who he was and suggesting some special treatment.[179] He wrote to Marinetti at the same time, suggesting that he might co-sign Pratella's letter to give it greater weight.[180] In a subsequent letter, presumably fearful of the potentially negative optics of Cangiullo's request, Marinetti coached Pratella in what he should write to Valazzi. It should communicate to Valazzi "chi è Cangiullo, il suo grande valore e pure i riguardi che la sua sensibilità artistica meravigliosa merita ed esige" (who Cangiullo is; his great, pure value; the respect his marvellous artistic sensibility merits and demands). However, Marinetti repeatedly stressed that the letter was not about "raccomandare un soldato al suo superiore, ma di presentare un poeta geniale altamente italiano al suo capitano intelligentissimo" (recommending a soldier to his superior, but about introducing a brilliant, supremely Italian poet to his very intelligent captain).[181]

While their receipt of special concessions such as these indicates that the Futurists were generally respected by their superior officers, it is more difficult to ascertain the reactions of other soldiers and officers to the Futurists. Certainly, among the ranks of the Volunteer Cyclists the Futurist figures were well received and well integrated, and they participated fully in the social life of the battalion. The Volunteer Cyclists were stationed in Gallarate, near Milan, between the end of May and 20 July 1915, where they underwent training exercises. Before they departed for the front lines at the end of July, the volunteers organized two benefit performances for the battalion and the people of Gallarate. In both cases the "decorazione semifuturista" (semi-Futurist decoration)[182] of the theatre was remarked upon; it had been executed by Boccioni, Russolo, Sant'Elia, and others.[183] *La Gazzetta dello Sport* described the "ridda orgiastica di colori, così cara al temperamento dei pittori futuristi che si sono sbizzarriti a caricaturizzare corse folli di moto, sgroppate di volontari ciclisti, motivi di ruote, cadute capitombolari, affannose riparazioni di macchine" (orgiastic jumble of colours, so dear to the temperament of the Futurist painters who went wild drawing mad races in automobiles, racing of the volunteer cyclists, motifs of wheels, headlong falls, exhausting repairs of machines).[184] Marinetti also declaimed Futurist poetry on both occasions, including his own "Bombardamento di Adrianopoli." A local newspaper reported that Marinetti's performance aroused much curiosity in the audience, and noted that "fu salutato forse per la prima volta da applausi incontrastanti" (he was greeted, maybe for the first time, with undisputed applause).[185] He received a similar reaction at the second performance the following week when he was "ripetutamente e, crediamo, sinceramente applaudito" (repeatedly and, we believe, sincerely applauded).[186] Certainly, Futurist ideas made a strong impression on members of the battalion. At a celebratory meal in November 1915 to mark their success at Dosso Casina, a humorous song in Lombard dialect was performed whose title was "Zum … tu … tum," a clear reference to Futurist *parole in libertà*.[187] At another banquet the following week Marinetti was lightly made fun of in a rhyming song where it was claimed that "dopo l'avanzata – è meno futuretti" (after the advance – he is less *futuretti*).[188] In a third song, written to mark the disbandment of the battalion, the anonymous author recounted memories of the time spent at the front lines, with a verse dedicated to the leader of Futurism:

Ricorderem gli scoppi – del fiero MARINETTI
L'assegio d'Adrianopoli – gli scatti i grandi affetti
Dei bulgari la marcia – le vampe e i boati
I colpi dei cannoni – l'assalto dei soldati!

(We will remember the explosions – of the proud MARINETTI
The siege of Adrianpoli – the gestures the great affection
Of the Bulgarians the march – the flames and the rumbles
The bang of the cannons – the assault of the soldiers!)[189]

Such an enthusiastic response to the Futurists was perhaps unsurprising in a battalion as positively inclined in favour of the war as was the Lombard Battalion of Volunteer Cyclists.

In other battalions and divisions, interventionists reported the displays of hostility shown towards them for their support of the war. Ottone Rosai recalled such instances in his letters. He noted that "io […] che voglio la guerra sono uno dei più malvisti fra tutto questo ammasso di merda" (I […] who desire the war am one of the most unpopular in all of this heap of shit).[190] However, there were apparently also situations in which the opposite occurred, such as the case of Mario Carli. In summer 1915 he reported to his father: "i miei camerati mi vogliono molto bene: ho trovato fra loro qualche giovane d'ingegno, letterati, avvocati, ingegneri. La mia ciocca bianca è diventata popolare e io sono chiamata comunemente *'il futurista.'* Oggi tre colleghi si sono litigati seriamente per poter leggere il mio libro." (My fellow soldiers like me a lot: I have found among them a few talented young people, intellectuals, lawyers, engineers. My white tuft of hair has become popular and I am generally called *"the Futurist."* Today three colleagues seriously fought with each other to be able to read my book.)[191]

Unfortunately, in the absence of additional evidence, it is impossible to ascertain to what extent either extreme was representative of Futurist experiences in the army.

Futurist Coping through *Parole in Libertà* and Letter Writing

Aside from certain material benefits that Futurism afforded, of more significance was the role that it played in the psychological well-being and resilience of combatant Futurists. As seen above in the case of the Volunteer Cyclists, battle was regarded as the ultimate expression of Futurism. The attitude of Angelo Rognoni was similar: "Io sono più futurista che mai in questo ambiente che sa di polvere di cannone. Faccio delle galoppate meravigliose." (I am more Futurist than ever in this atmosphere that smells of cannon powder. I do marvellous gallops.)[192] When Pratella learned that Jannelli was an artillerist, he told him, "Mi piacete molto così; siete al vostro posto futurista di battaglia" (I like you a lot like that; you are in your Futurist battle position).[193] Marinetti, unsurprisingly, also regarded the war as the fullest expression of Futurism, declaring, "Io sono in pieno futurismo sotto le parabole rombando delle bombe, aspettando la grande Ora ferocissima e massacrante!" (I am in full Futurism under the roaring trajectory of the bombs, waiting for the great ferocious and massacring Hour!)[194] In the context of British and German soldiers, Alexander Watson has argued that "by imposing an imagined structure and order on the frightening and unpredictable environment in which they operated, soldiers made it seem less chaotic and threatening and provided themselves with a sense of security and empowerment crucial for mental health."[195] The structure and order to which Watson was referring consisted of positive illusions, humour, and religion, but for the Futurists the "imagined structure" was Futurism itself.

Futurism offered a ready-made code with which to interpret the conflict and extract meaning from it, and this is particularly true of the Futurists' ability to confront the "bombardamento sensoriale" (sensorial bombardment)[196] brought about by technological advancements in weaponry. The First World War has been considered a turning point in the history of the landscape of sound "because of the unceasing, obsessive, and to contemporaries intolerable, omnipresence of noise."[197] This "symphony of the front" – the overwhelming assault on soldiers' auditory sensations that occurred in the trenches during the First World War – is well documented in the historiography of the conflict.[198] In line with the experiences of other soldiers, the Futurist sensorial experience of the First World War was dominated by the auditory. Luigi Russolo concluded in his 1916 work *L'arte dei rumori* (The art of noises), which was inspired by his time fighting with the Alpine soldiers in 1915, that "nella guerra moderna, meccanica e metallica l'elemento visivo è quasi nullo; infiniti invece vi sono il senso, il significato e l'espressione dei rumori" (in modern mechanical metallic war, the visual element is almost nothing; on the other hand the sense, meaning and expression of noises is infinite).[199]

Marinetti had long been interested in battlefield noises, and indeed his first large-scale *parole in libertà* experiment, *Zang Tumb Tumb*, was based on the experience of war noises. Words in freedom was the most widely used method of conveying the sounds of bombardments to others. Russolo wrote in 1916: "La guerra moderna non può essere espressa liricamente, se non coll'istrumentazione rumoristica delle parole in libertà futuriste [...] I poeti futuristi [...] sono i soli che rendano colle parole in libertà l'essenza rumoristica delle battaglie d'oggi." (Modern war cannot be expressed lyrically, if not with noisemaking instruments of Futurist words in freedom [...] The Futurist poets [...] are the only ones who can render with words in freedom the noisy essence of today's battles.)[200]

Similarly, Paolo Buzzi commented that "la guerra è rumore" (war is noise) and that "i bombardamenti, i treni blindati, i duelli d'artiglieria, le cariche, i reticolati elettrizzati non hanno nulla a che fare colla poesia tradizionale, archeologica, georgica, nostalgico [*sic*] erotica" (bombardments, armoured trains, artillery duels, explosive charges, electric barbed wire have nothing to do with traditional poetry – archaeological, pastoral, nostalgic, erotic). For this reason the *parole in libertà* constituted a successful vehicle for the Futurists at the front to communicate their experiences.[201] Three years previously Marinetti had already provided similar advice about the efficacy of words-in-freedom techniques in conveying war experiences. In the 1913 manifesto "Distruzione della sintassi, Immaginazione senza fili, Parole in libertà" (Destruction of syntax, Wireless imagination, Words in freedom), Marinetti asked the reader to imagine a friend who was recounting a dramatic experience, whether it be a revolution, a war, a shipwreck, or an earthquake. Instinctively, Marinetti argued, he will begin eschewing syntax and punctuation, preferring instead to convey the visual, aural, and olfactory sensations of the story.[202] Thus, according to Marinetti, the appropriate manner for a Futurist to deal with an overwhelming experience, including war, was through words in freedom. The evidence of Futurist soldiers who fought during the First World War is that they followed Marinetti's advice.[203] The Futurist journal, *L'Italia Futurista*, published between June 1916 and February 1918, contained a page of *parole in libertà* drawings in almost every issue, featuring those that followed the Futurist pattern of conveying war noises through complex typography and layout.[204]

By filtering their experiences through words-in-freedom compositions, the Futurists were able to intellectualize them and distance themselves from the reality of the trenches. Eric Leed has written about the link between the constant noise in the trenches and instances of mental breakdown, arguing that "for the vast majority of Europeans who fought in the war, noise meant nothing but chaos; it caused nothing but fear, stupefactions, and dull resignation. Precisely because there was no cultural convention to call forth an appropriate switch of the soldier's 'inner state' during the transition from order to noise during the war, the barrage most often effected a transition into neurosis, breakdown, or mental disorder."[205]

In contrast to the picture painted by Leed, the Futurists, owing to their pre-war exposure to war noises, did possess a "cultural convention" that could be employed in order to interpret the chaos of noise, namely words in freedom. By intellectualizing their experiences and interpreting the noise of the bombardments according to Futurist codes, the Futurists were able to construct meaning from the chaos. Mary R. Habeck has discussed how many soldiers would compare the noises to human sounds or to aspects of their pre-war lives as a way of making sense of their experiences.[206] Marinetti, for example, recounted to Pratella his experience of a "Battaglia ferocissima con balzi violenti cadenze infinite, ritmi grandiosi, ritorni furenti brutali, martellamenti selvaggi, che mi ricordavano la tua Grande Sinfonia futurista al Costanzi" (ferocious Battle with violent leaps infinite cadences, impressive rhythms, raging brutal choruses, wild hammering, that reminded me of your Great Futurist Symphony at the Costanzi [Theatre]).[207] The Futurist use of *parole in libertà* can be viewed in analogous terms, in that they helped protect the Futurists from the more extreme psychological disorders that afflicted so many of the men who fought in the trenches of the Great War.[208]

In addition to the creative outlet that Futurism could provide for its members, the movement also, and perhaps more importantly, provided emotional support by fostering a sense of belonging and group identity. With combatant Futurists stationed all over the "zona di Guerra,"[209] their primary method of communication, as it was for all others serving in the army, was letters.[210] The possibility of promoting group identity through letters had been recognized by Marinetti even before the beginning of the war,[211] but once he was at the front in August 1915, he quickly understood the importance that letter writing would assume for both Futurist soldiers and Futurists on the home front. Thus, he began to ruminate on the possibility of Futurism engaging in this unprecedented epistolary urge and decided to impose a Futurist framework on the movement's war-time communication in order to promote group cohesion. Already by September 1915 Marinetti had written to Cangiullo of his desire to overhaul the process of letter writing:

Ho pensato alla grande grandissima utilità di scriversi con parole in libertà semplificate e chiare molto chiare. Voglio riformare lo stile epistolare ora assolutamente passatista pedante lungo monotono carico ridicolo! Laconismo + segni aritmetici + varietà calligrafica espressiva = lettere futuriste.

(I have been thinking about the terrific usefulness of writing with simplified and clear (very clear) words in freedom. I want to reform the epistolary style that is today absolutely passéist pedantic long monotonous heavy

ridiculous! Brevity + arithmetic signs + expressive calligraphic variety =
Futurist letters.)[212]

Cangiullo took up the challenge and designed the "lettera tipo-
Cangiullo" and the "cartolina tipo-Cangiullo."[213] In both cases, the
space for writing was divided into different subject boxes: those of the
postcard into Futurism, War, News and Business, Pleasures, Women,
Travel and Appointments, and Greetings or Insults; and those of the letter into almost identical headings. In a letter of 12 September Marinetti
advised Buzzi on how best to use the new letters and postcards:

Nelle lettere e cartoline (meglio queste perche impongono laconismo
e sintesi) ti consiglio di servirti molto della valutazione numerica (+ −
x =) e musicale [...] Utile scrivere con parole in libertà a tutti gli amici.
Propagare. Risolvere problema della lettera diventata ridicola nella sua
vecchia forma.

(In the letters and postcards (these are better because they impose brevity
and synthesis) I advise you to use numeric (+ − x =) and musical signs a
lot [...] Useful to write with words in freedom to all your friends. Spread
the word. Resolve the problem of the letter that has become ridiculous in
its old form.)[214]

Sometime around September or October Boccioni requested more
of Cangiullo's "moduli geniali" (terrific forms) as they had used them
all.[215] The predefined subject headings in these Futurist letter and postcard templates were an attempt to both enforce a Futurist interpretation
of the war experience and develop group camaraderie between combatant and non-combatant Futurists.

Over and above this rather rigid use of correspondence, combatant
Futurists engaged intensely in letter writing, both with other Futurists
at the front and with those on the home front. Much has been written
about the functions of letter writing for combatants in French, British,
and Italian contexts,[216] and numerous scholars have stressed the importance of letters in identity construction and maintenance for soldiers
and officers. Jay Winter has argued that the importance of letter writing for soldiers lay in the fact that they "reminded soldiers who they
had been before and who (God willing) they would be after the war."[217]
Gibelli is even more insistent about the significance of letters for soldiers, as they provide "l'unico rifugio in una situazione totalmente

inospitale e precaria, quasi come l'unica fonte di identità in una condizione disorientante" (the only refuge in a completely inhospitable and precarious situation, virtually the only source of identity in a disorientating situation).[218]

Correspondence fulfilled such a role for Futurists in uniform. In the Italian context Caffarena has noted the frequent cases of older men trying to control, from a distance, their business affairs, their farms, and their children, "cercando di riaffermare il ruolo di capo famiglia messo in discussione dalla lontananza" (trying to reassert their role as head of the family, which had been called into question by their absence).[219] The evidence of Marinetti's letters suggests that, in addition to the emotional support mentioned earlier, this was one of their primary functions for him. Marinetti needed to be constantly informed about the activities of other Futurists and needed his news to be passed on to them, and he was directly involved in the management of Futurism throughout his army service. During his training period at the Scuola Bombardieri at Susegana near Treviso, Marinetti wrote frequent letters to Angelo Rognoni and Gino Soggetti,[220] advising them about their journal *La Folgore Futurista*,[221] and he often solicited content for *L'Italia Futurista* from other Futurists on the front lines.[222] He was instrumental in shaping the direction of *Roma Futurista* in autumn 1918 while he was still at the front, frequently offering advice to Mario Carli in Rome.[223]

Letter writing performed different roles for other combatant Futurists. Their letters were filled with information about Futurist activity on the home front, and there was a feverish sharing of the addresses of other combatant and non-combatant Futurists.[224] Receiving news of this type helped them to feel less alone at the front, a point explicitly mentioned in some Futurist correspondence. Following the death of Boccioni, Gerardo Dottori[225] asked Marinetti to write to him: "fatemi sentire che siamo ancora molti e forti [...] Ò bisogno di ritrovarmi un po' a contatto con voi." (Make me feel that we are still many and strong [...] I need to be in contact with you all again.)[226] Giuseppe Sprovieri[227] was anxious for news while he was at the front, writing to Folgore that "vorrei sapere tante cose di Roma, vorrei partecipare a tutto il movimento d'arte di cui i giornali mi portano di tanto in tanto qualche notizie" (I want to hear lots from Rome, I want to participate in the whole art movement about which the newspapers bring me news from time to time).[228] As has been noted in the case of Marinetti, exchanging correspondence also represented a way for the men to offer and receive much-needed emotional support during their time in combat. In the

wake of Boccioni's death, Valentinelli wrote to Marinetti, both expressing his own sorrow and attempting to offer solace:

> Sono immensamente addolorato per la morte del grande e simpatico
> futurista Boccioni. Immaginandomi il suo grande dolore mi permetto di
> scriverLe per tentar di lenirlo almeno in minima parte, se è possibile, con
> l'esprimerLe ancora una volta l'affezione e l'ammirazione grandissima
> che tutti i futuristi irredenti sentono verso di Lei.

> (I am immensely sad about the death of the great and good Futurist
> Boccioni. Imagining your great sorrow I am taking the liberty of writing to
> you to try and alleviate it even a little, if that is possible, by expressing to
> you once again the great affection and admiration that all the irredentist
> Futurists feel for you.)[229]

Sprovieri identified Folgore's letters as a significant source of support
for him in dealing with the difficulties of life at the front lines:

> Ho visto quindi spettacoli di morte, di valore, di tenacia, indimenticabili
> [...] ho ricevuto la tua lettera. Te ne ringrazio. Ha per me un contenuto
> ideale più grande di quanto tu non immagini, ed ha un contenuto di vita
> inestimabile. Era una voce che appagava in me il senso della vita dopo la
> morte contemplata assai da vicino. Le notizie che in essa mi dài mi han
> fatto sorridere e ridere.

> (I have thus seen unforgettable displays of death, of virtue, of tenacity.
> I received your letter. Thank you. For me it has an ideal content greater
> than you can imagine, and it contains an inestimable amount of life. It was
> a voice that filled me with a sense of life after contemplating death from
> up close. The news in the letter made me smile and laugh.)[230]

Corresponding with Marinetti assumed a particular significance for
Paolo Orano. He regarded Marinetti as an "esempio solare di forza"
(cheerful example of strength)[231] and wrote that "il tuo entusiasmo e la
tua energia sono in questo momento tutto ciò che può controbilanciare
la debolezza di altri" (your enthusiasm and energy are at the moment
everything that can balance out the weakness of others).[232] Letters could
also function as talismans: Marinetti himself told Cangiullo that he had
carried a letter by him and Balla while he was engaged in fighting in
May 1917, during which he sustained an injury, and that "certamente

portate fortuna!" (you certainly bring good luck!).[233] The final function of correspondence for combatant Futurists was to assert and maintain their roles and identities as Futurists within the movement. Cesare Cerati sent a drawing to Balla that featured him in the uniform of the Arditi troops, signed "Cerati, futurista."[234] Numerous Futurists sent words-in-freedom drawings to publications like *L'Italia Futurista*, signing them "*futurista al fronte* (Futurist at the front)" and thereby affirming their commitment to the movement. Statements of Futurist identity could also take the form of offering explicit support for the movement, as Valentinelli did to Marinetti. On behalf of all Futurist irredentists he stated: 'Soldati, non possiamo noi ora esplicare nel Futurismo tutta la nostra attività, ma dopo la guerra tutte le nostre forze le daremo al meraviglioso movimento, il faro del XX secolo." (As soldiers, we cannot now carry out all of our activities for Futurism, but after the war we will give all of our efforts for the marvellous movement, the beacon of the 20th century).[235]

Although Futurism could help combatant Futurists to cope with the war, the war itself was a traumatic interruption of Futurist artistic life on the home front, causing considerable tension among those who were not actively engaged in it. It was this tension between military duty and the development and promotion of Futurism that plagued the movement throughout the war years. From 1916 onwards Marinetti sought to tie Futurism's artistic direction ever more closely to the war effort so that these two conflicting demands could be reconciled.

3 *Futurismo moderato*: Re-imagining Futurism for a War-Time Society

Group Tensions on the Home Front

As soon as Italy entered the war in May 1915, all Futurist activity stopped. The Futurist leadership marked this moment by publishing the manifesto "Per la guerra, sola igiene del mondo" (For the war, sole hygiene of the world), which declared that "il movimento futurista letterario, pittorico e musicale è attualmente sospeso, causa l'assenza del poeta Marinetti, recatosi sul teatro della Guerra" (the Futurist movement in literature, art and music is currently suspended, because of the absence of the poet Marinetti, who has departed for the theatre of war).[1] The manifesto continued:

> Finchè duri la guerra, lasciamo da parte i versi, i pennelli, gli scalpelli e le orchestre! Son cominciate le rosse vacanze del genio! Nulla possiamo ammirare, oggi, se non le formidabili sinfonie degli *shrapnels* e le folli sculture che la nostra ispirata artiglieria foggia nelle masse nemiche.

> (For as long as the war lasts, let's leave poetry, paintbrushes, chisels and orchestras to one side! The red holidays of genius have begun! It is not possible, today, to admire anything except the fantastic symphonies of shrapnel and the crazy sculptures that our inspired artillery forges in the enemy masses.)[2]

Initially this is exactly what happened, and without Marinetti the movement was left rudderless and floundered.[3] Carrà and Balla, neither of whom had volunteered, were not convinced by Marinetti's fixation on seeing active combat. Carrà viewed the Battalion of Volunteer

Cyclists as a "BURLA!" (JOKE!),[4] arguing that if anyone wanted to fight seriously, they should sign up for the navy or the regular army; anything else was "fesserie" (nonsense), which could have a certain moral or political importance but no military value.[5] Carrà continued this theme in a letter to Papini of June 1915, writing that Marinetti's followers "non vedono che le divise militari di onorevole in questo momento anche se chi le indossa non fa un cazzo di buono per la Patria" (see only military uniforms as honourable at this time even if those who are wearing them aren't doing any fucking good for the country).[6] As soon as Balla learned that Marinetti was at the front, he wrote to the Angelini sisters, Marinetti's secretaries and maids, imploring them to keep him informed of Marinetti's well-being: "Voi non potete immaginarvi il mio dispiacere di vedere un uomo così grande andare al fronte come un altro qualunque!!!!! Ho la speranza che Egli venga subito notato e preso subito in alta considerazione dai superiori." (You can't imagine my displeasure at seeing such a great man going to the front like a nobody!!!!! I hope that he will be noticed immediately and looked upon favourably by his superiors.)[7]

Those who remained on the home front, primarily Buzzi and Pratella but also Settimelli, were concerned about Marinetti's prioritization of his military service over the promotion of Futurism. In June 1915, when Marinetti was still recovering from his hernia operation, Buzzi wrote to Pratella that "Marinetti è nervoso, per l'arte mi sembra al momento un trapassato. Non vede che sparare." (Marinetti is tense; for the moment I think art is dead and gone. He is only interested in shooting.)[8] During his short-lived military service in June 1915 Settimelli had already expressed his annoyance at Marinetti's neglect of the movement, writing:

> Anch'io non ho nessuna notizia da Milano. La grande organizzazione marinettiana crolla così miseramente davanti ad 'un fatto serio'? Io sono incazzato, ve lo confesso, ed esagero perciò […] Anch'io sono già soldato e faccio già le mie marce e le istruzioni, ciononostante, come vedete, riesco a tenere i miei affari e a scrivere agli amici.

> (I haven't had any news from Milan either. Does the great Marinettian organization collapse so pathetically in front of "something serious"? I'm pissed off, I'll admit, and that's why I am exaggerating […] I'm a soldier already too and I am already taking orders and marching, and still, as you see, I manage to keep my affairs in order and to write to my friends.)[9]

In September 1915 Buzzi confided to Pratella that he hoped Marinetti and Boccioni would soon see "la loro ora di gloria e di stravita la bianca morte, così, li restituirà abbronzati e vibranti per l'altra battaglia della quale noi prepariamo, forse, le munizioni" (their hour of glory and intensified life so that the white death will return them tanned and vibrant for that other battle for which we are perhaps preparing the ammunition).[10] In November Pratella appealed directly to Boccioni, writing, "Senza intenzione di offendere i tuoi ideali, [...] proprio in questo momento io preferirei saperti nel tuo studio attorno alla tua meravigliosa arte" (Without offending your ideals, [...] at this precise moment I would prefer to know that you were in your studio surrounded by your wonderful art).[11]

Marinetti and Boccioni were aware of the impact that their absence with the Volunteer Cyclists would have on the movement. Boccioni appealed to Cangiullo to ensure that "il nome dei futuristi legati alla guerra non venga oscurato per il loro lontano dovere o meglio per il dovere verso la Patria che li tiene lontani" (the names of Futurists involved in the war are not forgotten because of their distant duty or, better, because of their duty towards the Nation that keeps them far away).[12] After he had left for the front, Marinetti put in place a contingency plan for the management of the movement. On 20 August 1915 he appointed Pratella as his unofficial deputy, writing: "Ti prego di legare insieme con lettere continue i diversi e migliori futuristi [...] Rianima e consolida con lettere continue la fede in tutti i futuristi ai quali puoi scrivere." (I ask you to tie together all the different and best Futurists with constant letters [...] Reignite and strengthen the faith of all the Futurists to whom you can write with constant letters.)[13] He reiterated this point a few weeks later, stating: "Ti prego ancora una volta di tenere legati insieme con lettere ardenti ed energiche i migliori futuristi. Non trascurare quelli che sono episodicamente o parzialmente futuristi. Sono qualche volta *trasformabili*." (I am asking you again to keep all the best Futurists tied together with passionate and energetic letters. Do not neglect those who are episodically or partially Futurists. Sometimes they can be *converted*.)[14]

Buzzi was also encouraged to keep writing to all his Futurist friends.[15] However, these efforts were insufficient to replace Marinetti's energy and drive in overseeing Futurist activity. Folgore confessed that "il futurismo passa qui in Italia ore di nervosimo terribile, aggravato da dissidi interni" (Futurism here in Italy is experiencing a time of terrible tension, aggravated by internal disagreements),[16] and in December 1915 Pratella complained: "Il movimento futurista, come organizzazione, è completamente arenato […] Il momento presente è preziosissimo ed unico per la ricostruzione futurista. Io faccio del mio meglio, ma non posso bastare solo per tutti; basto per il mio campo e non per gli altri." (The Futurist movement, as an organization, has completely run aground […] This present moment is extremely precious and unique for the Futurist reconstruction. I'm doing my best but on my own I cannot replace everyone; I'm enough for my field, but not for the others.)[17]

Once the Battalion of Volunteer Cyclists had been disbanded, there was a shared hope that Marinetti would now turn his attention back towards Futurism, which had suffered in his absence. Balla's suggestion that Marinetti was too good for ordinary combat was echoed by Pratella and Valentinelli. In December 1915 Pratella wrote to Settimelli that he did not know what Marinetti would do now: "Batterà nell'esercito regolare? Non glielo auguro e non me lo auguro" (Will he fight in the regular army? I don't wish that for him or for myself).[18] Ennio Valentinelli expressed similar sentiments, writing from the front to Carrà, pleading with him to

> persuadere Marinetti Boccioni e li altri giù [a Milano] che ne ànno una giustificata occasione di starsene a casa a combattere contro i passatisti li austriacanti i neutralisti l'imbellici che formicolano dopo la morte dei più saldi campioni dell'intelligenza. È una campagna per la quale ci vogliono l'intelligenti mentre in trincee bastano anche i fessi, purchè abbiano dei buoni muscoli. Per flagellare i nemici interni ci vogliono uomini di tempra futurista. Non lasciate l'Italia in balia dei farabutti mentre noi combattiamo al fronte.

> (persuade Marinetti Boccioni and the others down there [Milan] that they have a justified opportunity to stay at home to fight against the passéists, pro-Austrians, neutralists, the idiots that swarm about after the death of the firmest examples of intelligence. It is a campaign for which intelligent men are needed, while in the trenches even idiots are enough as long as they have strong muscles. To flog the internal enemies, men of a Futurist temperament are required. Don't leave Italy at the mercy of crooks while we fight at the front.)[19]

Marinetti was fully aware of the dissatisfaction among many of the Futurists. After returning to Milan in December 1915, he sought to reassure Pratella, telling him: "Spero essere sottotenente d'artiglieria fra un paio di mesi. Intanto, come vedi, ho ripreso energicamente la lotta e i lavori [...] Sto preparando cose importanti per il Futurismo." (I hope to be a second lieutenant in the artillery in a couple of months. In the meantime, as you can see, I have energetically resumed the struggle and our work [...] I am preparing important things for Futurism).[20] As the war was promising to stretch on longer than originally anticipated, Marinetti began to understand that Futurism could not survive an extended hiatus, and he realized the impossibility of suspending Futurism completely for the duration of the war.

The Birth of Moderate Futurism

When he returned from combat with the Volunteer Cyclists, Marinetti commented that "la stampa è singolarmente migliorata per noi Futuristi" (the press has strangely improved for us Futurists).[21] It was primarily the status of the protagonists of the movement – Marinetti, Boccioni, Russolo, and Sant'Elia – as volunteer soldiers that had elicited this positive judgment from the mainstream media, which was evident from as early as July 1915 and continued for the duration of the war.[22] An article commenting on the participation of intellectuals in the war highlighted that these men, the Futurists included, had put aside "ogni veste di superiorità, per rientrare nelle file di quell'enorme livellatore di uomini che è un esercito in Guerra" (every vestige of superiority, in order to re-enter the lines of that enormous leveller of men, the army at war).[23] The Futurists – "bravi giovanotti" (good young men) – were also praised for having put their interventionist words into action, by volunteering as soldiers,[24] which was a common theme in articles of the time. Valeria Vampa in *Gran Mondo* praised the Futurists,

> i quali dopo avere tentato con lo sforzo e [...] con lo scherno di creare una nuova corrente d'idee e di ideali nel campo sconfinato delle arti, dopo aver tentato che non siano stroncate ed offuscate le sfolgoranti ali del genio con i vieti sofismi di decrepite scuole o scuolette, convergono tutta la forza del loro braccio, tutta l'attività del loro intelletto, sui campi eruenti [*sic*] dove tuttavia si decidono i migliori destini dell'umanità.

> (who after having tried with great effort and [...] with mockery to create a new current of ideas and ideals in the immense field of the arts, after having tried so that their dazzling wings of genius would not be torn down and obscured by the old sophistry of decrepit little schools, unite all

the strength of their arms, all the activity of their intellect, on the erupting fields where the best destinies of humanity are decided.)[25]

Similarly, an article of *La Libreria Economica* claimed that the Futurists' war service would be their finest hour:

Chi conosce il loro fervore e la loro audacia non dubita ch'essi compiranno appieno il loro dovere di uomini e d'artisti (poichè per loro le due funzioni s'integrano e s'identificano) e che questo sarà, se non l'ultimo [...] il loro canto più bello e più alto.

(Anyone who knows their fervour and audacity is in no doubt that they will fully do their duty as men and as artists (because for them the two functions are integrated and identified with one another) and that this will be, if not their last [...] their most beautiful and loudest song.)[26]

Marinetti was singled out for praise in most reports on the Volunteer Cyclists. *La Stampa* journalist Carlo Scarfoglio wrote that Marinetti's volunteering "manifesta una grande forza di volontà, perché, [...] non brilla più del fiore velluto della prima giovinezza" (shows great willpower, because he is no longer in the first flower of youth [he was thirty-seven at the time]).[27] The series of reports that Renzo Codara wrote about the battalion for *La Gazzetta dello Sport* was unstinting in its praise of the Futurist soldiers. Marinetti's sporting prowess and his willingness to live up to his warmongering rhetoric by volunteering were admired.[28] Russolo was lauded as a "soldato docile, obbediente, esemplare" (docile, obedient, exemplary soldier), and Marinetti was singled out for his "geniale esuberanza" (wonderful exuberance).[29] He was described as a "modello di disciplina agli altri, [che] compie scrupolosamente il suo dovere ed è certamente tra i migliori soldati" (model of discipline for the others, [who] scrupulously does his duty and is certainly among the best soldiers).[30] The Futurists' military service had yielded great dividends, and upon his return to Milan at the end of 1915 Marinetti realized the importance of continuing to highlight his status as a soldier and a veteran of the war in order to maintain the public's favourable opinion of his movement. Faced with this unprecedented, positive reaction, Marinetti saw the value of altering his own attitude towards the Italian public by reaching out to new audiences with a toned-down version of Futurism. He sought to accomplish these aims through two manifestos: "L'unica soluzione del problema finanziario"

(The only solution to the financial problem), of December 1915,[31] and "L'Orgoglio Italiano" (Italian pride), of January 1916.[32]

The December manifesto is the earliest indication of Marinetti's willingness to compromise central aspects of his Futurist program in the service of the Italian war effort. The manifesto expanded on ideas that he had expressed in an interview with the *Standard* of London in November 1913,[33] but key differences between the 1913 and the 1915 statements highlight Marinetti's altered attitude towards mainstream public opinion. In both instances Marinetti proposed the sale of Italy's major works of art and sculpture, which would provide money for the navy and agriculture (1913) or for the war effort (1915). Although in 1913 Marinetti wished that "every picture, every statue, every bronze in all the museums and the palaces of Italy leave by the next post," thus freeing Italians from the *"hantise du passé,"* his proposals in 1915 were less extreme. He proposed a gradual sale, one so slow that people would barely notice at first, and, rather than merely wanting to rid Italy of these symbols of the past, Marinetti stated that the works of art would be "la più efficace delle réclames al genio creatore della nostra razza" (the most effective publicity [abroad] of the ingenious creativity of our race).[34] He also showed an esteem for Italy's curators and art historians that ran counter to all of his previous pronouncements on the academy – "[la] fetida cancrena di professori, d'archeologi, di ciceroni e d'antiquarii" ([the] stinking cancer of professors, archaeologists, tour guides and antiquarians) of earlier manifestos.[35] The attitude towards great Italian artists of the past was also markedly different in the two statements. In 1913 Marinetti had complained that foreigners who came to Italy were interested only in Michelangelo, Titian, and Cellini, leading them to "despise our new Italian art." By selling off Italy's treasures, Marinetti wished to show that "we have among us men who could be greater than Michelangelo, greater than Titian, greater than Cellini [… but who] are weighed down by this exploitation, this adoration of the past, and of fixed forms."[36] In 1915, however, he explicitly claimed Giotto, Botticelli, Cellini, Michelangelo, and Raffaello as "futuristi geniali del loro tempo" (brilliant Futurists of their time), openly embracing Italy's artistic tradition rather than dismissing it.[37] In both statements Marinetti proposed new archaeological digs to refill the museums, comparing Italy's troves of antiquities to the coal mines of Britain. In 1915, far from rejecting the past, Marinetti believed that these new antiquities would represent "il passato galvanizzato" (the past galvanized) in order to "risorger[e] per partecipare al gran progresso nazionale" (rise again to participate in great national progress).[38] In the conclusion to the manifesto Marinetti identified these ideas as a *futurismo moderato* (moderate Futurism), a term that aptly captured Marinetti's new approach for the remainder of the war, as he sought to balance the demands of war-time society and propaganda with the literary and artistic requirements of the Futurist movement.

A month later, in January 1916, Marinetti published "L'Orgoglio Italiano," co-signed by Boccioni, Russolo, Sant'Elia, Sironi, and Piatti, which represented the first comprehensive discussion of their combat experiences. Marinetti focused on the way in which "giovani pittori e poeti italiani possano trasformarsi in audaci, rudi, instancabili alpini" (young Italian painters and poets can transform themselves into daring, rough, tireless Alpini).[39] This manifesto was then supplemented by two long articles for *La Gazzetta dello Sport* and numerous interviews with newspapers, all with the aim of raising public awareness of the Futurists' military service with the Volunteer Cyclists.[40]

At this point, as well as promoting the war experiences of the Futurists, Marinetti began to actively promote the movement and was at pains to underline just how much he was doing to further the Futurist cause. Marinetti opened the manifesto "La declamazione dinamica e sinottica" (Dynamic and synoptic declamation), published on 11 March 1916, with a description of all the cultural activities in which the Futurists were engaged, including an exhibition of interventionist paintings by Balla in Rome; a talk by Boccioni on painting at the Istituto di Belle Arti, Naples; the manifesto by Boccioni to Southern painters; another talk by Boccioni on Futurist painting in Mantua; an afternoon of talks and declamations by Marinetti, Cangiullo, Jannelli, and Corra at the Istituto di Belle Arti, Naples; the publication *Vela Latina*; and eight *serate futuriste* on the art of noises, by Russolo and Piatti in Marinetti's house.[41] These activities notwithstanding, and wishing to carve out a new position for Futurism within mainstream Italian culture, Marinetti diverted his attention away from the promotion of Futurist art. Severini disapproved of his modus operandi during the war, writing that for Marinetti "l'elemento arte, nel suo valore totale, tende a divenire sempre più piccolo mentre in me è il contrario. Questa è la chiave della nostra divergenza" (the artistic element, in its total value, tends to become ever smaller, while for me it is the opposite. This is the key to our divergence).[42] There was no collective Futurist exhibition for the duration of the war, and Severini complained that "le nostre vendite ingrossate enormemente da Marinetti furono sempre il risultato di un caso e, adesso che il caso non è più aiutato dalle frequenti esposizioni, le vendite sono scomparse all'orizzonte" (our sales, swollen enormously by Marinetti, were always the result of chance, and now that this chance is no longer assisted by frequent exhibitions, the sales have disappeared from the horizon).[43] The war years were thus characterized by a decline in the importance of painting within the movement, in favour of theatrical performances and periodical publication.

Reaching Out to New Audiences: *Teatro Futurista Sintetico* and *L'Italia Futurista*

Having bolstered the positive public opinion towards Futurism, Marinetti next turned his attention towards the theatre, a forum in which he could continue to promote Futurism as a movement intimately engaged in the war effort. In the manifesto "Il teatro futurista sintetico," written during the interventionist period, Marinetti had disingenuously referred to it as a political genre, even though any content of a political nature was conspicuously absent from the first tour of 1915. The manifesto stated:

> La guerra, Futurismo intensificato, c'impone di marciare e di non marcire nelle biblioteche e nelle sale di lettura. **Noi crediamo dunque che non si possa oggi influenzare guerrescamente l'anima italiana, se non mediante il teatro**. Infatti il 90% degl'italiani va a teatro, mentre soltanto il 10% legge libri e riviste.

> The war – intensified Futurism – forces us to march and not to rot in libraries and reading rooms. **We believe therefore that today it is only possible through theatre to render the Italian soul more belligerent**. Indeed, 90% of Italians go to the theatre, while only 10% read books and magazines.[44]

The second Futurist synthetic-theatre tour, in the spring of 1916, was based around this belief and was markedly different from the tour of the interventionist period. In fact, there were two tours happening simultaneously, visiting the cities of Vercelli, Genoa, La Spezia, Imperia, Pavia, Venice, Livorno, Lucca, Viareggio, Siena, Pistoia, Florence, and Naples. At each of these events a selection of *sintesi* was performed, and Marinetti concluded the performance with a speech about his impressions of the war.

Marinetti had come to the realization that the success of these tours depended on his identity as a soldier and on his ability to tap into the patriotic spirit of the audience. Emanuela Scarpellini has noted that plays with war themes were very popular in Milan from 1915, although many were appreciated for their nationalistic sentiments rather than for the quality of their content.[45] To an extent this was also true of the Futurist material. In a letter to Pratella of March 1916 Marinetti wrote that unfortunately the short plays by Pratella and Buzzi had been "*momentaneamente* sacrificati" (*momentarily* sacrificed) because "fu necessario non dare che delle sintesi antitedesche e patriottiche" (it was necessary to perform only anti-German and patriotic *sintesi*).[46] Thus, the revised program of the second synthetic-theatre tour featured new *sintesi*, including *L'arresto* (The arrest), *Il soldato lontano* (The faraway soldier), and *La camera dell'ufficiale* (The officer's room) by Marinetti, which were all performed for the first time on 8 March 1916 at the Teatro Niccolini in Florence.

These *sintesi* by Marinetti are revealing of a new-found maturity in his representation of war, far removed from the bombast of his pre-war works such as *Le monoplan du pape*. The *sintesi* do not attempt to dramatize the conflict; rather they emphasize the unknowability of the war. The three micro-plays represent the point of view of Marinetti's imagined audience on the home front – women, and the cowardly men who had not volunteered for service. There is no celebration of war, only an acknowledgment of the emotional and psychological distress that it caused both the soldiers and their loved ones. This approach was quite atypical in the theatre of the time. For the most part, political and military plays related to the Risorgimento, rather than to the current war, and Scarpellini has commented that "sui palcoscenici non giunse una realistica rappresentazione della guerra in corso" (a realistic representation of the unfolding war did not appear on stage).[47] Instead, "heroic" plays were favoured that hid "la durezza reale e la guerra sofferta" (the real hardship and sufferings of war).[48]

La camera dell'ufficiale is a more sophisticated and reflective incarnation of the *dramma d'oggetti* (drama of objects), a genre of *sintesi* first unveiled by Marinetti in 1915, which sought to breathe life into inanimate objects.[49] There are no characters and no dialogue, and the play consists of a single setting. It is night-time, and through a window in a dark room the audience surveys a mountain landscape. A sentry with a bayonet passes under the window at regular intervals, and a light signal flashes from time to time. The audience hears, coming from the room next-door (which remains unseen), the sound of a typewriter, papers rustling, and footsteps, as well as the distant rumble of cannons. Suddenly a telephone rings in the darkened room. Footsteps and banging doors are heard from the adjacent room, before the deafening sound of a grenade is heard striking the next room, causing the ceiling to collapse. The door swings open, revealing an unmade camp bed, a pack of medicines, a letter and a photograph on the pillow, a revolver and a notebook on a crate, a pair of boots, and a balaclava.[50] The officer's life is distilled into a few objects, which highlight the harsh Alpine conditions, illness, and homesickness. The audience does not witness the grenade attack, a reminder that those on the home front will only ever be able to experience the war at a remove and can never have first-hand knowledge of its realities. Whereas the officer was absent in *La camera dell'ufficiale*, in *Il soldato lontano* the soldier is present but invisible to the other characters, further emphasizing the inaccessibility of the war to non-combatants. His mother and lover sit in a room, knitting warm clothes for the soldier in the trenches, while he sits beside them, unseen, in his uniform, holding his bayonet.[51]

L'arresto is a play within a play, whose setting shows a small stage and an audience in evening dress. The "first spectator" explains that all the actors and the authors are soldiers who have returned from the front, and claims that the play will be an "esecuzione [...] vissuta" (lived [...] performance).[52] The audience members include an anti-war philosopher, a pro-intervention critic who had stayed at home rather than volunteering, and a translator of Nietzsche whose physical ailments had prevented him from enrolling in the army. The curtain opens to show Alpine soldiers digging a trench. The critic complains about the accuracy of the scene, causing the actor playing the captain to challenge the critic to act onstage instead. The critics are pushed onstage by the actor-soldiers, who take their places in the audience. The play constitutes a rather unsubtle reminder to the audience members of the Futurists' own stance as veterans and of their superiority as witnesses of the true "theatre of war."

Overall, this second tour received a more positive response from audiences and critics than had the spring tour of 1915. Marinetti declared that the first performance in March 1916 succeeded "magnificamente sotto tutti i punti di vista poiché il pubblico (divenuto decisamente favorevole a noi e molto rispettoso) ascoltò tutte le sintesi in un silenzio assoluto, senza mai interrompere [...] e applaudì freneticamente quelle più avanzate" (magnificently in all respects because the audience (which has become decidedly favourable towards us and very respectful) listened to all the *sintesi* in absolute silence, without ever interrupting [...] and wildly applauded the most advanced ones).[53]

Reviews of the synthetic-theatre tours in 1916 often referred to the audience's behaviour, not least because it was frequently in stark contrast to that which had characterized the Futurist *serate* of the prewar and interventionist years.[54] Commenting on the synthetic-theatre performance held in Florence in March 1916, the critic Baccio Bacci observed:

Noto che la folla è migliorata: non si sono ripetute quelle ignobili becerate passatiste che deplorammo sinceramente, allorchè fu data al Teatro Verdi una grande serata futurista. Allora trionfò il becerismo e udimmo soltanto il rumore di oggetti che volavano. Ieri sera no. Abbiamo ascoltato, applaudito e anche fischiato. Ma decentemente.

(I noticed that the audience has improved: those vile, boorish, passéist scenes that we sincerely deplored back at the big Futurist *serata* at the Teatro Verdi were not repeated. Back then, boorishness triumphed and we heard only the noise of flying objects. That did not happen last night. We listened, applauded and also booed. But decently.)[55]

Another critic reported that there was "qualche timido applauso di consenso, molti applausi ironici, molte risate, qualche fischio e suoni variati ... all'ultimo" (a bit of timidly approving applause, lots of ironic applause, lots of laughter, a few boos and other sounds ... at the end).[56] Although the performance was by no means met with universal approval, the nature of the dissent was markedly different from that which both the Futurists and the critics had come to expect. It cannot be denied, however, that these *sintesi* still constituted challenging theatrical performances for the general public. One critic stated that the audiences "abandoned" the Futurists when *Il soldato lontano* and *La camera dell'ufficiale* were performed, but he blamed this primarily on difficulties with staging. *L'arresto* would have been "uno schietto successo" (a straightforward success) had it been performed in a more suitable theatre, but it nonetheless displayed "arguzia, ironia, e soprattutto molto ingegno" (wit, irony, and above all a lot of talent).[57]

One reason for this new-found positivity towards the Futurists was that a number of their performances were held in aid of charitable war causes, with the proceeds being donated to the Red Cross and the

Famiglie dei Richiamati (Families of the Enlisted).[58] Reviews of the time commented on the fact that the Futurist benefit performances in Florence in March and May 1916 were sold out.[59] Such charity performances were a common feature of war-time theatre and provided theatre-goers with a means of proving their commitment to the war effort. Audiences wanted to "esprimere apertamente la volontà di partecipare al ritrovato clima di concordia nazionale ed il teatro poteva fornire [...] il palcoscenico più idoneo" (to openly express their desire to participate in the new-found climate of national accord, and the theatre provided [...] the most suitable stage).[60] Another significant reason behind the change in audience reaction towards Futurism was that many of the patriotic *sintesi* being performed had been written by Futurist soldiers, such as Boccioni, a fact to which Marinetti alluded in *L'arresto*. Thus, it would have been unthinkable for the audience to pelt the performers with objects, as had occurred during the first synthetic-theatre tour, in 1915. As a member of the army, Marinetti could not be ridiculed as he had been when he had been merely the leader of a provocative and marginal artistic movement. Indeed, Marinetti's status as a soldier explicitly drew comment in reviews: "Marinetti, Settimelli, Corra, Boccioni, Chiti, sono uomini di talento e di coraggio [...] Marinetti è reduce dal fronte e vi tornerà a pagare il suo tributo di fede e di sangue. È gente che vive: con rumore, con stranezza, con segni esagerati di esistenza. Ma vive." (Marinetti, Settimelli, Corra, Boccioni, [and] Chiti are talented and courageous men [...] Marinetti is a war veteran and he will return to the front, to pay his dues in faith and bloodshed. They are people who live: noisily, strangely, with exaggerated signs of existence. But they live.)[61]

In the same way that Futurist theatre began to flourish in 1916, so too was it "un momento di particolare vivacità nella produzione di giornali legati al gruppo" (a particularly lively moment for the production of newspapers linked to the group)[62] during the war years. From the days of the interventionist crisis Marinetti had been searching for a publication that would serve as the movement's mouthpiece, but both *Lacerba* and *La Balza Futurista* had failed to achieve this aim. The two pages of *Vela Latina* edited by Cangiullo in Naples between October 1915 and March 1916 initially appeared to fill this gap. Cangiullo sought to strike a balance between the promotion of the Futurists' war service and the promotion of their cultural activities, but ultimately the magazine was focused on "Arte d'avanguardia" (avant-garde Art)[63] and aimed at an audience of like-minded intellectuals. In February 1916 Marinetti boasted that "le pagine futuriste di *Vela* sono ora *molto molto* lette" (the

Futurist pages of *Vela* are now *very widely* read).[64] Marinetti helped to fund the endeavour, but Cangiullo admitted to feeling oppressed by his presence "dietro le quinte" (behind the scenes) and to having had "vivacissimi battibecchi" (very lively quarrels) with him for the first time.[65] In April 1916 Ferdinando Russo, the overall editor of the journal, was forced to discontinue publication owing to the high costs and the lack of availability of paper,[66] and Futurism was once again without an official publication. Marinetti finally realized his dream of an independent Futurist newspaper in June 1916 when *L'Italia Futurista* was launched, edited at various stages by Settimelli, Corra, Conti, Chiti, Arnaldo Ginna,[67] and Maria Ginanni.[68] Many aspects of the Futurist pages in *Vela Latina* were continued in *L'Italia Futurista*, including both the publication of *parole in libertà* by Futurists at the front and a focus on synthetic theatre. However, there was a new focus on the war effort and on war-related material aimed at non-Futurist audiences, although this content has been called "the least interesting part of the journal."[69]

The mission of the newspaper was to re-engage with the artistic side of life, which had been neglected at the outbreak of the war. As Settimelli explained in the first issue's editorial, the Futurists initially intended to re-start their "idolatrate esplorazioni liriche, le nostre innovatrici idee sulla vita" (idolatrous lyrical explorations, our innovative ideas about life) only after the end of the war. However, they had realized that "il genio artistico è una leva di conquista più formidabile talvolta di una flotta e di un esercito. È sempre l'anima che fa e vince le guerre" (artistic genius is sometimes a stronger instrument of conquest than a fleet or an army. It is always the soul that wages and wins wars).[70] One month after the newspaper's launch Settimelli wrote to Pratella that twenty thousand copies of each issue were being printed, with between twelve hundred and fifteen hundred being sold in Florence alone.[71] The newspaper vendors were apparently "sbalorditi" (amazed),[72] but, as always, Futurist declarations of their own success must be taken with a grain of salt. Both Ardengo Soffici and Massimo Bontempelli wrote to Settimelli praising the newspaper and citing its relevance at the front and in the contemporary political climate.[73]

The ideal reader of *L'Italia Futurista* was the soldier fighting at the front. As Settimelli outlined,

Avrà dei redattori combattenti, degli abbonati in trincea, dei critici *in cantina* (*al sicuro* dagli areoplani [*sic*]), dei propagandisti aviatori. Correrà dal fronte all'interno e sarà compilato e discusso al fronte nella caserma, nell'ospedale, nella trincea. Da questo flusso e riflusso dovrebbe trarre nuove ispirazioni e suggestioni.

(It will have combatant editors, subscribers in the trenches, critics in the *cellar* (*sheltered* from aeroplanes), aviator propagandists. It will move from the front to the home front and will be drafted and discussed at the front in the barracks, in the hospital, in the trenches. It will take new inspiration and suggestions from this ebb and flow.)[74]

The newspaper functioned both as a source of information for the Futurists, communicating news about the injuries of Marinetti and Russolo and the deaths of Boccioni and Sant'Elia, and as an advertisement of Futurist heroism for the general public. Combatant contributors were given the label *futurista al fronte*, and they submitted articles and *parole in libertà*, which were often direct accounts of their war experiences. Featuring Futurists at the front allowed Marinetti to parade the movement as being fully engaged with the realities of the war and also helped to stave off any criticisms of their being "imboscati" (shirkers) for producing a newspaper instead of fighting. Marinetti was contemptuous of "il pensatore italiano, che fisicamente valido, [...] si chiude nell'arte come in un sanatorio o in un lazzaretto di colerosi" (the Italian thinker, who physically able, closes himself off inside his art as if in a sanatorium or a lazaret for cholera sufferers), saying that they deserved punches, kicks, and shots in the back.[75]

Despite the *parole in libertà* compositions that were featured in *L'Italia Futurista*, the newspaper is a manifestation of moderate Futurism. The ideological line was not far removed from public opinion, and the newspaper focused also on contributions from prominent intellectuals who were not attached to Futurist circles, such as Ada Negri, Grazia Deledda, and Salvatore Quasimodo. In fact, the most experimental aspects of *L'Italia Futurista* were those unconnected to the war effort, to the extent that the strictly Futurist content of the journal has been deemed its most "conformist" element.[76] The so-called *pattuglia azzurra* (blue patrol), comprising Corra, Ginna, Ginanni, Chiti, and others, dedicated a significant amount of the journal's attention to exploring proto-surrealist themes of the occult and mysticism.[77]

The content of *L'Italia Futurista* displayed a departure from the naivety of the Futurist visions of an apocalyptic war, which was summed up by Settimelli's admission that their prediction of war as one-quarter trenches and three-quarters bayonets had proved untrue.[78] Nino

SINTESI PAROLIBERA

1915   1916

CANTI
+
CANTI
+
CANTI

MAGGIO
mese
r o s e o
delle rose
e
della speranza

CADAVERI
CADAVERI
CADAVERI
+
DENUDATI

MAGGIO
offensiva austriaca
mese
ROSSO
delle migliori
vite recise
della realtà

NINO FORMOSO
futurista ferito al fronte.

FRAGILITÀ

Strisciare sui piani dell'inesplorabile appoggiandomi alle trasparenze MASSICCE   ad ogni passante un grappolo di glicine   il mio l'ho posto nel vaso d'argento ove raccolgo tutti i sorrisi perduti

poi una manata di bonbons — festevolezza argento oro azzurro verde dalle vetrine di cristallo

Se ogni desiderio fosse un fiore diafano vorrei preparare un letto di petali per la tua bellezza defunta.

VIERI
Futurista al fronte.

PIAZZA BRA

Piazza Bra   solidità soffice cielo azzurrone buio

gocce di luce violetta sospese nell'oscurità = albicocche paonazze   grossi cerchi di luce candida intravvisti dentro le fessure

fanali spenti = grossi grani di ribes rigati opacità ombre cinesi   grappoli di piccoli chicchi   serenità frammentazioni d'aureole spezzettature di cadeiloscopio

danze serpentine di collane luminose

1 bnffo d'aria fresca irrompere nella piazza a destra il mio passo sboccare a sinistra   estuario questa sera mi sento elastico   2 pugni di piombo pieni di sangue caldo mi tengono ben tese le braccia gambe leggere volano s'alzano evaporizzano cassa toracica aereata   altalena

ore 1 e 9 incomincia il mio turno di servizio alla stazione di Porta Nuova

Piazza Bra si distende nel vuoto   aggramparsi al costone scalcinato dell'Arena   misurata dall'eco dei miei passi che s'allontanano.

ACCIAI
Futurista al fronte

Pubblicazioni imminenti nelle Edizioni dell' Italia Futurista dirette da Maria Ginanni:

Fuochi di bengala

di ANTONIO BRUNO

preceduti

da un razzo

di EMILIO SETTIMELLI

Mascherate futuriste

di EMILIO SETTIMELLI

In preparazione:

SCIENZA ed ARTE OCCULTA

di ARNALDO GINNA

Figure 3.1. Nino Formoso, "Sintesi parolibera" (Free-word synthesis), *L'Italia Futurista*, 3 June 1917, 3. Courtesy of Museo d'arte moderna e contemporanea di Trento e Rovereto, Archivio del '900.

Formoso's "Sintesi parolibera" revealed the changes that had occurred between the first and second years of the war, in the transformation of the "canti" (songs) of 1915 into the "cadaveri" (bodies) of 1916.[79]

Mario Carli wrote in 1917 that at the start of the war it was easier "quando non si conoscevano i mezzi di difesa del nemico [e] si navigava fra illusioni e nozioni di seconda mano" (when we did not know the enemy's defence apparatus [and] we navigated our way through delusions and second-hand information).[80] By mid-1917 he argued that there could not any more be "l'illusione, la montatura, il contagio del brivido" (illusion, the crescendo, the contagious thrill), and yet the soldiers fought with "più foga dei primi giorni" (more fire than in the first days).[81] In its stridently pro-war stance *L'Italia Futurista* desired to speak to soldiers and to inspire them to greater acts of heroism and courage. Although in the pages of the journal the Futurists were unable to ignore the realities of the unfolding war, there was a concerted effort, particularly on Marinetti's part, to present a mythic version of the war, concentrating on its modern, technological aspects and inculcating an indifference towards death and a glorification of injury. The first issue featured a long manifesto by Marinetti, meditating on the "nuova religione-morale della velocità" (new moral-religion of speed) and on "divine" places and objects such as "i campi di battaglia. Le mitragliatrici, i fucili, i cannoni, i proiettili […] Le mine" (the battlefields. The machine guns, the rifles, the cannons, the bullets […] The mines).[82] Lucia Re has astutely pointed out that this manifesto constituted an attempt by Marinetti "to suppress the opposite, all-too-real experience of war: that of agonizing slowness, of waiting, of contemplation, of fear."[83] While battle scars were to be glorified, not least through the label *futurista ferito al fronte* (Futurist injured at the front), death had a more ambiguous role in the journal, which was brought into sharp focus by Boccioni's demise in August 1916. His death was marked in *L'Italia Futurista* by triumphalism, and in December of that year Marinetti stated categorically that "è impossibile che l'*Italia futurista* contenga dei necrologi" (it is impossible for *L'Italia Futurista* to contain obituaries). He continued:

> In Italia occorre un'energia sempre pronta contro quella schifosa tendenza che spinge tutti a mettersi comodamente a tavola sul corpo di un artista morto. *Dobbiamo dare l'esempio. I vivi, i vivi soltanto sono sacri. Il Futurismo*, malgrado l'immensa spaventosa scomparsa del povero Boccioni e di tanti altri, *è più vivo che mai.*

(Italy requires an energy that is always ready against that disgusting tendency that pushes everyone to sit comfortably around the body of a dead artist. *We must set the example. The living, only the living are sacred. Futurism,* notwithstanding the immense and painful loss of poor Boccioni, and many others, *is more alive than ever.*)[84]

The need to forget the dead was bound up with Marinetti's drive for positivity and "artificial optimism," but also with his need not to remind the public that Futurism was losing some of its greatest members. Marinetti restated the ban on obituaries to Mario Carli in summer 1917 so that *L'Italia Futurista* would distinguish itself from all other Italian newspapers "per una assoluta mancanza di soffietti, di critiche pedanti, di recensioni e di piagnistei" (for the absolute absence of puff pieces, pedantic critiques, reviews and whining).[85]

The pages of *L'Italia Futurista* also became the home to debates about the role of women in society during the war. The depiction of women, however, sought to appeal to the journal's primary audience of soldiers. Women contributed to the newspaper, and Maria Ginanni was also its editor for a few months, but their views were not always taken seriously by the male Futurist hierarchy.[86] A number of contradictory stances towards women were put forward in the journal: they were full of flaws,[87] they should be afforded the right to vote,[88] they were immensely stupid.[89] In an open letter to Ada Negri of autumn 1917 Marinetti was highly critical of the behaviour of women during the war, ordering them to stop complaining about its duration. He made sure to point out that he was not referring to mothers, wives, and sisters, but the words of his letter contradict this statement. He told women to stop "rimpinzare le vostre lettere ai soldati di stupidissimi piagnistei! I combattenti si sforzano di rassicurare le loro donne con lettere piene di buon umore e di serenità. Ma ricevono in cambio lettere deprimenti e scoraggianti che parlano di notti lagrimose e disperate!" (stuffing your letters to the soldiers with stupid whining! The combatants try to reassure their women with letters full of good humour and calm. But in return they receive depressing and discouraging letters that recount tearful and desperate nights!)[90] Even in an article such as his "Donne, dovete preferire i gloriosi mutilati!" (Women, you must prefer the glorious amputees!), purporting to address female readers, Marinetti in reality was seeking to reassure injured soldiers of their continued virility and masculinity, claiming that there was "niente di più bello di una manica vuota e fluttuante sul petto" (nothing more beautiful than an empty sleeve flapping on a chest).[91] The article concluded with a goading taunt to the women that they should also be forced to serve in the trenches in order to experience the soldiers' plight.

One of Marinetti's major concerns during the war was to recruit younger Futurists to the movement, and he was far more insistent about this target audience than that of women. During the interventionist crisis Marinetti had reissued the manifesto "In quest'anno futurista" (In this Futurist year), which was addressed to Italian students whom he encouraged to "scopare fuori dalle università i vecchi bidelli tedescofili" (sweep the old Germanophilic custodians out of the universities).[92] From its first issue *L'Italia Futurista* included a section entitled "I Giovanissimi" (The young ones), which featured *parole in libertà* by Futurists aged between sixteen and twenty-two. Throughout the war Marinetti continued to target young people,[93] but this indulgent approach was not appreciated by the other protagonists of the movement. Soon after the launch of *L'Italia Futurista* even Boccioni, Marinetti's closest ally, had reservations about Marinetti's strategy, writing to Pratella: "è terrible il peso di dovere elaborare in sé un secolo di pittura. Tanto più quando si vedono i nuovi arrivati al futurismo afferrare le idee inforcarle e correre a rotta di collo stropiandole." (It is terrible to have to carry the weight alone of developing a century of painting. Even more so when I see the new arrivals to Futurism grabbing onto the ideas, upending them and running at breakneck speed distorting them.)[94] Pratella agreed with Boccioni, stating that "il futurismo è diventato oramai il *somaro di battaglia degl'imbecilli*" (by now Futurism has become the *flagship for imbeciles*).[95]

In spite of the internal tensions caused by his tactics, the success of *L'Italia Futurista* was intimately linked to Marinetti's presence and involvement. Just before his departure for the war zone in December 1916 Marinetti wrote to Pratella that he felt it "necessario bello piacevole fare così tutto il mio dovere-piacere; ma spero, voglio *ritornare*. Mi sento indispensabile, ma credo anche che il Futurismo ormai può anche vivere di vita propria" (necessary beautiful pleasant to do all of my duty-pleasure; but I hope, I want to *return*. I feel indispensable, but I also believe that by now Futurism can survive on its own).[96] After his departure the editors of *L'Italia Futurista* briefly considered ceasing publication of the journal. Chiti told Carli that they had produced the final issue because Marinetti was absent again and Settimelli was engaged in the new tour of the *teatro sintetico*.[97] Corra admitted to Pratella in January 1917 that "la partenza di Marinetti ci ha scombussolato parecchio" (Marinetti's departure really turned us upside down)[98] but that, "ripensandoci, abbiamo deciso di continuare ad ogni costo *l'Italia Futurista*" (on second thoughts, we have decided to continue with *L'Italia Futurista* at all costs).[99] Thus, after a break of almost two months, publication resumed at the start of February 1917.

Best-Selling Futurism

In reaching out to new audiences through *L'Italia Futurista* and acquiescing to the public's need for patriotic plays during the theatre tours of 1916, Marinetti found his vision of a moderate Futurism slowly beginning to take shape. From 1917 this orientation towards mainstream tastes became more pronounced through that year's theatre tours and through the first Futurist forays into mass-market, popular literature.

In January 1917 two extraordinary performances of the *teatro futurista sintetico* were held in Florence in aid of military families, organized by the Comitato Studentesco di Beneficienza. The program began with *Il dramma del futurista* (The drama of the Futurist), which consisted of four *sintesi* by Settimelli and Corra. As a reviewer commented, "si tratta di un nuovo tentativo di teatro futurista, più accessibile alle menti ed ai gusti degli spettatori che si ostinano a rimaner passatisti" (it is a new attempt at Futurist theatre, more accessible to the minds and tastes of the audience who insist on remaining passéist).[100] The four·*sintesi* largely conformed to the norms of traditional dramas and were essentially short one-act plays with a clear narrative structure and traditional staging, all focusing on the figure of Italo, a young Futurist poet and volunteer in the war.[101] The first *sintesi*, "Dichiarazione di guerra" (Declaration of war), was a reminder of the interventionist "radiant days of May" and of Futurism's involvement in those events. Italo, the willing volunteer, is faced with friends who care more about their poetry than the war, and with those who believe Italy should fight alongside the Central powers. The final *sintesi*, "Attaco di aeroplani austriaci" (Attack of Austrian aeroplanes), features Italo who has returned from war with bandaged legs and unable to walk. He wishes that he could be the Futurist "uomo meccanico dalle parti smontabili" (mechanical man of removable parts) and that he could be given new legs.[102] An Austrian air raid begins, and Italo observes it from the window, admiring the Italian planes. He sees his own regiment pass by and wants to take up his place again. He rushes to the door but collapses. This small movement is a huge triumph for Italo because he had been told he would never walk again, and is proof that "occorre liberarsi dalle schiavitù del nostro corpo!" (it is necessary to free ourselves from the slavery of our bodies!).[103] At the end of the *sintesi* he is proud to have surpassed his physical handicaps and dies content. Reviewers of the peformances noted that all the *sintesi* had "un relativo sapore futurista" (a relative Futurist flavor)[104] but were effective. They were "assai applaudite" (quite well received)[105] and "accettati dal pubblico con una certa simpatia" (accepted by the audience with a certain enjoyment).[106] The same critic observed that there were "poche risate ironiche e niente commestibili ... Il futurismo progredisce forse perché il pubblico si è un po' più avvicinato a lui" (few ironic laughs and no edible projectiles ... Futurism is making progress maybe because the audience has come a bit closer to it).[107] However, the Futurists were also reducing the distance between themselves and their audiences by appealing to mass tastes and by jettisoning the more avant-garde impulses in scripting and staging that had been on show during the tours of 1915 and 1916. The 1917 plays bore little resemblance to the earlier manifestations of the genre.

At the same performances the first Futurist film, *Vita Futurista* (Futurist life), was shown. Although Italy's cinema industry had been booming for years (by 1914, Italy, along with Denmark, was the third-largest exporter of films in the world),[108] before the war Marinetti had never shown any interest in the medium. But in November 1916, as part of his drive to reach wider audiences for Futurism, Marinetti (with Corra, Settimelli, Ginna, Balla, and Chiti) published the manifesto "La cinematografia futurista" in *L'Italia Futurista*.[109] *Vita Futurista* was met with great success: "interessò e suscitò una ilarità rumorosa: e veramente in alcune sue parti essa è di una comicità esilarante" (people were interested and it provoked noisy laughter: and certainly some parts of it are exhilaratingly funny).[110] The Futurists admitted that the film was not widely seen, but their intention was that "domani apparirà anche alle masse" (tomorrow it will also be shown to the masses).[111] These 1917 performances were far more focused on pure entertainment value than had been the previous iterations of the genre, and, while still featuring a war-themed program, the Futurists addressed the public's need for escapism. One reviewer remarked:

In uno spettacolo futurista tutto è interessante, anche il pubblico. Questo aveva oggi l'aria di pensare: "Su da bravi futuristi! Non siamo in vena di risse, nè di pugilati! La guerra ahimè, altrove e le patate costano un po' care! Siate voi, artisti o guastamestieri, non siamo qui per combattere una battaglia letteraria, ma per ridere, sia alle vostre spalle, sia alle nostre!" I futuristi, dal canto loro, per corrispondere al desiderio del pubblico, gli hanno ammannita tutta roba di primissima qualità ... futurista.

(At a Futurist performance, everything is interesting, even the audience. Today it made you think, "Come on, good Futurists. We're not·in the mood for fights and punch-ups. Alas, the war continues elsewhere and potatoes are a bit expensive! Whether you are artists or incompetents, we are not here to fight a literary battle, but to laugh, whether it is behind your backs, or our own!" The Futurists, for their part, in order to respond to the audience's desires, dished out top-quality Futurist stuff.)[112]

Contemporaneously to this new-found solicitude towards the audience in the realm of theatre, a new Futurist attitude developed with regard to book publishing. Part of Marinetti's initial response to the outbreak of war and to Italy's neutrality had been to increase the activity of the publishing wing of the movement, Edizioni futuriste di "Poesia", which specialized in publishing the experimental *parole in libertà* of major Futurists and was financed entirely by Marinetti. In total, seven volumes were published during the interventionist months, but as the war progressed, Marinetti turned his attention away from these niche publications.[113] Part of the motivation was practical: book production in Italy halved during the war years (from 11,523 to 6,902),[114] and, as the cost of paper rose, restrictions were introduced. Thus, Marinetti directed his financial resources to supporting high-impact, crowd-pleasing books, issued by major publishing companies. Instead of publishing whole volumes of *parole in libertà* compositions, these more experimental forms were placed on the pages of Futurist journals.

Over and above practicality, the new focus on popular literature was also an embodiment of Marinetti's war-time strategy of moderate Futurism. These novels eschewed the experimental aspects of Futurist literature in order to appeal to a mainstream audience, in particular soldiers and officers.[115] Seeking to rely on already established editorial markets, Futurist popular literature was placed with large commercial publishers. The first Futurist mass-market publication was Marinetti's *Come si seducono le donne* (How to seduce women; 1917), which was followed by a host of genre novels (mystery, detective story, erotic) by Futurists such as Carli, Corra, and Settimelli in the final war years and the immediate post-war period. Here I will concentrate only on those works published before the end of the war, which were consumed by soldiers and officers at the front: *Come si seducono le donne* by Marinetti, *Io ti amo* (I love you; released in March 1918) by Corra,[116] and Marinetti and Corra's *L'isola dei baci* (The island of kisses; 15 August 1918).

Come si seducono le donne is a short "self-help" manual, aimed at both educating and entertaining active soldiers and officers. The tone is light-hearted and comic, filled with accounts of Marinetti's numerous successes in sexual and romantic liaisons, as well as practical "how-to" guides on seducing women, which feature declarations such as "dopo un violentissimo bombardamento di frasi infuocate, lancio risolutamente le fanterie delle mani" (after a violent bombardment of impassioned words, I unwaveringly launch the infantry of my hands).[117] Interspersed between humorous anecdotes of Marinetti's seduction techniques are indictments of women's behaviour during war-time and the inevitable betrayal that soldiers would experience. Marinetti warned that, though a woman would fall in love with a strong and courageous volunteer who was departing for the front, she would betray him "col primo venuto, *acerbo, riformato, o vecchio*" (with the first newcomer, *immature, a military reject, or old*) who came her way.[118] Thus, Marinetti sought to persuade his readers that "il combattente deve preferire una bottiglia di vino a qualsiasi lettera innamorata" (the combatant must prefer a bottle of wine over any love letter).[119] He also condemned the flipside of female infidelity: male jealousy, "lugubre, atroce e schifosa malattia passatista [che] è [...] una specialità italiana" (gloomy, atrocious, disgusting passéist disease [that] is [...] an Italian speciality).[120] In this way, Marinetti deemed it absolutely necessary to destroy the obsession with "la donna unica l'uomo unico" (one woman one man).[121] The book's conclusion was a call to the men of Italy's army to abandon the strictures of traditional love and marriage, which could only hold them back in times of war. Marinetti declared his support of "divorzio facile. Svalutazione e abolizione graduale del matrimonio [...] Ridicolizzazione sistematica e accanita della gelosia. Libero amore" (easy divorce. Devaluation and gradual abolition of marriage [...] Systematic and dogged ridicule of jealousy. Free love).[122]

Bruno Corra's novel *Io ti amo* recounts the story of Carlo, an intellectual, and Anna, a young bourgeois woman, who fall in love and marry. Faced with money and marital troubles, Carlo begins to edit a cinema journal financed by lawyer Pasquale De Rosa, while Anna becomes an actress for De Rosa's film company. Carlo experiences growing contempt for Anna as she blossoms in her new role. When Anna shoots her first film on the Riviera, and Carlo remains in Milan, he becomes consumed by jealousy. She persuades him that she has not been unfaithful, and they vow to do away with physical jealousy and personal attachment, "calpestare tutti i pregiudizi della morale Borghese" (to trample on all the prejudices of bourgeois morality),[123] and "liberarsi dalla decrepita concezione dell'amore che vuole legare, limitare, trattenere, impiccolire [*sic*], tener vicino" (free themselves from the decrepit concept of love that wants to tie down, limit, hold back, make smaller, hold close).[124] Shortly afterwards, however, when his father dies, Carlo realizes that a man is never reborn through love but "attraverso il dolore o attraverso lo sforzo: in mezzo a uno sconvolgimento naturale o sopra un campo di battaglia, in un duello di vita o in una camera funebre" (through pain or through effort: amidst a natural disaster or on a battlefield, in a duel or in a funeral room).[125] He finally understands the bind of marriage and decides to kill himself, but before he can go through with his resolution, he hears the sounds of a military parade outside his window, experiences a moment of revelation, and joins the crowd. In the act of marching with the anonymous masses Carlo feels himself liberated from all of his sorrow and enlists for the war, which is revealed in the novel's last line to be the war currently unfolding in Italy. The novel concludes with news of Carlo's death "mortalmente colpito da granata nemica" (mortally wounded by an enemy grenade).[126]

L'isola dei baci, co-authored by Marinetti and Corra,[127] is a fictional account of a trip that Corra and Marinetti take to Capri as a break from "la troppo intensa partecipazione alla vita febbrile della nostra epoca guerresca e rivoluzionaria" (the too-intense participation in the frenzied life of our warlike and revolutionary epoch).[128] The Futurists are joined on their boat ride to Capri by a mysterious group of men who are taking part in a political meeting on the island. The extravagant behaviour of these men and the fact that it is an international group (comprising French, English, Italian, a Dalmatian, and others who are possibly Austrian or German) lead the Futurists to believe that they are hiding "tenebrosi benchè indecifrabili scopi politici" (mysterious but incomprehensible political aims).[129] Marinetti and Corra meet Paolo Castretta, who has been following the group for five years to try and discover who they are. The group members are all anti-war and anti-Futurism. Castretta appeals to the Futurists for help in his quest, declaring that "questa riunione di gente sospetta se era già equivoca in tempo di pace è divenuta veramente pericolosa da che siamo in Guerra" (this meeting of shady men, already suspicious in peacetime, has become truly dangerous when we are at war).[130] Corra, Marinetti, and Castretta sneak into a meeting at the Grotta Azzurra. The president of the group is Paul De Ritten, indisputably the most handsome of them all. De Ritten rails against all modern and "Futurist" inventions (electric light, trains, bicycles, cars) and states his wish to bring an end to the war. They proclaim Capri to be "l'unica terra paradisiacamente neutrale e internazionale" (the only earthly paradise, neutral and international)[131] and state that all women must be expelled from the island. At that point a woman's voice interrupts the gathering. The wife of De Ritten accuses the men of being sex maniacs and homosexuals and then shoots herself. At her funeral the men gather around once more, stating that they are the best and most able politicians because they are not distracted by women. Women are castigated because they love heroes, who are badly dressed and have dirty hands. By contrast, "noi amiamo la vigliaccheria, la pace ad ogni costo, le passeggiate archeologiche, gli amorevoli conversari tra uomini, l'antica Grecia e la sterilità" (we love cowardice, peace at any cost, archaeological strolls, loving conversations between men, ancient Greece, and sterility).[132] At the novel's conclusion Paolo Castretta sends a telegram to his superiors, saying that his mission has been completed. He excludes various hypotheses regarding the group's motivations, including an anarchic plot, an international workers' committee, and a meeting of representatives of neutral countries, and declares that "trattasi fondazione Nuova Religione Internazionale invertiti omosessuali. Pericolo minore ma non trascurabile" (it is the foundation of a New International Religion of inverts and homosexuals. A lesser danger but not one to be neglected).[133]

All three of these works achieved levels of commercial success that were unprecedented for the Futurist movement. *Come si seducono le donne* was first published by Edizioni da Centomila Copie in September 1917, and, according to the publicity in *L'Italia Futurista*, thousands of copies had been sold in a month and the second edition was being prepared.[134] In fact, we know from a letter written on 21 August 1917 that, although Corra and Settimelli had enough paper for five thousand copies, they initially only printed two thousand.[135] Either the Futurists did not expect the book to be so successful, or they decided to manipulate the market by producing few copies in the first edition, allowing them to quickly herald a second.[136] In his study of popular Italian literature Michele Giocondi recorded that *Come si seducono le donne* and *Io ti amo* each sold approximately fifty thousand copies during the period 1917–43, qualifying them as best-sellers.[137] *L'isola dei baci* was also a huge success for Corra and Marinetti. At Corra's suggestion, they decided to print five thousand copies (at their own expense) and to place it with the publisher Facchi, who would coordinate the launch.[138] The novel was released in August 1918, and, according to Corra, by 1 September, thirty-five hundred copies had already been sold and he was preparing the second edition.[139]

Each of these three books belongs to a different literary genre – the self-help novel, the love story, and the detective-mystery story – designed to appeal to soldiers at the front, many of whom were quite unused to reading. Despite high levels of illiteracy in the Italian army, as Giorgio Pasquali wrote in the 1930s, "in our country people had probably never read as much as they did during the war, in the trenches."[140] Although the messages of these books by Marinetti and Corra were inherently Futurist, they were wrapped in an accessible form using simple language, humour, and mildly titillating content. Marinetti reported on the success of *Come si seducono le donne* among the soldier population, noting that "a pezzi era letto portato da squadrone a squadrone [...] con staffette. Mentre uno leggeva un episodio, l'altro spediva a cavallo l'episodio letto" (it was read in pieces carried from squadron to squadron by a courier. As one was reading one episode, the other sent the finished bit on by horse).[141] If *L'Italia Futurista* is to be believed, the announcement of the imminent publication of *Come si seducono le donne* struck a chord with soldiers: "Gli uomini mandano dal fronte allegre frasi di attesa e già pensano che il libro sia un terribile vendicatore di tutto ciò che quasi ogni uomo ha sofferto per le donne." (The men send us happy and expectant words from the front and already think the book will be a great avenger of everything that almost every man has suffered at women's hands.)[142] *L'isola dei baci* was also firmly marketed towards a populist audience. Corra wrote in the preface that it was positioned "fuori dalla letteratura" (outside literature)[143] and that literary types would show contempt for the book and "si rifiuteranno di chiamarlo *romanzo*, per non offendere gli altri veri romanzi bene educati e *come si deve*" (they will refuse to call it a *novel*, so as not to offend the other real novels, who are well behaved as they *ought to be*).[144] For the same reasons, the novel would appeal to those who were "lontani dalla letteratura" (distant from literature).[145] In the list of those who would appreciate it the first category mentioned was officers.[146] The imagined audience for *Io ti amo* was undoubtedly the same; indeed Remo Chiti reported seeing a soldier at the military school reading the novel in August 1918.[147]

As Lucia Re has discussed at length with regard to *Come si seducono le donne*, "the image of the sensual woman became a source of paranoia, and a scapegoat for all the fears and uncertainties generated by the war."[148] The main rhetorical goal of *Come si seducono le donne* was to "alleviate the male fear of betrayal" by their wives while they were at the front.[149] By dismissing the validity of the concepts of fidelity and jealousy, soldiers would find women's behaviour on the home front to be irrelevant. *Io ti amo* can be regarded as a fictionalized reiteration of many of the key arguments presented in Marinetti's earlier work.[150] Corra's statement in the preface to *Come si seducono le donne* that it encapsulated one of the most daring Futurist concepts, namely "la liberazione dall'amore come fenomeno capace di *unicità, eternità e fatalità*" (the liberation of love as a phenomenon capable of *uniqueness, eternity and destiny*),[151] could also have described the content of his own later novel. In both works women's betrayal is seen as liberating, and the war provides a mechanism for male rebirth. Carlo, in *Io ti amo*, is brought back from the brink of death by the prospect of war, and Marinetti claimed in *Come si seducono le donne* that "per tutti gli uomini dai 35 ai 50 anni la guerra è una seconda giovinezza. Militarizzazione dei muscoli e dei nervi logorati dalla vita." (For all men between 35 and 50, the war is a second youth. The militarization of muscles and nerves worn out by life.)[152]

In her discussion of *Come si seducono le donne* Re has discussed the echoes of the "homoerotic tradition of the Platonic dialogue"[153] in the image of Marinetti dictating his book to Corra, whose beautiful blonde hair is often praised. At the same time she notes the "distinctly homophobic allusions" in the book and interprets them as a "reflection of the homosexual panic" that men experienced in the intimate spaces of the trenches.[154] It is this theme and aspect of Marinetti's "self-help" guide that Corra takes up in his novel *L'isola dei baci*, which Marinetti declared to be a "romanzo utile, ora utilissimo" (useful book, now extremely useful).[155] The homosexuals are explicitly vilified as a group of depraved and cowardly men, whose physical beauty is a reminder of their cowardice and lack of patriotism in refusing to fight in the war. By equating physical beauty and cowardice, Corra implicitly praises the mutilated body of the war veteran, just as Marinetti had in *Come si seducono le donne*.

These novels and *L'Italia Futurista* were two methods employed by the Futurists to engage those soldiers serving at the front lines and to promote an understanding and appreciation of Futurist concepts among them. When Marinetti returned to active service in January 1917, he began in earnest to address soldiers and officers, as did a number of other Futurists.

4 How to Seduce Soldiers: Futurist Propaganda and Politics

Promoting Futurism at the Front

After spending most of 1916 in Milan, Marinetti arrived at the front on 20 February 1917 as part of the Seventy-Third Bombardiers' Battery, Eleventh Division, in the area of Gorizia.[1] He would spend the rest of 1917 and 1918 serving in various battalions and regiments in and around the front lines.[2]

Marinetti quickly began to consider the question of the promotion of Futurism at the front, and particularly among the officer population, in order to continue the courting of military personnel that had begun in the pages of *L'Italia Futurista*. He decided on a publicity campaign that involved sending Futurist manifestos, literary texts, and copies of *L'Italia Futurista* to dozens of individual officers and groups who were serving in other parts of the war zone. He sent detailed instructions to Nina Angelini to post copies of Boccioni's *Pittura e scultura futurista*, Russolo's *L'arte dei rumori*, and his own *Zang Tumb Tumb*, among many other texts. Between 27 February and 3 May, Marinetti sent numerous letters related to the diffusion of Futurist texts, in which he named over forty recipients who were serving in the army.[3] The impact and success of this endeavour are unfortunately hard to judge. Whatever its efficacy, this approach was soon abandoned, just days after Marinetti had made his first propaganda speech to officers at the front; perhaps he realized that promoting Futurism and the war effort through persuasive rhetoric would be more effective than providing officers with experimental, and at times impenetrable, literary texts.

Marinetti: A Propaganda Pioneer

Marinetti has been criticized by scholars for his behaviour as an officer during the last two years of the war. Giovanni Antonucci has accused him of favouring propaganda activity over his combat duties,[4] and Günter Berghaus has commented that "Marinetti's active service at the front did not resemble in the least that of a common soldier. He was allowed to move in and out of the war zone more or less as it pleased him."[5] In fact, apart from sanctioned leave and convalescence, Marinetti did not move out of the war zone in 1917 and 1918. There is an implicit suggestion in the comments of Antonucci and Berghaus that Marinetti was shirking his real war-time duties in favour of promoting Futurism. In reality Marinetti only became involved in propagandist activity on the orders of General Luigi Capello, who has been described by Mario Isnenghi as one of the pioneers of the Italian Army's efforts in the area of war-time propaganda.[6] Indeed, given that Marinetti was formally involved in propaganda activities on the front lines from as early as March 1917, he was himself a pioneer of Italian pursuits in that area.

Italian state-run war propaganda was virtually non-existent for the first two and a half years of the war "when neither the state nor the army made even the most minimal effort to 'sell' the conflict to those being called upon to fight it."[7] Giuseppe Prezzolini remarked that, in the early years of the war, propaganda consisted of "ordinare dei soldati sull'attenti in un cortile, dopo otto ore di fatiche e lì, togliendo loro un'ora di libertà, obbligarli a sentire la chiacchierata d'un avvocato inabile alle fatiche di Guerra" (ordering the soldiers to stand to attention in the courtyard after eight hours of work, taking away an hour of their free time, obliging them to listen to the chatter of a lawyer who was deemed unfit for war service).[8] The official beginning of the Servizio Propaganda (known as the Servizio P.) can be dated to a circular written by General Armando Diaz in February 1918, which stated: "Alcuni Comandi, con giusta intuizione dei bisogni del momento, hanno studiato e concretato un programma di propaganda patriottica fra le truppe [... con] iniziative, le quali incontrano pienamente il favore di questo Comando." (Some Commands, with a precise intuition of the needs of the present moment, have researched and put into action a program of propaganda among the troops [... with] initiatives, which are fully supported by this Command.)[9] General Capello of the Second Army was certainly one of the enterprising Commands to which Diaz referred.

As soon as he took charge of the Zona di Gorizia in March 1917, Capello set about creating an informal propaganda machine. His major innovation was the decision not to use the highest-ranking officers or political civilian figures but rather lower-ranking officers to address the troops "giacchè il soldato preferisce sempre ascoltare il suo ufficiale col quale si trova giornalmente a contatto, legato dalla stima e dall'affetto che nascono dalla comunità delle privazioni e dei rischi" (since the soldier always prefers to listen to his own officer with whom he is in daily contact, to whom he is linked through the respect and affection that are born from a shared experience of deprivation and risks).[10] Capello favoured an informal style of speech, with some humour, so that officers would feel as though they were listening to a conversation,[11] and stated that the speeches to the troops were the propaganda strategy that had proven "di maggior rendimento" (the most effective).[12] Capello selected approximately eighty men, comprising both officers and civilians, to raise troop morale through speeches and rhetoric,[13] and Marinetti was one of his chosen recruits.

On 13 March 1917 Marinetti was invited to meet with Capello, who spoke to him about the troops as follows (according to Marinetti's notes at the time):

> Lo spirito delle mie truppe è buono ma lo voglio migliore. Bisogna che l'impeto delle fanterie sia *travolgente*. Prendere una trincea non significa niente. Bisogna andare avanti. Molti si credevano assolutamente fuori d'ogni pericolo. Classi anziane richiamate ora e perciò senza preparazione bellica. Bisogna infiammarli e persuaderli della necessità di dare all'attacco un impulso *travolgente* feroce [...] Tutti gli ufficiali assisteranno a questi discorsi – Tutti! Reggimento per reggimento.

> The spirit of my troops is good but I want it to be better. The enthusiasm of the infantry must be *overwhelming*. Capturing a trench doesn't mean anything. We must move forwards. Many believed themselves to be absolutely out of any danger. Older men called up now and therefore with no war preparation. We must excite them and persuade them of the necessity to give a fierce, *overwhelming* impetus to the attack [...] All the officers will attend these speeches – All of them! Regiment by regiment.[14]

Clearly Marinetti's reputation had preceded him, for Capello told Marinetti, 'Io conosco molto lei e le sue teorie che mi piacciono. Ma non ho mai avuto occasione di venirla a sentire!' (I know a lot about you and I like your theories. But I've never had the chance to come and hear you speak!).[15] Marinetti's first assignment took place in April 1917 when he was tasked with providing "una scossa di eloquenza" (a jolt of eloquence) to a group of officers.[16]

In a memo of March 1917 Capello had laid out the scope of his propaganda campaign and specified the topics that the officers should cover in their speeches:

1 The moral reasons for going to war;
2 The necessity of the war;
3 The disadvantages of a quick peace;
4 The duty of every Italian towards the pursuit of freedom and Italian civilization;
5 Remembering the past and reflecting on the present, the Italian soldier must loathe the enemy;
6 Discipline brings about victory;
7 The friendly camaraderie and mutual trust between officers and soldiers is a source of cohesion and strength;
8 Defecting to the opposite side is the most ignominious act a man can commit;
9 Aggressive spirit.[17]

There is a striking overlap between these topics and the messages that Marinetti had been pedalling since the start of the war, particularly in the pages of *L'Italia Futurista*. Given this convergence of positions, Marinetti took to his new task with gusto, and the content of his first engagement loyally reflected Capello's approved topics: "Invito a finirla fuori col nemico schifoso massacrandolo e sfondandolo definitivamente" (I suggest finishing off the disgusting enemy, massacring him, and definitively breaking him).[18]

Capello's vision did not only extend to formal delivery of speeches; he also recommended frequent informal visits by propaganda officers to places of socialization at the front lines, especially the canteen.[19] Even before he was approached by Capello, this had been Marinetti's modus operandi. He grasped every opportunity to speak with small groups of officers and noted in his diary that the discussion invariably turned to Futurism in some way. No matter where he went – the huts, the brothel, the hospital – Marinetti reported finding "molti simpatizzanti futuristi" (lots of Futurist sympathizers).[20] As Alan Kramer has noted, "the private and the political were quite deliberately intertwined by Marinetti,"[21] and his propaganda duties for the army provided the perfect platform for him to merge his two identities, which up to that point had often been in conflict with one another. Immediately after his first official speech, for example, at lunch with some Neapolitan officers he spoke about Futurism and noted excitedly that "tutti diventano futuristi! o sembrano diventare, colla meravigliosa superficiale elasticità improvvisatrice meridionale" (everyone is becoming Futurist! or they seem to be, with the wonderful superficial improvised flexibility of Southerners).[22]

There were, however, some restrictions on the acceptable topics that could be addressed in the formal propaganda speeches. On one occasion in September 1917 Marinetti wrote that he had held a talk on Futurism and the war in front of a crowd of officers, captains, and a colonel, at which he recited some of his Futurist *parole in libertà*, to great acclaim.[23] Just a few days later, though, he complained about "la *legge* (che vuole che se porto un manoscritto in tasca non ho poi l'occasione né la possibilità di declamarlo)" (the *rules* (which state that if I have a manuscript in my pocket I won't have the possibility or the occasion to read it)),[24] but he boasted of his success in flouting these regulations. Possibly in reaction to this incident, although Marinetti was certainly not the only culprit, on 8 October 1917 Capello issued a circular that reprimanded those who were dealing with philosophical or literary subjects in their speeches, which demonstrated that "che non tutti i conferenzieri [...] si rendono conto dello scopo unico delle conferenze [...]: farsi comprendere interamente dalla massa dei soldati ed avvincerne l'animo" (not all the speakers [...] understand the only aim of the talks [...]: to be completely understood by the masses of soldiers and to bring their souls closer).[25]

Futurist Responses to Caporetto

Before Marinetti could be compelled to put Capello's directive into practice, the twelfth battle of the Isonzo began on 24 October 1917. Better known as Caporetto, it was a stunningly effective assault by approximately 350,000 Austrian and German troops on the Italian front line.[26] Their tactic was for small units to quickly penetrate the Italian lines and then attack from the rear, surprising Italian soldiers who believed themselves to be miles from the front. The assault succeeded beyond the expectations of the Central powers, bringing about the collapse of the Italian front line at the Isonzo River, resulting in 10,000 dead,

30,000 injured, 265,000 Italian prisoners of war, and 350,000 men who deserted or were separated from their units.[27] Between 24 October and 9 November the front was pushed back 150 kilometres from the Isonzo River to the Piave River, which effectively "nullified the extraordinary effort and expense of two years of war."[28] The unexpected attack resulted in chaos behind the Italian lines with instances both of Italian soldiers retreating without fighting, and of units engaging in combat as long as they could until they were forced to retreat. Despite this, Luigi Cadorna, leader of the Italian Army, declared on 28 October that the rout was caused by soldiers' refusal to fight, leading to widespread fears of "disfattisti"' (defeatists) in the ranks.[29] Caporetto had an enormous impact on the soldiers' morale and belief in the war. Armando Diaz, Cadorna's replacement, instigated a series of improvements in soldiers' conditions, including better rations and leave, as well as the establishment of the Servizio P., tasked with increasing the well-being of the troops.

Marinetti was at the Isonzo front when he heard the "notizia tragica" (tragic news) of the retreat at Caporetto.[30] He waited anxiously in his barracks to see if he would also be ordered to retreat. When the order came, Marinetti was distraught: "Mi sento morire. Dolore acuto al cuore. Sfacelo nelle vene. La mia forza interna è presa brutalmente a schiaffi pedate a pugni a martellate." (I feel like dying. Sharp pain in my heart. Destruction in my veins. My internal strength is being brutally slapped, kicked, punch, pounded.)[31] He began to dismantle his position, burning the telephone cables and destroying vehicles and munitions, and tried to delay his departure from the front for as long as possible. He experienced grenade attacks and shoot-outs with Austrian troops. Scenes of infernal chaos greeted him at Udine: "Disordine panico. Feriti e malati sgombrati in furia. Barelle. Feriti. Grida di terrore. Carri. Ambulanze. Ronzare di aeroplani [...] Cannoni rovesciati. Incendi. Incendii [*sic*]." (Disorder panic. Injured and sick hastily cleared out. Stretchers. Injured. Cries of terror. Wagons. Ambulances. Buzzing of airplanes [...] Overturned cannons. Fires. Fiires [*sic*].)[32]

When it became clear that the army could not defend the Tagliamento River (located between the Isonzo and the Piave Rivers), Marinetti began a retreat march in heavy rain and fog along with fourteen thousand other men, going several days "senza bere mangiare e dormire coll'acqua alla cintola" (without drinking eating and sleeping with water up to our belts).[33] Despite the difficult conditions and the rumours of betrayal that were circulating, Marinetti praised the Italian troops: "Tutti facciamo il nostro dovere. Ordine perfetto." (We all do our duty. Perfect order.)[34] During all this time Marinetti was suffering from jaundice, and so, on arrival at the Piave, he was ordered to a hospital in Padua for treatment.[35] Upon his release he sought to be reunited with his company of bombardiers and soon organized a unit of trench builders (*zappatori*), comprising bombardiers who had been separated from their units. Newly promoted to lieutenant, Marinetti was once again present at the front lines by 18 December 1917.[36]

With Marinetti otherwise engaged, it fell to Settimelli, editor of *L'Italia Futurista*, to issue a Futurist response to Caporetto. He hoped that the armies of the United States and Japan would soon be present in Europe, and declared that "è giunta l'ora di AVVICINARE la vittoria usufruendo nel minor tempo possibile di tutte le grandi riserve non ancora intaccate" (the time has come to bring victory CLOSER exploiting in as short a time as possible all the great reserves that have not yet been tapped).[37] A few weeks later Settimelli sought to protect Italy's hurt pride, stating that the French and British troops were not coming to help Italy but to "AIUTARE la causa comune" (HELP the common cause). He accepted the criticisms of those who said that victory was linked to resistance and that in comparison to the French, British, and Americans the Italians had shown a much weaker capacity to resist the enemy. However, he reminded his readers that England had been unified for centuries, France was a very wealthy country, and the United States had only just entered the war, so "gli italiani non hanno nessuna ragione di sentirsi per questo diminuiti di fronte all'Estero" (Italians have no reason to feel diminished against foreign powers).[38]

Marinetti's response to the disaster at Caporetto was one of "ottimismo artificiale" (artificial optimism), a phrase that he had first coined in 1914.[39] In an undated notebook entry from the war, entitled "Un tentativo di guarigione futurista" (Attempt at a Futurist cure), Marinetti made this recommendation: *"Stabilire un ponte coll'ottimismo artificiale* […] *tra un avvenimento buono e un altro avvenimento buono,* scavalcando il vallone dell'avvenimento cattivo" (*Build a bridge with artificial optimism* […] *between one positive event and another positive event*, passing over the valley of the unpleasant event).[40] Thus, Marinetti avoided public discussion of Caporetto, the one exception being an open letter to Settimelli, published in *L'Italia Futurista* on 9 December 1917. While he did wonder whether the defeat was due to "debolezza o tradimento" (weakness or betrayal), his primary message was one of optimism, hope, and reassurance. Marinetti praised the bravery of the Italian troops and stated that the Italian Army "ha piegato temporaneamente sotto lo sforzo di questo esercito rinforzato da tre altri eserciti" (temporarily folded under the might of this army reinforced by three other armies [Germany, Ottoman Empire, and Bulgaria]).[41] He was, however, still realistic in his estimation of the defeat, acknowledging: "Naturalmente la ritirata non fu quella che si sperava. Un esercito vittorioso al quale si ordina di abbandonare per ragioni strategiche delle terre sanguinosamente conquistate subisce un crollo morale pericolosissimo." (Of course the retreat was not what we had hoped for. A victorious army that is ordered, for strategic reasons, to abandon lands that have been bloodily conquered suffers a very dangerous collapse in morale.)[42]

Marinetti made no further public comment about Caporetto in *L'Italia Futurista*, although his own morale had been dealt a severe blow. In January 1918 he would note his difficulty in remaining optimistic in the face of such defeat: "Sono triste angosciato aspiro a un folle grande assoluto eroismo solitario nel crollo nuovo aggiunto a molti crolli del mio *ottimismo*. È ancora in piedi ma il suo tetto è sforacchiato!" (I am sad and anguished, I strive for a crazy great absolute isolated heroism in the new collapse added to the many other collapses of my *optimism*. It is still standing but its roof is leaking!)[43]

Notwithstanding these feelings, upon his return to the front in December 1917 he launched immediately into propagandizing again on behalf of both the war effort and Futurism.

The Servizio Propaganda

Caporetto taught the Italian high command that "bisognava badare al soldato" (it was necessary to take care of the soldier).[44] Soldiers' treatment quickly improved: rations and leave were increased, and concessions were made to agricultural workers who needed to return home for harvests.[45] Another important aspect of this new solicitude towards the soldier was the establishment of the Servizio Propaganda (Servizio P.) in the first months of 1918. Its objective was "la rieducazione del soldato: l'assistenza, la vigilanza morale, la propaganda alle linee" (the rehabilitation of the soldier: support, surveillance of morale, propaganda at the front).[46] The establishment of the Servizio P. marked a change in the position of the intellectual within the army and his return "al suo posto distinto da quello anonimo delle masse [e un] ritrovamento di un mandato sociale e di una funzione di utilità pubblica" (to his distinguished place from the anonymity of the masses [and a] rediscovery of his social mandate and a publicly useful role),[47] although Marinetti had already been engaged in propaganda duties for almost a year.

After the catastrophe of Caporetto, Marinetti continued his speaking engagements to hundreds and sometimes thousands of officers at a time. He spoke "con violenza eloquente delle ragioni della guerra della Germania che straccia i trattati non fa onore alla sua firma e ordina di silurare senza *lasciare traccia*" (with eloquent violence about Germany's reasons for war, a Germany that tears up treaties, does not honour its signature, and orders torpedoes that don't *leave a trace*).[48] However, it seems that Marinetti was no longer subject to the earlier restrictions regarding the promotion of Futurism within his formal propaganda speeches.[49] In March 1918 he spoke to several hundred officers about Italy "liberata dal suo passato e dal forestiero" (liberated from her past and from foreigners) and about "anticlericalismo futurista feroce per il dopo Guerra" (a fierce Futurist anticlericalism after the war), before explaining *parole in libertà* and declaiming one of his own compositions.[50] Marinetti's propagandizing was apparently so successful that Lombardo Radice of the Servizio P. was afraid of losing his own position to him, although Marinetti assured him that he would never accept a formal role in the propaganda service or "nessun posto consimile imboscato" (any other similar shirker role).[51] .

The Birth of the Futurist Political Party

As the Italian Army sought to regain its momentum following Caporetto, in February 1918 the manifesto of the Futurist Political Party was published on the front page of the final issue of *L'Italia Futurista*, although the party itself would only be established in November 1918 after the war. The circumstances of the birth of the party have always been rather unclear. Gentile commented that the idea of a political party began to mature in 1917 "anche se non si può dire a chi spetti la sua paternità" (even if one can't say whose the idea was).[52] Berghaus has suggested that the manifesto was "written, presumably, during Marinetti's army leave from 27 January to 8 February 1918."[53] In fact, it was in April 1917 while he was at the front that Marinetti first jotted down ideas for a "programma politico sociale" (social political program), which bore many similarities to the manifesto that was finally published almost a year later. In these notes he proposed the abolition of marriage and the introduction of divorce; the expulsion of the papacy from Rome; the abolition of the parliament; the abolition of higher education; and the abolition of police stations in favour of a situation in which every armed citizen would defend themselves.[54] The manifesto itself, however, was not drafted until a few months later during Marinetti's summer leave in 1917. Writing from Ravenna on 21 August 1917, Corra informed Settimelli that Marinetti was there with him and "mi ha parlato dei vostri progetti di organizzazione" (has spoken to me about your plans). The plan was that Paolo Orano's manifesto on Dalmatia would appear in *L'Italia Futurista* on 1 September, and the political manifesto would appear in the following issue, on 15 September, which they would try to "fare apparire integralmente dalla Censura" (get published untouched by the Censor).[55] Although Orano's manifesto did appear in September, the publication of the political manifesto was delayed for six months until February 1918. At least part of the motivation for this long delay must have been the inappropriate timing of such a publication following the defeat at Caporetto.

As Berghaus has observed, Marinetti's "aesthetic program of renewal was always complemented by a political engagement."[56] Before 1917, however, Marinetti's interest in engaging directly in parliamentary politics had been half-hearted at best. During the general election of March 1909 Marinetti had issued a flyer entitled "Elettori futuristi!" that urged Italy's young people to engage in "una lotta ad oltranza contro i candidati che patteggiano coi vecchi e coi preti" (a struggle to the bitter end against candidates who have any truck with the traditionalists and with the priests).[57] In the pre-war years, political engagement by the Futurists had remained largely an excuse for rowdy violence and cheap publicity (for example, the irredentist *serate* in 1910 and the interventionist demonstrations in 1914). During the 1913 general elections, 100,000 copies of the third Futurist political manifesto had been printed, leading to speculation that Marinetti would stand for election, but he denied that this was his immediate intention.[58] A 1911 manifesto had declared Futurism to be against parliamentarianism, a view that Marinetti reiterated in an interview of 23 February 1915 with *L'Avvenire*. Although he firmly identified Futurism as a movement of art and artists, Marinetti admitted: "Non possiamo [...] non aspirare ad una nostra forza nel Parlamento [...] Io aspetto di svolgere una vera azione politica fra poco ponendo una candidatura per una lotta tipica. Dovrò conquistare alla baionetta un collegio di prim'ordine." (We cannot [...]

not aspire to having our own voice in Parliament [...] I expect to soon carry out some real political action by putting myself up as a candidate for a typical struggle. I must win a first-class seat with a bayonet.)[59] In spite of these claims Marinetti showed no interest in parliamentary politics for the next three years. As Maddalena Carli has rightly pointed out, "il credo prebellico dei futuristi non andava certo nella direzione di una professionalizzazione (e normalizzazione) della militanza politica" (pre-war Futurist beliefs were certainly not headed in the direction of a professionalization (and normalization) of political militancy).[60]

However, for a year before the publication of the manifesto of the Futurist Political Party, Settimelli had been reflecting on the changes in Italian society in the pages of *L'Italia Futurista*. As living conditions worsened on the home front from the beginning of 1917, spontaneous popular protests began all over Italy. De Felice estimated that approximately five hundred demonstrations took place between 1 December 1916 and 15 April 1917, in which hundreds of thousands of women participated. This unrest continued throughout the summer, culminating in the August riots in Turin.[61] With Marinetti at the front, it was Settimelli who first captured and understood this change in the public mood and the possible consequences for Futurism, and it was he who first considered the idea of a political turn for the Futurist movement. Thus, he sought to shape Futurism and Marinetti accordingly. In February 1917 Settimelli wrote: "Ogni italiano vive oggi intensamente la vita dell'Italia e cerca di scrutare quali sono i suoi interessi. Questa educazione politica è un bene enorme. Non dovrà essere perduta quando – dopo la guerra un grande partito nazionale darà il ritmo della nuova vita italiana." (Today every Italian intensely lives the life of Italy and tries to examine what Italy's interests are. This political education is an enormous benefit. It must not be lost when – after the war – a great national party will decide the rhythm of the new Italian life.)[62]

During the following month Settimelli chose to publish the "Programma Politico Futurista" (a reprint of Marinetti's 1913 manifesto) on the front page of *L'Italia Futurista*, indicating Settimelli's vision that Futurism might indeed become the "great national party" to lead Italy after the war. This manifesto declared Futurist politics to be irredentist, anti-clericalist, and anti-socialist; it advocated a cult of progress and physical fitness, a minimum of doctors, professors, and lawyers, and more farmers, engineers, and producers.[63]

Part of this heightened political consciousness in *L'Italia Futurista* revolved around discussions and predictions about the end of the war.[64]

Marinetti's voice was conspicuously absent from these discussions, the one exception being an interview with Settimelli in March 1917. Even though the discussion about the end of the war was limited to one paragraph, Settimelli sought to position Marinetti as a voice in this unfolding debate by entitling the article "Intervista con Marinetti sulla fine della guerra" (Interview with Marinetti on the end of the war). Following is the entirety of Marinetti's statement on the topic:

> Entriamo nella fase finale. Le condizioni della Germania e dell'Austria sono *certamente* disperate. È molto probabile che in ottobre si depongano le armi per un armistizio e s'incominci a trattare la Pace. Noi siamo in condizioni formidabili. Di tutto si può dubitare fuori che della vittoria per l'Italia.

> (We are entering into the final phase. The situation of Germany and Austrian is *certainly* desperate. It is very probable that in October weapons will be laid down in an armistice and Peace negotiations will begin. We are in a very strong position. You can doubt everything except Italy's victory.)[65]

Already, just nine months after the journal's launch, a growing political sensitivity was becoming evident, as was Settimelli's desire to mould Marinetti into the mouthpiece for a post-war political movement. In this March interview Settimelli claimed: "Questo poeta bizzarro e ossessionato da ricerche nuovissime e da clamorosi gesti artistici sembrava il più disadatto e il più lontano dalla politica. Gli avvenimenti ce l'hanno mostrato *il più vicino*." (This odd poet, obsessed with innovative research and noisy artistic actions, seemed the most inappropriate and the furthest from politics. The war has shown him to be *the closest*.)[66] This marked a startling about-face from the position of *L'Italia Futurista* at its launch in the previous year. In the journal's second issue, in June 1916, Marinetti had issued an invective against parliamentary politics, praying for an Austrian battery to be aimed at the Italian parliament at Montecitorio,[67] and Settimelli had declared that Marinetti was "il più eccentrico degli spiriti italiani, il più bizzarro dei poeti italiani, il più *lontano dalla politica*" (the most eccentric of Italian spirits, the oddest of Italian poets, the *furthest from politics*).[68] At that stage Settimelli had sought to establish Marinetti as a bulwark against, and as an alternative to, traditional politics, but he seemed unclear as to how Marinetti would be able to play an effective role in Italian life while still remaining outside of politics. Thus, Settimelli opted to leave it to the Italian people to decide how they would make use of Marinetti's "titanica passione [… e] l'audacia del suo Genio rigeneratore" (titanic passion [… and] the audacity of his regenerative Genius) after the war.[69] By spring 1917 it was clear that both Settimelli and Marinetti had realized that the latter could perhaps launch himself and Futurism into the arena of parliamentary politics.

Although Marinetti and Settimelli were preparing to launch a political wing of the Futurist movement, the general public was deemed not yet willing to accept the possibility of a Futurist political party. Thus, the task fell to Settimelli to convince the readers of *L'Italia Futurista* that Marinetti could be a serious political contender. In July 1917 Settimelli republished the 1909 and 1913 political manifestos but grouped them under the headline "Movimento politico futurista" (Futurist political movement). In an article published on 12 August Settimelli claimed that the Futurists were "forse gli uomini più calunniati dalla ignoranza, dalla imbecillità, dalla malvagità pubblica" (possibly the men most vilified by ignorance, stupidity, and public cruelty)[70] and sought to redeem them in the eyes of the public. He wrote that art was only "una parte del programma futurista. Sarà la più sviluppata, ma non è certo la più importante" (one part of the Futurist program. It is the most developed, but it is definitely not the most important).[71] Gentile has previously identified this article as marking a turning point because, "senza rinnegare nulla delle idee precedenti, proponeva un orientamento notevolmente diverso e, per aspetti significativi, anche nuovo per la politica del futurismo" (without denying any of their previous ideas, it proposed a noticeably different and, in significant ways, new direction for political Futurism).[72] However, given that by 21 August the political manifesto was ready, or at least at an advanced drafting stage, and due for imminent publication (according to the letter by Corra), it is likely that this article by Settimelli and the manifesto were conceived and drafted at the same time, and so it cannot be claimed with any certainty that Settimelli's article provided the impetus for Futurism's political turn. However, in stating that art was only one part of the Futurist program, Settimelli was paving the way for similar declarations that Marinetti would make in the manifesto. Until the end of 1917 Settimelli remained the public face of "political" Futurism through the pages of *L'Italia Futurista*.

In December of that year Settimelli explicitly mentioned the Futurist Political Party for the first time (in July it had been a "movement"), writing: "Il partito politico futurista che stiamo elaborando ci porterà in contatto con le masse e varerà il nostro grande sogno nella intera compagine nazionale rendendolo aspirazione di popolo." (The Futurist political party that we are developing will bring us into contact with the masses and will launch our great dream to the whole nation, making it the desire of the people.)[73] This article essentially sought to train the readership to buy into the concept of Futurism as a political movement and was certainly written in preparation for the publication of the political manifesto, which occurred two months later. Settimelli continued, stating that Marinetti and the other Futurists fighting in the trenches "aspettano di passare alla vita politica, di vivere a contatto con le maggioranze" (are waiting to move into political life, to live in contact with the masses). The Futurists would attack all the most difficult problems, but "per ottenere tutto questo bisognerà che il pubblico non li scarti *a priori* per la loro multipla funambolica, colorita profondamente italiana duttilità" (to obtain all of this the public must not reject them *a priori* for their multiple acrobatic, colourful and deeply Italian adaptability).[74]

Eventually, in the final issue of *L'Italia Futurista*, in February 1918, the "Manifesto del Partito Politico Futurista" was published. It had been considerably expanded from the notes that Marinetti had made in his diary in April 1917, and some of those points had been toned down. He was still in favour of introducing divorce and "free love," but the gradual abolition of marriage was reduced to a gradual devaluation instead.[75] The transformation of education that he had proposed at that time (abolition of illiteracy, obligatory primary education, and gymnastics in schools) remained largely unchanged in 1918, although the proposal to abolish higher education completely was tempered to the abolition of only "molte Università inutili" (many useless Universities). The proposal that the police force should be abolished in favour of armed citizens was abandoned, as was the outright abolition of Parliament. Instead, Parliament would be transformed through an equal participation of industrialists, farmers, engineers, and businessmen and a reduction in the numbers of lawyers and teachers serving in it. However, Marinetti did reserve the right to abolish the parliament and introduce a technocratic government if the remodelled parliament were to fail. The manifesto of 1918 also featured a number of additional points related to the necessity of creating a strong and free Italy and to the importance of maintaining a strong army and navy – "tutti pronti" (all at the ready) – to keep Italy on a war footing for any possible war or revolution. A significant portion of the manifesto was devoted to provisions for ex-combatants, including the establishment of "un patrimonio agrario dei combattenti" (an agricultural fund for combatants), acknowledgment of military service in the calculation of pensions, and job competitions in the public administration that would be open exclusively to veterans.[76]

The manifesto also provided important clarifications for the future of the Futurist movement. As has already been observed, since the interventionist crisis Marinetti's interest in military service and the war had alienated certain members of the movement and had caused tension within its ranks. Despite his best efforts he had not been able to satisfactorily balance the demands of Futurism as an artistic and literary avant-garde movement with his competing desire to mobilize Futurism in favour of the Italian war effort. Thus, he made a radical decision in the manifesto of the political party. He declared that "il partito politico futurista che noi fondiamo oggi, e che organizzeremo dopo la guerra, sarà nettamente distinto dal movimento futurista artistico" (the Futurist political party that we are founding today, and that we will organize after the war, will be clearly distinct from the Futurist artistic movement).[77] Dividing the movement into two parallel strands was an extreme departure from Futurism's foundational rhetoric that had expressed the need for art to engage fully with life – famously expressed as the introduction of "il pugno nella lotta artistica" (the fist into the artistic struggle).[78] Marinetti explained the reason behind his decision:

Questo [il lato artistico] continuerà nella sua opera di svecchiamento e rafforzamento del genio creatore italiano. Il movimento artistico futurista, avanguardia della sensibilità artistica italiana, è necessariamente sempre in anticipo sulla lenta sensibilità del popolo. Rimane perciò una avanguardia spesso incompresa e spesso osteggiata dalla maggioranza che non può intendere le sue scoperte stupefacenti, la brutalità delle sue espressioni polemiche e gli slanci temerari delle sue intuizioni. Il partito politico futurista invece intuisce i bisogni presenti e interpreta esattamente la coscienza di tutta la razza nel suo igienico slancio rivoluzionario. Potranno aderire al partito politico futurista tutti gli italiani, uomini e donne d'ogni classe e d'ogni età, anche se negati a qualsiasi concetto artistico e letterario.

(This [the artistic side] will continue its work of rejuvenating and strengthening Italian creative genius. The Futurist artistic movement, the avant-garde of Italian artistic sensibility, is necessarily always ahead of the slow sensibility of the people. It will remain therefore an avant-garde, which is often misunderstood and often opposed by the majority who cannot understand its amazing discoveries, the brutality of its polemical statements, and the bold passion of its intuitions. The Futurist political party on the other hand understands present needs and interprets exactly the consciousness of a whole race in its hygienic, revolutionary passion. All Italians, men and women of every class and age, can join the Futurist political party, even if they reject all artistic and literary concepts.)[79]

Just as earlier in the war Marinetti had been willing to sacrifice some artistic integrity in favour of promoting the war effort through Futurism, here his desire to reach out to a broader audience (primarily soldiers, officers, and veterans) overrode the requirements of Futurism as an artistic movement and, in effect, relegated artistic concerns into second place after politics.

Initially, however, this division of Futurism into two strands seemed to precipitate a halt to Futurist action in either sphere between February and August 1918. *L'Italia Futurista* had published its final issue; no Futurist books were published, and no theatre performances or exhibitions are recorded as having occurred during this time. The nascent political party was also stalled. At the front lines, however, Marinetti was still enjoying success in his part-time work as a propagandist. No longer was he a figure of fun, but rather he was being taken increasingly seriously by his military commanders. Marinetti recalled an encounter in early 1918 with a number of high-ranking officers "che mi avevano ricevuto con una certa alterigia. Ora sono pieni d'ossequio" (who had received me with a certain superiority. Now they are full of respect).[80] It was perhaps because of his increasingly positive reputation that Benito Mussolini reached out to Marinetti in the summer of 1918 in search of new political allies.

These meetings between Marinetti and Mussolini were the first meaningful contact between the two men since their brief interactions during the interventionist demonstrations of spring 1915, when Mussolini had been rather cool towards the Futurists' overtures. In May 1917, as Marinetti was recovering from his battlefield injury, he had attempted once more to gain favour with Mussolini. Mussolini was also convalescing in hospital, in Milan,[81] and sent him a telegram wishing him a speedy recovery. Marinetti, although he was in a military hospital in Udine, did not want to let this opportunity pass him by. Thus, he tasked Nina Angelini with buying "dei *bellissimi garofani rossi*" (*beautiful red carnations*) and delivering them to Mussolini.[82] He reiterated these instructions a few days later: "Dirai a Mussolini portandogli i garofani rossi che *Il Futurismo italiano glieli manda*. Gli dirai che sono ansioso di saperlo *guarito* e che tutti noi futuristi gli vogliamo molto bene." (You'll tell Mussolini, bringing him the red carnations, that *they were sent by Italian Futurism*. You will tell him that I am anxious to know he is *getting better* and that all of us Futurists are very fond of him.)[83] The visit between Angelini and Mussolini occurred on 1 June 1917 but appears not to have been a success. The only available information is unfortunately tantalizingly brief: "Visita a Mussolini male eseguita senza precisione. Basta non ne parliamo più." (Visit to Mussolini badly executed without precision. Enough, we won't say anything more about it.)[84]

The two men had no further contact until Mussolini reached out to Marinetti in July 1918. Marinetti wrote in his diary that "Benito Mussolini mi ha mandato a dire che desiderava tanto rivedermi [...] Desidera parlare a lungo con me." (Benito Mussolini sent word that he very much wanted to see me again [...] He wants to speak at length with me.)[85] They met twice in the following days, and Marinetti's view of Mussolini was very favourable. He praised his "bella faccia violenta chiara forte intelligente sana ma agitata da smorfie passionali" (nice violent clear strong intelligent face healthy but agitated by passionate grimaces).[86] They discussed defeatist artists and intellectuals, Giovanni Papini's neutralist articles, and combatants' organizations. Finally, unlike during the interventionist crisis, Marinetti could truthfully declare that Mussolini "è pieno di idee futuriste" (is full of Futurist ideas).[87] Nonetheless, no formal alliance transpired between the two men until after the end of the war.[88]

Roma Futurista and *Il Montello*

From February 1918, when *L'Italia Futurista* ceased publication, no Futurist periodical existed that was aimed at a soldier audience. In August Mario Carli complained to Marinetti about this state of affairs:

Il momento mi sembra anche favorevolissimo alla ripresa di un'azione futurista energica e significativa. Basta uno sguardo sommario per capire che il Futurismo è prossimo a naufragare nel silenzio e nell'incuriosità generale [...] Credi tu che sia patriottismo questa rinuncia alla lotta futurista, o non piuttosto disfattismo?

(Right now seems a very favourable moment for the resumption of energetic and meaningful Futurist action. We need only take a quick glance to understand that Futurism is nearly drowning in silence and a general lack of curiosity [...] Do you think that this sacrifice of the Futurist struggle is patriotism, or not rather defeatism?).[89]

Thus, on 20 September 1918, the magazine *Roma Futurista* appeared, edited by Carli, Settimelli, and Marinetti. On the same day, whether by coincidence or by design, a second Futurist magazine appeared: *Il Montello*. These two magazines can be regarded as sister publications, achieving the same ends by different means. Both sought to court a military audience: *Il Montello* was a "giornale di trincea" (trench newspaper) funded by the Servizio P. and aimed at ordinary soldiers and low-ranking officers, while *Roma Futurista* was directed towards the elite of the Italian Army, the Arditi soldiers.

Both newspapers point to the compromises that the Futurists were willing to make in order to extend their supporter base and attract new audiences, and both publications diverged significantly from the model of *L'Italia Futurista*. While the earlier publication had sought to achieve a fusion of Futurism's artistic and political objectives, such an approach was not followed in *Roma Futurista*. It was designed to be devoid of any literary content. *Il Montello*, in spite of boasting a Futurist editorial team, contributors, and content, was compelled to erase virtually all easily identifiable traces of Futurism from its pages. Nonetheless, in a letter to Primo Conti in September 1918, Marinetti triumphantly stated that "*Il Montello* [...] è futurista" (*Il Montello* [...] is Futurist).[90] Later, again discussing *Il Montello*, Marinetti passionately declared to Soggetti, "Come vedi il futurismo lotta e vince!" (As you can see, Futurism struggles and wins!).[91] Walter Adamson has commented that Marinetti's "elitist convictions were manifest above all in the futurist mode of participating in World War 1, in which they functioned to support group solidarity at whatever cost to general camaraderie."[92] However, Marinetti's enthusiastic support of a publication like *Il Montello*, designed to reach out to ordinary soldiers, would seem to contradict this point of view. Both newspapers demonstrate an adaptability on the part of Futurism, which has already been observed in other aspects of Futurist war-time production, and thus they are highly significant documents with regard to the progressively less confrontational stance adopted towards non-Futurist audiences.

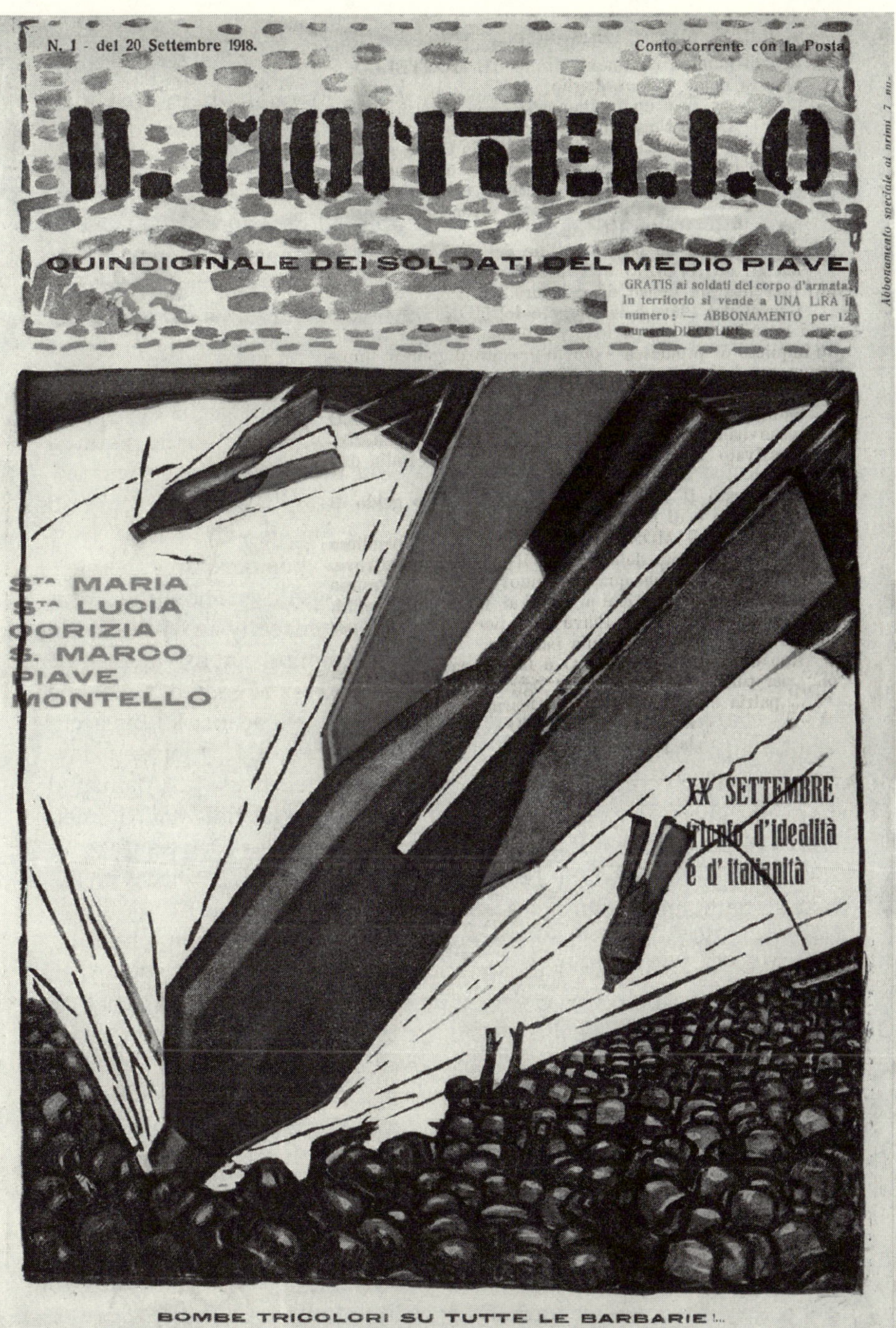

Figure 4.1. *Il Montello*, 20 September 1918. Courtesy of Biblioteca Storica Moderna e Contemporanea, Rome.

The elitist aspect of Futurism's activity manifested itself in their interest in the Arditi, one of the primary audiences of *Roma Futurista*. The Arditi corps, officially established on 26 June 1917, comprised elite soldiers and officers who served in assault divisions. Engaged in the most dangerous military tasks, they suffered losses and casualties that were significantly higher than those of the regular army. To compensate for their exposure to higher risks, the Arditi soldiers enjoyed better conditions than did the average private soldier. Their rations were of better quality and more generous; they received a higher rate of pay; and they were exempt from camp chores, trench duty, long marches, and carrying a heavy backpack. Their training consisted of physical and psychological tests designed to weed out those who were lacking the required nerve and bravery.[93] Their attitude towards military discipline was lax, and there were reports of Arditi attacking supply depots with hand grenades in order to procure extra rations, cigarettes, and wine.[94] They were also rumoured to be criminals, and one of their nicknames was *teppisti* (hooligans). Far from disagreeing with this description, the Arditi embraced it. In his book *Noi Arditi*, published early in 1919, Mario Carli, an ardito himself, defended the corps, stating that its "teppismo" was merely "un eccesso di generosità" (an excess of generosity) as the Arditi had always sought to defend the weak. He dismissed the accusations of "pollai saccheggiati, [...] alberi decimati, [...] focolari devastati" (ransacked chicken coops, [...] decimated trees, [...] damaged homes) as being part of the fabric of life during war-time and claimed that the Arditi were not the only ones responsible for such acts.[95] Similarly, Ottone Rosai entitled his 1919 memoir about his service with the assault battalions *Il libro di un teppista* (Book of a hooligan).[96]

Prior to the formal establishment of the Arditi divisions in June 1917, Capello's Second Army had designated certain exceptional soldiers in this way.[97] Marinetti was called upon to deliver a speech to a group of them in May 1917: "Esalto gli *arditi* parlo del coraggio e della *paura*. Insegno l'orgoglio di essere e dichiararsi *arditi* d'un reggimento e la vergogna d'esser *paurosi*." (I glorify the *arditi*, I speak about courage and about *fear*. I teach the pride of being and declaring yourself an *ardito* in a regiment and the shame of being *fearful*.)[98] Marinetti, however, had no further contact with the Arditi until more than a year later, when he was in Verona to testify in the trial of some of them who were accused of drunken behaviour. Marinetti robustly defended their actions against the carabinieri.[99] He highlighted the need to judge them according to the codes of war rather than the morality of peace. With their love of battle, and the emphasis on speed and danger in their attack strategies, it is not difficult to understand why the Futurists saw the Arditi as kindred spirits. Marinetti's admiration for their troops was undeniable; in a letter to Carli, Marinetti expressed his "simpatia per questa rossa gioventù futurista d'Italia" (fondness for this red Futurist youth of Italy)[100] and in his notebook admitted that he would like to command an Arditi division because they were "la nuova Italia giovane irruente rivoluzionaria *futurista*" (the new young Italy, impulsive, revolutionary, *Futurist*).[101] In *Noi Arditi*, Carli identified the ardito as "il futurista della guerra, l'avanguardia scapigliata e pronta a tutto, [...] che scaglia le bombe fischiettando i ricordi del Varietà" (the Futurist of the war, the dishevelled avant-garde, ready for anything, [...] who flings bombs whistling tunes from a Variety show).[102] Indeed he concluded in his book that while the ardito was "*il futurista della Guerra*" (*the Futurist of the war*), the Futurist was "*l'ardito delle battaglie artistiche e politiche*" (*the ardito of the artistic and political battles*).[103]

It was in August 1918, during Marinetti's summer leave, that the idea of courting the Arditi began in earnest. In Rome to discuss *Roma Futurista*, Marinetti, Carli, and Settimelli initially intended the newspaper to have the subtitle "*Giornale per tutti gli arditi*" (*Newspaper for all the Arditi*)[104] and to feature the "esaltazione in ogni numero del corpo degli *arditi*" (glorification of the *Arditi* corps in every issue).[105] Then, from September 1918, Marinetti began publicly to link the Arditi to the Futurists. In a speech of 15 September to Arditi officers Marinetti praised them as the "parte migliore della razza italiana quella che ha più vigore più sangue più eroismo più coscienza d'Italianità" (the best part of the Italian race, which has more vigour, more blood, more heroism, more awareness of Italianness)[106] and admired their "amore di novità spirito futurista novatore [...] amore della violenza della guerra e del bel gesto eroico" (love of novelty, innovative Futurist spirit [...] love of violence of war and of the beautiful heroic gesture).[107] In a letter to Pratella of 29 September Marinetti wrote that "la testata lega i futuristi arditi della nazione agli arditi futuristi dell'esercito" (the newspaper links the Futurists, arditi of the nation, to the Arditi, Futurists of the army).[108]

Roma Futurista ultimately sought to strike a balance between reaching out to the Arditi and not alienating other soldiers and officers. The newspaper's subtitle was "Giornale del partito politico futurista" (Newspaper of the Futurist political party), a more inclusive label than the one originally intended to single out the Arditi. The first issue's editorial did not mention the Arditi explicitly but appealed to "forze giovani, violente, antitradizionali e ultra italiane" (young, violent, anti-traditional and ultra-Italian forces) and expressed the desire to "risolvere praticamente e prontamente tutti i problemi inerenti al benessere e alla glorificazione degli autentici combattenti e dei mutilati" (practically and quickly resolve all the problems relevant to the well-being and glorification of the authentic combatants and war-injured).[109] Even Carli's article on the Arditi in the first issue offered a somewhat inclusive perspective, seeking to reach out to anyone who embodied the Arditi's ideals even if he was not part of the elite squad. He issued a spiritual call to "tutti gli 'arditi' d'Italia, tutti coloro che hanno anima di combattenti, orgoglio di italiani, energia di futuristi" (all the "arditi" of Italy, all those who have the soul of a combatant, the pride of an Italian, the energy of a Futurist).[110] Nonetheless, the Arditi did have a special position in the pages of *Roma Futurista*, and they were praised as Italy's saviour from her enemies, both internal and external, and would return from the front to construct "i nuovi valori della politica, dell'arte e della ricchezza nazionale" (the new values of politics, art and national wealth).[111]

Much as had been the case in *L'Italia Futurista*, with its parade of contributions by *futuristi al fronte*, a recurring element of *Roma Futurista* was its reminders of the Futurists' tireless service with the Italian Army. Indeed, when he had first suggested the idea of founding a new journal, Carli had stressed to Marinetti the importance of their records of war service, stating, "Io sono *Ardito* e *ferito*, e quindi inattaccabile, [...] tu ti sei gloriosamente battuto molte e molte volte, e sei stato *ferito*, mettendoci in una condizione di assoluta superiorità" (I am an *Ardito* and *injured*, and therefore untouchable, [...] you have fought gloriously many times, and you have been *injured*, which puts us in a position of absolute superiority).[112] Just as Settimelli had encouraged readers of *L'Italia Futurista* to take the Futurists seriously and not to dismiss them as buffoons, the editors of *Roma Futurista* faced their detractors head-on, playing the indisputable trump card of admirable records of military service:

> I nostri nemici tenteranno vanamente di screditarci evocando i nostri burrascosi comizi artistici. I futuristi [...] sono oggi i primi fra i primi sul campo di battaglia. I futuristi, questi artisti bizzarri, hanno saputo battersi, vincere e morire. I nostri nemici cercheranno anche di aggirarci con le loro subdole simpatie, insinuando che degli artisti anche se geniali non possono fare della politica; e noi li smentiremo con la nostra indagine precisa, pratica, inesorabile contro i traditori e i truffatori della patria.

(Our enemies will vainly try to discredit us by bringing up our stormy artistic rallies. The Futurists […] are today the first on the battlefield. The Futurists, these odd artists, know how to fight, win and die. Our enemies will also try to bypass us with deceitful congeniality, insinuating that even talented artists cannot be involved in politics; and we will prove them wrong with our precise, practical, relentless investigation against the traitors and cheaters of the nation.)[113]

In a cartoon on the front page of a later issue of the journal Roberto Iras Baldessari[114] even went so far as to suggest that pre-war hostility from the public had prepared the Futurists for life in the trenches.

Readers of *Roma Futurista* were reminded of the Futurists' war service at every opportunity, most prominently on the front page of every issue in a list of the Futurist dead and injured.[115] The Futurists had to prove their war-time credentials in order to convince the Arditi (and other military personnel), who may not have been previously sympathetic to the movement, to join the Futurist Political Party.

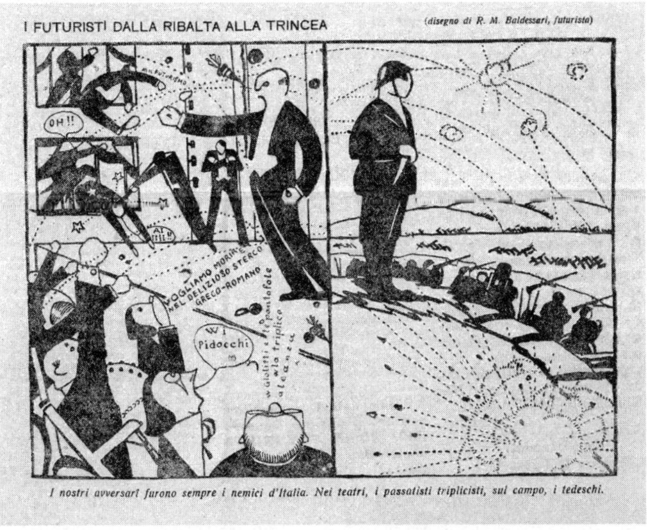

Figure 4.2. Roberto Iras Baldessari, "I futuristi dalla ribalta alla trincea" (The Futurists from the stage to the trench), *Roma Futurista*, 20 November 1918, 1. Courtesy of Museo d'arte moderna e contemporanea di Trento e Rovereto, Archivio del '900.

The editors were aware of the potentially alienating effect that the Futurist reputation for artistic extravagance and experimentation could have on a group such as the Arditi, which was not known for its intellectual abilities. Thus, as in the "Manifesto del Partito Politico Futurista" (faithfully republished in every issue of *Roma Futurista*), the first issue's editorial distanced the new journal from Futurism's artistic past, with this opening: "Il futurismo che fino ad oggi esplicò un programma specialmente artistico, si propone una integrale azione politica per collaborare a risolvere gli urgenti problemi nazionali." (Futurism, which up to now has carried out above all an artistic program, proposes complete political action to collaborate in resolving urgent national problems.)[116] The declarations of *Roma Futurista* and the promise of a new political party to be established after the war certainly struck a chord with its target audience. Enthusiastic missives of support and party membership were received from dozens of soldiers and officers in the trenches, most of them Arditi. There were those like Cesare Cerati,[117] Auro d'Alba,[118] and Massimo Bontempelli[119] who were already Futurists or working closely alongside them; those like Federico Pedrazzini and Alberto Cauli who had followed "con sempre crescente entusiasmo il movimento futurista in Italia" (with ever-increasing enthusiasm the Futurist movement in Italy);[120] and those like Franco Ciarlantini who regarded *Roma Futurista* as "un martello perforatore ed esplosivo e piace per tre quarti del suo programma anche a chi come me, non fu mai futurista" (an explosive drill hammer, and three-quarters of the program is appealing even to people like me who have never been Futurists).[121] The party received support from generals, majors, officers, soldiers, and students,[122] although, as Berghaus has discussed, the real reach of the party was undoubtedly exaggerated by the Futurists.[123]

While *Roma Futurista* could freely advertise its Futurist ideology, *Il Montello*, as a state-funded newspaper for soldiers, did not enjoy the same freedom. In spite of its boast of a Futurist editorial team, contributors, and content, virtually all evidence of this Futurist allegiance was removed from the magazine's pages. The trench newspapers were one of the most significant methods of persuasion aimed at soldiers in the trenches that were adopted by the Servizio P.[124] Trench newspapers were ostensibly produced to appeal to the ordinary soldier, to entertain him at the front, and to distract him from his environment, although in reality they were often read by the officer corps.[125]

Il Montello, a biweekly newspaper for the soldiers of the Eighth Army, was edited by Massimo Bontempelli and Mario Sironi.[126] The first issue was launched on 20 September 1918, and three further issues were published before the end of the war in November.[127] The newspaper was distributed free to soldiers of the Eighth Army but was also available for one lira to other readers. The editors were keen to show that *Il Montello* would speak for all soldiers, no matter where they were based.

Sironi and Bontempelli were the two driving forces behind *Il Montello* and were assigned to the Servizio P. from other military divisions. It seems likely that Margherita Sarfatti, journalist and mistress of Mussolini, was responsible for Sironi's new assignment. Sironi had been with the Corps of Photoelectrical (Railroad) Engineers, but Sarfatti had requested "that he be given a task more appropriate to his training as a painter, such as illustrating for a propaganda journal or working for the camouflage design unit,"[128] and soon afterwards he was present with the propaganda division of the Eighth Army.[129] Bontempelli approached Folgore about becoming part of the editorial team and also expressed a desire for Cangiullo to take part.[130] Contributors included Marinetti, Carrà, Folgore, Carli, Settimelli, Cangiullo, Corra, and Jamar 14.[131]

Marinetti first heard of *Il Montello* from Bontempelli in August 1918. On summer leave in Milan, he recorded in his notebook that "Bontempelli mi parla del giornale di trincea a tinta futurista" (Bontempelli spoke to me about a soldiers' newspaper with a Futurist slant); he also asked Marinetti for some material.[132] On 1 September Corra sent Marinetti a copy of the first issue of *Il Montello* and on 19 September informed him that he had just sent him three hundred copies to distribute.[133] According to Corra, the print run was twenty thousand copies.[134] In the absence of independent evaluations, we must rely on Futurist pronouncements about the success of the journal. The first issue was apparently "piaciutissimo" (very well liked),[135] and "il terzo numero […] fa furore, gli abbonamenti si susseguono l'uno all'altro" (the third issue is doing very well, the subscriptions keep flowing in).[136]

Il Montello sought to strike a balance in terms of its readership and to appeal to both the ordinary soldier with his limited literacy skills and to the officer classes. Half of the journal's pages comprised illustrations and humorous cartoons, which were more suitable for common soldiers, "digiuni di cultura e assai poco abituati alla lettura" (starved of culture and very unused to reading).[137] A page in the first issue explained military strategies and tactics with amusing drawings: a frontal attack consisted of the butt of a gun being thrust into the face of an Austrian soldier; a "ritirata strategica" (strategic retreat) showed an Austrian's head being shoved into a toilet bowl (*ritirata* means both "retreat" and "latrine"); and a surprise attack consisted of an Italian soldier creeping up on an Austrian officer who was sitting atop a piano and drinking wine.[138] Alongside contributions such as these were essay competitions, clearly aimed at educated officers, with titles such as "Why did America enter the war?" and "What is courage?"[139]

The version of Futurism displayed in the pages of *Il Montello* was more ambiguous and surreptitiously conveyed than was the case in other periodicals such as *L'Italia Futurista*. In spite of the Futurist editorial team and content, nowhere in any issue of *Il Montello* is the newspaper explicitly aligned with Futurism.[140] Mario Isnenghi has argued that in *Il Montello* "il timbro specifico del futurismo" (Futurism's specific stamp)[141] was lost and that Futurism was "del tutto marginale, o emarginato" (completely marginal or marginalized).[142] His assertion is correct up to a point. Isnenghi argued that Futurism was absent from *Il Montello* because its ideology conflicted with the general thrust of the propaganda mission of the trench newspapers. He continued that "l'immaginario futurista è eminentemente polemico, fondato sul tropo dell'antitesi" (the Futurist imaginary is eminently polemical, founded on antithesis) and that as a result it was "male utilizzabile, perché sfasato, rispetto all'immaginario dei fogli di trincea" (not very usable, because it was out of sync, with respect to the imaginary of the trench newspapers).[143] They were designed to pedal a protective and reassuring message to the troops, thus the destructive, aggressive world of Futurism was not suitable for the populist stance of the trench newspapers.[144] However, as was argued in the previous chapter, from 1917 onwards the Futurist movement had been gradually shedding its most provocative and avant-garde elements and had been approaching a more mainstream position. Similarly, the version of Futurism conveyed in the trench newspaper was more ambiguous in character and was toned down in certain respects in order to appeal to a more mainstream audience. *Il Montello* shows evidence of a concerted attempt by leading Futurists to produce a more palatable version of Futurism, which would be less antagonistic and more acceptable to the ordinary soldier.

References to Futurism are evident in *Il Montello*, but the editors camouflaged its presence. In the first issue a full-colour image entitled "Sintesi della guerra mondiale" appears. It is a reworking of the black-and-white image "Sintesi futurista della guerra" that had been produced by Carrà during the early days of the interventionist crisis and signed by Marinetti, Boccioni, Carrà, Russolo, and Piatti. In the version

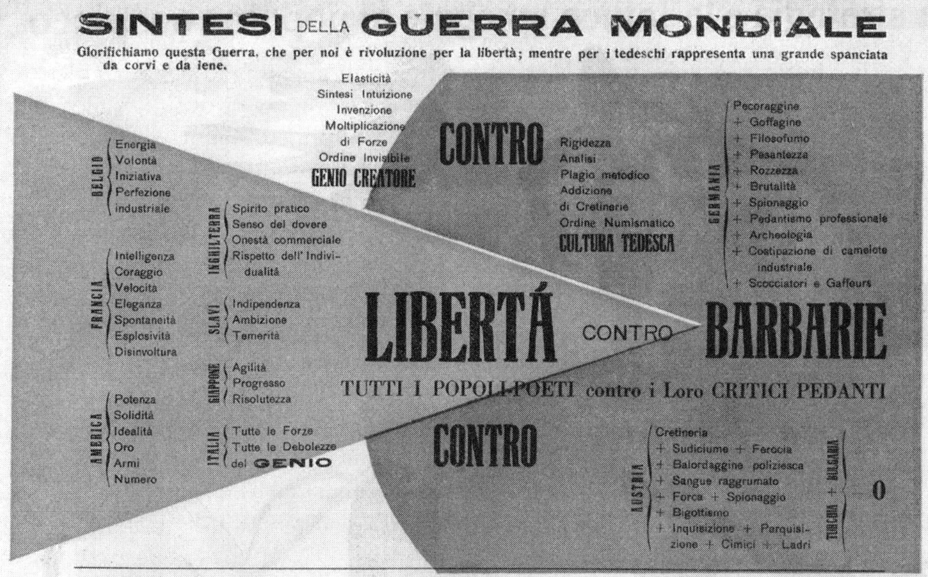

Figure 4.3. "Sintesi della guerra mondiale" (Synthesis of the world war), *Il Montello*, 20 September 1918, 2. Courtesy of Biblioteca Storica Moderna e Contemporanea, Rome.

in *Il Montello* all references to Futurism have been removed, and the central struggle of the original 1914 version between "Futurismo" and "Passatismo" has been recast as a conflict between "Libertà" and "Barbarie." In 1914 the Futurists had declared war to be "la sola igiene del mondo" (the sole hygiene of the world), and in 1918 it was cast as "rivoluzione per la libertà" (revolution for freedom). On the same page was a short story called "Trincee di pane!" (Trenches of bread!), which featured a soldier's invalid father, a war widow, an unemployed refugee, an orphan, a veteran who had lost his legs, and another who had been poisoned by gas.[145] The story was published anonymously, but in fact it had been written by Marinetti and published in *L'Italia Futurista* in August 1916.[146]

The reasons behind the erasure of Futurism from *Il Montello* are two-fold. First, all soldier newspapers were subject to military censorship, and all contributors had to write anonymously. Once the war was over,

Jamar 14 was able to tell Folgore that "Il Montello ora uscirà non anonimo" (Il Montello will now not be issued anonymously).[147] As Isnenghi has indicated, there was also perhaps trepidation among the Servizio P. hierarchy regarding the Futurists. Writing to Folgore about the failed attempt to have him join the editorial staff, Sironi commented: "[Non] so il perché del fallito risultato […] Forse un secondo futurista nella famiglia li terrorizza?!" (I don't know why it didn't work out […] Maybe the idea of a second Futurist in the family horrifies them?!)[148]

The second motivation was one of perception, in what has been defined as the "authenticity effect" in relation to the trench newspaper *La Ghirba*, edited by Ardengo Soffici.[149] In the first issue of *Il Montello* Bontempelli wrote about the mission and aims of the journal:

> Questo primo numero non rivela che una parte infinitesimale della potenzialità artistica e giornalistica del … Fanteria [*sic*], la quale non tarderà ad avere affermazioni così spettacolose che ogni giorno il direttore nostro si troverà sul tavolo un monte anzi un *Montello* di manoscritti, disegni, ecc.

> This first issue only reveals a tiny part of the artistic and journalistic potential … of the Infantry, which will not have to wait long for spectacular affirmation, because the editor finds every day on his desk a mountain, no a *Montello*, of manuscripts, drawings, etc.[150]

Given that Bontempelli's intention was to showcase the artistic and literary talents of the ordinary soldier, it would certainly have been counterproductive to make it clear that the first issue was populated by contributions from prominent figures of one of Italy's best-known cultural movements.

Aside from these surreptitious references to Futurist ideas, the content of *Il Montello* adhered to patterns of other periodicals produced by the Servizio P.. In relation to attitudes towards women and peace, *Il Montello* provided a direct contrast to the positions of *Roma Futurista*, as befitting the different audience for each publication. Women in *Il Montello* were not portrayed as whining obstacles to victory or as erotic objects to be conquered; rather their depiction was in line with that of other trench newspapers; she was a "presenza assidua, di tutela e ricatto emotivo, alle spalle di ogni militare" (constant presence, of protection and emotional blackmail, behind every soldier).[151] The editors of *Il Montello* continuously praised the mothers, sisters, wives, and daughters of the war, who had sacrificed their loved ones for the sake

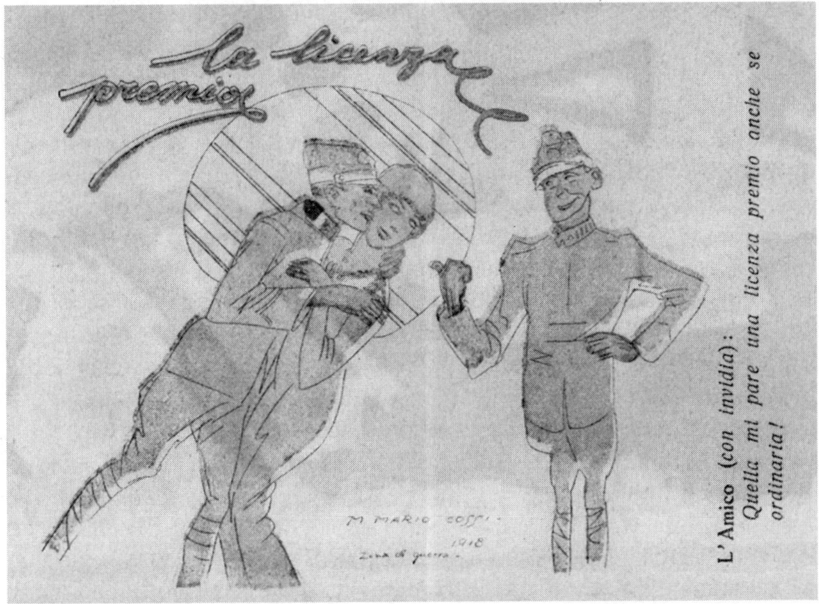

Figure 4.4. Mario Cossi, "La licenza premio" (Bonus leave), *Il Montello*, 20 September 1918, 6. Courtesy of Biblioteca Storica Moderna e Contemporanea, Rome.

of Italy's glory and victory.[152] The only drawings featuring women were lightly humorous and romantic.

One text featured a soldier character who objected to being told by his commanding officers that he must fight and win for "Costanza" and "Letizia" (Tenacity and Joy, also women's names), because he was in love with Nina and not those others. He wished to win "con chi e per chi mi pare" (with whom and for whom I choose) and refused to fight on behalf of unknown women – "What if they're ugly?" he asked.[153] The portrayal of women in *Roma Futurista* was far less sentimental, verging between blaming "donne piagnucolose" (whining women), among others, for the defeat at Caporetto[154] and stating the editors' belief in equal rights for women, although their praise for the female sex was far from effusive: "Se ella ha minori qualità dell'uomo nel senso della politica e del progresso collettivo, deve *solo* per questa sua deficienza rimanere in un posto secondario, non per leggi restrittive imposte dalla nostra prepotenza maschile." (If she has fewer qualities than men do in terms of politics and collective progress, this deficiency is the *only* reason for which she must remain in a secondary position, not because of restrictive laws imposed by our masculine arrogance.)[155]

The final issue of *Il Montello*, published after the Italian victory at Vittorio Veneto, praised the soldiers for a war that had been won "pienamente, gloriosamente, gioiosamente" (fully, gloriously, joyously) and reassured their readers that they would soon be returning to the familiarity of their families and their farms.[156] *Roma Futurista* of 10 November 1918 hailed victory but sought to appeal to the violent instincts of the Arditi soldiers, by stating that this was only the beginning of the realization of the Futurist dream.[157] It would be necessary to be alert to the internal threats of traitors, and combatants' organizations would work to protect and develop all that had been acquired during the war.[158]

The End of the War

When the armistice between Italy and Austria-Hungary was signed on 4 November 1918, Carli and Settimelli, accompanied by other soldiers, paraded through the streets of Rome, triumphantly waving an Italian tricolour. More and more soldiers joined in the parade, which Carli led to the "Altar of the Nation" complex at the Campidoglio in the city centre, before retiring to a café where he spoke briefly "con violenza futurista" (with Futurist violence).[159] In keeping with the belligerent tone of *Roma Futurista*, he declared:

> Abbiamo stritolato l'Austria, il suo esercito è in pezzi. Trieste, Trento, Fiume, le isole Dalmatiche sono in nostra mano:
> MA NON BASTA!
> Bisogna invadere la Baviera! Gridate con me: guerra alla Germania!
> OGGI PIÙ CHE MAI!

> (We have smashed Austria, her army is in pieces. Trieste, Trent, Fiume, the Dalmatian islands are in our hands:
> BUT THAT IS NOT ENOUGH!
> We must invade Bavaria! Shout with me: War on Germany!
> TODAY MORE THAN EVER!)[160]

While Carli and Settimelli marched through the streets of Rome, Marinetti was still at the front. He had been actively involved in the decisive battle of Vittorio Veneto that took place in late October and early November, and sent joyful missives about the Italian victory to his Futurist friends and a number of newspapers.[161]

The Futurist movement in November 1918 was radically different from that which had existed at the start of the European conflict in August 1914. Futurism now stood as a nascent political party – a move intimated by Marinetti since 1913 but never launched. In contrast to the paralysis that had struck Marinetti in August and early September 1914, the Futurists ended the war with a clear mission and a new supporter base. During the interventionist months Marinetti had been adamant that Futurism remained first and foremost an artistic movement, and throughout the war years he grappled with the uneasy balance of artistic, political, and military demands within one integrated movement. By the end of the war Marinetti was facing a different challenge, that of managing and promoting two separate and often competing branches of the same movement – one political and one artistic.

Epilogue

On 22 March 1919, at the Galleria Centrale d'Arte at the Palazzo Cova in the centre of Milan, Marinetti opened the *Grande Esposizione Nazionale Futurista*, the first collective Futurist exhibition to be held in Italy since the outbreak of war. The following day, close by at Piazza San Sepolcro, a stone's throw from the Piazza del Duomo, Marinetti was present at the establishment of Benito Mussolini's Fasci di Combattimento. These two events encapsulate the state of Futurism in the immediate post-war period, when Marinetti was dividing himself between the needs of artistic Futurism on the one hand and political Futurism on the other. On 1 February 1919 he had written to Cangiullo that "l'immenso lavoro impostomi dai Fasci Politici Futuristi non mi vieta di riprendere il lavoro artistico" (the immense amount of work imposed on me by the Futurist Political branches does not prevent me from restarting artistic work).[1] Since the war's end in November 1918 Marinetti had been attempting to keep these two strands of Futurism operating in parallel to each other, which proved to be a demanding task.

As he sought to manage these distinct sides of his movement, Marinetti (with Settimelli and Carli) published in *Roma Futurista* an important document that set out the vision for post-war Futurism. "Che cos'è il futurismo? Nozioni elementari" (What is futurism? Basic ideas) appeared for the first time on 16 February 1919 and was republished consistently in *Roma Futurista*.[2] Three different modes of Futurist identification were offered: one who was "futurista nella vita" (Futurist in life); one who was "futurista nella politica" (Futurist in politics); and one who was "futurista nell'arte" (Futurist in art).[3] This document is a stronger and clearer restatement of the conclusion of the "Manifesto del Partito Politico Futurista," which had allowed for somebody to be a believer in political Futurism but to have no inclination towards the movement's artistic branch. The conclusion of "Che cos'è il futurismo?" declared unequivocally for the first time that "il movimento futurista artistico è separato dal movimento futurista politico" (the Futurist artistic movement is separate from the Futurist political movement).[4] During the war Marinetti had hoped that Futurism could thrive as one unitary movement spanning both art and politics, but he ultimately found himself incapable of achieving this aim.

Although the "Manifesto del Partito Politico Futurista" had been published in February 1918, and *Roma Futurista*, the party newspaper, had been launched in September of that year, the Futurist Political Party only came into being after the end of the war. On 30 November 1918 the first branch of the party was formed in Florence and was followed by branches (*fasci*) in other Italian cities, including Milan, Naples, and Bologna. The research of Günter Berghaus has demonstrated that the actual number of adherents to the party was very low at this stage.[5] Nonetheless, Futurist links with the Arditi continued to thrive, and many of them joined the party. On 1 January 1919 Mario Carli established the Associazione fra gli Arditi d'Italia in Rome, and later that month its Milanese branch was formed at Marinetti's house.[6] Contemporaneously, the relationship between Marinetti and Mussolini strengthened as Mussolini also wished to attract some of the Arditi to his soon-to-be-established Fasci di Combattimento. When the latter was finally launched on 23 March 1919, there was a strong Futurist presence. Marinetti, Corra, and Carli were all in attendance, and Marinetti was elected to the Central Committee. Marinetti and Mussolini each felt that his group had something to gain from the alliance, but nonetheless a "mutual distrust and antipathy" persisted between the two men.[7]

While this alliance was being forged, Marinetti was also furiously attempting to relaunch Futurism as a vital force in the artistic world after the war. It was originally planned that the *Grande Esposizione Nazionale Futurista* would travel to four locations in Italy – Milan, Genoa, Florence, and Venice[8] – but the iterations of the exhibition in the final two locations never took place.[9] It opened in the Galleria Centrale d'Arte in Milan on 22 March 1919 and remained there until 9 May, before transferring to Genoa where it opened on 24 May and remained for two months.[10]

In the exhibition catalogue Marinetti wrote that "il movimento futurista artistico, che subì durante la guerra un rallentamento forzato, riprende oggi il suo dinamismo eccitatore e rinnovatore" (the Futurist artistic movement, which experienced an enforced slowdown during the war, today reclaims its electrifying and renewing dynamism).[11] The exhibition was a reflection of the pronouncements made by Marinetti in 1917 about an appropriate art for a post-war society. In a 1917 article in *L'Italia Futurista* Marinetti was critical of passéist critics who were preparing for official commemorations and historical investigations of the war. He believed:

> L'arte dopo la guerra sarà in gran parte diretta a un *superamento* dell'atmosfera dolorosa di oggi, verso una sempre maggiore allegria, vivacità, originalità e spensieratezza. L'arte del dopoguerra sarà fatta di libertà, di audacia, di entusiasmo giovanile, di velocità, di varietà di colore e di impreveduto [...] Come è necessario ora fare con energia la guerra, senza rievocare nostalgicamente la pace passata e senza piagnucolare, con forza, tenacia e ottimismo fino alla vittoria completa, così si dovrà poi, nei relativi riposi pacifici dell'umanità, lavorare e vivere intensamente aerandosi i cervelli con sempre nuove e inattese forme d'arte ultraallegre, ultrasorprendenti e ultraspensierate, senza rievocare gli orrori della guerra, e senza rievocare sotto un bombardamento di discorsi e di statue balorde i numerosissimi autentici eroi della nostra guerra.

> Art after the war will in large part be directed at *overcoming* the painful atmosphere of today, towards an ever-greater happiness, vivacity, originality and light-heartedness. Post-war art will be made up of freedom, audacity, youthful enthusiasm, speed, colourful variety and the unexpected [...] Just as now it is necessary to energetically engage in war, without nostalgically remembering past peace and without whining, with strength, tenacity and optimism towards complete victory, in the same way afterwards, in the peaceful breaks for humanity, we will have to intensely work and live airing out our brains with always new and unexpected forms of ultra-happy, ultra-surprising, and ultra-carefree art, without remembering the horrors of war, without recalling, under a bombardment of speeches and stupid statues, the innumerable authentic heroes of our war.[12]

In the introduction to the 1919 exhibition catalogue Marinetti provided an account of Futurism's activities during the war years, making reference to the many dead and injured Futurists but without dwelling on these aspects. The version of Futurism presented in the exhibition was both one that was intimately connected to the war that had just ended and one that wished to signal an independence from war-time Futurism.

As Giovanni Lista has commented, the exhibition marked a "svolta fondamentale del futurismo" (a fundamental turning point for Futurism).[13] This is true both of the Futurists who were included in the show and of the works that they exhibited. Works by thirty-five Futurists were exhibited, and a further nineteen were represented in the catalogue. Giacomo Balla and Luigi Russolo were the only "original" Futurist painters to be included. Others such as Francesco Cangiullo, Fortunato Depero, and Mario Sironi had joined after 1912 and were active prior to the outbreak of the war in 1914. The majority of the exhibitors, however, had become affiliated with Futurism only from 1915.

Even before the war Marinetti's willingness to open the ranks to new members had angered some of the movement's original protagonists, particularly Carlo Carrà and Gino Severini, but also Umberto Boccioni.[14] Marinetti, however, did not take their concerns seriously, either during the war or after it. His objective in the *Grande Esposizione Nazionale Futurista* was to present his movement as a dynamic and lively force in Italy's cultural life. As Fabio Benzi has pointed out, "più artisti esso coinvolge, tanto più il verbo futurista risulterà vittorioso e condiviso, assorbito da ogni strato della società" (the more artists it involves, the more the word Futurism will emerge victorious and shared, absorbed by every stratum of society).[15] War themes were prominent in the works on display, and one of the free-word artists represented was General Capello who had first incorporated Marinetti into the propaganda service. In the catalogue Marinetti declared that Italian Futurism was "l'anima della nuova generazione che ha combattuto contro l'impero austroungarico e l'ha vittoriosamente annientato" (the soul of the generation that fought against the Austro-Hungarian Empire and victoriously annihilated it),[16] and in an article for *Il Popolo d'Italia* he highlighted the fact that almost all of the painters had carried out "eroicamente il loro dovere sui campi di battaglia" (heroically their duty on the battlefield).[17] However, absent from the roll call of the exhibition was any Futurist who had lost his life in the conflict, including Boccioni and Sant'Elia. The message was clear: Futurism and its members had survived the war intact. It would appear that Marinetti's strategy was successful. A number of articles on the exhibition presented Futurism as a movement that had been revitalized rather than decimated by the war. According to the critic D.B. for *Perseveranza*, the exhibition constituted "un voler contarsi, a guerra finita, fra i pittori avanguardisti" (a need for reckoning, at the war's end, of avant-garde painters). Although the war had killed some of them, he commented, "ne ha generati molti di nuovi" (it has generated many new ones).[18] Similarly, an article in *La Sera* began with this triumphant statement: "La guerra è finita: i futuristi ritornano." (The war is over: the Futurists return.)[19]

By all accounts the exhibition was well attended. One Milanese critic remarked on the "enorme successo di curiosità destata dal semplice annuncio della mostra [...] coll'affluenza di una vera folla" (the enormous curiosity aroused by the simple announcement of the exhibition [...] with the influx of a real crowd),[20] and an advertisement in the Futurist magazine *Dinamo* claimed that the exhibition in Milan welcomed 2,000 visitors every day, of which 1,990 were "simpatizzanti intelligenti" (intelligent sympathizers) while ten were "critici, professori, pittori passatisti, velenosamente esasperati" (critics, professors, passéist painters, poisonously exasperated).[21] Marinetti considered the exhibition to be a triumph: "Folla enorme, entusiasmo [...] Tutta la stampa ha marciato. Molti giornali favorevoli." (Huge crowd, enthusiasm [...] The whole press is on board. Many newspapers in favour.)[22] Press reactions were indeed on the whole very positive, based on three major factors: the Futurists' status as war veterans; their improved attitude towards the public; and the optimistic outlook of the exhibition.

Reports responded positively to the Futurists' status as ex-combatants. An article from *Il Caffaro* of 25 May 1919 summed up the prevailing response to the Futurist exhibitions. Marinetti told the journalist that some Futurist painters had not been able to participate in the exhibition because they were still on active duty with the army, leading the reporter to acknowledge that "i futuristi hanno manifestato in ogni campo la loro attività battagliera" (the Futurists have demonstrated their fighting activity in every field) and to ask, "Come negare tutta la simpatia a questi combattenti di ieri?" (How can we deny our deepest affection towards yesterday's combatants?).[23] Marinetti made sure that the Futurists' military involvement was prominently featured at the exhibitions. At the inauguration of the Milanese show, Mario Carli, by now a captain with the Arditi, gave a speech about the elite division, which was warmly applauded.[24] His status as a volunteer and the injuries he had sustained were both highlighted in a short article. Although his judgment of the exhibition's content was negative, the journalist from the *Rivista di Milano* could not criticize the Futurists' combat record; he acknowledged that Futurism "non ha fatto che la guerra in questi ultimi anni e l'ha fatta da valoroso" (has engaged in nothing but war in the last few years and it has done so bravely).[25]

Not only did the exhibition mark a clear break with the protagonists of pre-war Futurism, but it also broke with earlier conceptions of Futurist art. Paintings gave way to free-word tables, which were heavily represented in the exhibition, following the trend that Marinetti had begun during the war years. The exhibition was divided into four sections (paintings, drawings, plastic complexes, and Futurist plastic theatre; free-word tables; surprise alphabet; and architecture), and four trends in Futurist art were identified by Marinetti: pure painting; plastic dynamism; dynamic Futurist decorativism; and coloured states of mind, without plastic concerns.[26] The fact that Boccioni's beloved plastic dynamism constituted only one of the four trends (and listed only second, at that) is further evidence of Marinetti's desire to shift the focus from Futurism's pre-war incarnation.

Newspaper reports frequently remarked on a new-found accessibility in the Futurist artworks, on the curiosity and interest of the members of the public, and, in turn, on the Futurists' improved attitude towards their audience. The hostility towards the Futurists that had been evident in the pre-war years was almost entirely absent in the reactions to the 1919 exhibition, a fact that drew comment in a number of reports. One journalist reminded readers that before the war people followed Marinetti's movement "con un sorrisetto sulle labbra" (with a little smile on their lips),[27] while another recalled the situation of just a few years previously when the Futurists received nothing but "balorde curiosità o stupido dileggio" (foolish curiosity and stupid mockery) from the public.[28] Now, by contrast, people flocked to the exhibition "in una predisposizione dello spirito di benevola, ansiosa e caparbia determinazione di comprendere, disposizione ben diversa da quella di un tempo non lontano!" (benevolently predisposed, with an anxious and stubborn determination to understand, a very different disposition to the way it was not long ago!).[29] The public was by all accounts eager to engage with the movement. The student newspaper, *La Fiamma Verde*, confidently asserted that "il visitatore resta piacevolmente meravigliato di trovarvi, in luogo delle astruse pazzie che aveva temuto, delle opere quasi tutte facilmente comprensibili" (the visitor will be pleasantly amazed to encounter, instead of the abstruse madness he had feared, works that are almost all easily understood),[30] and the *Rivista di Milano* critic agreed but was less enthusiastic of the outcome, writing, "I mezzi di espressione forse nell'intenzione di farsi semplici, sono diventati poveri" (The expressive measures, maybe in the attempt to simplify, have been impoverished).[31] The critics were not incorrect in identifying an attempt by the Futurists to be less opaque in their artwork. As we have seen, already in November 1914, Marinetti had advised Severini to extend the reach of Futurist art by producing less abstract and more realistic paintings.

Nevertheless, the critic from the Genoese newspaper *Il Caffaro* claimed that the visitor would be unable to understand anything of the works on view but that this did not matter. He informed his readers that "per intendere un quadro non si vuole che rappresenti qualche cosa: [...] di pittura che tali cose rappresentano ce n'è tanti che non si può dar torto a questi bravi artisti futuristi che hanno finalmente il coraggio di presentarsi in diverso modo" (to understand a painting it does not have to represent something: [...] there are so many paintings that represent something, that we cannot criticize these great Futurist artists for having finally had the courage to present themselves differently).[32]

Marinetti was also praised for his availability to visitors and for his willingness to explain the artworks on display, which was a markedly different approach from that which had characterized the riotous Futurist *serate* of 1910 and 1911. Marinetti was "di una cortesia inalterabile" (unassailably polite)[33] at the inauguration of the Genoa exhibition, moving from one room to the next, rendering the atmosphere "più movimentata" (more energized).[34]

In fact, references to the positive and dynamic atmosphere of the exhibition were common in newspaper reports. The critics responded well to the works on display, judging them to be an appropriate response to the three years of war that Italy had just endured. Comprehensibility of the artworks was regarded as less important than the viewer's emotional response to them. Upon entry into the gallery, "siete subito attorniati da una vera ridda di colori. Vi trovate in un vortice nel quale rappresentate centro" (you are immediately surrounded by a real jumble of colours. You find yourself in a vortex of which you are the centre).[35] The exhibition delivered "una sensazione di piacere. Sarà forse un piacere che non dà riposo, un godimento un po' eccitante, ma alla fine sempre una sensazione" (a sense of pleasure. It might be a pleasure that is not relaxing, an excited enjoyment, but at the end it is always a sensation).[36] The works displayed "una gioia di colori e di forme, una gaiezza decorativa, che avvolgano in una atmosfera di ottimismo il visitatore" (a joy of colour and form, a decorative gaiety, that envelop the visitor in an atmosphere of optimism).[37] There was a sense among the critics that the Futurist movement, as represented by the exhibition, had tapped into the public mood in spring 1919 as Italy emerged from a state of war. According to one, Futurism "ci porta in un mondo nuovo" (brings us to a new world), and another declared that "il futurismo è l'arte sola e vera che saprà imporsi domani" (Futurism is the only true art that can impose itself on tomorrow).[38]

The experience of the *Grande Esposizione Nazionale Futurista* demonstrated to Marinetti that he had been incorrect in February 1918 to declare that Futurism as an avant-garde would be "spesso osteggiata" (often opposed) by the Italian public. Perhaps in response to this unexpected positivity towards artistic Futurism, Marinetti's desire to keep both aspects (art and politics) of the movement alive and running simultaneously was already waning by the summer of 1919. After the exhibition had closed in Genoa, he wrote to Gerardo Dottori that "con la più energica decisione ed elasticità futurista, noi riprendiamo il movimento artistico, senza lasciarci sopraffare dall'attuale caoticissimo momento politico" (with the most energetic and elastic Futurist conviction, we will resume the artistic movement, without letting ourselves be overwhelmed by the chaos of this political moment).[39] In October 1919 Giuseppe Bottai[40] complained that Marinetti was not committed to the work of the political party. He wrote to Carli that in Rome "molto c'è da lavorare. Marinetti però se ne infischia" (there is a lot of work to do. Marinetti doesn't care though).[41]

Despite this ambivalence regarding Futurism's political destiny, Marinetti was one of three Futurists who stood for election as a Fascist candidate in the November 1919 elections. Mussolini's party performed disastrously, achieving only 4,657 votes, equivalent to 1.72 per cent of the total vote in Milan.[42] The election results marked a decisive turning point for Futurist political engagement. Balla complained that "quelle rompiscatole elezioni ànno guastato molti interessi e anche il nostro à subito alterazioni" (those pesky elections have ruined many interests, and also ours has undergone alterations).[43] Within two months Futurism had withdrawn from the political arena, and the Futurist Political Party was no more. On 22 December Marinetti wrote in his notebook that he had discussed the transformation of *Roma Futurista* with the editors Balla, Bottai, Gino Galli,[44] and Enrico Rocca.[45] He wished it to be "artistica parolibera plastica musicale rumorista e politica" (artistic, free-word, plastic, musical, noise-making and political). He specifically wanted to abolish articles and reviews, in favour of "un giornale a sorpresa, carico di novità e di creazioni" (a surprise newspaper, full of novelty and creation).[46] The first issue of the new *Roma Futurista* appeared on 4 January 1920, carrying a new subtitle. No longer was it the newspaper of the Futurist Political Party but rather the "settimanale del Movimento Futurista" (weekly paper of the Futurist Movement). In an article entitled "Programma a sorpresa pel 1920" (Surprise program for 1920) the editors of the journal described the new vision for the movement, following the ideas that Marinetti had prescribed. They wrote that Futurist artists had returned to their "fervido lavoro creativo" (fervent creative work), mentioning Russolo's work on new noise-tuner machines and his upcoming concert in Paris, a synthetic-theatre tour of Europe, and the successful exhibitions in Milan and Genoa. These activities brought about a "conseguente necessità di trasformare *Roma Futurista*" (consequent necessity to transform *Roma Futurista*),[47] which was suggested as if this move were entirely divorced from Marinetti's recent political failure. From now on, *Roma Futurista* "non sarà più un organo esclusivamente politico ma bensì: plastico, letterario, parolibero, musicale, rumorista, sportivo, cinematografico e politico" (will not be an exclusively political organ any more but rather: plastic, literary, free-word, music, noisy, sporty, cinematic and political). The journal would no longer publish "il monotono e abbrutente rubinetto di articoli politici" (the monotonous and demeaning flow of political articles), although it would remain "l'organo dell'Ardito e del Fascismo" (the mouthpiece of the Ardito and of Fascism). In practice, however, the journal ceased to engage with political issues and devoted itself entirely to artistic matters. Bottai and Rocca had wanted to retain at least the front page for political content, but they met with "opposizione feroce, assoluta, testarda" (fierce, absolute, stubborn opposition) from Marinetti.[48] When Bottai attempted to publish a political article, Marinetti arrived in Rome and ranted for two hours, declaring, "Niente politica! politica niente! politica un c…" (No politics! no politics! f*** politics).[49]

Since the movement's inception Marinetti had desired a fusion of art and politics under the umbrella of Futurism, a stance that only intensified during the years of the First World War. He initially believed that he could achieve this by tethering all Futurist artistic production to the war effort, but he realized in 1918 that such a fusion was both impractical and impossible, leading him to split the movement into two separate strands. He toyed with this separation between 1918 and 1919 but quickly understood that Futurism could only effectively function in one realm or the other. By 1920 it was clear that Marinetti had opted for art. The year 1920 marked his official and definitive retreat from parliamentary politics, and this turn away from political Futurism defined the course of "secondo futurismo" in the 1920s and 1930s. In the 1920s Marinetti emphasized that the Futurists were "più che mai devoti alle idee ed all'arte, lontani dal politicantismo" (more devoted than ever to ideas and to art, far removed from politicking)[50] and that "il Futurismo è un movimento artistico e ideologico. Interviene nelle lotte politiche soltanto nelle ore di grave pericolo per la Nazione" (Futurism is an ideological and artistic movement [that] intervenes in political struggles only in moments of grave danger for the Nation).[51] This retreat into art at the beginning of the 1920s was a viable possibility for the movement only because of the profound change it had experienced during the war years. On the one hand, the strategy of futurismo moderato had allowed the Futurists to move closer to mainstream tastes. On the other, their status as volunteers, combatants, and veterans, assiduously cultivated during the war, had earned them acceptance among the Italian people. Marinetti and the Futurists would subsequently harness this new-found public respect and exploit it for the following twenty-five years.

Abbreviations

ADF *Archivi del futurismo*. Edited by Maria Drudi Gambillo and Teresa Fiori. Vol. 2. Rome: De Luca, 1962.

APICE Archivi della Parola, dell'Immagine e della Comunicazione Editoriale, Università degli Studi, Milan.

BRB Beinecke Rare Book and Manuscript Library, Yale University, Connecticut.

BSF Giacomo Balla. *Scritti futuristi*. Edited by Giovanni Lista. Milan: Abscondita, 2010.

CC-AS Carlo Carrà and Ardengo Soffici. *Lettere 1913–1929*. Edited by Massimo Carrà and Vittorio Fagone. Milan: Feltrinelli, 1983.

CC-GP Carlo Carrà and Giovanni Papini. *Il carteggio Carrà–Papini: Da "Lacerba" al tempo di "Valori Plastici."* Edited by Massimo Carrà. Milan: Skira, 2001.

CG-FTM Corrado Govoni. *Lettere a F.T. Marinetti*. Edited by Matilde Dillon Wanke. Milan: Scheiwiller, 1990.

CP Francesco Balilla Pratella. *Caro Pratella: Lettere scelte e commentate*. Edited by Gianfranco Maffina. Ravenna: Edizioni del Girasole, 1980.

FBP *Lettere ruggenti a Francesco Balilla Pratella*. Edited by Giovanni Lugaresi. Milan: Quaderno dell'Osservatore, 1969.

FMST Fondazione Museo Storico del Trentino, Trento.

FPC Fondazione Primo Conti, Fiesole.

FTM-AP Filippo Tommaso Marinetti and Aldo Palazzeschi. *Carteggio con un'appendice di altre lettere a Palazzeschi*. Edited by Paolo Prestigiacomo. Milan: Mondadori, 1978.

FTM and BCM   Papers of F.T. Marinetti and Benedetta Cappa
Marinetti, Getty Research Institute, Los Angeles.

FTM-FC   Filippo Tommaso Marinetti and Francesco Cangiullo.
Lettere (1910–1943). Edited by Ernestina Pellegrini.
Florence: Vallecchi, 1989.

FTMT   Filippo Tommaso Marinetti. *Taccuini 1915–1921.*
Edited by Alberto Bertoni. Bologna: Il Mulino, 1987.

GRI   Getty Research Institute, Los Angeles.

LF   Claudia Salaris. *Luciano Folgore e le avanguardie: Con
lettere e inediti futuristi.* Scandicci, Italy: La Nuova
Italia, 1997.

LF-FTM   Luciano Folgore and Filippo Tommaso Marinetti.
Carteggio futurista. Edited by Francesco Muzzioli.
Rome: Officina Edizioni, 1987.

MART   Museo d'arte moderna e contemporanea di Trento e
Rovereto, Rovereto.

MC-FTM   Mario Carli and Filippo Tommaso Marinetti. *Lettere
futuriste tra arte e politica.* Edited by Claudia Salaris.
Rome: Officina Edizioni, 1989.

MSIG   Museo Storico Italiano della Guerra, Rovereto.

PPF   *Prefuturismo e primo futurismo in Sicilia (1900–1918).*
Edited by Giuseppe Miligi and Umberto Carpi.
Messina: Sicania, 1989.

TIF   Filippo Tommaso Marinetti. *Teoria e invenzione
futurista*, 6th ed. Edited by Luciano De Maria. Milan:
Mondadori, 2005.

UBLF   Umberto Boccioni. *Lettere futuriste.* Edited by
Federica Rovati. Rovereto: Egon / MART, 2009.

VdelF   *Le vestali del futurismo.* Edited by Virginio Giacomo
Bono. Voghera, Italy: Edo Edizioni Oltrepò, 1991.

Notes

Introduction

1 Paraphrased from Filippo Tommaso Marinetti, *Le monoplan du pape: Roman politique en vers libres* (Paris: E. Sansot, 1912).

2 Marinetti was born in Alexandria in Egypt and was fluent in both French and Italian. He wrote exclusively in French until 1912 and had his secretary, Decio Cinti, translate his works into Italian. On Marinetti's linguistic background see Maria Pia De Paulis-Dalembert, "F.T. Marinetti: La réecriture de l'imaginaire symboliste et futuriste entre le francais et l'italien," *Chroniques italiennes* 12 (2007): 1–30; and Brunella Eruli, *Dal futurismo alla patafisica: Percorsi dell'avanguardia* (Ospedaletto, Italy: Pacini, 1994), 14.

3 Marinetti, "Fondazione e Manifesto del Futurismo (1909)," in *Teoria e invenzione futurista*, 6th ed., ed. Luciano De Maria (1968; Milan: Mondadori, 2005), 7–14, here 11 (hereafter cited as *TIF*). Unless indicated otherwise, all translations are by the author.

4 Marinetti, "La guerra elettrica (1911)," in *TIF*, 319–25, here 324.

5 The following year he collected the articles that he had written for the Paris-based newspaper *L'Intrasigéante* in a small book called *Le bataille de Tripoli (26 octobre 1911) vécue et chantée* (Milan: Edizioni futuriste di "Poesia," 1912).

6 It has long been reported by scholars that Marinetti was an eyewitness to the Battle of Adrianople. See for example Giovanni Lista, *Les futuristes* (Paris: H. Veyrier, 1988), 29. However, recent research by Günter Berghaus and Ton van Kalmthout indicates that this was not the case. When reciting his free-word poem "Bombardamento di Adrianopoli" around Europe in 1913, Marinetti informed his audiences that he had observed the battle first-hand, but at a performance in Delft in the Netherlands an army

captain, who had travelled with Marinetti to the battle zone, privately contradicted Marinetti's statement, saying, "Neither he nor I was ever admitted to the front by the Bulgarians." See "Wereldgeschiedenis," *De Hollande Revue*, 1 October 1919, 573–4, in Ton van Kalmthout, "Futurism in the Netherlands, 1909–1940," *International Yearbook of Futurism Studies* (2014): 165–201, here 182. On this same point, see also Günter Berghaus, review of *Dramaturgy of Sound in the Avant-Garde and Postdramatic Theatre*, by Mladen Ovadija, *International Yearbook of Futurism Studies* (2015): 541–9.

7   See Marinetti, "Manifesto tecnico della letteratura futurista (1912)," in *TIF*, 46–54; Jeffrey T. Schnapp, "On *Zang Tumb Tuuum*," in *Italian Futurism 1909–1944: Reconstructing the Universe*, ed. Vivien Greene, exhibition catalogue, New York, 21 February – 1 September 2014 (New York: Guggenheim Museum, 2014), 156–8.

8   See Marinetti, "Movimento politico futurista (1915)," in *TIF*, 337–41. Marinetti republished the political manifestos of 1909, 1911, and 1913 in the 1915 volume *Guerra sola igiene del mondo*, included in *TIF*, 235–41.

9   Italy entered the war against Austria-Hungary only and did not declare war on Germany until 28 August 1916.

10   Carlo Dalmazzo Carrà (1881–1966), Futurist painter and free-word artist. He met Marinetti in February 1910 and signed a number of early manifestos, including the "Manifesto dei pittori futuristi" and "Contro Venezia passatista" (both 1910), and published the interventionist volume *Guerrapittura* in 1915. He served first as a private soldier and later as an officer in the infantry. He suffered a nervous breakdown during the war and spent time in a military psychiatric hospital outside Ferrara. Early in 1917, after meeting with Giorgio De Chirico, he moved away from Futurism and towards a metaphysical style of painting.

11   Gino Severini (1883–1966), Futurist painter. A key figure in early Futurist painting, he was a signatory of the "Manifesto dei pittori futuristi" (1910) and featured heavily at pre-war Futurist exhibitions. He spent the war years in Paris, where he completed a number of Futurist war-inspired paintings during 1915, which he exhibited the following year. Before the war was over, however, he had distanced himself from Marinetti's movement.

12   Umberto Boccioni (1882–1916), Futurist painter. The movement's most famous painter, Boccioni volunteered for the war in May 1915 and served in the Lombard Battalion of Volunteer Cyclists and Motorists, Eighth Platoon. He saw action during the capture of Dosso Casina near Malcesine in October 1915. The battalion was disbanded in December 1915, and Boccioni was discharged from the army. In July 1916 he was called up with

his category and was enrolled in the 29th Artigliera da Campagna. He began training on horseback but, on 17 August, fell from his horse, hit his head, and died at the military hospital in Verona.

13 Antonio Sant'Elia (1888–1916), Futurist architect. Initially a member of the Nuove Tendenze group in 1914, he quickly left them to join the ranks of the Futurists and, in July 1914, published the "Manifesto dell'architettura futurista," which had been in part crafted by Marinetti. He served alongside the other Futurists in the Lombard Battalion of Volunteer Cyclists in 1915 and in the following year was promoted to second lieutenant in the infantry. In July 1916, he was awarded a silver medal for bravery after an engagement at Monte Zebio. In October of the same year, he was promoted to lieutenant and was commander of a company. He was killed on 10 October 1916 during the eighth battle of the Isonzo at Monfalcone, when he was shot in the forehead with a machine-gun bullet.

14 Maurizio Calvesi, "Profilo del futurismo (1965)," in *Studi sul futurismo*, vol. 1 of *Le due avanguardie* (Milan: Lerici, 1966; Bari: Laterza, 1971), 47–51, here 51. Citations refer to the Laterza edition.

15 Marianne W. Martin, *Futurist Art and Theory, 1909–1915* (Oxford: Clarendon Press, 1968; New York: Hacker Art Books, 1978), 204. Citations refer to the Hacker edition.

16 The years 1909–15 are often called the heroic years of the movement, while everything that came afterwards is generally labelled "secondo futurismo." On the historiography of the movement's development, see Walter L. Adamson, "Contexts and Debates: Fascinating Futurism; The Historiographical Politics of an Historical Avant-Garde," *Modern Italy* 13, no. 1 (2008): 69–85, here 71–3.

17 Stephen Kern, *The Culture of Time and Space, 1880–1918*, 2nd ed. (Cambridge, MA: Harvard University Press, 2003), 299.

18 Walter L. Adamson, "The End of an Avant-Garde? Filippo Tommaso Marinetti and Futurism in World War 1 and Its Aftermath," in *The History of Futurism: The Precursors, Protagonists, and Legacies*, ed. Geert Buelens, Harald Hendrix, and Monica Jansen (Lanham, MD: Lexington, 2012), 299–318, here 304–5.

19 See for example Claudia Salaris, "The Invention of the Programmatic Avant-Garde," in Greene, *Italian Futurism, 1909–1944*, 22–49, specifically 42, and Enrico Crispolti, *Storia e critica del futurismo*, 2nd ed. (Bari: Laterza, 1987), 21.

20 See Giovanni Lista, *Arte e politica: Il futurismo di sinistra in Italia* (Milan: Multhipla, 1980); Gian Battista Nazzaro, *Futurismo e politica* (Naples: J.N. Editore, 1987); Emilio Gentile, "Il futurismo e la politica: Dal nazionalismo

modernista al fascismo (1909–1920)," in *Futurismo, cultura e politica*, ed.
Renzo De Felice (Turin: Fondazione Giovanni Agnelli, 1988), 105–60;
Angelo D'Orsi, *L'ideologia politica del futurismo* (Turin: Il Segnalibro, 1992);
and Günter Berghaus, *Futurism and Politics: Between Anarchist Rebellion and
Fascist Reaction, 1909–1944* (Providence, RI: Berghahn, 1996).

21 Marinetti, "Battaglie di Trieste (1910)," in *TIF*, 245–53, here 246.

22 Luciano De Maria, introduction to *TIF*, xxix–c, here lxv. De Maria wrote
that "la guerra intesa come festa […] trova la sua più radicale espressione"
(war as celebration […] finds its most radical expression) in Marinetti's
Zang Tumb Tumb (1914), (lxvi).

23 Mario Isnenghi, *Il mito della grande guerra da Marinetti a Malaparte*, 6th ed.
(Bari: Laterza, 1969; Bologna: Il Mulino, 2007), 179. Citations refer to
the Mulino edition. *Guerra Festa* was also the title of a 1925 tapestry by
Fortunato Depero. Because of the chronological scope of this book, *L'alcova
d'acciaio* will not form part of the analysis. See Filippo Tommaso Marinetti,
L'alcòva d'acciaio: Romanzo vissuto (Milan: Vitagliano, 1921).

24 Günter Berghaus, "Violence, War, Revolution: Marinetti's Concept of a
Futurist Cleanser for the World," in "A Century of Futurism, 1909–2009,"
ed. Federico Luisetti and Luca Somigli, special issue, *Annali d'italianistica*
27 (2009): 23–43, here 34.

25 Marja Härmänmaa, "The Dark Side of Futurism: Marinetti and War," in
Back to the Futurists: The Avant-Garde and Its Legacy, ed. Elza Adamowicz
and Simona Storchi (Manchester: Manchester University Press, 2013),
255–71, here 264. Claudia Salaris used "guerra festa" as the subtitle for
her section on Marinetti's combat experiences, in *Marinetti: Arte e vita
futurista* (Rome: Editore Riuniti, 1997), 160. Adamson has written that
Marinetti viewed the war "as something to be approached playfully, even
toyed with, despite the fact that he regarded the stakes with the utmost
seriousness." "Futurism and Italian Intervention in World War 1," in
Greene, *Italian Futurism 1909-1944*, 175–7, here 177.

26 For art-historical accounts of Futurist war-time art, see Richard Cork,
A Bitter Truth: Avant-Garde Art and the Great War (New Haven, CT: Yale
University Press in association with Barbican Art Gallery, 1994); and
Massimo Libardi, Fernando Orlandi, and Maurizio Scudiero, *Qualcosa di
immane: L'arte e la grande guerra* (Scurelle, Italy: Silvy, 2012).

27 Many of the published letters cited in this book have appeared in
epistolaries but have not been comprehensively considered in
scholarship.

28 John Horne, "Soldiers, Civilians, and the Warfare of Attrition:
Representations of Combat in France, 1914–18," in *Authority, Identity, and*

the Social History of the Great War, ed. Frans Coetzee and Marilyn Shevin-Coetzee (Providence, RI: Berghahn, 1995), 223–49, here 225.

29 See Enrico Crispolti, ed., *Ricostruzione futurista dell'universo*, exhibition catalogue, Turin, June–October 1980 (Turin: Museo civico di Torino, 1980).

30 Calvesi, "Importanza di Marinetti (1964)," in *Studi sul futurismo*, 170–6, here 174.

31 Adamson, "The End of an Avant-Garde?," 307.

32 Fortunato Depero (1892–1960), Futurist artist. Depero was an Italian-speaking citizen of Austria-Hungary. In 1913 he founded the "circolo futurista trentino" in Rovereto. When war broke out in summer 1914, he departed for Rome, where he quickly made contact with Giacomo Balla, Francesco Cangiullo, and others. Upon Italy's intervention in the war, Depero volunteered for the Italian Army and by June 1915 was serving as a private soldier with the infantry. A month later he was at the front but remained there for only six weeks before being discharged on medical grounds. He spent the rest of the war holding exhibitions (in Rome and Capri) and creating his *Balli plastici* for the theatre. From the 1920s to the 1940s, Depero was one of the most important and most famous exponents of Futurist art, working in advertising, sculpture, tapestry, and ceramics.

33 Mario Carli (1889–1935), Futurist writer. Although he was exempted from military service on medical grounds, by July 1915 he had volunteered for service in the infantry and received training to become an officer. In June 1916, he was identified as a *"futurista al fronte"* (Futurist at the front) by *L'Italia Futurista*. For most of 1917 and 1918 he served with a battalion of *zappatori* (diggers), building military structures in and around the front lines. In 1918, he volunteered to become a member of the Arditi and was injured on 24 June at the Piave River, for which he received a silver medal. While recuperating in a hospital in Rome, he co-founded and edited *Roma Futurista*. After the war he was also instrumental in the Futurist Political Party and Arditi associations and was present in Fiume with Gabriele D'Annunzio.

34 Giuseppe Steiner (1898–1964), Futurist poet and playwright. His first free-word composition appeared in *L'Italia Futurista* in October 1916, where he was identified as a *"giovanissimo futurista"* (very young Futurist). By January 1917 he was serving in an engineers' corps, and he continued to contribute Futurist work to *L'Italia Futurista* and *La Folgore Futurista*. In June 1917, he was identified as a *"futurista al fronte"* (Futurist at the front) in *L'Italia Futurista*, and was included in the list of Futurist war-injured in the first issue of *Roma Futurista* in 1918. After the war he published a

poetry collection, *La chitarra del fante* (1920), on his war experiences. He continued to be associated with Futurism throughout the 1920s and 1930s.

35 Angelo Rognoni (1896–1957), Futurist free-word poet and playwright. He became involved in the Futurist circle in Pavia in 1916 and began contributing to *L'Italia Futurista*. In January and February 1917, he was the editor of *La Folgore Futurista*, alongside Gino Soggetti. He volunteered for the war and served in the artillery battalion in 1917. In 1918, he was captured and spent fourteen months as a prisoner of war in a camp near Hanover. In 1921, he made a public break with Futurism but continued to associate himself with the movement up to the 1930s.

36 In this book I do not consider the *lacerbiani* Giovanni Papini and Ardengo Soffici to any great extent, although their interactions with Marinetti during the interventionist crisis are discussed in chapter 1. See Giovanni Papini and Ardengo Soffici, *Carteggio*, ed. Mario Richter (Rome: Edizioni di storia e letteratura, 1991), and Walter L. Adamson, *Avant-Garde Florence: From Modernism to Fascism* (Cambridge, MA: Harvard University Press, 1993), 205–17.

1. Futurist Non-belligerence

1 On Italy's public memory of the First World War, see John Foot, *Italy's Divided Memory* (New York: Palgrave MacMillan, 2009), 31–53.

2 Antonio Gibelli, *La grande guerra degli Italiani* (Milan: Rizzoli, 1998), 71.

3 Historical accounts of interventionism by scholars of the First World War diverge significantly from those in Futurist scholarship. For example, in their comprehensive study *La Grande Guerra 1914–1918* (Bologna: Il Mulino, 2008), Mario Isnenghi and Giorgio Rochat make no mention of Futurism with regard to interventionism, highlighting instead the actions of Filippo Corridoni, Cesare Battisti, Gabriele D'Annunzio, and Benito Mussolini as having been most influential in the shaping of public opinion (117–27). In Marco Mondini's discussion of the various forces pushing for Italy's intervention, Marinetti barely merits a passing reference. See *La guerra italiana: Partire, raccontare, tornare 1914–18* (Bologna: Il Mulino, 2014), 36–57.

4 D'Orsi, *L'ideologia politica del futurismo*, 48.

5 Emilio Gentile, *Le origini dell'ideologia fascista 1918–1925* (Bari: Laterza, 1978), 120.

6 Biblioteca di storia moderna e contemporanea, *Diverse guerre in una: La cultura italiana dell'interventismo*, exhibition catalogue, Rome, 9 March–9 May 1987 (Rome: Biblioteca di storia moderna e contemporanea, 1987), 115.

7 Francesco Cangiullo (1884–1977), Futurist writer and playwright. Cangiullo joined the movement in 1912 and led the Futurist group based in Naples.

From October 1915 to March 1916 he edited the "Futurist Pages" in the
Neapolitan journal *Vela Latina*, and in early 1916 he organized a number of
Futurist events that Marinetti and Boccioni attended in the city. Cangiullo
was called up to the army as a private soldier in July 1916 and was assigned
to the Eighty-Second Infantry Regiment based in Rome, but he never served
at the front. During the war he published *Piedigrotta* under the auspices
of the Edizioni futuriste di "Poesia" and contributed to *L'Italia Futurista*
and *Il Montello*. After the war he invented the Futurist genre "Teatro della
Sorpresa" with Marinetti but in 1924 publicly left the movement.

8 Giacomo Balla (1871–1958), Futurist painter. He was a signatory of the
   "Manifesto dei pittori futuristi" and "La pittura futurista: Manifesto
   tecnico" (both in 1910). He completed a series of paintings in 1915
   inspired by the interventionist demonstrations in Rome but, owing to his
   age, did not serve in the army. In 1916 he co-signed the "Manifesto della
   cinematografia futurista" and served as an editor of *Roma Futurista* from
   1920.

9 Balla's manifesto was first published in French on 20 May 1914, entitled
   "Le vêtement masculin futuriste: Manifeste," and then in Italian, retitled
   "Il vestito antineutrale: Manifesto futurista" (The anti-neutral suit: Futurist
   manifesto) on 11 September 1914. Balla's original appeal for more dynamic
   men's clothing was transformed by Marinetti into an interventionist, anti-
   neutrality statement, suggesting that the suit should be made in a white,
   green, and red coloured material to echo the colours of the Italian flag. See
   Eugenia Paulicelli, "Fashion and Futurism: Performing Dress," in Luisetti
   and Somigli, "A Century of Futurism," 187–207, specifically 194–5.

10 Claudia Salaris, *Filippo Tommaso Marinetti* (Scandicci, Italy: La Nuova
   Italia, 1988), 140. See also Mario Verdone, *Il Futurismo* (Rome: Newton &
   Compton, 2003), 18.

11 Lawrence Rainey, "Introduction: F.T. Marinetti and the Development of
   Futurism," in *Futurism: An Anthology*, ed. Lawrence Rainey, Christine
   Poggi, and Laura Wittman (New Haven, CT: Yale University Press, 2009),
   1–39, here 19.

12 Berghaus, *Futurism and Politics*, 79.

13 Ruth Ben-Ghiat, Luciano Cafagna, Ernesto Galli della Loggia, Carl Ipsen,
   David I. Kertzer, and Mark Gilbert, "History as It Wasn't: The Myths of
   Italian Historiography," *Journal of Modern Italian Studies* 6, no. 3 (2001):
   402–19, here 417. In this article they discuss *Miti e storia dell'Italia unita*,
   ed. Giovanni Belardelli, Luciano Cafagna, Ernesto Galli della Loggia, and
   Giovanni Sabbatucci (Bologna: Il Mulino, 1999).

14 Francesco Balilla Pratella, "Il Futurismo e la Guerra: Cronistoria sintetica,"
   Vela Latina, 18–24 November 1915, 1. A slightly modified version entitled

"Il Futurismo e la Guerra: Cronaca sintetica," dated 11 December 1915, is printed in *TIF*, 554–61. See also Marinetti, "Movimento politico futurista," in *TIF*, 341. The mythologizing was also present in Marinetti's collection of manifestos published towards the end of 1915, *Guerra sola igiene del mondo*, in *TIF*, 235–341; in the "Manifesto del partito politico futurista," *L'Italia Futurista*, 11 February 1918, 2; in the post-war *Democrazia futurista* (1919), in *TIF*, 345–469; and in *Futurismo e Fascismo* (1924), in *TIF*, 491–572. For a facsimile reproduction of *L'Italia Futurista*, see "*L'Italia Futurista: Firenze, 1916–1918*," ed. Luciano Caruso (Florence: SPES, 1992).

15 In addition to the sources already quoted above, see Anne Bowler, "Politics as Art: Italian Futurism and Fascism," *Theory and Society* 20, no. 6 (1991): 763–94; Julie Dashwood, "Futurism and Fascism," *Italian Studies* 27, no. 1 (1972): 91–103, specifically 95 and 103; Salaris, *Filippo Tommaso Marinetti*, 139–40; David D. Roberts, "Croce and Beyond: Italian Intellectuals and the First World War," *International History Review* 3, no. 2 (1981): 201–35, specifically 206; Richard Wohl, *The Generation of 1914* (Cambridge, MA: Harvard University Press, 1979), 170. D'Orsi and Berghaus have alluded to the Futurists' role in the "mythopoeia" of the interventionist crisis and to some exaggerations on the part of Marinetti regarding the significance of Futurist actions. See D'Orsi, *L'ideologia politica del futurismo*, 39, and Berghaus, *Futurism and Politics*, 74–5. Gentile has noted that "adottando un criterio di effettualità, si possono avere dubbi plausibili sulla serietà e persino sulla esistenza di una politica futurista" (adopting a parameter of effectiveness, one can have credible doubts about the seriousness, and even the existence, of a political Futurism), although he does not develop this line of argumentation. "Il futurismo e la politica," 106.

16 Cork, *A Bitter Truth*, 61–3; Luigi Sansone, "F.T. Marinetti emblema del futurismo," in *F.T. Marinetti = Futurismo*, ed. Sansone, exhibition catalogue, Milan, 12 February–7 June 2009 (Milan: Federico Motta, 2009), 19–51, on interventionist actions, 29; Crispolti, *Storia e critica del futurismo*, 178 and 193–7.

17 Biblioteca di storia moderna e contemporanea, *Diverse guerre in una*, 116.

18 Gentile is unusual in highlighting that the "effettualità [della politica del futurismo], come capacità di conseguire risultati concreti corrispondenti ai propositi, fu molto scarsa" (effectiveness [of Futurist politics], in its ability to obtain concrete results aligned with its aims, was negligible). "Il futurismo e la politica," 106.

19 Foot, *Italy's Divided Memory*, 18.

20 Balla to Marinetti, 17 July 1914, in Giacomo Balla, *Scritti futuristi*, ed. Giovanni Lista (Milan: Abscondita, 2010), 164–5 (emphasis in the original; hereafter cited as *BSF*).

21 Corrado Govoni (1884–1965), Futurist poet. Govoni joined Futurism's ranks between 1910 and 1911 and published a number of Futurist-inspired collections of poetry before the war: *Poesie elettriche* (1911), *L'inaugurazione della primavera* (1915), and *Rarefazioni: Parole in libertà* (1915). He did not volunteer for the army but was later called up to serve. Already by the beginning of the war he had distanced himself from Futurism and from Marinetti.

22 Govoni to Marinetti, 20 August 1914, in Govoni, *Lettere a F.T. Marinetti*, ed. Matilde Dillon Wanke (Milan: Scheiwiller, 1990), 80 (hereafter cited as *CG-FTM*).

23 Papini to Carrà, 25 August 1914, in Carlo Carrà and Giovanni Papini, *Il carteggio Carrà-Papini: Da "Lacerba" al tempi di "Valori Plastici"*, ed. Massimo Carrà (Milan: Skira/MART, 2001), 195 (hereafter cited as *CC-GP*).

24 Soffici to Carrà, after 25 August 1914, in Carrà and Soffici, *Lettere 1913–1929*, ed. Massimo Carrà and Vittorio Fagone (Milan: Feltrinelli, 1983), 61 (hereafter cited as *CC-AS*).

25 Fortunato Depero, *Motorumorista, Futurista, Mimismagico, Astrattista Formidabile, Architetto e Poeta* (Milan: Edizioni del Naviglio, 1986), 4.

26 Depero to Rosetta Amadori, 5 August 1914, Museo d'arte moderna e contemporanea di Trento e Rovereto (hereafter referred to as MART), Archivio del '900, Fondo Depero, Dep. 3.3.1.3.16.

27 He received permission from Innsbruck to depart for Italy on 22 August 1914. MART, Archivio del '900, Fondo Depero, Dep. 1.1.2.

28 Depero to Amadori, 7 August 1914, MART, Archivio del '900, Fondo Depero, Dep. 3.3.1.3.16 (emphasis in the original).

29 Depero was officially admitted into the Futurist ranks in the spring of 1915. It was announced in a letter to Balla signed by Marinetti, Boccioni, Carrà, and Russolo. MART, Archivio del '900, Fondo Depero, Dep. 1.1.3.

30 Severini to Marinetti, 6 August 1914, in *Futurismo 100: Illuminazioni; Avanguardie a confronto; Italia, Germania, Russia*, ed. Ester Coen, exhibition catalogue, Rovereto, 17 January–7 June 2009 (Milan: Electa, 2009), 79.

31 Severini to Carrà, 10 August 1914, in Coen, *Futurismo 100*, 293.

32 Severini to Marinetti, 6 August 1914, in Coen, *Futurismo 100*, 79.

33 Severini to Carrà, 10 August 1914, in Coen, *Futurismo 100*, 293.

34 Severini to Marinetti, 6 August 1914, in Coen, *Futurismo 100*, 79. He reiterated this sentiment in another letter dated 19 August 1914, in Coen, *Futurismo 100*, 79.

35 Unsigned article, [headline partially absent] "proibito per l'art. 113 Marinetti parte per la guerra," *Il Piccolo Giornale d'Italia* (Rome), 7 August

1914, in Papers of F.T. Marinetti and Benedetta Cappa Marinetti, Getty Research Institute (hereafter referred to as Papers of FTM and BCM, GRI), Libroni, box 38, accession no. 920092. In total, 9,425 Italians volunteered to fight in the French foreign legion during the war, including six grandsons of Giuseppe Garibaldi. Some Italians living in France had already enlisted by 5 August. See Hubert Heyriès, "I volontari italiani in Francia durante la Grande Guerra," in *Volontari italiani nella Grande Guerra*, ed. Fabrizio Rasera and Camillo Zadra (Rovereto: Museo della Guerra, 2008), 81–96.

36 Unsigned article, [headline partially absent] "proibito per l'art. 113 Marinetti parte per la guerra," *Il Piccolo Giornale d'Italia* (Rome), 7 August 1914, in Papers of FTM and BCM, GRI, Libroni, box 38, accession no. 920092.

37 Giuseppe Ungaretti to Marinetti, 9 August 1914, F.T. Marinetti Papers, Beinecke Rare Book and Manuscript Library (hereafter referred to as FTM Papers, BRB), box 17, folder 1087.

38 Marinetti to Francesco Balilla Pratella, 12 August 1914, in *Lettere ruggenti a Francesco Balilla Pratella*, ed. Giovanni Lugaresi (Milan: Quaderni dell'Osservatore, 1969), 49 (hereafter cited as *FBP*). In his "Il Futurismo e la Guerra: Cronistoria sintetica," published in *Vela Latina*, 18–24 November 1915, Pratella mentioned a demonstration on 20 August. There is no further mention of this in any Futurist correspondence; most probably he was referring to the demonstration on 6 August.

39 Marinetti to Cangiullo, 11 August 1914, in Filippo Tommaso Marinetti and Francesco Cangiullo, *Lettere (1910–1943)*, ed. Ernestina Pellegrini (Florence: Vallecchi, 1989), 77 (hereafter cited as *FTM-FC*).

40 Marinetti to Pratella, 12 August 1914, in *FBP*, 49.

41 Marinetti to Cangiullo, 13 August 1914, in *FTM-FC*, 78. The demonstration was most likely a reaction to the Socialist anti-war demonstrations that had taken place in Milan between 29 July and 3 August with crowds of between twenty thousand and forty thousand in attendance. See Marco Gervasoni, "La nascita della retorica interventista: Dalla 'Plebe' alla 'Patria,'" in *Combattere a Milano 1915–1918: Il corpo e la guerra nella capitale del fronte interno*, ed. Barbara Bracco (Milan: Il Ponte, 2005), 7–13, here 11.

42 Marinetti to Cangiullo, 11 August 1914, in *FTM-FC*, 78 (emphasis in the original).

43 Marinetti to Cangiullo, 13 August 1914, in *FTM-FC*, 78.

44 Marinetti to Pratella, 19 August 1914, in *FBP*, 50.

45 Papini to Carrà, after 25 August 1914, in *CC-GP*, 52.

46 Papini to Marinetti, 17 September 1914, in FTM Papers, BRB, box 14, folder 845. The only manifesto issued between August and November

1914 was the Italian translation of Balla's clothing manifesto, "Il vestito antineutrale," on 11 September.

47 Marinetti to Soffici, undated, in *Archivi del futurismo*, ed. Maria Drudi Gambillo and Teresa Fiori (Rome: De Luca, 1962), vol. 2, 344–5 (hereafter cited as *ADF*). Drudi Gambillo and Fiori suggest that the letter was written between August and December 1914. Considering the animosity between the editors of *Lacerba* and Marinetti from October 1914, it is more likely that this letter dates from August or September 1914.

48 Luciano Folgore (1888–1966), pseudonym of Omero Vecchi, Futurist poet. Folgore was already an active member of the movement before Italy's entry into the war, having published two volumes of poetry in the collection Edizioni futuriste di "Poesia" – *Canto dei motori* (1912) and *Ponti sull'oceano* (1914). In 1916 he was assigned to an artillery regiment in Rome but was discharged on medical grounds. After a nine-month wait in expectation of being declared medically unfit for duty, he instead was mobilized again in July 1917 and stationed as part of the anti-aerial division guarding the Venice Lido. During his military service he contributed to the Futurist soldier newspaper, *Il Montello*. Although he continued to write after the war, he was no longer affiliated with the Futurist movement.

49 Marinetti to Folgore, 25 August 1914, in Claudia Salaris, *Luciano Folgore e le avanguardie: Con lettere e inediti futuristi* (Scandicci, Italy: La Nuova Italia, 1997), 242 (hereafter cited as *LF*). Marinetti was not the only Futurist with this idea. Ugo Tommei expressed a similar desire in a letter to Giovanni Papini in the summer of 1914. See Fabrizio Bagatti, Gloria Manghetti, and Silvia Porto, eds., *Futurismo a Firenze 1910–1920*, exhibition catalogue, Florence, 18 February–8 April 1984 (Florence: Sansoni, 1984), 119.

50 Francesco Balilla Pratella (1880–1955), Futurist composer. Already a well-regarded composer, Pratella joined Marinetti's movement in 1910, writing the "Manifesto dei musicisti futuristi" (1910) and the "Manifesto tecnico della musica futurista" (1911). He did not volunteer for the army but was called up on 1 May 1916. He could have become an officer because of his level of education but decided to remain a private solider. He was assigned to a territorial (non-mobilized) battalion in Rimini, where he was responsible for the musical instruction of the soldiers. After a few months he was assigned to his home town of Lugo so that he could continue to manage the local music school. He was exempted from most duties in the barracks and given ample free time to manage the school and to write. His regiment was mobilized in January 1917, but, after a medical visit deemed him unfit for combat, he spent the remainder of the war working in an

administrative capacity in Cesena near his home town. He was discharged on 1 December 1918 and continued his musical work in conjunction with Futurism.

51 Pratella to Guglielmo Jannelli, 31 August 1914, Fondazione Primo Conti, Fiesole (hereafter referred to as FPC), Fondo Pratella, Corrispondenza SC X/INS 2/CAM D.

52 Luigi Russolo (1885–1947), Futurist painter and musician. One of the earliest protagonists of the movement, Russolo was a signatory of the "Manifesto dei pittori futuristi" and "La pittura futurista: Manifesto tecnico," both in 1910. He wrote the manifesto "L'arte dei rumori" in 1913, which was published in expanded book form in 1916. He volunteered with the Lombard Battalion of Volunteer Cyclists in 1915 and, after its disbandment, remained with the Battalion of Alpine Volunteers. In 1916, he was promoted to second lieutenant and transferred to the Fifth Alpine Regiment "Val Brenta." He received a serious head injury during an engagement at Monte Grappa in December 1917 and spent the following eighteen months recovering in various hospitals around Italy. He received a silver medal for bravery and a special recognition because of his war injuries. In 1919 he was declared permanently exempt from military service. He remained close to the Futurist movement for the rest of his life.

53 See the register of enrolments in the Battaglione Lombardo di Volontari Ciclisti e Automobilisti, in Fondo Volontari, Museo Storico Italiano della Guerra, Rovereto (hereafter referred to as MSIG). In his revised "cronaca sintetica" published with the manifesto "L'Orgoglio Italiano" on 11 December 1915, Pratella states that this happened on 3 August 1914, but this is incorrect. Collezione Reggi, Archivi della Parola, dell'Immagine e della Comunicazione Editoriale, Università degli Studi, Milan (hereafter referred to as APICE). Available at http://apicesv3.noto.unimi.it/site/reggi/. The receipt and two guarantees for the bicycles, dated 29 August 1914, are held in the Papers of FTM and BCM, GRI, box 4, folder 6, accession no. 920092. A condition of enrolment with the battalion was that each volunteer had to be in possession of his own bicycle.

54 Renzo De Felice has commented that the Futurists "al contrario dei nazionalisti non avevano avuto a questo proposito [l'idea di scendere in piazza] alcun tentennamento" (unlike the Nationalists had no hesitation in this regard [at the idea of demonstrating in public]), which as we have seen is not an entirely accurate portrayal of Marinetti's initial reaction to the outbreak of war. *Mussolini il rivoluzionario 1883–1920* (Turin: Einaudi, 1965), 474.

55 Armando Mazza (1884–1964), Futurist writer. Mazza joined the movement
   in 1910 and participated in the early *serate futuriste* around Italy. Active in
   Futurist interventionist activities, he signed the manifesto "Sintesi futurista
   della guerra" (1914) and during the war contributed to *Vela Latina*, *L'Italia
   Futurista*, and other publications. He was called up for military service in
   1918 and spent several months at an officers' training course in Modena.
   In August 1918 he was awaiting his appointment as a second lieutenant
   in the infantry, and soon after saw active service. He continued his
   involvement with Futurism in the post-war period.

56 Filippo Tommaso Marinetti, *La grande Milano tradizionale e futurista: Una
   sensibilità italiana nata in Egitto*, ed. Luciano De Maria (Milan: Mondadori,
   1969), 110. See also Marinetti, "I futuristi primi interventisti," in *Marinetti e il
   futurismo* (1929), in *TIF*, 595–600, on the September demonstrations 595–8.

57 Ugo Piatti (1880–1953), Futurist musician. Piatti was part of the core
   Futurist group from 1911, and from 1913 he collaborated with Russolo
   to build his famous "noise-tuner" instruments. He was a signatory of
   the manifesto "Sintesi futurista della guerra" (1914) and enrolled with
   the Lombard Battalion of Volunteer Cyclists in 1915; he was named as a
   co-author of the manifesto "L'Orgoglio Italiano" (1915). He volunteered for
   service again in 1916 and was assigned to coastal surveillance in Pesaro.
   Later he served as a lieutenant of the *bersaglieri ciclisti* (cyclists in the rifle
   regiment) at the Piave, where he was injured. He was listed among the
   injured Futurists in the first issue of *Roma Futurista* on 20 September 1918.
   In the 1920s he progressively distanced himself from Futurism and moved
   towards the Novecento group.

58 A brief report in *Il Giornale* (Turin) on 19 September 1914 ("I 'futuristi'
   in carcere") stated that Gabriellino D'Annunzio, the son of the famous
   author, had been involved in the demonstration but had evaded arrest
   by the police. Papers of FTM and BCM, GRI, Libroni, box 38, accession
   no. 920092. On their time in prison, see Francesco Cangiullo, *Le serate
   futuriste: Romanzo storico vissuto* (Milan: Ceschina, 1961), 145–52;
   Marinetti, *La grande Milano tradizionale e futurista*, 112–13; Umberto
   Boccioni's letters to his family, dated 16 September, 19 September,
   and 22 September, in Umberto Boccioni, *Lettere futuriste*, ed. Federico
   Rovati (Rovereto: Egon/MART, 2009), 126–9 (hereafter cited as *UBLF*);
   Marinetti's letters to Nina Angelini, dated 18 September, 19 September,
   and 21 September, in *Le vestali del futurismo*, ed. Virginio Giacomo Bono
   (Voghera, Italy: Edo Edizioni Oltrepò, 1991), 61 (hereafter cited as
   VdelF).

59 To put the actions of the Futurists into context, a few days later in Rome, on 20 September 1914, an irredentist and pro-intervention demonstration saw fifty thousand people take part. See Mondini, *La guerra italiana*, 48.

60 See De Felice, *Mussolini il rivoluzionario*, 249.

61 Police Report, Archivio dello Stato Rome, cited in Gentile, "Il futurismo e la politica," 117n36.

62 On the role of the press in the interventionist struggle, see Mondini, *La guerra italiana*, 36–45.

63 "'La Fanciulla del West' al Dal Verme," *Corriere della Sera* (Milan), 16 September 1914, 3.

64 Berghaus, *Futurism and Politics*, 74.

65 "Futuristi, nazionalisti, ed attori drammatici," *La Sera* (Milan), 17 September 1914, Papers of FTM and BCM, GRI, Libroni, box 38, accession no. 920092.

66 "Una piccola dimostrazione in Galleria," *Corriere della Sera* (Milan), 17 September 1914, 4.

67 Police Report, Archivio dello Stato Rome, cited in Gentile, "Il futurismo e la politica," 117n36. In response to the *La Sera* article of 17 September 1914, Umberto Notari, a friend of Marinetti, wrote to the newspaper, claiming that the demonstration did not have "quei limiti microscopici che il giornale […] ha voluto porre in rilievo" (those microscopic dimensions that the newspaper […] wanted to highlight), but, on the balance of probabilities, the reports of the police and the newspapers provide the most accurate accounts. See Notari, "A proposito di 'pagliacciate,'" *La Sera* (Milan), no date but shortly after 17 September 1914, Papers of FTM and BCM, GRI, Libroni, box 38, accession no. 920092.

68 "Marinetti e Boccioni al Cellulare. Altri agenti feriti," *Il Secolo* (Milan), 18 September 1914; and "La prossima scarcerazione di Marinetti e comp," *La Sera* (Milan), 21 September 1914, Papers of FTM and BCM, GRI, Libroni, box 38, accession no. 920092.

69 "Baraonda in Galleria a Milano," *L'Adriatico* (Venice), 17 September 1914, Papers of FTM and BCM, GRI, Libroni, box 38, accession no. 920092.

70 "La scarcerazione di Marinetti, Boccioni e compagni," *La Stampa* (Turin), 22 September 1914, 5.

71 "Marinetti in gattabuia," *Il Piccolo Giornale d'Italia* (Rome), article written on 19 September 1914, date of publication unclear; and "I futuristi milanesi in gattabuia," *Il Successo* (Genoa), 27 September 1914 – both in Papers of FTM and BCM, GRI, Libroni, box 38, accession no. 920092.

72 "L'Italia rompe la neutralità," *Il Centesimino: Quotidiano Pupazzettato*,
18 September 1914, Papers of FTM and BCM, GRI, Libroni, box 38,
accession no. 920092.

73 Ibid.

74 Boccioni to his family, 22 September 1914, in *UBLF*, 128.

75 Marinetti to Soffici, 14 September 1914, in *ADF*, 345.

76 Telegram from Marinetti, Boccioni, Piatti, and Russolo to Soffici, 23
September 1914, in *ADF*, 348.

77 This planned *serata* in Montecatini is just one example of the Futurists'
mythologizing of their interventionist activities, as it was recorded in their
accounts of their pro-war engagement, without the crucial information that the
event never took place. It is mentioned in Pratella, "Il Futurismo e La Guerra:
Cronistoria sintetica," *Vela Latina*, 18–24 November 1915, 1. This error has been
repeated in Futurist scholarship, for example Verdone, *Il Futurismo*, 18.

78 Marinetti to Jannelli, 6 November 1914, in *Prefuturismo e primo futurismo in
Sicilia (1900–1918)*, ed. Giuseppe Miligi and Umberto Carpi
(Messina: Sicania, 1989), 300 (hereafter cited as *PPF*).

79 The only letters that mention the manifesto date to the first week of
November 1914, in which Marinetti asks others to help him distribute and
promote the manifesto, indicating that it had only recently been released.
See Marinetti to Cangiullo, 6 November 1914, in *FTM-FC*, 79–80; Marinetti
to Folgore, 5 November 1914, in Luciano Folgore and Filippo Tommaso
Marinetti, *Carteggio futurista*, ed. Francesco Muzzioli (Rome: Officina,
1987), 70 (hereafter cited as *LF-FTM*).

80 In Emilio Gentile, *La nostra sfida alle stelle: Futuristi in politica* (Rome:
Laterza, 2009), 35, there is a reproduction of the manifesto, which gives the
300,000 figure, while in a letter to Folgore of 5 November 1914 Marinetti
gave the 20,000 figure and reported on the reception in the universities
of Genoa and Pavia. *LF-FTM*, 70. On the reception of the manifesto,
Marinetti told Cangiullo that it had "grande ripercussione negli ambienti
studenteschi" (a big impact in student circles). Marinetti to Cangiullo, 6
November 1914, in *FTM-FC*, 79–80. Jannelli wrote in January 1915 that
in Messina "lanciai 500 manifesti Sintesi dal Teatro Mastrojeni: grande
interesse, discussioni, pugilati" (I threw 500 of the Sintesi manifestos from
the Teatro Mastrojeni: huge interest, discussion, fistfights). Jannelli to
Folgore, 1 January 1915, in *LF*, 231.

81 See letter from Ugo Tommei to Carrà, 26 January 1915, MART, Archivio
del '900, Fondo Carrà, Car.1.143. He asks, "Posso avere un po' di quelle
cartoline tricolori che avete messe fori ora?" (Can I have a few of those
tricolour postcards that you've just released?) The earliest reference to the

postcard that I have been able to trace is a letter from Marinetti to Jannelli, undated but between the end of November and early December 1914, in *PPF*, 301.

82 See Cangiullo, *Le serate futuriste*, 211–19; "I futuristi alla Sapienza: Un rumoroso incidente all'Università di Roma," *Corriere della Sera* (Milan), 11 December 1914, 4; "Nuovi disordini all'Università di Roma provocati dai futuristi," *Corriere della Sera* (Milan), 12 December 1914, 4.

83 Once again, a comparison of other interventionist events unfolding at the same time help put the Futurist demonstrations into context. On 6 January 1915 the funeral of Bruno Garibaldi in Rome (who had volunteered for service in France) turned into a pro-interventionist demonstration of 200,000 people. See Mondini, *La guerra italiana*, 47.

84 See for example, "Il futurista Marinetti in casacca tricolore provoca dimostrazioni antineutraliste all'Università di Roma," *La Stampa* (Turin), 12 December 1914, 4. Despite indication to the contrary in the headline of this article, it was Cangiullo, not Marinetti, who actually wore the tricolour suit.

85 Mario Carli to Emilio Settimelli, 12 December 1914, FPC, Fondo Settimelli, Corrispondenza SC I/INS 7/CAM A (emphasis in the orginal).

86 Biblioteca di storia moderna e contemporanea, *Diverse guerre in una*, 116–17.

87 D'Orsi, *L'ideologia politica del futurismo*, 29.

88 [Jannelli], "La guerra attuale è il più bel poema futurista apparso finora, dice Marinetti," *Il Piccolo Giornale d'Italia* (Rome), 11 December 1914, Papers of FTM and BCM, GRI, Libroni, box 38, accession no. 920092. A version of this interview was reprinted in *L'Avvenire* (Messina) and published on 23 February 1915, in *PPF*, 267–72.

89 These comments appear in the version of the interview published in *L'Avvenire*, in *PPF*, 272.

90 Marinetti to Cangiullo, 6 November 1914, in *FTM-FC*, 80.

91 Marinetti to Severini, 20 November 1914, in *ADF*, 349. Severini was living in Paris, and thus it was possible for Marinetti to stretch the truth by stating that they "continually" held demonstrations, as it would have been difficult for Severini to confirm this.

92 Marinetti to Pratella, 27 November 1914, in FPC, Fondo Pratella, Corrispondenza SC VII/INS 13/CAM B.

93 See Marinetti to Folgore, 5 November and 27 November 1914, in *LF-FTM*, 70 and 72 respectively.

94 Marinetti, "1915: In quest'anno futurista (1914)," in *TIF*, 328–36, here 333 (emphasis in the original).

95 Ibid., 334–5.

96 On Balla's interventionist paintings, see Christine Poggi, "Folla/Follia: Futurism and the Crowd," *Critical Inquiry* 28, no. 3 (2002): 709–48, here 736–40; on Boccioni and Carrà's works, see Poggi, *In Defiance of Painting: Cubism, Futurism and the Invention of Collage* (New Haven, CT: Yale University Press, 1992), 237–43.

97 Marinetti to Severini, 20 November 1914, in *ADF*, 349.

98 Ibid.

99 Ibid., 349–50. Severini followed Marinetti's advice and produced a number of pro-war paintings, in a less abstract style, one of which was based on a photograph of a Belgian armoured train (*Treno blindato in azione*, 1915). See Christine Poggi, *Inventing Futurism: The Art and Politics of Artificial Optimism* (Princeton: Princeton University Press, 2009), 176.

100 Cangiullo, *Le serate futuriste*, 219.

101 Marinetti to Severini, 26 March 1915, in *ADF*, 356.

102 Pratella, "Il Futurismo e La Guerra: Cronistoria sintetica," *Vela Latina*, 18–24 November 1915, 1.

103 Marinetti to Folgore, 2 January 1915, in *LF-FTM*, 75.

104 Unsigned article, "Una serata futurista," *Urbis et Orbis* (Rome), 31 January 1915, Papers of FTM and BCM, GRI, Libroni, box 38, accession no. 920092.

105 Pratella, "Il Futurismo e La Guerra," 1.

106 This *serata futurista* in Ravenna is unknown to scholars of Futurism. It is absent from Berghaus's comprehensive account of Futurist theatre (1996) and has not been cited in subsequent scholarship. An original flyer for the event was recently unearthed by the Libreria Antiquaria Pontremoli in Milan. See *Futurismo: Collezione Mughini* (Milan: Libreria Antiquaria Pontremoli, 2014), 188.

107 Paolo Buzzi (1874–1956), Futurist poet. He joined the Futurist movement in 1909 and published several collections of poetry before Italy entered the war: *Aeroplani* (1909), *Versi Liberi* (1913), and *L'elisse e la spirale* (1915). He worked in an administrative capacity for the region of Lombardy and thus was exempted from military service during the war.

108 Giannetto Malmerendi (1893–1968), Futurist painter. He first came into contact with the Futurists in January 1914 on the occasion of a Futurist conference at Bologna university, and he joined the movement the same year. In January 1915 Malmerendi held a small exhibition in Faenza, which was opened by Marinetti. In the same month he enrolled voluntarily with the army and was assigned to the Telegraph Engineers' Corps in Florence. While serving in the army, he participated in some

exhibitions (both affiliated with Futurism and not), but by 1919 he had distanced himself from Marinetti's movement.

109 Boccioni expressed his regret at not being able to attend. See Boccioni to Malmerendi and Armando Cavalli, 18 January 1915, in *UBLF*, 132–4.

110 L.B., "La Conferenza Marinetti – Mostra Futurista," *Il Socialista* (Faenza), 14 January 1915, MART, Archivio del '900, Documenti Malmerendi, no classification.

111 Ibid.

112 Unsigned article, "Marinetti a Faenza," *Il Piccolo* (Faenza), 10 January 1915, MART, Archivio del '900, Documenti Malmerendi, no classification. Predictably, the version of events presented in the pro-interventionist newspaper *Il Lamone* (Faenza), a mouthpiece of the Partito Repubblicano Italiano, reported that Marinetti's praise of the war was met with "il miagolio piagnucoloso di qualche neutral-pacifista" (the weepy meows of a few pacifist neutrals). See Achille Cenni, "Conferenza Marinetti. Mostra d'arte futurista," *Il Lamone* (Faenza), 10 January 1915, MART, Archivio del '900, Documenti Malmerendi, no classification.

113 Alberto Presenzini-Mattòli (1892–1984), Futurist writer. He was associated with the Futurist group based in Perugia prior to the outbreak of the war. He was deemed unfit for military service because of a delicate constitution but nonetheless succeeded in serving in the army after the Battle of Caporetto. He was a contributor to *L'Italia Futurista* and *Roma Futurista*, and from 1920 he co-edited the journal *Griffa!*.

114 Giovanni (Giannino) Mariotti (1894–1943), Futurist writer. He was associated with the Futurist group based in Perugia prior to the outbreak of the war. Owing to his professional position with the Ministero degli Esteri, in 1914 he was stationed in Marseilles, and later in Stuttgart, and had no further involvement with Futurism.

115 Unsigned article, "Il tumultuoso comizio di ieri al Turreno," *L'Unione Liberale* (Perugia), 29–30 December 1914; unsigned article, "Il comizio Caroti al Turreno," *La Battaglia* (Perugia), 31 December 1914; unsigned article, "La conferenza neutralista dell'On. Caroti," *Il Popolo, settimanale repubblicano* (Perugia), 2 January 1915. These reports are quoted in *Umbria Futurista, 1912–1944*, ed. Domenico Cialfi and Antonella Pesola, exhibition catalogue, Terni, 20 February–30 April 2009 (Arrone, Italy: Thyrus, 2009), 13–23 and 20.

116 See unsigned postcard to Giannina Pironi, 25 December 1914, in Sansone, *F.T. Marinetti = Futurismo*, 234. It is a "bandiera futurista" postcard, with a newspaper clipping describing Cangiullo's arrest pasted on the reverse.

117 Filippo Granato to Marinetti, 1 April 1915, Marinetti Student Notebooks and Other Papers, GRI, box 1, folder 25, accession no. 890122.

118 Berghaus, *Futurism and Politics*, 79. Marinetti advised Jannelli to discuss in *La Balza Futurista* the need to encourage Futurists "ad essere sempre alla testa delle dimostrazioni interventiste" (to be always at the head of interventionist demonstrations). Marinetti to Jannelli, 16 April 1915, in *PPF*, 308. Jannelli did not follow this piece of advice.

119 Cangiullo, *Le serate futuriste*, 219.

120 Guglielmo Jannelli (1895–1950), Sicilian Futurist free-word poet and playwright. He first met Marinetti in 1911 during the *serata futurista* in Palermo and again in 1913. He was a strong supporter of Futurist interventionist action, and in 1915 he founded the magazine *La Balza Futurista* with Luciano Nicastro and Vann'Antò. By June 1915 he was already serving in the war zone as a second lieutenant in the artillery. He contributed to *L'Italia Futurista* as a *"futurista al fronte"* and to *La Folgore Futurista*. In 1919 he co-founded the Messina branch of the Futurist Political Party.

121 Auro D'Alba (1888–1965), pseudonym of Umberto Bottone, Futurist poet and playwright. He published a collection of poems, *Baionette*, for the Edizioni futuriste di "Poesia" in 1915 and was actively involved in interventionist demonstrations. During the war years he contributed to *Lacerba* and *L'Italia Futurista*. He served as an officer in the *bersaglieri* (rifle regiment) and received a silver medal and war cross.

122 Pratella, "Il Futurismo e la Guerra," 1.

123 See unsigned article, "Dimostrazioni interventiste sciolte dalla forza pubblica a Roma. Marinetti arrestato e rilasciato," *La Stampa* (Turin), 19 February 1915, 2. A photograph of Marinetti being arrested was featured on the front page of *La Tribuna* (Rome) on 19 February 1915. In a letter to his wife, Cangiullo noted that the demonstration was also reported in *Il Mattino* (Naples). Cangiullo to Margherita Cangiullo, no date, FPC, Fondo Cangiullo, Corrispondenza SC I/INS 1/CAM E.

124 "Dimostrazioni interventiste," *La Stampa* (Turin), 19 February 1915, 2.

125 "Serata di dimostrazioni a Milano," *La Stampa* (Turin), 1 April 1915, 7.

126 Cangiullo, *Le serate futuriste*, 235.

127 "Una dimostrazione al 'Fossati' contro l'operetta Viennese," *Il Secolo* (Milan), 2 April 1915, Papers of FTM and BCM, GRI, Libroni, box 39, accession no. 920092.

128 See report in *Corriere della Sera* (Milan), 12 April 1915, cited in Berghaus, *Futurism and Politics*, 90n95.

129 Marinetti to Folgore, 21 April 1915, in *LF-FTM*, 80. For a further account, see Marinetti, *La grande Milano tradizionale e futurista*, 144.

130 "Tumultuosi tentativi di pubblici comizi a Roma. L'arresto di Benito Mussolini e del futurista Marinetti," *La Stampa* (Turin), 12 April 1915, 5. Bruno Corra and Emilio Settimelli were also arrested on this occasion, according to Pratella, "Il Futurismo e la Guerra: Cronaca sintetica," 11 December 1915, Collezione Reggi, APICE.

131 "Comizi, Dimostrazioni, Arresti," *Due Soldi* (Milan), 17 April 1915, Papers of FTM and BCM, GRI, Libroni, box 39, accession no. 920092.

132 Biagio, "Dimostrazioni interventiste," *L'Illustrazione Italiana* (Milan), 19 April 1915, Papers of FTM and BCM, GRI, Libroni, box 39, accession no. 920092.

133 "Mussolini e Marinetti," *La Voce del Popolo* (Brescia), 16 April 1915, Papers of FTM and BCM, GRI, Libroni, box 39, accession no. 920092.

134 Biblioteca di storia moderna e contemporanea, *Diverse guerre in una*, 122. Drudi Gambillo and Fiori also mention the frequency with which Mussolini and Marinetti acted alongside each other during this period, in *ADF*, 490.

135 Günter Berghaus, in Filippo Tommaso Marinetti, *Critical Writings*, ed. Berghaus, trans. Doug Thompson (New York: Farrar, Straus & Giroux, 2006), 471–2n13. In the same volume Berghaus also reported that Marinetti and Mussolini were arrested in Piazza della Pilotta in Milan at an unspecified date (463n1), but this event never took place. The error possibly arose as a result of Settimelli's faulty memory. See "Resistenza colorata (Lettera aperta a BM)," in Emilio Settimelli, *Inchiesta sulla vita italiana* (Rocca San Casciano, Italy: Cappelli, 1919), 167.

136 Crispolti, *Storia e critica del futurismo*, 197.

137 De Felice, *Mussolini il rivoluzionario*, 474.

138 See Paul O'Brien, *Mussolini in the First World War: The Journalist, the Soldier, the Fascist* (Oxford: Berg, 2005), 31–58.

139 Unsigned article, written by Jannelli, "La guerra attuale è il più bel poema futurista apparso finora, dice Marinetti," *Il Piccolo Giornale d'Italia* (Rome), 11 December 1914, Papers of FTM and BCM, GRI, Libroni, box 38, accession no. 920092.

140 Ibid.

141 Ibid.

142 Mussolini to Cangiullo, 24 February 1915, in *ADF*, 353–4. Mussolini did write a letter to Paolo Buzzi, dated 21 November 1914, in which he stated that he both sympathized and identified with the Futurist cause, but this

did not turn into any formal allegiance. The letter is quoted in Alberto Schiavo, *Futurismo e Fascismo* (Rome: Giovanni Volpe, 1981), 17.

143 See Papini, "Il cerchio si chiude," *Lacerba*, 15 February 1914, 1–2; Boccioni, "Il cerchio non si chiude!," *Lacerba*, 1 March 1914, 3–5; Papini, "Cerchi aperti," *Lacerba*, 15 March 1914, 3–5.

144 Luca Somigli, "Past-Loving Florence and the Temptations of Futurism," in *The Oxford Critical and Cultural History of Modernist Magazines*, vol. 3, *Europe, 1880–1940*, ed. Peter Brooker, Sascha Bru, Andrew Thacker, and Christian Weiskorp (Oxford: Oxford University Press, 2013), 469–90; on *Lacerba*, 470–8; here, 476.

145 For more on the history of *Lacerba*, see Claudia Salaris, *Storia del futurismo: Libri, giornali, manifesti* (Rome: Riuniti, 1985), 71–9; Adamson, *Avant-Garde Florence*, 166–81 and 193–203; Alessandro Del Puppo, *"Lacerba," 1913–1915* (Bergamo: Lubrina, 2000), 234–52; and Dante Della Terza, "F.T. Marinetti e i futuristi fiorentini: L'ipotesi politico-letterario di *Lacerba*," *Italica* 61, no. 2 (1984): 147–59.

146 Marinetti to Soffici, 6 August 1914, in *ADF*, 343.

147 Marinetti to Pratella, 12 August 1914, in *ADF*, 344.

148 Adamson, *Avant-Garde Florence*, 193.

149 On 17 August 1914 Balla wrote a letter to Jannelli, stating, "LACERBA dato il movimento guerra è diventata per volontà di Marinetti politica / scrivi tu di politica momento opportuno" (LACERBA because of the war movement has become political owing to Marinetti's wishes / you should write about politics, it is the right time). *BSF*, 146.

150 Soffici to Aldo Palazzeschi, 15 August 1914, in Filippo Tommaso Marinetti and Aldo Palazzeschi, *Carteggio con un'appendice di altre lettere a Palazzeschi*, ed. Paolo Prestigiacomo (Milan: Mondadori, 1978), 158 (hereafter cited as *FTM-AP*).

151 Soffici to Marinetti, no date but end of 1914, cited in Claudia Salaris, *Marinetti editore* (Bologna: Il Mulino, 1990), 152.

152 Soffici to Palazzeschi, 15 April 1914, in *FTM-AP*, 155.

153 Papini to Carrà, 25 August 1914, in *CC-AS*, 195.

154 Pratella to Jannelli, 31 August 1914, in *PPF*, 229–30 (emphasis in the original).

155 Salaris, *Storia del futurismo*, 71.

156 The exact circulation is hard to determine, and figures in letters of the time ranged from 8,000 to 20,000 copies. Marinetti purchased 3,000 of copies of each issue. See Salaris, *Marinetti editore*, 142–4.

157 Marinetti, "Il massacro dei sottomarini," *Lacerba*, 1 September 1914, 4–5.

158 Soffici to Carrà, 29 September 1914, in *CC-AS*, 62.

159 Caroline Tisdall and Angelo Bozzolla, *Futurism* (1977; repr. London: Thames and Hudson, 2003), 177.

160 Papini to Marinetti, 17 September 1914, in F.T. Marinetti Papers, BRB, box 14, folder 845.

161 Soffici to Carrà, 29 September 1914, in *CC-AS*, 62 (emphasis in the original).

162 Ibid. (emphasis in the original).

163 Ibid., 63 (emphasis in the original).

164 Pratella to Jannelli, 17 October 1914, in *PPF*, 231. Pratella wrote that he could not recognise *Lacerba* "come *organo futurista*, spero che tutto sia per finire tra noi e *Lacerba*" (as a *Futurist authority*. I hope everything between us and *Lacerba* is about to finish) (emphasis in the original). On 24 October 1914 Balla wrote to Marinetti: "Disgraziata *Lacerba* / abbandonata dai veri futuristi" (Disgraceful *Lacerba* / abandoned by the real Futurists). *BSF*, 165.

165 Papini and Soffici, "Lacerba, il Futurismo e Lacerba," *Lacerba*, 1 December 1914, 3–5, here 5.

166 Salaris, *Storia del futurismo*, 72.

167 Papini and Soffici, "Lacerba, il Futurismo e Lacerba," 5. In a letter of December 1914 Carrà wrote to Papini, "Mi pare poi ingiusto, come fate nella vostra dichiarazione, diminuire l'importanza e il valore politico che ebbe la dimostrazione contro l'Austria, dimostrazione che fu violentissima come lo provano i numerosi arresti" (I think it is unfair how you undermine, in your declaration, the importance and political value of the demonstration against Austria, which was very violent and resulted in numerous arrests). *CC-GP*, 56.

168 Palazzeschi, Papini, and Soffici, "Futurismo vs Marinettismo," *Lacerba*, 14 February 1915, 1–3. On this debate, see Shirley Vinall, "Marinetti, Soffici, and French Literature," in *International Futurism in Arts and Literature*, ed. Günter Berghaus (Berlin: De Gruyter, 2000), 15–38.

169 Palazzeschi, Papini, and Soffici, "Futurismo vs Marinettismo," 1–3.

170 Elettrone Rotativi [Soffici], "Adampetonismo," *Lacerba*, 24 April 1915, 1–3, here 2.

171 Ibid.

172 Ibid.

173 Marinetti to Folgore, 5 November 1914, in *LF-FTM*, 70 (emphasis in the original).

174 Marinetti to Severini, 26 March 1915, in *ADF*, 356. Earlier that month (5 March) Marinetti had written to Mario Betuda, stating that if Italy's entry into the war were to be delayed any longer, they would establish a Futurist newspaper immediately in Milan. See Marinetti to Betuda, 5 March 1915, MART, Archivio del '900, Fondo Carrà, Car.I.88.2.

175 Remo Chiti (1891–1971), Futurist playwright and journalist. Chiti was
exempted from military service on medical grounds. During the war
he collaborated with *L'Italia Futurista* and *La Folgore Futurista* and
wrote numerous *sintesi*. He was also a signatory of the "Manifesto della
cinematografia futurista" in 1916. In 1919 he served as editor of *Dinamo*
(with Carli and Settimelli), and with Balla founded the Roman branch of
the Futurist Political Party.

176 Chiti to Carli, 10 May 1915, MART, Archivio del '900, Fondo Carli,
Carli.3.2.2.22.

177 Marinetti to Folgore, 16 January 1915, in *LF-FTM*, 77.

178 Mario Sironi (1885–1961), Futurist painter. Active in Futurist circles
from 1912, Sironi joined the movement in spring 1915 and soon after
began serving with the Lombard Battalion of Volunteer Cyclists. He
was a co-signatory of the "L'Orgoglio Italiano" manifesto (1915). In
1916 he enrolled once more as a volunteer and underwent an officers'
training course for the engineers' corps in Turin, leaving in spring 1917
as a second lieutenant. He served with the engineers' corps in the war
zone, before joining the Servizio Propaganda in 1918, where he edited
the Futurist soldier newspaper *Il Montello*. He continued exhibiting as a
Futurist painter for many years after the war.

179 The one exception is an unsigned review of Carrà's book *Guerrapittura* in
the issue published on 23 May 1915 (p. 6), just before Italy's entry into the
war. Pratella had a column about music, and Boccioni one about painting,
while Sironi contributed cartoons and humorous drawings. After Italy's
entry into the war a drawing by Cangiullo entitled *Milano – Dimostrazione
(Sensazione futurista)* was published. See *Gli Avvenimenti*, 19–26 December
1915, no page number.

180 Notari to Cangiullo, 4 February 1915, in *ADF*, 352.

181 Cangiullo to Pratella, 27 March 1915, FPC, Fondo Pratella,
Corrispondenza SC III/INS 5/CAM B.

182 Luciano Nicastro (1895–1977), Futurist free-word poet. He joined
Futurism in 1914, and in spring 1915 he edited *La Balza Futurista* with
Vann'Antò and Jannelli. He was called up in summer 1915 and served as
an officer with the *bombardieri* (bomber corps) for the duration of the war.
He contributed to *Vela Latina* and *L'Italia Futurista* during this time. In
1919 he founded the Messina branch of the Futurist Political Party with
Jannelli.

183 Vann'Antò (1891–1960), pseudonym of Giovanni Antonio Di Giacomo,
Futurist free-word poet. He became involved in Futurism during the
interventionist campaign and edited *La Balza Futurista* with Nicastro

and Jannelli in Messina. He was called up for military service almost immediately following Italy's entry into the war and during the war contributed *parole in libertà* compositions to *L'Italia Futurista* as a *"futurista al fronte."* He was listed among the Futurist war-injured in the first issue of *Roma Futurista* on 20 September 1918, but by 1920 had disassociated himself from the movement.

184 Pratella to Jannelli, 17 March 1915, in *PPF*, 233 (emphasis in the original).

185 Ibid., 235 (emphasis in the original).

186 Pratella to Jannelli, 6 April 1915, in *PPF*, 236 (emphasis in the original).

187 Marinetti to Jannelli, 20 March 1915, in *PPF*, 303–4; Balla to Jannelli, undated but April 1915, in *BSF*, 147.

188 Pratella to Jannelli, 17 May 1915, in *PPF*, 242.

189 Nicastro to Pratella, 16 June 1915, FPC, Fondo Pratella, Corrispondenza SC VIII/INS 31/CAM A.

190 Ibid. Pratella urged the editors to produce at least one more issue following Italy's intervention, but this did not occur. See Pratella to Jannelli, 26 May 1915, FPC, Fondo Pratella, Corrispondenza SC X/INS 3/ CAM A.

191 Salaris, *Storia del futurismo*, 80.

192 Salaris, *Marinetti: Arte e vita futurista*, 165.

193 Giusi Baldissone, *Filippo Tommaso Marinetti* (1986; repr. Milan: Mursia, 2009), 203.

194 Marinetti, Settimelli, and Corra, "Il teatro futurista sintetico," 11 January 1915, in *TIF*, 113–29, here 113.

195 Emilio Settimelli (1891–1954), Futurist writer and playwright. Loosely associated with the movement from 1914, Settimelli joined Futurism in January 1915 when he co-signed, with Marinetti and Bruno Corra, the Futurist synthetic theatre manifesto. He was a soldier only for a few weeks, before being discharged from all military service because of a heart defect. Instead he became a promoter of Futurism and the war effort on the home front. He was the founder and editor of *L'Italia Futurista* in 1916 along with Corra, and later of *Roma Futurista* with Mario Carli and Marinetti. He officially left Marinetti's movement in 1921, although he would remain affiliated with it for many years.

196 Bruno Corra (1892–1976), pseudonym of Bruno Ginanni Corradini, Futurist writer. Corra had collaborated with friends Carli and Settimelli on various projects since 1912, and then in 1915 he co-signed the Futurist synthetic theatre manifesto. He was exempted from military service on medical grounds and spent the war in Florence, editing *L'Italia Futurista*, organizing Futurist theatre performances, and writing novels,

such as *Sam Dunn è morto* (1917), *Io ti amo* (1918), and *L'isola di baci* (with Marinetti, 1918). After the war he began to distance himself from Futurism and became a best-selling novelist in the 1920s.

197 Marinetti, Settimelli, and Corra, "Il teatro futurista sintetico (1915)," in *TIF*, 114 (emphasis in the original).

198 Pratella, "Il Futurismo e la Guerra: Cronaca sintetica," 11 December 1915, Collezione Reggi, APICE.

199 See Giovanni Antonucci, *Cronache del teatro futurista* (Rome: Abete, 1975), 79–96.

200 Antonio Cervi, in *Il resto del Carlino* (Bologna), 6 February 1915, in Antonucci, *Cronache del teatro futurista*, 82; untitled article, in *La Provincia di Padova* (Padua), 10–11 February 1915, in Antonucci, *Cronache del teatro futurista*, 85.

201 Untitled article, *Il Caffaro* (Genoa), 23 February 1915, in Antonucci, *Cronache del teatro futurista*, 95.

202 The Futurists contributed to a special issue of *La Grande Illustrazione* in aid of the Belgian refugees. See *La Grande Illustrazione* 1, no. 13 (January 1915). Boccioni's *Carica di Cavalleria* was printed on page 4. On page 9 there was an excerpt from an unpublished poem of Marinetti's, "I Garibaldini." Aside from this activity the core group of Futurists did not undertake any charitable activities during the interventionist period. This would only occur during the theatre tours of 1916.

203 Sebastiano Sani in *L'Avvenire d'Italia* (Bologna), 5 February 1915, in Antonucci, *Cronache del teatro futurista*, 80 (emphasis in the original).

204 Untitled article, in *Il Secolo XIX* (Genoa), 23 February 1915, in Antonucci, *Cronache del teatro futurista*, 95.

205 Marinetti, Settimelli, and Corra, "Il teatro futurista sintetico (1915)," in *TIF*, 120 (emphasis in the original).

206 Breda, "Il teatro futurista sintetico," *I Pazzi*, 22 February 1915, 2, repr. in *Dossier futurista: Documenti (1910–1919)*, vol. 1, ed. Luciano Caruso (Florence: SPES, 1995).

207 P.B., in *L'Eco di Bergamo* (Bergamo), 20 February 1915, in Antonucci, *Cronache del teatro futurista*, 93.

208 Perhaps the most famous is Marinetti's *Le basi* (The bases), in which only the actors' legs and feet are seen.

209 They had planned a performance in Turin, but it was banned by the authorities. See Marinetti to Betuda, 5 March 1915, MART, Archivio del '900, Fondo Carrà, Car.I.88.2.

210 See Günter Berghaus, *Italian Futurist Theatre, 1909–1944* (Oxford: Oxford University Press, 1998), 193–7; Antonucci, *Cronache del teatro futurista*,

79–96; see articles in *Il Lavoro*, 23 and 24 February 1915, and *Il Caffaro*, 22 and 23 February 1915 (both Genoa) in Franco Ragazzi, *Marinetti: Futurismo in Liguria* (Genoa: De Ferrari, 2006), 58. The pro-Futurist newspaper *Gli Avvenimenti* provided a different view and reviewed the tour positively, suggesting that the days of the Futurists being interrupted and treated badly by audiences were over. See "Un nuovo genere di teatro: 'Il teatro sintetico,'" *Gli Avvenimenti*, 21 February 1915, 6. In an interview with Marinetti for *Il Caffaro* (Genoa, 22 February 1915) the reporter claimed that the tour had been greeted with enormous curiosity "non più baccanali, carenvaleschi non più volgari interruzioni incomposte, ma benevola attenta disposizione da parte del pubblico, interesse vivissimo, polemiche ardentissime dopo" (no longer bacchanalian, carnivalesque, no more rude vulgar interruptions, but a benevolent attentive attitude on the part of the audience, deep interest, passionate discussions afterwards), an account that is at odds with all others of the tour. Ragazzi, *Marinetti: Futurismo in Liguria*, 58.

211 Chiti to Carli, 6 February 1915, MART, Archivio del '900, Fondo Carli, Carli 3.2.2.13. Chiti was referring to the performance in Bologna on 4 February 1915.

212 E. Luciani, "Visti a Verona," in Various authors, *L'Arena: Il giornale di Verona; Centoventicinquesimo anniversario* (Verona: Athesis, 1991), 105.

213 Marinetti to Pratella, 17 February 1915, in *FBP*, 51–2. See also Marinetti to Cangiullo, 17 February 1915, in *FTM-FC*, 87.

214 Giovanni Antonucci, *Lo spettacolo futurista in Italia* (Rome: Nuova Universale Studium, 1974), 39.

215 Most famously, on 5 May 1915, D'Annunzio addressed a demonstration of 100,000 at Quarto at the unveiling of a commemorative monument to Garibaldi's Mille. Demonstrations with tens and hundreds of thousands of pro-intervention supporters were staged all over the country. See Mondini, *La guerra italiana*, 56–7; Brunello Vigezzi, "Le 'radiose giornate del maggio' 1915 nei rapporti dei prefetti," in Vigezzi, *Da Giolitti a Salandra* (Florence: Vallecchi, 1969), 111–201; and Mario Isnenghi, *L'Italia in piazza: I luoghi della vita pubblica dal 1848 ai giorni nostri* (Milan: Mondadori, 1994; Bologna: Il Mulino, 2004), 241–60. Citations refer to the Mulino edition.

216 Boccioni reported that the beginning of a hernia had been discovered and that Marinetti was refused for that reason. Boccioni to Guido Callegari, undated but before 17 May 1915, in *UBLF*, 142. A journalist reported that Marinetti was refused for an "imperfezione ventricolare" (heart defect). Renzo Codara, "Tra le file dei volontari ciclisti," *La Gazzetta dello Sport*

(Milan), 17 May 1915, in *Con Boccioni a Dosso Casina: I testi e le immagini dei futuristi in battaglia*, ed. Dario Bellini (Rovereto: Nicolodi, 2006), 31–2. Marinetti was still recovering at the beginning of June. See Buzzi to Pratella, 8 June 1915, FPC, Fondo Pratella, Corrispondenza SC II/INS 33/ CAM B.
217 "L'unica soluzione del problema economico in Italia secondo F.T. Marinetti (Nostra intervista)," *Gazzetta di Messina e delle Calabrie* (Messina), 28 February 1916, Papers of FTM and BCM, GRI, Libroni, box 39, accession no. 920092.
218 Ibid.

2. Futurism at the Front

1 In 1905 the Central Committee of Volunteer Cyclists and Motorists was established, which in 1908 became an auxiliary military corps officially recognized by the government. These groups engaged in military-style training, including shooting and marching practice and instruction on weapons, logistics, and military tactics. See *Regolamento per l'Applicazione dello Statuto del Corpo Nazionale dei Volontari Ciclisti ed Automobilisti* (Rome: Ministero della Guerra, 1912), Fondo Volontari, MSIG. The cyclists were recruited on a regional basis and were formed into platoons of between sixteen and thirty-two cyclists, which could then be grouped into larger battalions. All recruits had to be Italian citizens; over sixteen years of age; in possession of a bicycle, motorcycle, or automobile; and in good physical health.
2 They engaged in training activities at Gallarate from 31 May to 20 July. Marinetti was not present at this time as he was still recovering from his hernia operation. He joined the battalion on 20 July.
3 Unsigned article, "Entusiastiche manifestazioni cittadine per la partenza dei volontari ciclisti," *Corriere della Sera* (Milan), 22 July 1915, 5.
4 Codara, "I V.C.A. di Milano sono partiti per il fronte. Note e impressioni di un volontario," *Corriere della Sera* (Milan), 26 July 1915, in Bellini, *Con Boccioni a Dosso Casina*, 41.
5 "Entusiastiche manifestazioni cittadine," 5.
6 Marinetti wrote later of their annoyance at this celebratory departure: "I miei amici ed io fummo […] piuttosto seccati che contenti di quell'entusiasmo clamoroso. Pensavamo agl'innumerevoli eroi che già si erano slanciati spavaldi contro le mitragliatrici nemiche; già morti, forse, e ancora insepolti, senza un saluto, senza un fiore prima della battaglia né dopo." (My friends and I were […] more annoyed than happy at that noisy enthusiasm. We thought about the innumerable heroes who had already

hurled themselves cockily towards the enemy machine guns; already dead, maybe, and still unburied, without a good-bye, without a flower before the battle or after.) Marinetti, "Quinte e scene della campagna del Battaglione Lombardo Volontari Ciclisti sul Lago di Garda e sull'Altissimo," *La Gazzetta dello Sport* (Milan), part 1, 31 January 1916, in *Bolaffiarte* 79 (May 1978): 12–14, here 12. Boccioni, however, proudly recalled his mother's brave reaction: "Ci ha seguito in carrozza gridando w l'Italia! w i futuristi! w i volontari!" (She followed us in a carriage shouting Long live Italy! Long live the Futurists! Long live the volunteers!) See Boccioni to Balla, between 21 July and 16 August 1915, in *UBLF*, 143. Marinetti recounted the same episode in *La grande Milano tradizionale e futurista*, 145.

7 Advertisement issued by the Corpo nazionale dei volontari ciclisti e automobilisti, Comitato provinciale di Milano, August 1914, Fondo Volontari, MSIG. Volunteers were required to engage in "una solida ininterotta preparazione" (a solid, uninterrupted preparation) by attending an eight-day-long course, lessons, and refresher training so that they would be ready for Italy's entry into the war.

8 Marinetti to Jannelli, 31 August 1914, in *PFF*, 299.

9 Angeluccio Giudici (a member of the battalion), quoted in Luigi Sansone, *Futuristi a Dosso Casina*, exhibition catalogue, Riva del Garda, 12 July–2 November 2008 (Milan: Mazzotta, 2008), 16.

10 Marinetti, "Quinte e scene della campagna del Battaglione Lombardo Volontari Ciclisti," 31 January 1916, 12.

11 Marinetti to Notari, "Una lettera di F.T. Marinetti dal campo," *Gli Avvenimenti* (Milan), 7 August 1915, 2, in *UBLF*, 323.

12 Boccioni to Pratella, 17 August 1915, in *UBLF*, 143.

13 Codara, "La celebrazione sportiva e futurista del venti settembre fra i volontari ciclisti-automobilisti," *La Gazzetta dello Sport* (Milan), 27 September 1915, in Bellini, *Con Boccioni a Dosso Casina*, 74.

14 Marinetti, "Quinte e scene della campagna del Battaglione Lombardo Volontari Ciclisti," 31 January 1916, 13.

15 Boccioni to Sibilla Aleramo, 11 September 1915, in *UBLF*, 145.

16 Boccioni to Pratella, undated but before 12 September 1915, in *UBLF*, 145.

17 See "Il battaglione lombardo dei volontari ciclisti alla conquista del Dosso Casina," *Corriere della Sera* (Milan), 4 November 1915, and letter from Marinetti to Jannelli, cited in "Marinetti al fronte," *L'Avvenire* (Messina), 23 September 1915, both in Papers of FTM and BCM, GRI, Libroni, box 39, accession no. 920092; Boccioni to Callegari, 11 September 1915, in *UBLF*, 144.

18 Marinetti to Jannelli, 11 September 1915, in *PPF*, 312.

19 Ibid.

20 Umberto Boccioni, *Gli scritti editi e inediti*, ed. Zeno Birolli (Milan: Feltrinelli, 1971), 314.

21 Marinetti to Cangiullo, undated but mid-October 1915, in FTM Papers, BRB, box 26, folder 1365. See also Marinetti to Pratella, 19 October 1915, in *FBP*, 55–6, and Marinetti to Malmerendi [also signed by Boccioni], 12 October 1915, in MART, Archivio del '900, Documenti Malmerendi, no classification.

22 See illustration by Achille Beltrame, "I volontari ciclisti al fuoco. L'incontro con gli alpini alla conquista di Dosso Casina e Dosso Remit," *La Domenica del Corriere* (Milan), 14–21 November 1915, 9; Boccioni, *Gli scritti editi e inediti*, 316–17; Marinetti, "36 pagine dimenticate e inedite del diario di guerra di F.T. Marinetti," ed. Jean Pierre Andreoli de Villers, *Simultaneità* 1 (1997): 77–87; and Filippo Tommaso Marinetti, *Taccuini 1915–1921*, ed. Alberto Bertoni (Bologna: Il Mulino, 1987), 3–42 (hereafter cited as *FTMT*).

23 Boccioni to Vico Baer, undated but post 27 October, and undated but between 27 October and 3 November, in *UBLF*, 149–50 and 151–2; Marinetti, 26–27 October 1915, in *FTMT*, 18.

24 Boccioni to Vanna Piccini, undated but after 27 October 1915, in *UBLF*, 151.

25 Marinetti, 27 October 1915, in *FTMT*, 32.

26 Marinetti to Pratella, 31 October 1915, in *FBP*, 57–8.

27 Marinetti included this phrase in almost identical letters that he wrote to Cangiullo, undated, in *FTM-FC*, 90; to Orazia Prini, undated, reproduced in Sansone, *Futuristi a Dosso Casina*, back cover; and to Jannelli, published in *L'Avvenire* (Messina), 6 November 1915, Papers of FTM and BCM, GRI, Libroni, box 39, accession no. 920092. The expression first appeared in an undated letter to Malmerendi written before the battle of Dosso Casina on 12 October 1915, MART, Archivio del '900, Documenti Malmerendi, no classification.

28 See for example, Linda Landis, "Futurists at War," in *The Futurist Imagination: Word and Image in Italian Futurist Painting, Drawing, Collage, and Free-Word Poetry*, ed. Ann Coffin Hanson, exhibition catalogue, New Haven, 13 April–26 June 1983 (New Haven, CT: The Gallery, 1983), 60–75.

29 Enrico Crispolti, "Zang Tumb Tumb. I futuristi vanno alla guerra. Giochi, burle e travestimenti dei futuristi del battaglione ciclisti," *Bolaffiarte* 79 (May 1978): 10–11, here 11.

30 It is difficult to determine the exact number of Futurists who served in the Italian Army, both because of relatively scarce documentation of the period and because the term *Futurist* was often applied rather loosely by Marinetti during the war years as he was keen to swell the ranks of

his movement as much as possible. Of the thirty-six Futurists listed as members of the "Direzione del movimento futurista" between 1915 and 1917 in the publications of the Edizioni futuriste di "Poesia," at least twenty-three served in the army at some point. In addition, it has been possible to confirm the military service of another thirty-four Futurists who were active in the movement prior to 1918. In the post-war period in *Roma Futurista*, Marinetti began to list the names of numerous Futurists who had died or been injured in the war, but many of these had no Futurist association prior to autumn 1918 and were affiliated with the Futurist Political Party only. There were a number of reasons that some Futurists did not serve in the army: some were too old or too young, others were exempted on medical grounds, and some could delay military service because they were engaged in university study.

31 See Marco Mondini, "The Construction of a Masculine Warrior Ideal in the Italian Narratives of the First World War, 1915–18," *Contemporary European History* 23, no. 3 (2014): 307–27, here 308–10, and Vanda Wilcox, "Encountering Italy: Military Service and National Identity during the First World War," *Bulletin of Italian Politics* 3, no. 2 (2011): 283–302, here 289–90.

32 Boccioni to Piccini, undated but after 27 October 1915, in *UBLF*, 151.

33 Nicastro to Pratella, 15 December 1915, FPC, Fondo Pratella, Corrispondenza SC VIII/INS 31/CAM A.

34 Paolo Orano (1875–1945), Futurist writer. Orano's first official contact with Futurism occurred when his manifesto, "La Dalmazia è italiana e sarà italiana," was published on the front page of *L'Italia Futurista* in September 1917. He did not volunteer for the war but served as a second lieutenant from 1917 and delivered informal propaganda speeches to soldiers at the front. After the war he was heavily involved in the Fascist regime, becoming a senator in 1938.

35 Orano to Marinetti, 20 March 1917, Marinetti Student Notebooks and Other Papers, GRI, box 1, folder 18, accession no. 890122.

36 Cangiullo to Folgore, 8 July 1916, in *LF*, 207.

37 Chiti to Corra, Carli, and Settimelli, undated but 20 October 1913 added in different handwriting, MART, Archivio del '900, Fondo Carli, Carli. 3.2.2.7.

38 Chiti to Carli, 10 May 1915, MART, Archivio del '900, Fondo Carli, Carli. 3.2.2.23.

39 See Eva Cecchinato, "Sotto l'uniforme: I volontari nella Grande Guerra," in *La Grande Guerra*, ed. Mario Isnenghi and Daniele Ceschin (Turin: UTET, 2008), vol. 1, 176–86.

40 Athos Casarini (1883–1917), Futurist painter. He emigrated from Bologna
    to New York in 1909 and was the first to spread knowledge of the
    movement in America. In August 1915 he returned to Italy to volunteer for
    the army, and on 12 September 1917 died on the Carso.

41 The research for this book has uncovered the identity of the Futurist free-
    word poet who until now was known only as Acciaio: Ennio Valentinelli.
    Valentinelli was included in Ezio Godoli's *Dizionario del futurismo*, but
    there was no link made to the pseudonym Acciaio. See Maurizio Scudiero,
    "Ennio Valentinelli," in *Dizionario del futurismo*, ed. Ezio Godoli (Florence:
    Vallecchi, 2004), vol. 2, 1202. Guido Acciai was the *nome di guerra* of
    Valentinelli. Many of the volunteers from Trentino adopted a pseudonym
    to avoid execution for desertion if they were to be captured by the
    Austrians. See also "Documento della Commissione Centrale – Patronato
    dei Fuorusciti Adriatici e Trentini," undated, Archivio Commissione
    Centrale di Patronato dei Fuorusciti Adriatici e Trentini, Fondazione
    Museo Storico del Trentino, Trento (hereafter referred to as FMST), b.5, f.6,
    folder Valentinelli, doc. 1. Valentinelli was also identified as Acciaio in the
    signature to his free-word composition "Bar x alberi in fiore x chanteuse,"
    Vela Latina, 15 January 1916, 1. On Valentinelli, see Selena Daly, "Ennio
    Valentinelli: A Forgotten Futurist," *Modern Language Notes* 34, no. 2 (2016):
    103–15.

42 Umberto Maganzini (1894–1964), pseudonym Trilluci, Futurist free-
    word artist. He first came into contact with Futurism in Rovereto in 1913
    alongside Fortunato Depero. When the war broke out in summer 1914,
    his family moved to Italy, first to Lake Garda and then to Florence. In
    January 1915 he found himself in Rome, intending to study, but he became
    involved again with the Futurists, principally Depero and Balla, as well as
    Boccioni and Marinetti. He showed some work at Depero's exhibition in
    Rome in spring 1916 and later became part of the editorial team for *L'Italia
    Futurista*. He volunteered twice to go to the front in 1917 but was offered
    Libya as a destination because the high command was wary of the possible
    capture and execution of Austrian-born *trentini*. Maganzini refused and
    waited until summer 1918 when (under the pseudonym Ezio Forti) he
    enrolled in an Alpine regiment departing for the front. He returned as a
    second lieutenant and was awarded a war cross for his actions there.

43 This was the fate of Cesare Battisti, Fabio Filzi, and Damiano Chiesa, who
    were all captured, tried for high treason against the Austrian Empire, and
    hanged (Battisti and Filzi on 12 July 1916, Chiesa on 19 May 1916). After
    these high-profile executions the Italian authorities were more cautious

about accepting Austrian citizens from the "unredeemed territories" into the army.

44 Alessio Quercioli, "'Italiani fuori d'Italia': I volontari trentini nell'esercito italiano 1915–1918," in Rasera and Zadra, *Volontari italiani nella Grande Guerra*, 201–14, here 204. The volunteers were also very young: over half of the *trentini* who volunteered in 1915 were aged between twenty and twenty-nine. See Quercioli, "'Italiani fuori d'Italia,'" 208. In summer 1915 Depero was twenty-three years old, and Valentinelli was twenty-one. Maganzini was twenty in 1915.

45 Valentinelli to Commissione Centrale – Patronato dei Fuorusciti Adriatici e trentini, 3 February 1916, Archivio Commissione di Patronato dei Fuorusciti Adriatici e Trentini, FMST, b.5, f.6, folder Valentinelli, doc. 10.

46 Valentinelli to Ministero della Guerra (Direzione generale personale ufficiali, Roma), 3 September 1915, Archivio Commissione di Patronato dei Fuorusciti Adriatici e Trentini, FMST, b.5, f.6, folder Valentinelli, doc. 4; and Valentinelli to Commissione Centrale – Patronato dei Fuorusciti Adriatici e Trentini, 3 February 1916, Archivio Commissione di Patronato dei Fuorusciti Adriatici e Trentini, FMST, b.5, f.6, folder Valentinelli, doc. 10. He remained at the Commission until he began active service.

47 Depero to Amadori, 16 July 1915, MART, Archivio del '900, Fondo Depero, Dep. 3.3.1.4.5.

48 He bitterly regretted this turn of events and viewed this curtailment of his front-line experience as "una cosa molto seccante – avvilente" (something very annoying – depressing). See Depero to Amadori, 31 July 1915, MART, Archivio del '900, Fondo Depero, Dep. 3.3.1.4.13. He stated that he would return to "continuare le mie importantissime occupazioni artistiche" (continue my very important artistic business), although it was clear that this was an undesirable option compared to front-line service. See Depero to Amadori, 27 July 1915, MART, Archivio del '900, Fondo Depero, Dep. 3.3.1.4.10.

49 Depero to Amadori, 16 July 1915, MART, Archivio del '900, Fondo Depero, Dep. 3.3.1.4.5.

50 Gentile, *"La nostra sfida alle stelle,"* 35.

51 Valentinelli to Commissione Centrale – Patronato dei Fuorusciti Adriatici e trentini, 3 February 1916, Archivio Commissione di Patronato dei Fuorusciti Adriatici e Trentini, FMST, b.5, f 6, folder Valentinelli, doc. 10.

52 Valentinelli to Commissione Centrale – Patronato dei Fuorusciti Adriatici e trentini, 17 December 1915, Archivio Commissione di Patronato dei Fuorusciti Adriatici e Trentini, FMST, b.5, f.6, folder Valentinelli, doc. 5.

53 He received 300 lire a month. His salary notwithstanding, early in 1916 he had to reach out to the Central Commission in Rome for a loan of 100 lire for "oggetti di prima necessità, indispensabili nella mia qualità di sottotenente" (items of immediate necessity, essential for my role as a second lieutenant). See Valentinelli to Commissione Centrale – Patronato dei Fuorusciti Adriatici e Trentini, 7 February 1915, Archivio Commissione di Patronato dei Fuorusciti Adriatici e Trentini, FMST, b.5, f.6, folder Valentinelli, doc. 9.

54 Carli to Enea and Luisa Carli [his parents], 15 July 1915, MART, Archivio del '900, Fondo Carli, Carli 3.1.1.13.

55 Ibid.

56 Ibid.

57 Ibid.

58 Carrà to Marinetti, 10 September 1915, Marinetti Correspondence and Papers, GRI, box 2, folder 3, accession no. 850702.

59 Govoni to Marinetti, 20 May 1915, in *CG-FTM*, 99.

60 John Gooch, *The Italian Army and the First World War* (Cambridge: Cambridge University Press, 2014), 65–8, 114, 142–3. See also Barbara Bracco, *La patria ferita: Il corpo dei soldati italiani e la Grande Guerra* (Florence: Giunti, 2012), 39–46.

61 Mondini, *La guerra italiana*, 112–13.

62 Giovanna Procacci, *Soldati e prigionieri italiani nella grande guerra: Con una raccolta di lettere inedite* (Rome: Edizioni Riunite, 1993; Turin: Bollati Boringhieri, 2000), 121. Citations refer to the Bollati Boringhieri edition.

63 Isnenghi and Rochat, *La Grande Guerra*, 278. They report that in 1915 soldiers received a daily allowance of 750 grams of bread, 375 grams of fresh meat, 150 grams of rice or pasta, 350 grams of potatoes or vegetables, 15 grams of coffee, 20 grams of sugar, and a quarter-litre of wine. As the war continued, the rations of meat and potatoes were reduced; coffee was limited to a morning ration only, and a quarter-litre of wine was provided just three times a week. See p. 278n77.

64 Antonio Gibelli, *La grande guerra degli italiani 1915–1918* (Milan: Sansoni, 1998), 101.

65 See Nicola Labanca, "Trincea-trincee," in Isnenghi and Ceschin, *La Grande Guerra*, vol. 2, 620–9.

66 Marinetti, 4 October 1917, in *FTMT*, 140.

67 Marinetti, 18 December 1917–28 January 1918, in *FTMT*, 162–91.

68 Marinetti et al., "L'Orgoglio Italiano," *Vela Latina*, 15 January 1916, 1.

69 Marinetti to Nina Angelini, undated August 1915, and circa the end of October 1915, in *VdelF*, 62.

70 Marinetti, "Quinte e scene della campagna del Battaglione Lombardo Volontari Ciclisti," part 2, 7 February 1916, *La Gazzetta dello Sport* (Milan), in *Bolaffiarte* 79 (May 1978): 14–15, here 15.

71 Boccioni to Vico Baer, undated but between 27 October and 3 November 1915, in *UBLF*, 152.

72 Boccioni to Sig.ra L.F., 9 November 1915, in *UBLF*, 154. He expressed similar sentiments in a letter to Vico Baer, undated but after 27 October 1915, in *UBLF*, 149–50.

73 Marinetti, "Quinte e scene," 7 February 1916, 15. This reflection and other material collected in these articles were based on notes made by Marinetti while he was at the front. See Marinetti, "36 pagine dimenticate," 77–87.

74 Vann'Antò, "Trincea," *L'Italia Futurista*, 10 August 1916, 3.

75 Luciano Nicastro to his mother, 14 November 1917, in *La nostra salvezza: Lettere di guerra 1915–1918* (Florence: Libreria della Voce, 1918), 8.

76 Nicastro to his mother, 22 November 1917, in *La nostra salvezza*, 16.

77 Steiner, "Malaria," in *La chitarra del fante* (Piacenza, Italy: V. Porta, 1920), 41. Valentinelli [signed Acciaio] to Boccioni, 16 November 1915, Boccioni Papers, GRI, box 1, folder 15, accession no. 880380. On instances of diseases among Italian soldiers in the First World War, see Isnenghi and Rochat, *La Grande Guerra*, 276–9.

78 Boccioni to Lota Baer, between the start of September and 12 October 1915, in *UBLF*, 146.

79 Steiner, "La gioia," in *La chitarra del fante*, 29.

80 Marinetti to Pratella, 28 September 1917, in *FBP*, 64. See also Marinetti, 29 April 1917, in *FTMT*, 81–2.

81 Codara, "L'ora triste pei VCA. Congedo e scioglimento," *La Gazzetta dello Sport* (Milan), 6 December 1915, in Bellini, *Con Boccioni a Dosso Casina*, 166.

82 Gino Francioli, "Intervista con Marco Rossi Lecce [1980]," in Francesco Franco, "Il filo tenace di una ricerca 1978–2008: Da un ritaglio di giornale a un inedito video documentario sul futurismo," in Sansone, *Futuristi a Dosso Casina*, 37–41, here 40.

83 Marinetti, "Quinte e scene," 31 January 1916, 12; and 7 February 1916, 15.

84 Marinetti, "Quinte e scene," 31 January 1916, 12.

85 Marinetti, 25–26 July 1918, in *FTMT*, 290.

86 Ibid., 291.

87 Marinetti, 15 September 1918, in *FTMT*, 349 (emphasis in the original).

88 For further discussion of the Arditi see chapter 4.

89 Marinetti, 15 September 1918, in *FTMT*, 348.

90 Carlo Carrà, *La mia vita*, ed. Massimo Carrà (Milan: SE, 1997), 142.

91 Notari to Carrà, 18 January 1917, MART, Archivio del '900, Fondo Carrà, Car.I.97.2.

92 Valentinelli [signed Acciaio] to Boccioni, 16 November 1915, Boccioni
   Papers, GRI, box 1, folder 15, accession no. 8880380.

93 Marinetti, 18 December 1917, in *FTMT*, 164.

94 Marinetti, 7 January 1918, in *FTMT*, 179.

95 On the figure of the *alpino*, see Marco Mondini, *Alpini: Parole e immagini
   di un mito guerriero* (Bari: Laterza, 2008); Fabio Todero, "Alpini, guerra
   in montagna e letteratura: La nascita di un mito," in *Una trincea chiamata
   Dolomiti 1915–1917: Una guerra, due trincee / Ein Krieg, zwei Schützengräben*,
   ed. Willibald Rosner and Emilio Franzina (Udine: Gaspari, 2003), 81–90;
   and Maria Pia Critelli, "L'alpestre faccia dell'eroe: La montagna tra
   simbolo e panorama," in *Der Erste Weltkrieg im Alpenraum: Erfahrung,
   Deutung, Erinnerung / La Grande Guerra nell'arco alpino: Esperienze e
   memoria*, ed. Hermann J.W. Kuprian and Oswald Überegger (Innsbruck:
   Universitätsverlag Wagner, 2006), 61–72.

96 Ugo Tommei (1894–1918), Futurist writer. He worked in Libreria Gonnelli
   in Florence prior to the war, which was a meeting point for the city's
   intellectuals and Futurists. In 1913 he founded the avant-garde journal
   Quartiere Latino and later contributed articles to both *Lacerba* and *L'Italia
   Futurista*. He volunteered for the war in 1915 and by August was serving
   in the infantry at the front lines. He went missing in action on 14 January
   1918.

97 Tommei to Carrà, 8 August 1915, MART, Archivio del '900, Fondo Carrà,
   Car. 1.143.3.

98 Valentinelli [signed Acciaio] to Boccioni, 16 November 1915, Boccioni
   Papers, GRI, box 1, folder 15, accession no. 880380.

99 Luigi Russolo, *L'arte dei rumori* (Milan: Edizioni futuriste di "Poesia," 1916), 43.

100 Marinetti, speech to fellow soldiers, quoted in Codara, "La celebrazione
   sportiva e futurista del venti settembre fra i volontari ciclisti
   automobilisti," *La Gazzetta dello Sport* (Milan), 27 September 1915, in
   Bellini, *Con Boccioni a Dosso Casina*, 73–8.

101 Filippo Argenti, "Coi volontari lombardi sulle rive del Garda," *Vita
   nazionale*, 25 November 1915, Papers of FTM and BCM, GRI, Libroni,
   box 39, accession no. 920092. The article continued: "I concetti qualche
   volta erano forse un po' arditi. Che importa? […] I più entusiasti erano i
   territoriali di una compagnia che si trovava a Malcesine e che partecipava
   coi volontari alla festa." (The concepts were perhaps at times a little too
   daring. Who cares? […] The most enthusiastic were the territorial soldiers
   from a company stationed at Malcesine that took part in the celebrations
   alongside the volunteers).

102 Marinetti, speech to fellow soldiers, quoted in Codara, "La celebrazione
   sportiva e futurista," in Bellini, *Con Boccioni a Dosso Casina*, 77.

103 Ibid.
104 For a more detailed consideration of Marinetti's writings about his time with the Volunteer Cyclists, see Selena Daly, "'The Futurist Mountains': F.T. Marinetti's Experiences of Mountain Combat during the First World War," *Modern Italy* 18, no. 4 (2013): 323–38.
105 Giorgio Rochat, "The Italian Front, 1915–18," in *A Companion to World War 1*, ed. John Horne, trans. Paul O'Brien (Chichester, UK: Wiley-Blackwell, 2012), 82–96, here 85–7.
106 Tait Keller, "The Mountains Roar: The Alps during the Great War," *Environmental History* 14, no. 2 (2009): 253–74, here 260. Gibelli makes a similar argument about the Italian front; see *La grande guerra degli italiani*, 101.
107 Gas was used far less frequently by the Italians; Italy produced only 6,000 tons of gas compared to the 55,000 and 26,000 tons produced by Germany and France, respectively. See Rochat, "The Italian Front," 87.
108 Settimelli, "L'Italia Futurista," *L'Italia Futurista*, 1 June 1916, 1.
109 Carli, "Immagini da trincea," *L'Italia Futurista*, 12 August 1917, 3.
110 Marinetti to Carli, 2 October 1915, in Mario Carli and Filippo Tommaso Marinetti, *Lettere futuriste tra arte e politica*, ed. Claudia Salaris (Rome: Officina Edizioni, 1989), 44 (emphasis in the original; hereafter cited as *MC-FTM*).
111 Boccioni to Guido Callegari, before 11 September 1915, in *UBLF*, 144.
112 Vann'Antò, "Trincea," *L'Italia Futurista*, 10 August 1916, 3 (emphasis in the original).
113 Acciaio, "Artiglieria in azione," *L'Italia Futurista*, 1 November 1916, 3.
114 Ibid.
115 Ibid.
116 Labozzetta (1891–1917?), Futurist free-word poet. He was a contributor of free-word drawings to *L'Italia Futurista* as a *"futurista al fronte."* While recuperating in hospital in Udine in May 1917, Marinetti noted that Labozzetta came often to keep him company. On 27 January 1918 *L'Italia Futurista* listed him among the Futurist war-dead, but there is some uncertainty over whether he did actually die at the front, as he appears listed in some Futurist documents in the 1920s.
117 Luca Labozzetta, "Trincea," *L'Italia Futurista*, 26 August 1917, 3.
118 Guizzidoro (1896–?), pseudonym of Guido Orzi, Futurist free-word poet. He joined the group of Futurists in Rome in 1914 and contributed to *Lacerba*. In 1916 he volunteered for the army and was injured. He then contributed *parole in libertà* to *L'Italia Futurista* as a *"futurista ferito al fronte."* In 1918 he was captured by the Germans and interned in a prison camp near Hanover, with fellow Futurist Angelo Rognoni.

119 Guizzidoro, "Fate sschifo!," *L'Italia Futurista*, 29 April 1917, 1. The piece is dated 7 February 1917.

120 Marinetti, speech to fellow soldiers, quoted in Codara, "La celebrazione sportiva e futurista," in Bellini, *Con Boccioni a Dosso Casina*, 77–8.

121 Diego Leoni, "Guerra di montagna / Gebirgskrieg," in *La prima guerra mondiale*, ed. Stéphane Audoin-Rouzeau, Jean-Jacques Becker, and Antonio Gibelli (Turin: Einaudi, 2007), vol. 1, 237–46, here 241.

122 Marinetti, "La Guerra come complemento logico della natura," *L'Italia Futurista*, 25 February 1917, 1.

123 Ibid. In 1917 Carli expressed similar sentiments regarding mountain combat, writing that "a momenti sembra che le Montagne abbiano ritrovata, dopo tanti secoli di silenzio, un'anima d'acciaio da scaraventare contro delle rivali: e la lotta è quasi sempre fra di loro: lotta di Montagne rombanti" (sometimes it seems that the Mountains have rediscovered, after many centuries of silence, a soul of steel to hurl against their rivals: and the struggle is almost always between them: struggle of rumbling Mountains). See Carli, "Battaglia – Edificio di rumori," *L'Italia Futurista*, 21 October 1917, 2.

124 Filippo Tommaso Marinetti, *Come si seducono le donne* (Florence: Edizioni da Centomila Copie, 1917; Florence: Vallecchi, 2003), 37. Citations refer to the Vallecchi edition.

125 Ibid., 40.

126 Ibid.

127 Marinetti, "Noi rinneghiamo i nostri maestri simbolisti ultimi amanti della luna (1911)," in *TIF*, 302–6, here 303.

128 Marja Härmänmaa, "Futurism and Nature: The Death of the Great Pan?" in *Futurism and the Technological Imagination*, ed. Günter Berghaus (Amsterdam: Rodopi, 2009), 337–60, here 339.

129 On *Vela Latina*, see chapter 3.

130 John J. White, "Iconic and Indexical Elements in Italian Futurist Poetry: F.T. Marinetti's 'Words in Freedom,'" in *Signergy*, ed. Jac Conradie et al. (Amsterdam: John Benjamins, 2010), 129–56, here 129.

131 Johanna Drucker, *The Visible Word: Experimental Typography and Modernist Art (1909–1923)* (Chicago: University of Chicago Press, 1994), 131.

132 On depictions of the Alps in the nineteenth century, see Michael Wedekind and Claudio Ambrosi, eds., *Alla conquista dell'immaginario: L'alpinismo come proiezione di modelli culturali e sociali borghesi tra Otto e Novecento* (Treviso: Edizioni Antilia, 2007).

133 Mazza to Gino Soggetti, 15 June 1918, Gino Soggetti Papers, GRI, box 1, folder 2, accession no. 860387.

134 Walter Adamson, *Embattled Avant-Gardes: Modernism's Resistance to Commodity Culture in Europe* (Berkeley: University of California Press, 2007), 92.

135 Jamar 14 (1897–1987), pseudonym of Piero Gigli, Futurist free-word poet. At age sixteen, he began reading *Lacerba* and composing free-word drawings. By 1916 he was engaged in officers' training at the military academy in Modena, and contributed to *L'Italia Futurista* as a *"futurista al fronte."* He served as an ardito and in 1917 was injured (he subsequently received a silver medal for his service). In hospital in Udine he met Marinetti who was also recovering from his injury. By the early 1920s his Futurist phase had concluded.

136 Cesare Cerati (1898–1969), Futurist free-word poet and playwright. He was named as a *"giovanissimo futurista"* in *L'Italia Futurista* in 1916 and contributed to the short-lived journal *La Folgore Futurista* during the following year. He served with the Arditi troops during the war and was one of the founders of the Futurist Political Party in Milan.

137 Ottone Rosai (1895–1957), Futurist painter. Rosai first met the protagonists of Futurism in 1913 at the exhibition of Futurist paintings organized by *Lacerba* in Florence. In January 1915, during the interventionist period, he volunteered as a grenadier in the army and, after undergoing an accelerated training course, he fought at the front, where he was injured in the same year. He was subsequently injured twice in 1917 and received a silver and a bronze medal for his service. In July 1918 he requested to be transferred to an assault division, to serve as an ardito, an experience about which he wrote in *Il libro di un teppista* (1919). After the war's end he was involved in the establishment of the Futurist Political Party branches in Rome and Florence, and continued his affiliation with Futurism during the 1920s and 1930s.

138 Marinetti, "Il sessanta per cento dei futuristi feriti o mutilati," *Fronte Interno* (Rome), 24 January 1918, Papers of FTM and BCM, Libroni, box 40, accession no. 920092.

139 Nino Formoso, Futurist free-word poet. Originally from Sicily, he was based in Rome, in the orbit of Balla and Depero. He exhibited at a Depero exhibition held in Rome in May 1916. The same year he volunteered for the army, and he was injured in 1917. He contributed to *L'Italia Futurista* as a *"futurista ferito al fronte."* After the war he joined the Futurist Political Party in Rome but had abandoned the movement by 1924.

140 Ugo Cantucci (1896–1916), Futurist free-word poet. He became involved in the movement during the interventionist campaign. He served as a volunteer in the war and was awarded a silver medal, but he was killed early in 1916. His free-word compositions were

published posthumously in *Vela Latina* (February 1916) and *L'Italia Futurista* (June 1916).

141 Boccioni died on 16 August 1916. He had taken a horse to meet with friend and fellow Futurist Giorgio Ferrante. The horse bolted as a car passed, and threw Boccioni off. See the account by Ferrante reprinted in Cesare Biasini Selvaggi, "Sintesi diacronica del futurismo veronese," in *Futurismi a Verona: Il gruppo futurista veronese U. Boccioni*, ed. Giorgio Cortenova and Biasini Selvaggi, exhibition catalogue, Verona, 23 November 2002–30 March 2003 (Milan: Skira, 2002), 17–49, here 17.

142 Buzzi to Pratella, 19 August 1916, in Francesco Balilla Pratella, *Caro Pratella: Lettere scelte e commentate*, ed. Gianfranco Maffina (Ravenna: Edizioni del Girasole, 1980), 76 (hereafter cited as *CP*). Ferrante remembered meeting Marinetti at the train station in Verona and remarked that he looked "d'un colpo invecchiato e disperato" (suddenly aged and hopeless). See Biasini Selvaggi, "Sintesi diacronica del futurismo veronese," 17.

143 Gentile, *"La nostra sfida alle stelle,"* 43.

144 On Italian soldiers' emotions, see Vanda Wilcox, "'Weeping Tears of Blood': Exploring Italian Soldiers' Emotions in the First World War," *Modern Italy* 17, no. 2 (2012): 171–84.

145 Salaris, *Filippo Tommaso Marinetti*, 149.

146 Isnenghi, *Il mito della grande guerra*, 179. Berghaus makes a similar point in *Futurism and Politics*, 83.

147 The only moment at which any doubt crept into his self-presentation was the evening before the Volunteer Cyclists and the Alpini were due to launch their assault at Dosso Casina in October 1915. In a letter to Buzzi and Pratella, Marinetti's fear of death and the contemplation of his own mortality were evident for the first time: "La battaglia sarà seria. Sono felice di dare all'Italia nostra grande forte e gloriosa, la mia vita di Futurista Italiano, la mia vita che considero *importantissima*. Spero però di non essere ucciso domani per continuare a massacrare Austriaci e per vedere lo sfacelo dell'Austria passatista odiatissima nemica. Spero di non essere ucciso per potere riprendere con te la grande lotta futurista." (The battle will be serious, I am happy to give my Italian Futurist life to our great, strong and glorious Italy, my life which I consider to be of *great importance*. I hope I am not killed tomorrow, so that I can continue to slaughter Austrians and to see the undoing of passéist Austria, most hated enemy. I hope I am not killed tomorrow so that I can take up again with you the great Futurist struggle.) See Marinetti to Pratella and Buzzi, 22 October 1915, in *FBP*, 57 (emphasis in the original).

148 Marinetti to Cangiullo, between December 1916 and February 1917, in *FTM-FC*, 113 (emphasis in the original).

149 Marinetti to Cangiullo, 31 December 1916, in *FTM-FC*, 112–13 (emphasis in the original).

150 Pasqualino 13 anni (1900–75), pseudonym of Pasquale Cangiullo, Futurist free-word poet and younger brother of Francesco Cangiullo. Although Pasquale was already sixteen, Marinetti chose the name "Pasqualino 13 anni" for him, and he was named as a *"giovanissimo futurista"* in the second issue of *L'Italia Futurista* of 15 June 1916. He was a frequent contributor to *L'Italia Futurista* and in 1917, with his brother, produced a free-word drawing of Marinetti entitled *Marinetti ferito*. After the war he continued to show his work at numerous Futurist exhibitions.

151 Marinetti to Pasqualino Cangiullo (Pasqualino 13 anni), undated but after October 1916, FPC, Fondo Cangiullo, Corrispondenza SC II/INS 24/CAM B.

152 Marinetti to Cangiullo, undated but end of 1917, in *FTM-FC*, 116 (emphasis in the original). Marinetti frequently expressed his desire to see Pratella and recalled fond memories of time spent together in Pratella's house. See Marinetti to Pratella, 20 April 1917, 24 November 1917, and 1 January 1918, in *FBP*, 63–4. At the end of September 1917 he wrote of his desire to see Cangiullo. See Marinetti to Cangiullo, undated but end of September 1917, in *FTM-FC*, 119.

153 Marinetti to Pratella, 11 March 1918, in *FBP*, 65. Marinetti had no immediate family. His brother had died in 1897, his mother in 1902, and his father in 1907. His maidservants, Nina and Marietta Angelini, fulfilled these roles for him, providing practical support by sending clothes and food to the front, as well as emotional support.

154 Marinetti to Marietta Angelini, 25 April 1918, in *VdelF*, 84.

155 Fabio Caffarena, *Lettere dalla Grande Guerra: Scritture del quotidiano, monumenti della memoria, fonti per la storia; Il caso italiano* (Milan: Unicopli, 2005), 50. For example, in May 1917, when Marinetti was injured, he stopped writing to anybody except the Angelini sisters, because he was in pain and did not wish to reveal this to his Futurist friends.

156 Boccioni was very enthusiastic at the beginning of his service with the Volunteer Cyclists. He told Guido Callegari that "la mia salute e il mio umore sono eccellenti […] Io sono veramente felice" (my health and mood are excellent […] I am truly happy), and Sibilla Aleramo that "la mia salute è ottima malgrado sforzi terribili. L'entusiasmo è moltiplicato sono felice!" (my health is excellent despite the terrible exertions. My enthusiasm has multiplied I am happy!). See Boccioni to Callegari and to Aleramo, both before 11 September 1915, in *UBLF*, 144–5.

157 Boccioni to Ferruccio Busoni, 19 July 1916, in *UBLF*, 177.

158 Boccioni to Vittoria Colonna, 9 July 1916, in *UBLF*, 165.

159 Boccioni to Busoni, 19 July 1916, in *UBLF*, 177.

160 Primo Conti (1900–1988), Futurist painter. Conti first came into contact
     with the Futurists in Florence at the age of thirteen. He was a contributor
     to *L'Italia Futurista*, and his volume *Imbottigliature* was issued under
     the magazine's publishing wing in 1917. By early 1918 he had been
     entrusted with the editorship of *L'Italia Futurista*, but the magazine ceased
     publication in February 1918. Shortly afterwards, he enrolled in the army
     and was assigned to service in Mantua.

161 Conti to Francesco Meriano, 14 March 1918, in FPC, Fondo Meriano,
     Corrispondenza SC v/INS 18 (emphasis in the original).

162 Meriano to Folgore, 19 April 1917, in *LF*, 256.

163 Acciaio [written "Acciai"], "La terra sta male," *L'Italia Futurista*,
     10 February 1917, 3.

164 Steiner, "Gli scoiattoli," in *La chitarra del fante*, 15.

165 Folgore to Soffici, 15 July 1917, in *ADF*, 377.

166 Folgore, "Poema della Guardia," Folgore Papers, GRI, box 5, folder 19,
     accession no. 910141.

167 Marinetti to Pratella, 20 August 1915, in *FBP*, 61 (emphasis in the
     original). In this edition the letter is incorrectly dated 20 August 1916
     instead of 1915.

168 Boccioni to Lota Baer, undated but between the beginning of September
     and 12 October 1915, in *UBLF*, 146.

169 Carrà, *La mia vita*, 145.

170 Carrà to Meriano, 15 May 1917, MART, Archivio del '900, Fondo Carrà,
     Car.I.93.8.

171 Carli to Marinetti, August 1918, in *FTM-MC*, 52. In 1916 Pratella had
     complained to Jannelli: "Voi mi parlate di solitudine, io potrei cantarvi
     sullo stesso tono. Lavoro accanitamente nel silenzio, abbandonato
     dagli altri." (You speak to me of solitude, I could do the same. I work
     relentlessly in silence, abandoned by everyone else.) See Pratella to
     Jannelli, 23 July 1916, in *PPF*, 249.

172 Francesco Balilla Pratella, *Testamento: Prima edizione integrale*, ed.
     Rosetta Berardi and Francesca Serra (Ravenna: Edizioni del Girasole,
     2012), 192.

173 Pratella to Settimelli, 30 August 1917, FPC, Fondo Settimelli,
     Corrispondenza/SC I/INS 25/CAM A.

174 Boccioni to Colonna, 12 July 1916, in *UBLF*, 166 (emphasis in the original).

175 Boccioni to Colonna, 26 July 1916, in *UBLF*, 179.

176 Boccioni to Vico Baer, 29 July 1916, in *UBLF*, 180.

177 Boccioni to Busoni, 12 August 1916, in *UBLF*, 186.

178 Cangiullo to Marinetti, undated but August 1916, FPC, Fondo Pratella, Corrispondenza SC III/INS 5/CAM 1.

179 Cangiullo to Pratella, 12 August 1916, FPC, Fondo Pratella, Corrispondenza SC III/INS 5/CAM C.

180 Cangiullo to Marinetti, undated but August 1916, FPC, Fondo Pratella, Corrispondenza SC III/INS 5/CAM I.

181 Marinetti to Pratella, 17 August 1916, FPC, Fondo Pratella, Corrispondenza SC VII/INS 13/CAM D.

182 "La serata d'addio dei Volontari Ciclisti al Condominio," *Unione: Giornale della democrazia gallaratese* (Gallarate), 17 July 1915, 3.

183 For photographs of the Futurist decorations, see Sansone, *Futuristi a Dosso Casina*, 45.

184 Codara, "I V.C.A. di Milano sono partiti per il fronte," *La Gazzetta dello Sport* (Milan), 26 July 1915, in Bellini, *Con Boccioni a Dosso Casina*, 38. See also Luigi Russolo, "Un ricordo di Luigi Russolo," *La Martinella di Milano* (October 1958), in Bellini, *Con Boccioni a Dosso Casina*, 38.

185 "La serata di beneficienza dei volontari ciclisti al Condominio," *Unione* (Gallarate), 10 July 1915, 3.

186 "La serata d'addio dei Volontari Ciclisti al Condominio," *Unione* (Gallarate), 17 July 1915, 3.

187 "Zum… tu… tum," 3 November 1915, Fondo Volontari, MSIG.

188 "In occasione del banchetto dell'11 novembre 1915," 11 November 1915, Fondo Volontari, MSIG.

189 "L'addio agli ufficiali," Fondo Volontari, MSIG.

190 Rosai to Soffici, 5 March 1915, in Ottone Rosai and Ardengo Soffici, *Carteggio 1914–1951*, ed. Elena Pontiggia (Milan: Abscondita, 2010), 20.

191 Carli to Enea Carli, 17 July 1915, MART, Archivio del '900, Fondo Carli, Carli.3.1.1.14 (emphasis in the original).

192 Rognoni to Soggetti, undated but 1917, Soggetti Papers, GRI, box 1, folder 3, accession no. 860387.

193 Pratella to Jannelli, 17 May 1915, in *PPF*, 241.

194 Marinetti to Orano, 12 February 1917, Marinetti Correspondence and Papers, GRI, box 8, folder 5, accession no. 850702.

195 Alexander Watson, *Enduring the Great War: Combat, Morale, and Collapse in the German and British Armies, 1914–1918* (Cambridge: Cambridge University Press, 2008), 107.

196 Antonio Gibelli, *L'officina della guerra: La Grande Guerra e le trasformazioni del mondo mentale*, 3rd ed. (Turin: Bollati Boringhieri, 2007), 164–8.

197 Ludovic Tournès, "The Landscape of Sound in the Nineteenth and
      Twentieth Centuries [review article]," *Contemporary European History* 13
      (2004): 493–504, here 497.
198 The term *symphony of the front* appears in Glenn Watkins, *Proof through the
      Night: Music and the Great War* (Berkeley: University of California Press,
      2003), 61. On noise in the First World War, see Eric Leed, *No Man's Land:
      Combat and Identity in World War 1* (Cambridge: Cambridge University
      Press, 1979), 123–31; Gibelli, *La grande guerra degli italiani*, 37–42; and
      Gibelli, *L'officina della guerra*, 164–79. On Futurism and the noises of war,
      see Selena Daly, "Futurist War Noises: Coping with the Sounds of the
      First World War," in "Italian Sound," ed. Deanna Shemek and Arielle
      Saiber, special issue, *California Italian Studies* 4, no. 1 (2013): 1–16.
199 Russolo, *L'arte dei rumori*, 43.
200 Ibid., 43–4.
201 Buzzi, "I giovani poeti e la guerra," *L'Italia Futurista*, 1 December 1916,
      3–4. Nadia Marchioni has argued that the roots of the return to order in
      Futurist art of the 1920s are to be found in the sketches of soldiers in the
      trenches, such as those of Mario Sironi and Anselmo Bucci, which often
      featured the human figure. However, when these few sketches are viewed
      alongside the experimental *parole in libertà* drawings published in *L'Italia
      Futurista*, such a thesis seems less sustainable. See Marchioni, *La Grande
      Guerra degli artisti: Propaganda e iconografia bellica in Italia negli anni della
      prima guerra mondiale*, exhibition catalogue, Florence, 3 December 2005–25
      March 2006 (Florence: Pagliai Polistampi, 2005), 32–3.
202 Marinetti, "Distruzione della sintassi, Immaginazione senza fili, Parole in
      libertà (1913)," in *TIF*, 65–80, here 70.
203 There is also some evidence that the concepts of *parole in libertà*
      penetrated the consciousness of soldiers who were not officially affiliated
      with Marinetti's movement. *Il Resto del Carlino* published a letter in
      summer 1915 by a "soldato futurista" T.F., who recalled the sounds in the
      trenches as "Zsssss … punfff […] Trrrr." See untitled article, *Il Resto del
      Carlino* (Bologna), 25 July 1915. Another journalist identified a letter by
      a second lieutenant as being "quasi futurista" (almost Futurist) because
      of its use of mathematical symbols to express his impressions of the war.
      See "Il futurismo al campo," *Il Secolo* (Milan), 7 September 1915. Both in
      Papers of FTM and BCM, GRI, Libroni, box 39, accession no. 920092.
204 See Vieri Nannetti, "Piccolo Posti," *L'Italia Futurista*, 15 June 1916, 3;
      Vann'Antò, "Trincea," *L'Italia Futurista*, 10 August 1916, 3; Jamar 14,
      "Ferita + ospedale + etisia," *L'Italia Futurista*, 12 August 1917, 3; and
      Labozzetta, "Trincea," *L'Italia Futurista*, 26 August 1917, 3.

205 Leed, *No Man's Land*, 131.

206 See Mary R. Habeck, "Technology in the First World War: The View from Below," in *The Great War and the Twentieth Century*, ed. Jay Winter, Geoffrey Parker, and Mary R. Habeck (New Haven, CT: Yale University Press, 2000), 99–131, here 113.

207 Marinetti to Pratella, 25 May 1917, in *FBP*, 63.

208 On mental and psychiatric illness among Italian soldiers and officers, see Bruna Bianchi, "Delirio, smemoratezza e fuga: Il soldato e la patologia della paura," in *La Grande Guerra: Esperienza, memoria, immagini*, ed. Diego Leoni and Camillo Zadra (Bologna: Il Mulino, 1986), 73–104.

209 On different meanings of "zona di guerra" during the war, see Nicola Labanca, "Zona di guerra," in Isnenghi and Ceschin, *La Grande Guerra*, vol. 2, 606–19.

210 During the First World War, almost four billion letters and postcards were sent in Italy. Of these, approximately 2.1 billion were sent from the front lines to the rest of Italy, 1.5 billion from Italy to the front lines, and 263 million from one part of the war zone to another. See Caffarena, *Lettere dalla Grande Guerra*, 40.

211 Marinetti had long understood the importance of establishing a group identity through branded notepaper. See *Futurismi postali: Balla, Depero e la communicazione postale futurista*, ed. Maurizio Scudiero et al., exhibition catalogue Rovereto, 11 April–18 May 1986; Grado, 31 May–31 August 1986 (Rovereto: Longo, 1986), 29–30.

212 Marinetti to Cangiullo, undated but before 2 September 1915, in Sansone, *Futuristi a Dosso Casina*, 21.

213 The earliest example of a "lettera tipo Cangiullo" that I have been able to locate is dated 2 September. See Cangiullo to Pratella, 2 September 1915, in Luisa Bedeschi, "Dal carteggio di Francesco Balilla Pratella," in *Note futuriste: L'archivio Francesco Balilla Pratella e il cenacolo artistico lughese*, ed. Orlando Piraccini and Daniele Serafini (Bologna: Compositori, 2010), 35–40, here 36. Marinetti also experimented with a modest reform of the epistolary tradition during the war, by devising a template for a love letter, and a code to be used (i.e., 1= I love you a lot, 2= I will get my revenge!, 3= I desire you, etc.). See Salaris, *Filippo Tommaso Marinetti*, 165.

214 Marinetti to Buzzi, 12 September 1915, in Sansone, *Futuristi a Dosso Casina*, 21.

215 Boccioni to Cangiullo (also signed by Marinetti), September–October 1915, in Sansone, *Futuristi a Dosso Casina*, 28. The letter template was frequently used during the autumn of 1915 both by the Volunteer Cyclists (Marinetti, Boccioni, and Sant'Elia) and by Futurists on the home front (Buzzi and Cangiullo), but it was rarely used after the disbandment of the

battalion, perhaps because many of the movement's protagonists were not fighting in 1916, or because of the shortage of paper. The postcard continued to circulate until at least 1917, but Marinetti often ignored the predefined headings and used the postcards to write a brief message or communicate his new address to those at home. See for example Marinetti to Rognoni, 23 January 1917, in Rognoni Correspondence, GRI, box 2, folder 4a, accession no. 850150; Marinetti to Vieri Nannetti, 7 March 1917, in FPC, Fondo Nannetti, FC/NVN I.C.1; and Marinetti to Carrà, 5 May 1917, in MART, Archivio del '900, Fondo Carrà, Car. 1.88.4.

216 See Caffarena, *Lettere dalla Grande Guerra*; Martha Hanna, "A Republic of Letters: The Epistolary Tradition in France during World War 1," *American History Review* 108, no. 5 (2003): 1338–61; Martin Lyons, "French Soldiers and Their Correspondence: Towards a History of Writing Practice in the First World War," *French History* 17, no. 1 (2003): 79–95; Jessica Meyer, *Men of War: Masculinity and the First World War in Britain* (Basingstoke, UK: Palgrave Macmillan, 2009), 14–46.

217 Jay Winter, "The Practice of Metropolitan Life in Wartime," in *Capital Cities at War: Paris, London, Berlin, 1914–1919*, ed. Jay Winter and Jean-Louis Robert (Cambridge: Cambridge University Press, 2007), vol. 2, 1–19, here 2.

218 Gibelli, *L'officina della guerra*, 55.

219 Caffarena, *Lettere dalla Grande Guerra*, 69.

220 Gino Soggetti (1898–1958), Futurist free-word poet and playwright. As a student in 1916, he became active in Futurist circles in Pavia. In January and February 1917 he edited the journal *La Folgore Futurista* with Angelo Rognoni, before being called up for military service. In June he was training to be an officer with the infantry, by November he was at the front lines, and by April of 1918 he was serving as a second lieutenant at the front. After the war he participated in the "Grande esposizione nazionale futurista" and in other Futurist exhibitions and left the movement in 1924. He temporarily rejoined the movement almost a decade later.

221 See three letters from Marinetti to Rognoni, all undated but between late December 1916 and mid-February 1917, Rognoni Correspondence, GRI, box 2, folder 4, accession no. 850150.

222 Marinetti to Vieri Nannetti, undated but June 1917, FPC, Fondo Nannetti, FC/NVN I.C.1; Marinetti to Soggetti, undated but between 7 and 10 June 1917, Soggetti Papers, GRI, box 1, folder 1, accession no. 860387; Marinetti to Meriano, 24 July 1917, in Giovanni Lista, ed., "Francesco Meriano parolibero futurista: Con carteggio inedito di Marinetti," *Sì & No* 4 (March 1975): 104–19, here 116; Marinetti to Neri Nannetti, received 4 January 1918, FPC, Fondo Nannetti, FC/NVN I.C.1.

223 Marinetti to Carli, 26 September 1918, in *MC-FTM*, 57–8; three letters from Marinetti to Carli, all undated but October 1918, in *MC-FTM*, 62, 64, 66.

224 See for example, Carrà to Folgore, 11 May 1918, in *LF*, 209; and Mazza to Rognoni, 26 January 1917, Rognoni Correspondence, GRI, box 2, folder 5, accession no. 850150, in which he provided the addresses of Folgore, Depero, Balla, and Auro d'Alba, all based in Rome, as well as the addresses of Russolo, Sironi, Jannelli, and Carli, all serving with the army at that time.

225 Gerardo Dottori (1884–1977), Futurist painter and free-word poet. Dottori joined the movement at the end of 1911 or the beginning of 1912, having made contact with Balla in Rome. He organized the 1914 *serata futurista* in his home town of Perugia. In 1915 he departed for the front, where he remained for the duration of the war. During the conflict he contributed free-word compositions to *L'Italia Futurista* as a *"futurista al fronte,"* under the pseudonym G. Voglio. In the 1930s he became one of the most important exponents of Futurist *arte sacra* and *aeropittura*.

226 Dottori to Marinetti, 20 August 1916, Boccioni Papers, GRI, box 1, folder 24, accession no. 880380.

227 Giuseppe Sprovieri (1890–1988), Futurist gallery owner and critic. In December 1913 Sprovieri opened the first permanent Futurist gallery in Rome, and the following year a branch in Naples, which were the sites of numerous Futurist events. Both closed in August 1914 on account of the war. Already by early May 1915 Sprovieri was training to become a second lieutenant with the artillery and later with the bomber corps. By December 1916 he had received the grade of second lieutenant and served with both artillery and bombardier regiments during the war.

228 Sprovieri to Folgore, 10 April 1917, Folgore Papers, GRI, box 2, folder 49, accession no. 910141.

229 Valentinelli [signed Acciaio] to Marinetti, 22 August 1916, Boccioni Papers, GRI, box 1, folder 15, accession no. 880380.

230 Sprovieri to Folgore, 16 June 1916, in *LF*, 318.

231 Orano to Marinetti, 6 June 1917, Marinetti Student Notebooks and Other Papers, GRI, box 1, folder 18, accession no. 890122.

232 Orano to Marinetti, 22 March 1918, Marinetti Student Notebooks and Other Papers, GRI, box 1, folder 18, accession no. 890122.

233 Marinetti, quoted in Cangiullo, *Le serate futuriste*, 157.

234 Cesare Cerati to Balla, 28 April 1918, Letters to Balla, GRI, folder 1, accession no. 860388.

235 Valentinelli [signed Acciaio] to Marinetti, 22 August 1916, Boccioni Papers, GRI, box 1, folder 15, accession no. 880380.

3. *Futurismo moderato*

1 Marinetti, "Per la guerra, sola igiene del mondo," no date but May–June 1915, Collezione Reggi, APICE.

2 Ibid.

3 The war forced Giuseppe Sprovieri to close the two branches of his Permanent Futurist Gallery in Rome and Naples, which had been opened in December 1913 and May 1914, respectively. They remained closed until 1918. See Berghaus, *Italian Futurist Theatre*, 234. *La Balza Futurista* also ceased publication.

4 Carrà to Soffici, 26 May 1915, in *CC-AS*, 90.

5 Ibid. Carrà remained sceptical of the desire to voluntarily "abandon" one's artistic trenches for the front lines. See Carrà to Papini, undated but end of August 1915, in *CC-GP*, 63.

6 Carrà to Papini, 8 June 1915, in *CC-GP*, 61.

7 Balla to Nina and Marietta Angelini, 23 July 1915, in *BSF*, 106.

8 Buzzi to Pratella, 17 June 1915, in *CP*, 74.

9 Settimelli to Pratella, 5 June 1915, in *CP*, 84–5. Buzzi commented that Marinetti had ceased engaging in correspondence, which was exacerbated by the fact that his secretary and scribe Decio Cinti was also serving in the army. See Buzzi to Pratella, 17 June 1915, in *CP*, 74.

10 Buzzi to Pratella, 11 September 1915, in Bellini, *Con Boccioni a Dosso Casina*, 65.

11 Pratella to Boccioni, 3 November 1915, in *ADF*, 367.

12 Boccioni to Cangiullo, undated but autumn 1915, in Sansone, *Futuristi a Dosso Casina*, 28.

13 Marinetti to Pratella, 20 August 1915, in *ADF*, 361–2.

14 Marinetti to Pratella, 3 September 1915, in *FBP*, 55 (emphasis in the original).

15 Marinetti to Buzzi, 12 September 1915, in Paolo Buzzi, *Futurismo: Scritti, carteggi, testimonianze*, ed. Mario Morini (Milan: Palazzo Sormani, 1983), vol. 3, 295.

16 Folgore to Severini, no date but January 1916, in "Lettere e documenti," ed. Piero Pacini, *Critica d'arte* 17, no. 111 (May–June 1970): 8–56, here 47.

17 Pratella to Jannelli, 30 December 1915, in *PPF*, 248.

18 Pratella to Settimelli, 14 November 1915, FPC, Fondo Settimelli, Corrispondenza/SC I/INS 25/CAM A.

19 Valentinelli to Carrà, 21 December 1915, MART, Archivio del '900, Fondo Carrà, Car.I.146.1.

20 Marinetti to Pratella, 31 December 1915, in *FBP*, 59.

21 Ibid.

22 For a detailed consideration of the changing relationship between Futurism and the press during the war years, see Selena Daly, "Constructing the Futurist Wartime Hero: Futurism and the Public, 1915–1919," in "The Great War and the Modernist Imagination," ed. Luca Somigli and Simona Storchi, special issue, *Annali d'Italianistica* 33 (2015): 205–21.

23 Mario Fiorini, "Il genio in tutte le armi," *Il Secolo XX Ars et Labor* (Milan), July 1915, 655–62, here 655, Fondo Volontari, MSIG.

24 Ibid., 622.

25 Valeria Vampa, "I Futuristi in Azione," *Gran Mondo* (Rome), 25 October 1915, Papers of FTM and BCM, GRI, Libroni, box 38, accession no. 920092.

26 Dario Grammona, "I futuristi e la guerra," *La Libreria Economica*, 1 September 1915, Papers of FTM and BCM, GRI, Libroni, box 39, accession no. 920092.

27 Carlo Scarfoglio, "Il Benaco," *La Stampa* (Turin), 28 August 1915, 3.

28 See *Lo Sport illustrato e la Guerra* (Milan), 30 July 1915, 326, for an account of Marinetti's sporting achievements, probably written by Codara, and an extract from the "In quest'anno futurista" manifesto. See also in the same issue, Codara, "I Volontari Ciclisti ed Automobilisti," 321–3.

29 Codara, "Tra le file dei volontari cicilisti," *La Gazzetta dello Sport* (Milan), 17 May 1915, and "La celebrazione sportiva e futurista," *La Gazzetta dello Sport* (Milan), 27 September 1915, both in Bellini, *Con Boccioni a Dosso Casina*, 31 and 74 respectively.

30 Filippo Argenti, "Coi volontari lombardi sulle rive del Garda," *Idea Nazionale* (Rome), 25 November 1915, Papers of FTM and BCM, GRI, Libroni, box 39, accession no. 920092. A shortened version of this article entitled "Episodi e figure della guerra" appeared in *Corriere del Polesine* (Rovigo), 1 December 1915, Papers of FTM and BCM, GRI, Libroni, box 39, accession no. 920092. Photographs of the Futurists in action were also common. See "Il caposcuola del futurismo F.T. Marinetti, volontario," *La Domenica del Corriere* (Milan), 11 July 1915; "Marciare non marcire," *Bianco, Rosso, Verde* (Milan), 1 August 1915; "I futuristi alla guerra," *Gli Avvenimenti* (Milan), 12 December 1915, all Papers of FTM and BCM, GRI, Libroni, box 39, accession no. 920092. See also "I futuristi volontari al fronte," *Lo Sport illustrato e la Guerra* (Milan), 15 February 1916, 118.

31 Marinetti, "L'unica soluzione del problema finanziario," December 1915, Collezione Reggi, APICE. It subsequently appeared in *Vela Latina*, 19 February 1916, 1.

32 Marinetti, et al., "L'Orgoglio Italiano," *Vela Latina*, 15 January 1916, 1.

33 "Futurist View of the Past," *The Standard* (London), 18 November 1913, 11.

34 Marinetti, "L'unica soluzione del problema finanziario," December 1915, Collezione Reggi, APICE.

35 Marinetti, "Fondazione e Manifesto del Futurismo (1909)," in *TIF*, 11.

36 "Futurist View of the Past," *Standard* (London), 18 November 1913, 11.

37 Marinetti, "L'unica soluzione del problema finanziario," December 1915, Collezione Reggi, APICE.

38 Ibid.

39 Marinetti et al., "L'Orgoglio Italiano," 1. For a further discussion of this manifesto and of the Futurist experiences as Alpini, see Daly, "'The Futurist Mountains.'"

40 See Marinetti, "Quinte e scene della campagna del Battaglione Lombardo Volontari Ciclisti," 31 January and 7 February 1916. Interviews with Marinetti appeared in "Marinetti reduce dal fronte parla della guerra e del futurismo," *Giornale d'Italia* (Rome), 16 December 1915; "La guerra veduta da un futurista," *Il Secolo e il Giornale del Mattino* (Bologna), 23 December 1915; "L'unica soluzione del problema economica in Italia secondo F.T. Marinetti," *Gazzetta di Messina e delle Calabrie* (Messina), 28 February 1916; C.I. Ravida, "Marinetti reduce dal fronte," *Corriere di Mantova* (Mantua), 12 March 1916, all Papers of FTM and BCM, GRI, Libroni, box 39, accession no. 920092.

41 Marinetti, "La declamazione dinamica e sinottica," 11 March 1916, in *TIF*, 122–9, here 122.

42 Severini to Pratella, 23 August 1916, in *CP*, 71.

43 Ibid., 70. From May 1915 to November 1918 there were only eight Futurist exhibitions in Italy: two by Balla (December 1915 and October 1918), one posthumous one by Boccioni (December 1916–January 1917), three by Depero (April–May 1916, September 1917, and April 1918), one by Carrà (December 1917–January 1918), and one by Francesco and Pasqualino Cangiullo (November 1918). See Enrico Crispolti, ed., *Cataloghi di esposizioni* (Rome: De Luca / Consiglio nazionale delle ricerche, 2010), 112–43.

44 Marinetti, Settimelli, and Corra, "Il teatro futurista sintetico," 11 January 1915 and 18 February 1915, in *TIF*, 114 (emphasis in the original).

45 Emanuela Scarpellini, "Teatro e guerra," in *Milano in guerra 1914–1918: Opinione pubblica e immagini delle nazioni nel primo conflitto mondiale*, ed. Alceo Riosa (Milan: Unicopli, 1997), 153–79, here 159.

46 Marinetti to Pratella, 16 March 1916, referring to the premiere of the *teatro sintetico* tour at the Teatro Niccolini, Florence, March 1916, in *FBP*, 61 (emphasis in the original). In the same month Marinetti asked Jannelli for a new *sintesi* that would be "facilmente rappresentabile e potentemente patriottica e antitedesca" (easy to stage and powerfully *patriotic* and *anti-German*). See Marinetti to Jannelli, 24 March 1916, in *PPF*, 315 (emphasis in the original).

47 Scarpellini, "Teatro e guerra," 170.

48 Teresa Bertilotti, "Pratiche urbane, *entertainments* e rappresentazione della violenza," *Memoria e ricerca* 38 (2011): 41–55, here 45.

49 See for example, *Il teatrino dell'amore*, which features an animate children's toy theatre and sideboard, in Filippo Tommaso Marinetti, *Teatro*, ed. Jeffrey T. Schnapp (Milan: Mondadori, 2004), vol. 2, 547–50.

50 See Marinetti, *La camera dell'ufficiale*, in *Teatro*, vol. 2, 565–6.

51 See Marinetti, *Il soldato lontano*, in *Teatro*, vol. 2, 571–2.

52 See Marinetti, *L'arresto*, in *Teatro*, vol. 2, 567–9, here 567.

53 Marinetti to Pratella, 16 March 1916, in *FBP*, 61.

54 See Berghaus, *Italian Futurist Theatre*, 85–155.

55 Baccio Bacci, in *Il Nuovo Giornale* (Florence), 9–10 March 1916, in Antonucci, *Cronache del teatro futurista*, 101–2, here 101.

56 Y [Enrico Novelli], "La 'sintesi teatrale' al Niccolini," *La Nazione* (Florence), 10 March 1916, 3.

57 Y., "La 'sintesi teatrale,'" *La Nazione* (Florence), 10 March 1916, 3.

58 According to a report in *Il Nuovo Giornale* (Florence), 8–9 March 1916, in Antonucci, *Lo spettacolo futurista in Italia*, 182n4, the Futurist playwrights donated their royalty fees to the Red Cross, and the Ninchi-Rosa theatre company also donated a percentage to the Red Cross. A performance in Pavia on 14 April 1916 was in aid of the military hospital Filantropia in Livorno. See Berghaus, *Italian Futurist Theatre*, 200. In spring 1916 Marinetti gave a speech in Venice in support of the Red Cross. See Marinetti to Cangiullo, undated but beginning of May 1916, in *FTM-FC*, 109.

59 See Y., "Il teatro 'sintetico' al Niccolini," *La Nazione* (Florence), 8 March 1916, 2; and "La grande serata futurista di beneficienza al Teatro della Pergola," *La Nazione* (Florence), 8 May 1916, 3.

60 Scarpellini, "Teatro e guerra," 160.

61 Bacci, in *Il Nuovo Giornale* (Florence), 9–10 March 1916, in Antonucci, *Cronache del teatro futurista*, 102.

62 Salaris, *Marinetti editore*, 213.

63 [Ferdinando Russo], "Rinnovarsi o morire," *Vela Latina*, 14 October 1915, 1.

64 Marinetti to Pratella, 19 February 1916, in *FBP*, 60 (emphasis in the original). *Vela Latina* claimed a print run of twenty thousand copies. See *Vela Latina*, 5 February 1916, 1.

65 Cangiullo to Settimelli, 25 February 1916, FPC, Fondo Settimelli, Corrispondenza SC 1/INS 5/CAM A.

66 Russo, "Forza maggiore," *Vela Latina*, 4 March 1916, 1.

67 Arnaldo Ginna (1890–1982), pseudonym of Arnaldo Ginanni Corradini. Futurist artist. After writing a theoretical work, *L'arte dell'avvenire*, with

his brother, Bruno Corra, Ginna came into contact with the Futurists and began exhibiting with them. During the war he edited *L'Italia Futurista*, was involved in the production of the Futurist film *Vita Futurista*, and signed the "Manifesto della cinematografia futurista." He did not serve in the army. His allegiance to Marinetti and Futurism continued up to the 1940s.

68 Maria Ginanni (1891–1953), Futurist writer. Ginanni was the wife of Arnaldo Ginna and became active in Futurist circles during the war. She served as editor of *L'Italia Futurista* and edited the newspaper's book series, Edizioni de l'Italia Futurista (1917). In 1917 she published a novel, *Montagne trasparenti*. She continued working alongside the Futurists in the post-war period but abandoned the movement in the 1920s.

69 Somigli, "Past-Loving Florence," 483.

70 Settimelli, "L'Italia Futurista," *L'Italia Futurista*, 1 June 1916, 1.

71 Settimelli to Pratella, 8 July 1916, FPC, Fondo Pratella, Corrispondenza SC XII/INS 1/CAM B. In a letter to Meriano on 31 May 1916 (the day before its launch) Settimelli claimed that he had already had one thousand requests for the newspaper. See Bagatti et al., *Futurismo a Firenze*, 122.

72 Settimelli to Pratella, 8 July 1916, FPC, Fondo Pratella, Corrispondenza SC XII/INS 1/CAM B.

73 See Soffici, "'L'Italia Futurista' al fronte," *L'Italia Futurista*, 23 September 1917, 1, and Massimo Bontempelli, "Dalla prima linea," *L'Italia Futurista*, 9 December 1917, 3.

74 Settimelli, "L'Italia Futurista," *L'Italia Futurista*, 1 June 1916, 1.

75 Marinetti, "Schiaffi, calci e fucilate," *L'Italia Futurista*, 4 March 1917, 1.

76 See Maria Carla Papini, introduction to *"L'Italia Futurista" (1916–1918)*, ed. Maria Carla Papini (Rome: Edizioni dell'Ateneo e Bizzarri, 1977), 31–55, here 54.

77 See Mirella Bandini, "Elementi protosurrealisti nei testi di Mario Carli, Bruno Corra e Maria Ginanni," in Caruso, *"L'Italia Futurista,"* 15–18; Paola Sica, "Regenerating Life and Art: Futurism, Florentine Women, Irma Valeria," in Luisetti and Somigli, "A Century of Futurism," 175–85; and Lucia Re, "Maria Ginanni vs. F.T. Marinetti: Women, Speed, and War in Futurist Italy," in Luisetti and Somigli, "A Century of Futurism," 103–24.

78 Settimelli, "L'Italia Futurista," *L'Italia Futurista*, 1 June 1916, 1.

79 Formoso, "Sintesi parolibera," *L'Italia Futurista*, 3 June 1917, 3.

80 Carli, "L'ultima mobilitazione degli entusiasmi," *L'Italia Futurista*, 17 June 1917, 1.

81 Ibid.

82 Marinetti, "La nuova religione della velocità. Manifesto futurista," *L'Italia Futurista*, 1 June 1916, 1.

83 Re, "Maria Ginanni vs. F.T. Marinetti," 113.

84 Marinetti to Pratella, 20 December 1916, in *FBP*, 62 (emphasis in the original).

85 Marinetti to Carli, undated but summer 1917, in *MC-FTM*, 46.

86 While women did increasingly become associated with the movement during the war years, their activities were largely undertaken in psychic, proto-surrealist fields unrelated to the war effort. See Claudia Salaris, "Le donne futuriste nel periodo tra guerra e dopoguerra," in Leoni and Zadra, *La Grande Guerra*, 291–306. Of course, the increased involvement of women in the movement was directly linked to the changing social roles of women during the war. See Simonetta Ortaggi, "Italian Women during the Great War," in *Evidence, History, and the Great War*, ed. Gail Braybon (New York: Berghahn, 2003), 216–38; and Allison Scardino Belzer, *Women and the Great War: Femminity under Fire in Italy* (Basingstoke, UK: Palgrave, 2010).

87 Remo Chiti, "L'uomo femmina," *L'Italia Futurista*, 15 April 1917, 4.

88 Marinetti, "Contro l'amore e il parlamentarismo!," *L'Italia Futurista*, 1 April 1917, 1. This manifesto had been published first in 1910.

89 Corrado Morosello, "Salviamo la donna!," *L'Italia Futurista*, 27 May 1917, 2. The editors of the journal noted above this article that they did not always share the opinions of their contributors. On these articles and the attitude towards women in *L'Italia Futurista*, see Silvia Contarini, *La femme futuriste: Mythes, modèles et représentations de la femme dans la théorie et la littérature futuristes (1909–1919)* (Paris: Presses universitaires de Paris 10, 2006), 204–8.

90 Marinetti, "Donne, non piagnucolate: Lettera aperta a Ada Negri," *L'Italia Futurista*, 4 November 1917, 1. In his notebook he called the postal system a "rete di forze lussuriose che legano le donne nude agli uomini vestiti infangati in prima linea trincea" (web of lustful forces that tie naked women to mud-covered men in the front-line trenches). See Marinetti, 23 March 1917, in *FTMT*, 64. The open letter to Negri was possibly written around 11 October 1917 as he records similar ideas in his notebook on this date. See Marinetti, 11 October 1917, in *FTMT*, 145.

91 Marinetti, "Donne, dovete preferire i gloriosi mutilati," *L'Italia Futurista*, 15 June 1916, 1. For an analysis of the mutilated male body in Marinetti's work, particularly *L'alcova d'acciaio*, see Anthony Martire, "Il soggetto mutilato del futurismo: F.T. Marinetti e la costruzione dell'italiano futurista nel primo dopoguerra," *Memoria e Ricerca* 38 (2011): 99–110.

92 Marinetti, "1915. In quest'anno futurista (1914)," in *TIF*, 328–36, here 336.

93 He advised Boccioni to encourage the teenage editors of the semi-Futurist magazine *Gatto Nero*. See Marinetti to Boccioni, 14 May 1916, in *ADF*, 371. He also warned Carli in October 1918 never to criticize young people. See Marinetti to Carli, undated but October 1918, in *MC-FTM*, 64.

94 Boccioni to Pratella, 16 June 1916, in *UBLF*, 162.

95 Pratella to Boccioni, 20 June 1916, Boccioni Papers, GRI, box 1, folder 40 (emphasis in the original). The phrase *somaro di battaglia* is a play on the Italian expression *cavallo di battaglia* (war horse) meaning "strong suit" or "forte"; *somaro di battaglia* literally means "war donkey."

96 Marinetti to Pratella, 20 December 1916, in *FBP*, 62 (emphasis in the original).

97 Chiti to Carli, undated but late December 1916 or early January 1917, MART, Archivio del '900, Fondo Carli, Carli 3.2.2.41.

98 Corra to Pratella, 13 January 1917, FPC, Fondo Pratella, Corrispondenza SC IV/INS 10/CAM C.

99 Ibid.

100 "Gli spettacoli futuristi al Niccolini pro famiglie dei richiamati," *La Nazione* (Florence), 29 January 1917, reprinted in *L'Italia Futurista*, 10 February 1917, 2.

101 The four sintesi were *I corvi*, published in *L'Italia Futurista*, 18 March 1917, 4; *Uccidiamo il chiaro di luna*, published in *L'Italia Futurista*, 11 March 1917, 4; *Dichiarazione di guerra*, published in *L'Italia Futurista*, 8 April 1917, 4; and *Attacco di aeroplani austriaci*, by Settimelli only, published in *L'Italia Futurista*, 10 February 1917, 3.

102 In this, the *sintesi* echoes the conclusion to Marinetti's "Manifesto tecnico della letteratura futurista (1912)," in *TIF*, 46–54, in which he stated that the Futurists were preparing "la creazione dell'uomo meccanico dalle parti cambiabili" (the creation of a mechanical man with changeable parts), 54.

103 Settimelli, "*Attacco di aeroplani austriaci*," *L'Italia Futurista*, 10 February 1917, 3.

104 "Gli spettacoli futuristi al Niccolini," 2.

105 Ibid.

106 "Le rappresentazioni futuriste al Niccolini," *Il Nuovo Giornale* (Florence), 29 January 1917, reprinted in *L'Italia Futurista*, 10 February 1917, 2.

107 Ibid.

108 Pierre Sorlin, *Italian National Cinema, 1896–1996* (1996; repr. London: Routledge, 2005), 44. See also Giovanni Nobili Vitelleschi, "The Representation of the Great War in Italian Cinema," in *The First World War and Popular Cinema: 1914 to the Present*, ed. Michael Paris (New Brunswick, NJ: Rutgers University Press, 2000), 162–71.

109 On this manifesto and *Vita Futurista*, see Isabella Innamorati, "Un 'manifesto' fatto d'immagini," in Caruso, *"L'Italia Futurista,"* 31–6; and Günter Berghaus and Mario Verdone, *"Vita Futurista* and Early Futurist Cinema," in Berghaus, *International Futurism in Arts and Literature*, 398–421.

110 "Gli spettacoli futuristi al Niccolini," *La Nazione* (Florence), 29 January 1917, reprinted in *L'Italia Futurista*, 10 February 1917, 2.

111 Editors, "La prima nel mondo della Cinematografia Futurista," *L'Italia Futurista*, 10 February 1917, 2. The film was shown again in Rome on 14 and 15 June 1917.

112 "Le rappresentazioni futuriste al Niccolini," *Il Nuovo Giornale* (Florence), 29 January 1917, reprinted in *L'Italia Futurista*, 10 February 1917, 2.

113 The volumes published between August 1914 and May 1915 were *L'aeroplano del papa* by Marinetti, *Ponti sull'oceano* by Folgore, *L'elisse e la spirale* by Buzzi, *Guerrapittura* by Carrà, *Rarefazioni* by Govoni, *Guerra sola igiene del mondo* by Marinetti, and *Baionette* by Auro d'Alba. In 1916 four books were published: *Piedigrotta* by Cangiullo, *Equatore notturno* by Meriano, *L'arte dei rumori* by Russolo, and *Archi voltaici* by Volt. Only one was published in 1917 (*Sam Dunn è morto* by Corra), and none in 1918. Maria Ginanni established a book series, Edizioni de L'Italia Futurista, in 1917, which published nine volumes in total, although none of them addressed war-related themes.

114 David Forgacs, *Italian Culture in the Industrial era, 1880–1980: Cultural Industries, Politics, and the Public* (Manchester: Manchester University Press, 1990), 44.

115 Cinzia Sartini Blum has made a similar observation in reference to Marinetti's *Come si seducono le donne* and *L'alcova d'acciaio*. See *The Other Modernism: F.T. Marinetti's Futurist Fiction of Power* (Berkeley: University of California Press, 1996), 89.

116 See Corra to Marinetti, 13 March 1918, Papers of FTM, BRB, box 9, folder 351.

117 Marinetti, *Come si seducono le donne*, 34.

118 Ibid., 45 (emphasis in the original).

119 Ibid., 46.

120 Ibid., 74.

121 Ibid., 75.

122 Ibid., 110.

123 Bruno Corra, *Io ti amo: Romanzo dell'amore moderno* (Milan: Studio Editoriale Lombardo, 1918), 180.

124 Ibid., 176.

125 Ibid., 208.

126 Ibid., 251.

127 Unpublished letters from Corra to Marinetti cast some doubt on the
nature of the co-authorship of this novel. Corra's comments to Marinetti
strongly suggest that Corra penned the novel and then reached out
to Marinetti for help with financing the endeavour. In February 1918
he asked Marinetti "se accetti di dividere con me i rischi e vantaggi
dell'affare" (if you accept to share with me the risks and advantages of
this business) and then a few weeks later asked Marinetti again to let him
know "se intendi più partecipare alla cosa" (if you still intend to take part
in this). See Corra to Marinetti, 26 February and 13 March 1918, Papers
of FTM, BRB, box 9, folder 351. In reply, Marinetti told Corra that he was
"lieto di mettere questa volta le mie idee da parte e di combinare come
desideri l'edizione del nostro *L'isola dei baci*"(happy to put my ideas to
one side this time and to finish the edition of our *L'isola dei baci* as you
wish) and gave Corra instructions about the paper, font, and print run
of the novel. See Marinetti to Corra, 20 March 1918, Papers of FTM, BRB,
box 1, folder 8. The phrasing of an advertisement for the novel in *L'Italia
Futurista* also suggests that Corra was the primary author of the work. It
stated: "Bruno Corra ha ultimato con Marinetti il romanzo *L'isola dei baci*"
(Bruno Corra has finished the novel *L'isola dei baci* with Marinetti). See
L'Italia Futurista, 18 November 1917, 1.

128 Filippo Tommaso Marinetti and Bruno Corra, *L'isola dei baci: Romanzo
erotico-sociale* (Milan: Studio Editoriale Lombardo, 1918), 17.

129 Ibid., 31.

130 Ibid., 45.

131 Ibid., 90.

132 Ibid., 126.

133 Ibid., 137.

134 Advertisement, *L'Italia Futurista*, 2 December 1917, 4. The Futurists
launched a serious marketing campaign for *Come si seducono le donne* both
in *L'Italia Futurista* and in national newspapers. The first announcement
of *Come si seducono le donne* in *L'Italia Futurista* on 3 June 1917 proclaimed
it a "libro guerresco ed igienico!" (warlike and cleansing book!), and
stated its claim to "igiene! ilarità! futurismo! genialità!" (hygiene! hilarity!
Futurism! brilliance!). In the same issue Settimelli wrote an article about
it, saying that "coglierà tutto il pubblico più vivo, più giovane della più
giovane Italia" (it will seize the most lively audiences, the youngest of the
youngest Italians), and stressed that the book was intimately linked to the
war. See Settimelli, "*Come si seducono le donne*," *L'Italia Futurista*, 3 June

1917, 1. The hard sell continued through June and July (details of its high production values were given, including a photograph of Marinetti), and on 12 August there was a half-page advertisement with a photograph of Marinetti in uniform and the words "Affrettarsi a prenderlo – ENORMI RICHIESTE" (Hurry to get it – HUGE DEMAND), 4.

135 Corra to Settimelli, 21 August 1917, FPC, Fondo Settimelli, Corrispondenza SCI/INS 10/CAM A.

136 The second edition was published by Excelsior in 1918, and then an extended version, entitled *Come si seducono le donne e si tradiscono gli uomini* (How to seduce women and to betray men), by Sonzogno in 1920. It even spawned a parody. See Mari Annetta [Comtesse du Aubrun], *Come si seducono gli uomini* (How to seduce men) (Rocca San Casciano, Italy: Cappelli, 1918).

137 Michele Giocondi, *Lettori in camicia nera: Narrativa di successo nell'Italia fascista* (Messina: G. D'Anna, 1978), 21. The average number of copies sold for a work of fiction was two thousand; a work that sold five thousand copies could be considered a small success, and books that reached twenty thousand copies were rare (five or six a year). In his study Giocondi defined a successful book as one that reached around twenty thousand copies in four to seven years.

138 Corra to Marinetti, 26 February 1918 and 13 March 1918, Papers of FTM, BRB, box 9, folder 351; and Marinetti to Corra, 20 March 1918, Papers of FTM, BRB, box 1, folder 8.

139 Corra to Marinetti, 1 September 1918, Papers of FTM, BRB, box 9, folder 351. In his notebook Marinetti recorded that all four thousand copies of the first edition had been sold. See Marinetti, 24 September 1918, in *FTMT*, 355.

140 Giorgio Pasquali, "Esiste una crisi del libro?," *Il Libro Italiano: Rassegna bibliografica generale*, ed. Ministero di Educazione Nazionale e del Ministero della Cultura Popolare (1937), 58, in Forgacs, *Italian Culture*, 44. On reading in the army, see Piero Melograni, *La storia politica della Grande Guerra 1915–1918* (Bari: Laterza, 1969), 243–51.

141 Marinetti, 6 December 1918, in *FTMT*, 393.

142 Settimelli, "Marinetti e la seduzione delle donne," *L'Italia Futurista*, 10 June 1917, 1.

143 Corra, "Questo libro mi piace," in Marinetti and Corra, *L'isola dei baci*, 7–11, here 7.

144 Ibid., 8 (emphasis in the original).

145 Ibid., 9.

146 Ibid., 9 and 11.

147 Chiti to Settimelli, 7 August 1918, FPC, Fondo Settimelli, Corrispondenza SC I/ INS 8/ CAM A.

148 Lucia Re, "Futurism, Seduction, and the Strange Sublimity of War," *Italian Studies* 59, no. 1 (2004): 83–111, here 92.
149 Re, "The Strange Sublimity of War," 96.
150 Marinetti dictated *Come si seducono le donne* to Corra, and he is frequently cited in the book. There are many similarities, particularly between the chapter "La donna e il coraggio" of *Come si seducono le donne* and the plot of *Io ti amo*.
151 Corra and Settimelli, "Prefazione," in Marinetti, *Come si seducono le donne*, 9–18, here 17 (emphasis in the original).
152 Marinetti, *Come si seducono le donne*, 38–9.
153 Re, "The Strange Sublimity of War," 88.
154 Ibid., 89.
155 Marinetti to Pratella, 13 September 1918, FPC, Fondo Pratella, Corrispondenza SC/VII/INS 14/CAM A.

4. How to Seduce Soldiers

 1 Marinetti to Nina Angelini, 21 February 1917, in *VdelF*, 71; and Marinetti, 18–22 February 1917, in *FTMT*, 45. Between September and October 1916 Marinetti had served as a second lieutenant of the artillery at a fort at Bracciano, near Rome. This was his first assignment as an officer. See *Attendamento Bracciano IIIa Artiglieria, settembre–ottobre 1916* (Rome: Stabilimento Litografico A. Sampaolesi, 1916), Collezione Reggi, APICE. The author of this thirty-two-page pamphlet begins by stating: "La vita molto territoriale dell'attendamento di Bracciano è stata strinata di vivacità, di entusiasmo, di libera spensieratezza dall'arrivo di Marinetti e di Folgore." (The very territorial [i.e., non-combatant] life of the camp at Bracciano was scorched with liveliness, enthusiasm, and carefreeness by the arrival of Marinetti and Folgore.) See also Folgore, "Accampamento, parole in libertà," *L'Italia Futurista*, 11 February 1918, 3. After this period in Bracciano, Marinetti returned to Milan, and on 26 December 1916 he was called up to bombardiers' training college in Susegana near Treviso.
 2 Marinetti's return to the front was delayed in 1916: "perché il mio casellario penale portava la macchia del mio romanzo *Mafarka il futurista* sequestrato e condannato, e i carabinieri di Milano, ricordando i miei pugilati interventisti, mi dichiaravano dedito alla rissa, pensai di aspettare amnistia e nomina di sottotenente facendo dei bagni salubri a Viareggio" (because my criminal record had the stain of my novel *Mafarka il futurista*, which had been confiscated and found guilty, and the Milanese police, recalling my interventionist punch-ups, declared me to be committed to brawls, I decided to wait for an amnesty and my appointment as a second

lieutenant by having healthy swims at Viareggio). See Marinetti, *Come si seducono le donne*, 45.

3 See Marinetti to Nina Angelini, 27 February 1917 (Ang. 1.19); undated but before 6 March 1917 (Ang. 1.20); 20 March 1917 (Ang. 1.25); undated but after 15 March 1917 (Ang. 1.26); 28 March 1917 (Ang. 1.28); 23 April 1917 (Ang. 1.33); 29 April 1917 (Ang. 1.34); 3 May 1917 (two letters, Ang. 1.35 and Ang. 1.36) – all MART, Archivio del '900, Fondo Angelini. Such a generous attitude severely tested the movement's resources, causing Nina to write to Marinetti in March 1917 that they should try and save money by purchasing fewer books: "Bisogna cercare di fare poche spese anche in pacchi francobolli ecc." (We must try and have fewer expenses also for packages stamps etc.) See Nina Angelini to Marinetti, 6 March 1917, in *VdelF*, 89.

4 Antonucci, *Lo spettacolo futurista in Italia*, 47.

5 Berghaus, *Futurism and Politics*, 83.

6 Mario Isnenghi, *Giornali di trincea (1915–1918)* (Turin: Einaudi, 1977), 26.

7 Walter L. Adamson, "The Impact of World War 1 on Italian Political Culture," in *European Culture in the Great War: The Arts, Entertainment, and Propaganda, 1914–1918*, ed. Avial Roshwald and Richard Stites (Cambridge: Cambridge University Press, 1999), 308–29, here 313–14.

8 Giuseppe Prezzolini, *Vittorio Veneto* (Rome: Edizioni della Voce, 1920), 16.

9 Comando Supremo, "Propaganda patriottica," circular no. 1117/P, 1 February 1918, signed by Armando Diaz, in Gian Luigi Gatti, *Dopo Caporetto: Gli ufficiali P nella Grande Guerra: Propaganda, assistenza, vigilanza* (Gorizia, Italy: LEG, 2000), 48.

10 Second Army, Stato Maggiore, "Progetto per l'organizzazione di un corso di conferenze ai soldati," in Gatti, *Dopo Caporetto*, 52.

11 Luigi Capello, "Criteri per le conferenze," circular no. 2389/Op, 25 June 1917, in Gatti, *Dopo Caporetto*, 52.

12 Second Army / Capello, circular no. 1988/Op, 6 June 1917, in Gatti, *Dopo Caporetto*, 52.

13 Isnenghi, *Giornali di trincea*, 29–30. See also see Luigi Capello, *Caporetto, perché? La 2a Armata e gli avvenimenti dell'ottobre 1917* (Turin: Einaudi, 1967), 257.

14 Marinetti, 14 March 1917, in *FTMT*, 63 (emphasis in the original). Although Marinetti would have preferred to speak directly to the soldiers, Capello's system was aimed only at the officer population.

15 Ibid.

16 Marinetti, 22 April 1917, in *FTMT*, 73. The delay between Capello's first approach to Marinetti and the date of his first speaking engagement was due to Marinetti's hospitalization for bronchitis.

17 Capello, *Caporetto perché?*, 263.
18 Marinetti, 29 April 1917, in *FTMT*, 83.
19 Fifth Army, Stato Maggiore / Capello, "Relazione circa l'ufficio propaganda," circular no. 287/I.P., 11 June 1918, in Gatti, *Dopo Caporetto*, 54.
20 Marinetti, 3 March 1917, in *FTMT*, 56 (referring to a brothel). He found, for example, Futurist sympathizers "fra le baracche" (among the huts) on 25 February 1917, in *FTMT*, 52, and at a field hospital on 5 April 1917, in *FTMT*, 67–8.
21 Alan Kramer, *Dynamic of Destruction: Culture and Mass Killing in the First World War* (Oxford: Oxford University Press, 2007), 205.
22 Marinetti, 29 April 1917, in *FTMT*, 83.
23 Marinetti, 14 September 1917, in *FTMT*, 113.
24 Marinetti, 19 September 1917, in *FTMT*, 119 (emphasis in the original).
25 Second Army / Capello, circular no. 13636/SR, 8 October 1917, in Gatti, *Dopo Caporetto*, 53.
26 On Caporetto, see Nicola Labanca, *Caporetto: Storia di una disfatta* (Florence: Giunti, 1997).
27 Gooch, *The Italian Army and the First World War*, 245–6.
28 Nicola Labanca, "The Italian Front," in *The Cambridge History of the First World War*, ed. Jay Winter and Editorial Committee of the International Research Centre of the Historial de le Grande Guerre (Cambridge: Cambridge University Press, 2014), vol. 1, 266–96, here 286.
29 On the myth of Caporetto, see Isnenghi and Rochat, *La Grande Guerra*, 400–8.
30 Marinetti, 25–26 October 1917, in "Selections from the Unpublished Diaries of F.T. Marinetti," ed. Lawrence Rainey and Laura Wittman, *Modernism/ Modernity* 1, no. 3 (1994): 1–44, here 30.
31 Marinetti, [24 October 1917] in *FTMT*, 156. Marinetti wrote these notes on 18 December 1917, but they discussed the events at Caporetto between 24 October and the end of November 1917.
32 Marinetti, 28 October 1917, in "Selections from the Unpublished Diaries," 31.
33 Marinetti, undated but late October 1917, in *FTMT*, 159.
34 Ibid., 160.
35 Marinetti, undated but beginning of November 1917, in *FTMT*, 161.
36 He was promoted to lieutenant in mid-November 1917. See Marinetti to Pratella, 24 November 1917, in *FBP*, 64.
37 L'Italia Futurista [editorial team], "La Vittoria," *L'Italia Futurista*, 18 November 1917, 2.
38 Settimelli, "I diritti dell'Italia," *L'Italia Futurista*, 2 December 1917, 2.
39 Marinetti, "Lettera aperta al futurista Mac Delmarle (1913)," in *TIF*, 91–4. Marinetti wrote: "Il Futurismo è l'ottimismo artificiale nettamente opposto

a tutti i pessimisti cronici" (Futurism is artificial optimism clearly opposed to all the chronic pessimists), 94.

40 Marinetti, undated entry, in "Selections from the Unpublished Diaries," 38 (emphasis in the original). Rainey and Wittman suggest a date of around 1921 for this extract, but I believe it dates to early 1918.

41 Marinetti, "Teniamo duro. (Lettera aperta a Emilio Settimelli)," *L'Italia Futurista*, 9 December 1917, 1.

42 Ibid.

43 Marinetti, 8 January 1918, in *FTMT*, 181 (emphasis in the original). A few weeks later he compiled a list of his reasons for being optimistic as if he were trying to convince himself of the fact. See Marinetti, 19 February 1918, in *FTMT*, 196.

44 Giuseppe Prezzolini, "Il Servizio P.," in *Tutta la guerra: Antologia del popolo italiano sul fronte e nel paese* (Florence: Bemporad, 1918; Milan: Longanesi, 1968), 451–75, here 452. Citations refer to the Longanesi edition.

45 See Melograni, *La storia politica della Grande Guerra*, 501–2.

46 Giuseppe Lombardo Radice, *Nuovi saggi di propaganda pedagogica* (Turin: Paravia, 1922), ix. Lombardo Radice was one of the most important figures in the Servizio P.

47 Isnenghi and Rochat, *La Grande Guerra*, 413.

48 Marinetti, 10 January 1918, in *FTMT*, 184 (emphasis in the original).

49 Referring to the Servizio P. speeches, Lombardo Radice wrote that the high command "lasciava grandissima libertà di iniziativa." See Lombardo Radice, *Nuovi saggi di propaganda pedagogica*, 33.

50 Marinetti, 17 March 1918, in *FTMT*, 206. His successive speeches followed a similar pattern, mixing remarks on the war with commentary on Futurism, including references to *Come si seducono le donne*. See Marinetti, 23 April 1918 and 10 May 1918, in *FTMT*, 226 and 238–9 respectively.

51 Marinetti, 29 April 1918, in *FTMT*, 232.

52 Gentile, "Il futurismo e la politica," 120.

53 Berghaus, *Futurism and Politics*, 155.

54 Marinetti, 15 April 1917, in "Selections from the Unpublished Diaries," 25–6.

55 Corra to Settimelli, 21 August [year not stated, but 1917], FPC, Fondo Settimelli, Corrispondenza SC I/INS 10/CAM A.

56 Günter Berghaus, "The Futurist Political Party," in *The Invention of Politics in the European Avant-Garde (1906–1940)*, ed. Sascha Bru and Gunther Martens (Amsterdam: Rodopi, 2006), 153–82, here 153.

57 Marinetti, "Elettori futuristi! (1909)," in "Movimento politico futurista," in *Guerra sola igine del mondo* (1915), in *TIF*, 337–41, here 337–8.

58 He stated this in an interview with *Il Giornale d'Italia* (Rome) on 30 October 1913. See Marinetti, *Critical Writings*, 48. Marinetti issued short political manifestos in 1911 upon the outbreak of the war with Libya and in October 1913. See Marinetti, "Movimento politico futurista," in *TIF*, 337–41.

59 Marinetti, in Girav [Jannelli], "Il valore futurista della guerra," *L'Avvenire* (Messina), 23 February 1915, in *PPF*, 267–72, here 272.

60 Maddalena Carli, "'Un movimento artistico crea un partito politico': Il Futurismo italiano tra avanguardismo e normalizzazione," *Memoria e Ricerca* 33 (2010): 15–28, here 17.

61 Renzo De Felice, "Ordine pubblico e orientamenti delle masse popolari italiane nella prima metà del 1917," *Rivista storica del socialismo* (September–December 1963): 467–504, here 488. See also Melograni, *La storia politica della Grande Guerra*, 329–34.

62 Settimelli, 'Qual'è la nostra più grande Vittoria," *L'Italia Futurista*, 25 February 1917, 1–2, here 2.

63 Marinetti, "Programma politico futurista," *L'Italia Futurista*, 25 March 1917, 1. Settimelli added *"Futurista al fronte"* to Marinetti's signature, suggesting that this was penned by him at the front lines, and there is no indication that it is a re-publication of the words he wrote four years earlier. There is no evidence of correspondence between Settimelli and Marinetti about the reprinting of these manifestos.

64 A number of articles about the end of the war began to appear in *L'Italia Futurista* from February 1917. See Ginna, "Dopo la guerra," *L'Italia Futurista*, 25 February 1917, 4; Carli, "Le condizioni di pace," *L'Italia Futurista*, 22 April 1917, 1; Ginanni, "Quando finirà la guerra," *L'Italia Futurista*, 6 May 1917, 1; Ginanni, "Che cos'è la vittoria," *L'Italia Futurista*, 20 May 1917, 1.

65 Settimelli, "Intervista con Marinetti sulla fine della guerra," *L'Italia Futurista*, 4 March 1917, 2 (emphasis in the original).

66 Ibid. (emphasis added).

67 Marinetti, "La migliore batteria," *L'Italia Futurista*, 15 June 1916, 1. Marinetti attempted another critique of the parliament a month later, but it was censored. The sentence began "il parlamento non è che un illustre …" (the parliament is nothing but a famous …). See Marinetti, "Lettera aperta al Generale Cadorna," *L'Italia Futurista*, 10 July 1916, 1.

68 Settimelli, "D'Annunzio, Salandra, Orlando, L'Idea Nazionale, Futuristi," *L'Italia Futurista*, 15 June 1916, 2 (emphasis added).

69 Ibid.

70 Settimelli, "Il massacro dei Pancioni," *L'Italia Futurista*, 12 August 1917, 1–2, here 1.

71 Ibid.

72 Gentile, *"La nostra sfida alle stelle,"* 51.

73 Settimelli, "Duttilità futurista," *L'Italia Futurista*, 9 December 1917, 1.

74 Ibid.

75 Marinetti, "Manifesto del Partito Politico Futurista," *L'Italia Futurista*, 11 February 1918, 1–2, here 1.

76 Ibid.

77 Ibid.

78 Marinetti, "Prime battaglie futuriste (1911)," in *Guerra sola igiene del mondo* (1915), in *TIF*, 235–45, here 235.

79 Marinetti, "Manifesto del Partito Politico Futurista," *L'Italia Futurista*, 11 February 1918, 1–2, here 1.

80 Marinetti, 5 January 1918, in *FTMT*, 177.

81 See O'Brien, *Mussolini in the First World War*, 120–2. O'Brien's examination of Mussolini's medical records revealed that his war injury had been fabricated to hide his case of syphilis. He was in hospital between 2 April and 11 August 1917 and never returned again to the front.

82 Marinetti to Nina Angelini, 26 May 1917, in *VdelF*, 79 (emphasis in the original).

83 Marinetti to Nina Angelini, 28 May 1917, in *VdelF*, 79 (emphasis in the original).

84 Marinetti to Nina Angelini, undated but beginning of June 1917, in *VdelF*, 82.

85 Marinetti, 18 July 1918, in *FTMT*, 284.

86 Marinetti, 19 July 1918, in *FTMT*, 285–6.

87 Ibid., 286.

88 They did not meet again until after the war. By then Marinetti had changed his mind about Mussolini, calling him a reactionary. See Marinetti, between 28 November and 4 December 1918, in *FTMT*, 392.

89 Carli to Marinetti, undated but August 1918, in *MC-FTM*, 52.

90 Marinetti to Conti, undated but September 1918, in Filippo Tommaso Marinetti and Primo Conti, *Nei proiettori del futurismo: Carteggio inedito 1917–1940*, ed. Gabriel Cacho Millet (Palermo: Novecento, 2001), 70.

91 Marinetti to Soggetti, undated but "10 October 1918" added in a different hand, Soggetti Papers, GRI, box 1, folder 1, accession no. 860387.

92 Adamson, *Embattled Avant-Gardes*, 108.

93 On the Arditi, see Giorgio Rochat, *Gli arditi della Grande Guerra: Origini, battaglie e miti* (Milan: Feltrinelli, 1981; Gorizia, Italy: LEG, 2006).

94 Angelo Pirocchi, *Italian Arditi: Elite Assault Troops, 1917–1920* (Oxford: Osprey, 2004), 44.

95 Mario Carli, *Noi Arditi* (Milan: Facchi, 1919), 60.

96 See Ottone Rosai, *Il libro di un teppista* (Florence: Vallecchi, 1919).

97 On the early incarnations of the Arditi, see Gooch, *The Italian Army and the First World War*, 200–1.

98 Marinetti, 1 May 1917, in *FTMT*, 85 (emphasis in the original).

99 Marinetti, 10 July 1918, in *FTMT*, 278.

100 Marinetti to Carli, undated but July 1918, in *MC-FTM*, 50. In a letter to Cangiullo he called them "arditi gloriosi e simpatici che non amano i carabinieri!" (glorious and likeable arditi who do not love the police!). See Marinetti to Cangiullo, undated but July 1918, in *FTM-FC*, 120.

101 Marinetti, 26 August 1918, in *FTMT*, 320 (emphasis in the original).

102 Carli, *Noi Arditi*, 10.

103 Ibid., 64 (emphasis in the original).

104 Marinetti, 11 August 1918, in *FTMT*, 304.

105 Marinetti, 14 August 1918, in *FTMT*, 308.

106 Marinetti, 15 September 1918, in *FTMT*, 348.

107 Ibid., 349.

108 Marinetti to Pratella, 29 September 1918, FPC, Fondo Pratella, Corrispondenza SC VIII/INS 14/CAM A.

109 Roma Futurista [editorial team], "Roma Futurista," *Roma Futurista*, 20 September 1918, 1.

110 Carli, "A me, fiamme nere!," *Roma Futurista*, 20 September 1918, 3.

111 Ibid.

112 Carli to Marinetti, undated but August 1918, in *MC-FTM*, 53.

113 Roma Futurista [editorial team], "Roma Futurista," *Roma Futurista*, 20 September 1918, 1.

114 Roberto Marcello Iras Baldessari (1894–1965), Futurist painter. Born in Innsbruck, he moved to Rovereto in the early 1900s. When the war broke out, his family moved to Florence. There he came into contact with Futurists (including Rosai and Conti) at the Giubbe Rosse café, and he began working in a Futurist style. In December 1917 he was named in *L'Italia Futurista* as a member of the "gruppo pittorico futurista fiorentino." Although he did not serve in the army, he completed a number of war-inspired works while working in Padua during the war years, including *Treno dei feriti* (1918). He continued his Futurist collaboration into the 1940s.

115 This was first begun in *L'Italia Futurista* when a list of war-dead was featured on 15 July 1917 and again on 27 January 1918. The list of Futurist war-dead and -injured was carefully managed, with Marinetti instructing Carli from the front about whom to include in the list and

when. See Marinetti to Carli, two undated letters but both October 1918, in *MC-FTM*, 62 and 66. In the second of these letters Marinetti instructed Carli to publish a letter by Urrico Foà in *Roma Futurista*, which was important "perchè è stato 2 volte ferito e entra ora nel nostro partito" (because he has been injured twice and is now joining our party). He continued, "Non nominarlo però nell'elenco dei feriti. Lo faremo più tardi." (Don't include him in the list of the injured, though. We will do it later.) In an earlier letter Marinetti had explicitly stated that Carli must "riunire intorno al giornale i mutilati di guerra sostenendone gli interessi glorificandoli contro i disfattisti e gli imboscati" (gather the war-injured around the newspaper supporting their interests and glorifying them against the defeatists and shirkers). See Marinetti to Carli, 26 September 1918, in *MC-FTM*, 57.

116 Roma Futurista [editorial team], "Roma Futurista," *Roma Futurista*, 20 September 1918, 1. Popular forms of entertainment such as sport and cinema were proposed as integral parts of every branch of the Futurist Political Party. See Settimelli, "Il partito futurista," *Roma Futurista*, 30 September 1918, 3.

117 Cerati to Marinetti, "La voce degli arditi futuristi," *Roma Futurista*, 10 October 1918, 3.

118 Auro d'Alba to Carli, "Il Partito Futurista," *Roma Futurista*, 30 October 1918, 3. The letter was written in the trenches and dated 20 October 1918.

119 Bontempelli, "Aderisco," *Roma Futurista*, 10 November 1918, 3. Massimo Bontempelli (1878–1960), Futurist writer, briefly joined the Futurist ranks during the First World War. In 1917 he served in an artillery regiment, before moving in 1918 to work for the Servizio Propaganda as the editor of the Futurist soldier newspaper, *Il Montello*. He joined the Futurist Political Party's branch in Milan in 1918. By the 1920s Bontempelli had distanced himself from Futurism; in 1926 he co-founded the *900* magazine and began to experiment with "magic realism."

120 Federico Pedrazzini and Alberto Cauli to the editors of *Roma Futurista*, "La voce degli arditi futuristi," *Roma Futurista*, 10 October 1918, 3.

121 Franco Ciarlantini to the editors of *Roma Futurista*, "Il Partito Futurista," *Roma Futurista*, 10 October 1918, 3.

122 See General Gustavo Fara, "Adesioni," *Roma Futurista*, 20 October 1918, 3; Giacomo Soldi with the "*maggior parte* degli studenti cremonesi" (*majority* of the students of Cremona), "Adesioni," *Roma Futurista*, 20 October 1918, 3; Major Vanni Kessler to the editors of *Roma Futurista*, "Il Partito Futurista," *Roma Futurista*, 10 November 1918, 3–4; and Major Carlo Cisotti to Settimelli, "Il Partito Futurista," *Roma Futurista*, 10 November 1918, 3.

123 Berghaus, *Futurism and Politics*, 103–6.

124 On trench newspapers, see Isnenghi, *Giornali di trincea* and, for comparable European examples, Robert Nelson, *German Soldier Newspapers of the First World War* (Cambridge and New York: Cambridge University Press, 2011), and Stéphane Audoin-Rouzeau, *Men at War: National Sentiment and Trench Journalism in France during the First World War*, trans. Helen McPhail (Providence, RI: Berg, 1992).

125 Isnenghi, *Giornali di trincea*, 79.

126 The title of the journal alluded to the Montello mountain, which was a site of the second battle of the Piave in June 1918. *Il Montello* was a reimagining of the Eighth Army's previous trench journal, *San Marco*, which ran for eight issues between May and August 1918. The tone of *San Marco* was more serious than that of *Il Montello*, featuring dense text and limited illustrations, and its editors were criticized for being too highbrow. See "Il 'San Marco,'" *San Marco*, 10 June 1918, 6. Digitized copies are available via 14–18.it, "'Documenti ed Immagini della Grande Guerra," www.14-18.it/giornali-di-trincea.

127 These issues appeared on 1 October, 15 October, and 27 November. Digitized copies of the first three issues are available via 14–18.it, "Documenti ed Immagini della Grande Guerra," www.14-18.it/giornali-di-trincea. The day of publication did not appear on the cover of the fourth issue. In a letter written at the end of November Bontempelli stated that the fourth issue was being published that day *"con 30 giorni di ritardo"* (*with a 30-day delay*). See Bontempelli to Folgore, 27 November 1918, in *LF*, 194 (emphasis in the original). A fifth issue of *Il Montello*, designated a "numero straordinario" and also published in November 1918, does exist; however, it featured an entirely different layout and design, consisting of official communiqués from the Italian generals, and containing none of the humorous aspects of the previous four issues. It was clearly produced by a different editorial team. The final article was signed by Barba Piero, the pseudonym of Piero Jahier, the editor of another successful trench newspaper, *L'Astico*. In the 27 November letter to Folgore, Bontempelli stated that after the fourth issue *Il Montello* "cessa le sue pubblicazioni" (is ceasing publication), although a fifth issue of the Futurist *Il Montello* was planned. See Bontempelli to Folgore, 27 November 1918, in *LF*, 194. Jamar 14 also mentioned a planned fifth issue in a letter to Folgore, undated but late October or early November, in *LF*, 228. See also Sironi, *Battuto e Ladro*, a drawing shown at the exhibition *La guerra che verrà non è la prima 1914–2014* in Rovereto in 2014–15. The drawing is undated, but the subject matter (a defeated

German soldier stealing Italian treasures) clearly dates it to late October or early November 1918. In pencil on the drawing is "N. 5 – prima pagina" (No. 5 – front page), which must be understood as a reference to *Il Montello*. Drawings by Sironi appeared on the front page of each issue. See *La guerra che verrà non è la prima 1914–2014*, ed. Nicoletta Boschiero, exhibition catalogue, Rovereto, 4 October 2014–20 September 2015 (Milan: Electa / MART, 2014), 319.

128 In Emily Braun, *Mario Sironi and Italian Modernism: Art and Politics under Fascism* (Cambridge: Cambridge University Press, 2000), 231n44.

129 Bontempelli had previously been approached about joining the Sixth Army's propaganda team in March 1918, but this did not come to pass. See Faralli to Bontempelli, 4 March 1918, Bontempelli Papers, GRI, box 8, folder 13, accession no. 910147. When General Enrico Caviglia took command of the Eighth Army in June 1918, he found a very modest propaganda service in place and tasked Lombardo Radice with re-organizing it. See Gatti, *Dopo Caporetto*, 92–3.

130 See Bontempelli to Folgore, 25 August 1918, in *LF*, 191–2, and Bontempelli to Folgore, 4 September 1918, in *LF*, 192. Folgore wanted to join the editorial team and sent his documentation (a declaration of his medial visit) to the Command of the Eighth Army at Bontempelli's instigation in October 1918. See Bontempelli to Folgore, 3 October and 11 October 1918, in *LF*, 193. It was apparently Sironi's idea to recruit Folgore to the team, "come l'unico che a parer mio potesse benissimo integrare con le sue inesauribili risorse di rime e di spirito" (as the only person who, in my opinion, could fit in well with his inexhaustible resources of rhymes and wit). See Sironi to Folgore, undated but 1918, in *LF*, 306. In this letter he said that the attempt to have Folgore stationed with them had failed.

131 "Il Montello," *Roma Futurista*, 20 September 1918, 3. See also Bontempellli to Folgore, 25 August 1918, in *LF*, 191.

132 Marinetti, 21 August 1918, in *FTMT*, 310. Marinetti was an enthusiastic supporter of the journal. He told Folgore, "*Il Montello è bello*. Bravo!" (*Il Montello is nice*. Well done!) See Marinetti to Folgore, 28 September 1918, in *LF*, 244 (emphasis in the original).

133 Corra to Marinetti, 19 September [no year but 1918], Papers of FTM, BRB, box 9, folder 351.

134 Ibid.

135 Bontempelli to Folgore, 3 October 1918, in *LF*, 193.

136 [Illegible signature] to Bontempelli, 2 November 1918, Bontempelli Papers, GRI, box 9, folder 62, accession no. 910147. Another contributor, Jamar 14 (pseudonym of Piero Gigli), praised the content and noted

"piacerà moltissimo ai soldati" (the soldiers will really like it). See Gigli to Folgore, 7 October 1918, in *LF*, 228.

137 Gibelli, *La grande guerra degli italiani*, 134.

138 "La strategia e la tattica spiegate al popolo … austriaco," *Il Montello*, 20 September 1918, 4.

139 "I Concorsi del 'Montello,'" *Il Montello*, 20 September 1918, 6, and 1 October 1918, 6.

140 The only explicit indication of the alignment between *Il Montello* and Futurism appeared in the second issue in the form of an advertisement for a subscription offer to both *Il Montello* and *Roma Futurista*. See "Roma Futurista," *Il Montello*, 1 October 1918, 7. The first edition of *Roma Futurista* (also 20 September 1918) featured a similar advertisement for *Il Montello*, stating that it is "certamente il migliore dei giornali di guerra, e sembra destinato a esser letto con interesse anche fuori della Zona di Guerra" (certainly the best of the war newspapers, and seems destined to be read with interest also outside the War Zones). See "Il Montello," *Roma Futurista*, 20 September 1918, 3. The various collaborators to *Il Montello* are mentioned, but they are not identified as Futurists.

141 Isnenghi, *Giornali di trincea*, 70.

142 Ibid., 74.

143 Ibid., 71.

144 Ibid.

145 [Marinetti], "Trincee di pane!," *Il Montello*, 20 September 1918, 3.

146 Marinetti, "Trincee di pane!," *L'Italia Futurista*, 10 August 1916, 1.

147 Gigli (Jamar 14) to Folgore, undated but late October or early November 1918, in *LF*, 228.

148 Sironi to Folgore, undated but October 1918, in *LF*, 306.

149 See Koenraad Du Pont, "The 'Authenticity Effect': A Propaganda Tool in Trench Newspapers," in *The Great War in Italy: Representation and Interpretation*, ed. Patrizia Piredda (Leicester, UK: Troubadour, 2013), 3–12.

150 [Bontempelli], "Dai nostri reparti," *Il Montello*, 20 September 1918, 6.

151 Isnenghi, *Giornali di trincea*, 107.

152 "'Sono orgoglioso di offrire alla Patria tutta la mia carne e tutto il mio cuore!,'" *Il Montello*, 1 October 1918, 6. See also "La Posta Militare," *Il Montello*, 15 October 1918, 3.

153 Cussù, "Una protesta di Cussù," *Il Montello*, 15 October 1918, 6.

154 *Roma Futurista*, 20 September 1918, 3. It stated: "CAPORETTO = Socialisti ufficiali + preti + donne piagnucolose + burocrazia." (CAPORETTO = Socialist officers + priests + whining women + bureaucracy.)

155 Settimelli, "Il futurismo e la donna. Il disprezzo della donna," *Roma Futurista*, 30 September 1918, 1 (emphasis in the original).

156 "Soldati!," *Il Montello*, November 1918, 3.

157 Roma Futurista [editorial team], "Italia vittoriosa, addosso alla Germania!," *Roma Futurista*, 10 November 1918, 1.

158 Settimelli, "Azione futurista di dopo-guerra," *Roma Futurista*, 10 November 1918, 2.

159 *L'Epoca* (Rome), 5 November 1918, in "Le nostre prime dimostrazioni a Roma," *Roma Futurista*, 10 November 1918, 3. See also extracts from *Il Messaggero* (4 November) and *Il Piccolo* (4 November) published on the same page.

160 Carli, in *L'Epoca* (Rome), 5 November 1918, in *Roma Futurista*, 10 November 1918, 3. This theme had already been present in the pages of *L'Italia Futurista*. An article by Orano, entitled "La Dalmazia è italiana, sarà italiana," was printed on the front page of *L'Italia Futurista* on 9 September 1917.

161 See for example, "Il saluto di F.T. Marinetti," *Fronte Interno* (Verona), 13 November 1918, Papers of FTM and BCM, GRI, Libroni, box 39, accession no. 920092; "Lettere di vittoriosi," *Corriere Mercantile* (Genoa), 15 November 1918, and "Una lettera di Marinetti" (addressed to Mussolini), *Il Popolo d'Italia* (Milan), 16 November 1918, both in Papers of FTM and BCM, GRI, Libroni, box 40, accession no. 920092. See also Marinetti to Conti, November 1918, in Marinetti and Conti, *Nei proiettori del futurismo*, 75; Marinetti to Pratella, 12 November 1918, in *FBP*, 66–7; Marinetti to Neri Nannetti, undated but November 1918, FPC, Fondo Nannetti, Corrispondenza SC 1/INS 1/ CAM D; and Marinetti to Contessa Jole Nerazzini, undated but November 1918, in Erminio Jacona, "'Gentile amica, dopo le giornate sublimi del vittorioso massacro al fronte …': Nove lettere di Filippo Tommaso Marinetti – dal fronte italiano (1915–1918) – alla Contessa Jole Nerazzini," *Archivi del Nuovo* 14–15 (2004): 5–19, here 7.

Epilogue

1 Marinetti to Cangiullo, 1 February 1919, in *FTM-FC*, 125.

2 Between 16 February and 12 October 1919 this document appeared in all but six of the thirty-four issues of *Roma Futurista* that were published during the period. After the issue of 12 October 1919 the document did not appear again. *Roma Futurista*'s last issue appeared on 16 May 1920. A document entitled "Che cos'è il futurismo?" written by Marinetti

had appeared in February 1910 in *Il futurismo: Supplemento alla rassegna internazionale "Poesia."* However, aside from the title, this document does not resemble the 1919 piece. There was no suggestion in 1910 of Futurism being divided into separate artistic and political branches. See Marinetti, "Che cos'è il futurismo?," in *F.T. Marinetti futurista: Inedite, pagine disperse, documenti e antologia critica,* ed. ES (Naples: Guida, 1977), 33–6.

3 Marinetti, Settimelli, and Carli, "Che cos'è il futurismo? Nozioni elementari," *Roma Futurista,* 16 February 1919, 4.

4 Ibid.

5 Berghaus, *Futurism and Politics,* 104–6.

6 Carli, "Associazione fra gli Arditi d'Italia," *Roma Futurista,* 10 December 1918, 2.

7 Berghaus, *Futurism and Politics,* 118

8 See an advertisement for *Grande Esposizione Nazionale Futurista,* Papers of FTM and BCM, GRI, Libroni, box 41, accession no. 920092.

9 Scholars have claimed that the exhibition took place in Florence in May 1919 (Crispolti, *Cataloghi di esposizioni,* 144); June 1919 (see Micol Forti et al., eds., *Armonie e diarmonie degli stati d'animo: Ginna futurista,* exhibition catalogue, Rome 12 March–10 May 2009, Florence 23 June–20 September 2009 [Rome: Gangemi, 2009], 155); or summer 1919 (Maurizio Scudiero and Anna Maria Ruta, eds., *Futurismo e Futuristi a Firenze,* exhibition catalogue, Florence 15 April–15 May 2011 [Messina: G. D'Anna, 2011], 16). The dates May and June are certainly incorrect because the Genoa leg of the exhibition did not conclude until the end of July. August 1919 also seems highly unlikely. Marinetti wrote to Dottori in August 1919 that the exhibition "verrà aperta a Firenze dopo le elezioni" (will be opened in Florence after the elections), which took place in November 1919. See letter reprinted in Cialfi and Pesola, *Umbria Futurista,* 35. In an article in *Roma Futurista* in January 1920 there is a reference to the exhibition in Milan and Genoa but no mention of an event in Florence. See Balla, Giuseppe Bottai, Gino Galli, and Enrico Rocca, "Programma a sorpresa pel 1920," *Roma Futurista,* 4 January 1920, 1. On the proposed Venice leg of the exhibition, see Marinetti to Soggetti, undated but July 1919, Soggetti Papers, GRI, box 1, folder 1, accession no. 860387: "L'esposizione a Venezia non ha potuto aver luogo causa lo sfasciamento del padiglione costruito al Lido dall'impresario Moretti" (the exhibition could not be held in Venice because of the destruction of the pavilion that had been built at the Lido by the producer Moretti).

10 The exhibition closed at the end of July. See Marinetti, 24 July 1919, in *FTMT,* 427: "Genova. Serata di chiusura dell'Esposizione" (Genoa. Closing

event for the Exhibition), and "La chiusura dell'esposizione futurista," *Corriere Mercantile* (Genoa), 25 July 1919, Papers of FTM and BCM, GRI, Libroni, box 39, accession no. 920092.

11 Marinetti, in *Grande Esposizione Nazionale Futurista*, exhibition catalogue, Milan, Genoa, Florence, March–May 1919 [dates printed on catalogue], 4, reprinted in Crispolti, *Cataloghi di esposizioni*, 144–8, here 144.

12 Marinetti, "Imbecilli!," *L'Italia Futurista*, 24 June 1917, 1 (emphasis in the original).

13 Giovanni Lista, "Gli anni dieci: Il dinamismo plastico," in *Futurismo 1909–2009*, ed. Lista and Ada Masoero, exhibition catalogue, Milan, 6 February–7 June 2009 (Milan: Skira, 2009), 83–180, here 179.

14 See letters between Carrà and Severini, March–May 1914, in Coen, *Futurismo 100*, 282–8.

15 Fabio Benzi, *Il futurismo* (Milan: Motta, 2008), 237.

16 Marinetti, in *Grande Esposizione Nazionale Futurista*, exhibition catalogue, 5, reprinted in Crispolti, *Cataloghi di esposizioni*, 144.

17 Marinetti, "L'esposizione nazionale futurista che si apre oggi al Cova. Pittori futuristi combattenti e teatro plastico," *Il Popolo d'Italia* (Milan), 21 March 1919, Papers of FTM and BCM, GRI, Libroni, box 41, accession no. 920092.

18 D.B., "Leonardo Dudreville e la pittura futurista," *Perseveranza* (Milan), 26 March 1919, Papers of FTM and BCM, GRI, Libroni, box 41, accession no. 920092.

19 "La mostra di pittura futurista inaugurata oggi a Milano. Futurismo + dopoguerra," *La Sera* (Milan), 22 March 1919, Papers of FTM and BCM, GRI, Libroni, box 41, accession no. 920092.

20 "Esposizione futurista," *Il Secolo* (Milan), 24 March 1919, Papers of FTM and BCM, GRI, Libroni, box 41, accession no. 920092.

21 "Alla mostra futurista di Milano," *Dinamo* (Rome), March 1919, 1.

22 Marinetti to Cangiullo, 6 April 1919, in *FTM-FC*, 129.

23 P. de G., "L'inaugurazione della mostra futurista," *Il Caffaro* (Genoa), 25 May 1919, Papers of FTM and BCM, GRI, Libroni, box 41, accession no. 920092.

24 "Alla mostra futurista," *La Sera* (Milan), 23 March 1919, Papers of FTM and BCM, GRI, Libroni, box 41, accession no. 920092.

25 "L'esposizione futurista di Milano," *Rivista di Milano*, 5 May 1919, Papers of FTM and BCM, GRI, Libroni, box 41, accession no. 920092.

26 Marinetti, in *Grande Esposizione Nazionale Futurista*, exhibition catalogue, 6, reprinted in Crispolti, *Cataloghi di esposizioni*, 144.

27 "La mostra di pittura futurista inaugurata oggi a Milano. Futurismo + dopoguerra," *La Sera* (Milan), 22 March 1919, Papers of FTM and BCM, GRI, Libroni, box 41, accession no. 920092.

28 "La prima Mostra Nazionale Futurista," *Le Arti* (Milan), undated but March–April 1919, Papers of FTM and BCM, GRI, Libroni, box 41, accession no. 920092.

29 Ibid.

30 Edgardo Rebizzi, "L'Esposizione futurista a Milano," *La Fiamma Verde* (Milan), 20 May 1919, Papers of FTM and BCM, GRI, Libroni, box 40, accession no. 920092.

31 "L'esposizione futurista di Milano," *Rivista di Milano*, 5 May 1919.

32 P. de G., "L'inaugurazione della mostra futurista," *Il Caffaro* (Genoa), 25 May 1919.

33 Ibid.

34 Ang., "La mostra futurista," *Il Lavoro* (Genoa), 25 May 1919, Papers of FTM and BCM, GRI, Libroni, box 41, accession no. 920092. See also Pratella to Alceo Toni, April 1919, in *CP*, 110: "Vidi Marinetti all'esposizione futurista ma non mi fu possibile avvicinarlo. La ressa e le discussioni che provocano la sua presenza nella sala […] lo rendono inavvicinabile." (I saw Marinetti at the Futurist exhibition but I wasn't able to get close to him. The crowd and the discussions that his presence causes in the exhibition hall […] make him unapproachable.)

35 Ang. "La mostra futurista," *Il Lavoro* (Genoa), 25 May 1919.

36 Ibid.

37 "L'esposizione futurista di Milano," *Rivista di Milano* (Milan), 5 May 1919.

38 Carlo Otto Guglielmino, "L'esposizione futurista," *Il Piccolo* (Genoa), 3 June 1919, Papers of FTM and BCM, GRI, Libroni, box 41, accession no. 920092.

39 Marinetti to Dottori, undated but August 1919, in Cialfi and Pesola, *Umbria Futurista*, 35.

40 Giuseppe Bottai (1895–1959), Futurist Political Party member. He volunteered for the war in 1915 and served first as a second lieutenant in the infantry. He served at the Carso in 1916 and 1917 and was present with the Fourth Army during the retreat at Caporetto. In March 1918 he became an ardito. He had no involvement with Futurism prior to December 1918. In May 1919 he became a contributor to *Roma Futurista* and later began to edit the journal. He was affiliated with the Futurists only until 1920, at which point he turned to the Fascist movement.

41 Bottai to Carli, 22 October 1919, in Gentile, *"La nostra sfida alle stelle,"* 100.

42 Berghaus, *Futurism and Politics*, 146.

43 Balla to Virgilio Marchi, 28 November 1919, in *Marinetti e i futuristi a Roma*, ed. Rossana Bossaglia, exhibition catalogue, Rome, 4 March–22 May 1993 (Milan: Fidia Edizioni d'Arte, 1993), 60.

44 Gino Galli (1883–1954), Futurist artist. Galli had some limited engagement with Futurism (through Balla) in the pre-war period, but his significance grew only in the post-war period. He exhibited at the *Grande Esposizione Nazionale Futurista* in 1919 and began to edit *Roma Futurista* in the same year.

45 Enrico Rocca (1895–1944), Futurist journalist. Rocca was not affiliated with Futurism until after the end of the First World War although his name appeared in the list of Futurist war-injured in the 30 October 1918 issue of *Roma Futurista*. He joined the Fasci di Combattimento in Rome, led by Mario Carli, in 1919, and in June of that year he became one of the editors of *Roma Futurista*, also contributing articles to *Dinamo*. He resigned as editor in January 1920, however, in disagreement with Marinetti over the decision to turn *Roma Futurista* away from political affairs. He continued to work as a journalist throughout the 1920s and 1930s, founding and editing *L'Impero*, with Settimelli and Carli. Persecuted as a Jew under the Fascist racial laws, he took his own life in 1944.

46 Marinetti, 22 December 1919, in *FTMT*, 464.

47 Balla, Bottai, Galli, and Rocca, "Programma a sorpresa pel 1920," *Roma Futurista*, 4 January 1920, 1.

48 Bottai to Carli, 2 February 1920, in Gentile, *"La nostra sfida alle stelle,"* 99.

49 Ibid.

50 Marinetti, "Onoranze nazionali a Marinetti e Congresso futurista," in *Marinetti e il futurismo* (1929), in *TIF*, 614.

51 Marinetti, "Futurismo e Fascismo" (1924), in *TIF*, 494. Such claims were disingenuous at best, as throughout the years of the Fascist regime Marinetti and the movement's leaders engaged in informal political activity and explicit pro-regime propaganda. See Ernest Ialongo, "Filippo Tommaso Marinetti: The Futurist as Fascist, 1929–37," *Journal of Modern Italian Studies* 18, no. 4 (2013): 393–418. The meaning of this parapolitical engagement is a hotly debated topic, identified by some as evidence of Marinetti's being a "fervent Fascist" (Ialongo, "Filippo Tommaso Marinetti," 393, using the term Mussolini used to describe him) and by others as "opportunism" designed to secure Futurism's survival within the apparatus of the Fascist state. See Berghaus, *Futurism and Politics*, 220.

Bibliography

Archival Sources

14–18: Documenti e immagini della grande guerra, maintained by the
Ministero per i Beni e delle Attività Culturali

Giornali di trincea. www.14-18.it/giornali-di-trincea

Archivio del '900. Museo d'arte móderna e contemporanea di Trento e Rove-
reto. Rovereto
Angelini, Nina e Marietta, Fondo, circa mid-twentieth century to 1942
Carli, Mario–Dessy, Mario, Fondi, circa 1889–1995
Carrà, Carlo, Fondo, 1912–1966
Depero, Fortunato, Fondo, 1894–1960
Malmerendi, Giannetto, Documenti, [no date range]

Archivio della parola, dell'immagine e della communicazione editoriale,
maintained by Università degli Studi di Milano
Reggi, Sergio, Collezione '900, http://apicesv3.noto.unimi.it/site/reggi

Beinecke Rare Book and Manuscript Library, Yale University, Connecticut
Marinetti, Filippo Tommaso, Papers, 1888–1983

Fondazione Museo Storico del Trentino, Trento
Commissione Centrale di Patronato dei Fuorusciti Adriatici e Trentini,
1915–1920

Fondazione Primo Conti, Fiesole
   Cangiullo, Francesco, Fondo, 1884–1977
   Meriano, Francesco, Fondo, 1912–1934
   Nannetti, Neri e Vieri, Fondo, 1915–1919
   Pratella, Francesco Balilla, Fondo, 1910–1956
   Settimelli, Emilio, Fondo, 1910–1940

Getty Research Institute, Los Angeles
   Balla, Giacomo, Letters to, circa 1917–circa 1918 (860388)
   Boccioni, Umberto, Papers, 1899–1986 (880380)
   Bontempelli, Massimo, Papers, 1865–1991 (910147)
   Folgore, Luciano, Papers, 1890–1966 (910141)
   Marinetti, Filippo Tommaso, Correspondence and Papers, 1886–1974 (850702)
   Marinetti, Filippo Tommaso, Student Notebooks and Other Papers,
   1891–1943 (890122)
   Marinetti, Filippo Tommaso, and Marinetti, Benedetta Cappa, Papers of,
   1902–1965 (920092)
   Rognoni, Angelo, Correspondence, 1914–1957 (850150)
   Soggetti, Gino, Papers, circa 1916–circa 1930 (860387)

Museo Storico Italiano della Guerra, Rovereto
   Volontari, Fondo, 1905–1940

Published Primary Sources

Annetta, Mari [Comtesse du Aubrun]. *Come si seducono gli uomini*. Rocca San
   Casciano, Italy: Cappelli, 1918.
Attendamento Bracciano IIa Artigliera, settembre-ottobre 1916. Rome: Stabilimento
   Litografico A. Sampaolesi, 1916.
Balla, Giacomo. *Scritti futuristi*. Edited by Giovanni Lista. Milan: Abscondita,
   2010.
Bellini, Dario, ed. *Con Boccioni a Dosso Casina: I testi e le immagini dei futuristi in
   battaglia*. Rovereto: Nicolodi, 2006.
Boccioni, Umberto. *Lettere futuriste*. Edited by Federica Rovati. Rovereto:
   Egon / Museo d'arte moderna e contemporanea di Trento e Rovereto, 2009.
– *Gli scritti editi e inediti*. Edited by Zeno Birolli. Milan: Feltrinelli, 1971.
Bono, Virginio Giacomo, ed. *Le vestali del futurismo*. Voghera, Italy: Edo
   Edizioni Oltrepò, 1991.

Buzzi, Paolo. *Futurismo: Scritti, carteggi, testimonianze.* Edited by Mario Morini. 4 vols. Milan: Palazzo Sormani, 1983.

Cangiullo, Francesco. *Le serate futuriste: Romanzo storico vissuto.* Milan: Ceschina, 1961.

Capello, Luigi. *Caporetto, perché? La 2a Armata e gli avvenimenti dell'ottobre 1917.* Turin: Einaudi, 1967.

Carli, Mario. *Noi Arditi.* Milan: Facchi, 1919.

Carli, Mario, and Filippo Tommaso Marinetti. *Lettere futuriste tra arte e politica.* Edited by Claudia Salaris. Rome: Officina Edizioni, 1989.

Carrà, Carlo. *La mia vita.* Edited by Massimo Carrà. Milan: SE, 1997.

Carrà, Carlo, and Giovanni Papini. *Il carteggio Carrà–Papini: Da "Lacerba" al tempo di "Valori Plastici."* Edited by Massimo Carrà. Milan: Skira, 2001.

Carrà, Carlo, and Ardengo Soffici. *Lettere 1913–1929.* Edited by Massimo Carrà and Vittorio Fagone. Milan: Feltrinelli, 1983.

Caruso, Luciano, ed. *Dossier futurista: Documenti (1910–1919).* 2 vols. Florence: SPES, 1995.

Coen, Ester, ed. *Futurismo 100: Illuminazioni; Avanguardie a confronto; Italia, Germania, Russia.* Exhibition catalogue, Rovereto, 17 January–7 June 2009. Milan: Electa, 2009.

Corra, Bruno. *Io ti amo: Romanzo dell'amore moderno.* Milan: Studio Editoriale Lombardo, 1918.

Depero, Fortunato. *Motorumorista, Futurista, Mimismagico, Astrattista Formidabile, Architetto e Poeta.* Milan: Edizioni del Naviglio, 1986.

Drudi Gambillo, Maria, and Teresa Fiori, eds. *Archivi del futurismo.* Vol. 2. Rome: De Luca, 1962.

Folgore Luciano, and Filippo Tommaso Marinetti. *Carteggio futurista.* Edited by Francesco Muzzioli. Rome: Officina Edizioni, 1987.

Govoni, Corrado. *Lettere a F.T. Marinetti.* Edited by Matilde Dillon Wanke. Milan: Scheiwiller, 1990.

Jacona, Erminio. "'Gentile amica, dopo le giornate sublimi del vittorioso massacro al fronte …': Nove lettere di Filippo Tommaso Marinetti – dal fronte italiano (1915–1918) – alla Contessa Jole Nerazzini." *Archivi del Nuovo* 14–15 (2004): 5–19.

Libreria Antiquaria Pontremoli. *Futurismo: Collezione Mughini.* Milan: Libreria Antiquaria Pontremoli, 2014.

Lista, Giovanni, ed. "Francesco Meriano parolibero futurista: Con carteggio inedito di Marinetti." *Sì & No* 4 (March 1975): 104–19.

Lombardo Radice, Giuseppe. *Nuovi saggi di propaganda pedagogica.* Turin: Paravia, 1922.

234 Bibliography

Lugaresi, Giovanni, ed. *Lettere ruggenti a F. Ballila Pratella*. Milan: Quaderni dell'Osservatore, 1969.

Marinetti, Filippo Tommaso. "36 pagine dimenticate e inedite del diario di guerra di F.T. Marinetti." Edited by Jean Pierre Andreoli de Villers. *Simultaneità* 1 (1997): 77–87.

– *L'aeroplano del papa: Romanzo profetico in versi liberi*. Milan: Edizioni futuriste di "Poesia," 1914.

– *L'alcova d'acciaio: Romanzo vissuto*. Milan: Vitagliano, 1921.

– *Le bataille de Tripoli (26 octobre 1911) vécue et chantée*. Milan: Edizioni futuriste di "Poesia," 1912.

– *Come si seducono le donne*. Florence: Vallecchi, 2003. First published 1917 by Edizioni da Centomila Copie.

– *Critical Writings*. Edited by Günter Berghaus. Translated by Doug Thompson. New York: Farrar, Strauss & Giroux, 2006.

– *F.T. Marinetti futurista: Inediti, pagine disperse, documenti e antologia critica*. Edited by ES. Naples: Guida, 1977.

– *La grande Milano tradizionale e futurista: Una sensibilità italiana nata in Egitto*. Edited by Luciano De Maria. Milan: Mondadori, 1969.

– *Le monoplan du pape: Roman politique en vers libres*. Paris: E. Sansot, 1912.

– "Quinte e scene della campagna del Battaglione Lombardo Volontari Ciclisti sul lago di Garda e sull'Altissimo." *La Gazzetta dello Sport* (Milan), 31 January 1916 and 7 February 1916. *Bolaffiarte* 79 (May 1978): 12–15.

– "Selections from the Unpublished Diaries of F.T. Marinetti." Edited by Lawrence Rainey and Laura Wittman. *Modernism/Modernity* 1, no. 3 (1994): 1–44.

– *Taccuini 1915–1921*. Edited by Alberto Bertoni. Bologna: Il Mulino, 1987.

– *Teatro*. Edited by Jeffrey T. Schnapp. 2 vols. Milan: Mondadori, 2004.

– *Teoria e invenzione futurista*. 6th ed. Edited by Luciano De Maria. Milan: Mondadori, 2005. First published 1968 by Mondadori.

Marinetti, Filippo Tommaso, and Francesco Cangiullo. *Lettere (1910–1943)*. Edited by Ernestina Pellegrini. Florence: Vallecchi, 1989.

Marinetti, Filippo Tommaso, and Primo Conti. *Nei proiettori del futurismo: Carteggio inedito 1917–1940*. Edited by Gabriel Cacho Millet. Palermo: Novecento, 2001.

Marinetti, Filippo Tommaso, and Bruno Corra. *L'isola dei baci: Romanzo erotico-sociale*. Milan: Studio Editoriale Lombardo, 1918.

Marinetti, Filippo Tommaso, and Aldo Palazzeschi. *Carteggio con un'appendice di altre lettere a Palazzeschi*. Edited by Paolo Prestigiacomo. Milan: Mondadori, 1978.

Miligi, Giuseppe, and Umberto Carpi, eds. *Prefuturismo e primo futurismo in Sicilia (1900–1918)*. Messina: Sicania, 1989.

Nicastro, Luciano. *La nostra salvezza: Lettere di guerra 1915–1918*. Florence: Libreria della Voce, 1918.

Pacini, Piero, ed. "Lettere e documenti." *Critica d'arte* 17, no. 111 (May–June 1970): 8–56.

Papini, Giovanni, and Ardengo Soffici. *Carteggio*. Edited by Mario Richter. Rome: Edizioni di storia e letteratura, 1991.

Pratella, Francesco Balilla. *Caro Pratella: Lettere scelte e commentate*. Edited by Gianfranco Maffina. Ravenna: Edizioni del Girasole, 1980.

– *Testamento: Prima edizione integrale*. Edited by Rosetta Berardi and Francesca Serra. Ravenna: Edizioni del Girasole, 2012.

Prezzolini, Giuseppe. "Il Servizio P." In *Tutta la guerra: Antologia del popolo italiano sul fronte e nel paese*, edited by Giuseppe Prezzolini, 451–75. Milan: Longanesi, 1968. First published 1918 by Bemporad.

– *Vittorio Veneto*. Rome: Edizioni della Volpe, 1920.

Rosai, Ottone. *Il libro di un teppista*. Florence: Vallecchi, 1919.

Rosai, Ottone, and Ardengo Soffici. *Carteggio 1914–1951*. Edited by Elena Pontiggia. Milan: Abscondita, 2010.

Russolo, Luigi. *L'arte dei rumori*. Milan: Edizioni futuriste di "Poesia," 1916.

Salaris, Claudia. *Luciano Folgore e le avanguardie: Con lettere e inediti futuristi*. Scandicci, Italy: La Nuova Italia, 1997.

Settimelli, Emilio. *Inchiesta sulla vita italiana*. Rocca San Casciano, Italy: Cappelli, 1919.

Steiner, Giuseppe. *La chitarra del fante*. Piacenza, Italy: V. Porta, 1920.

Secondary Sources

Adamson, Walter L. *Avant-Garde Florence: From Modernism to Fascism*. Cambridge, MA: Harvard University Press, 1993.

– "Fascinating Futurism: The Historiographical Politics of an Historical Avant-Garde." *Modern Italy* 13, no. 1 (2008): 69–85.

– *Embattled Avant-Gardes: Modernism's Resistance to Commodity Culture in Europe*. Berkeley: University of California Press, 2007.

– "The End of an Avant-Garde? Filippo Tommaso Marinetti and Futurism in World War 1 and Its Aftermath." In *The History of Futurism: Precursors, Protagonists, and Legacies*, edited by Geert Buelens, Harald Hendrix, and Monica Jansen, 299–318. Lanham MD: Lexington, 2012.

– "Futurism and Italian Intervention in World War 1." In *Italian Futurism*, edited by Vivien Greene, 175–7.

– "The Impact of World War 1 on Italian Political Culture." In *European Culture in the Great War: The Arts, Entertainment, and Propaganda, 1914–1918*,

236 Bibliography

edited by Avial Roshwald and Richard Stites, 308–29. Cambrïdge: Cambridge University Press, 1999.

Antonucci, Giovanni. *Cronache del teatro futurista*. Rome: Abete, 1975.

– *Lo spettacolo futurista in Italia*. Rome: Nuova Universale Studium, 1974.

Audoin-Rouzeau, Stéphane. *Men at War: National Sentiment and Trench Journalism in France during the First World War*. Translated by Helen McPhail. Providence, RI: Berg, 1992.

Bagatti, Fabrizio, Gloria Manghetti, and Silvia Porto. *Futurismo a Firenze 1910–1920*. Exhibition catalogue, Florence, 8 February–8 April 1984. Florence: Sansoni, 1984.

Baldissone, Giusi. *Filippo Tommaso Marinetti*. Milan: Mursia, 1986. Reprint 2009.

Bandini, Mirella. "Elementi protosurrealisti nei testi di Mario Carli, Bruno Corra e Maria Ginanni." In *"L'Italia Futurista,"* edited by Luciano Caruso, 15–18.

Bedeschi, Luisa. "Dal carteggio di Francesco Balilla Pratella." In *Note futuriste: L'archivio Francesco Balilla Pratella e il cenacolo artistico lughese*, edited by Orlando Piraccini and Daniele Serafini, 35–40. Bologna: Compositori, 2010.

Belardelli, Giovanni, Luciano Cafagna, Ernesto Galli della Loggia, and Giovanni Sabbatucci, eds. *Miti e storia dell'Italia unita*. Bologna: Il Mulino, 1999.

Belzer, Allison Scardino. *Women and the Great War: Femininity under Fire in Italy*. Basingstoke, UK: Palgrave Macmillan, 2010.

Ben-Ghiat, Ruth, Luciano Cafagna, Ernesto Galli della Loggia, Carl Ipsen, David I. Kertzer, and Mark Gilbert. "History as It Wasn't: The Myths of Italian Historiography." *Journal of Modern Italian Studies* 6, no. 3 (2001): 402–19.

Benzi, Fabio. *Il futurismo*. Milan: Motta, 2008.

Berghaus, Günter. *Futurism and Politics: Between Anarchist Rebellion and Fascist Reaction, 1909–1944*. Providence, RI: Berghahn, 1996.

– "The Futurist Political Party." In *The Invention of Politics in the European Avant-Garde (1906–1940)*, edited by Sascha Bru and Gunther Martens, 153–82. Amsterdam: Rodopi, 2006.

–, ed. *International Futurism in Arts and Literature*. Berlin: De Gruyter, 2000.

– *Italian Futurist Theatre, 1909–1944*. Oxford: Clarendon Press, 1998.

– Review of *Dramaturgy of Sound in the Avant-Garde and Postdramatic Theatre*, by Mladen Ovadija. *International Yearbook of Futurism Studies* (2015): 541–9.

– "Violence, War, Revolution: Marinetti's Concept of a Futurist Cleanser for the World." In *"A Century of Futurism,"* edited by Federico Luisetti and Luca Somigli, 23–43.

Berghaus, Günter, and Mario Verdone. "*Vita Futurista* and Early Futurist Cinema." In *International Futurism in Arts and Literature*, edited by Günter Berghaus, 398–421.

Bertilotti, Teresa. "Pratiche urbane, *entertainments* e rappresentazione della violenza." *Memoria e ricerca* 38 (2011): 41–55.

Bianchi, Bruna. "Delirio, smemoratezza e fuga: Il soldato e la patologia della paura." In *La Grande Guerra*, edited by Diego Leoni and Camillo Zadra, 73–104.

Biasini Selvaggi, Cesare. "Sintesi diacronica del futurismo veronese." In *Futurismi a Verona: Il gruppo futurista veronese U. Boccioni*, edited by Giorgio Cortenova and Cesare Biasini Selvaggi. Exhibition catalogue, Verona, 23 November 2002–30 March 2003. Milan: Skira, 2002.

Biblioteca di storia moderna e contemporanea. *Diverse guerre in una: La cultura italiana dell'interventismo*. Exhibition catalogue, Rome, 9 March–9 May 1987. Rome: Biblioteca di storia moderna e contemporanea, 1987.

Blum, Cinzia Sartini. *The Other Modernism: F.T. Marinetti's Futurist Fiction of Power*. Berkeley: University of California Press, 1986.

Boschiero, Nicoletta, ed. *La guerra che verrà non è la prima 1914–2014*. Exhibition catalogue, Rovereto, 4 October 2014–20 September 2015. Milan: Electa / Museo d'arte moderna e contemporanea di Trento e Rovereto, 2014.

Bossaglia, Rossana, ed. *Marinetti e i futuristi a Roma*. Exhibition catalogue, Rome, 4 March–22 May 1993. Milan: Fidia Edizioni d'Arte, 1993.

Bowler, Anne. "Politics as Art: Italian Futurism and Fascism." *Theory and Society* 20, no. 6 (1991): 763–94.

Bracco, Barbara. *La patria ferita: Il corpo dei soldati italiani e la Grande Guerra*. Florence: Giunti, 2012.

Braun, Emily. *Mario Sironi and Italian Modernism: Art and politics under Fascism*. Cambridge: Cambridge University Press, 2000.

Caffarena, Fabio. *Lettere dalla Grande Guerra: Scritture del quotidiano, monumenti della memoria, fonti per la storia; Il caso italiano*. Milan: Unicopli, 2005.

Calvesi, Maurizio. *Studi sul futurismo*. Vol. 1 of *Le due avanguardie*. Bari: Laterza, 1971. First published 1966 by Lerici.

Carli, Maddalena. "'Un movimento artistico crea un partito politico': Il Futurismo italiano tra avanguardismo e normalizzazione." *Memoria e Ricerca* 33 (2010): 15–28.

Caruso, Luciano, ed. "*L'Italia Futurista*": *Firenze 1916–1918*. Florence: SPES, 1992.

Cecchinato, Eva. "Sotto l'uniforme: I volontari nella Grande Guerra." In *La Grande Guerra*, vol. 1, edited by Mario Isnenghi and Daniele Ceschin, 176–86.

238 Bibliography

Cialfi, Domenico, and Antonella Pesola, eds. *Umbria Futurista 1912–1944.* Arrone, Italy: Thyrus, 2009.

Contarini, Silvia. *La femme futuriste: Mythes, modèles, et représentations de la femme dans la théorie e la littérature futuristes (1909–1919).* Paris: Presses universitaires de Paris 10, 2006.

Cork, Richard. *A Bitter Truth: Avant-Garde Art and the Great War.* New Haven, CT: Yale University Press in association with the Barbican Art Gallery, 1994.

Crispolti, Enrico, ed. *Cataloghi di esposizioni.* Rome: De Luca / Consiglio nazionale delle ricerche, 2010.

–, ed. *Ricostruzione futurista dell'universo.* Exhibition catalogue, Turin, June–October 1980. Turin: Museo civico di Torino, 1980.

– *Storia e critica del futurismo.* 2nd ed. Bari: Laterza, 1987.

– "Zang Tumb Tumb: I futuristi vanno alla Guerra; Giochi, burle e travestimenti dei futuristi del battaglione ciclisti." *Bolaffiarte* 79 (May 1978): 10–11.

Critelli, Maria Pia. "L'alpestre faccia dell'eroe: La montagna tra simbolo e panorama." In *Der Erste Weltkrieg im Alpenraum: Erfahrung, Deutung, Erinnerung / La Grande Guerra nell'arco alpino: Esperienze e memoria*, edited by Hermann J. W. Kuprian, and Oswald Überegger, 61–72. Innsbruck: Universitätsverlag Wagner, 2006.

De Paulis-Dalembert, Maria Pia. "F.T. Marinetti: La réecriture de l'imaginaire symboliste et futuriste entre le français et l'italien." *Chroniques italiennes* 12 (2007): 1–30.

Daly, Selena. "Constructing the Futurist Wartime Hero: Futurism and the Public, 1915–1919." In "The Great War and the Modernist Imagination," edited by Luca Somigli and Simona Storchi, special issue, *Annali d'Italianistica* 33 (2015): 205–21.

– "Ennio Valentinelli: A Forgotten Futurist." *Modern Language Notes* 34, no. 2 (2016): 103–15.

– "'The Futurist Mountains': F.T. Marinetti's Experiences of Mountain Combat during the First World War." *Modern Italy* 18, no. 4 (2013): 323–38.

– "Futurist War Noises: Coping with the Sounds of the First World War." In "Italian Sound," edited by Deanna Shemek and Arielle Saiber, special issue, *California Italian Studies* 4, no. 1 (2014): 1–16.

Dashwood, Julie. "Futurism and Fascism." *Italian Studies* 27, no. 1 (1972): 91–103.

De Felice, Renzo, ed. *Futurismo, cultura e politica.* Turin: Fondazione Giovanni Agnelli, 1988.

– *Mussolini il rivoluzionario 1883–1920.* Vol. 1 of *Mussolini.* Turin: Einaudi, 1965.

– "Ordine pubblico e orientamenti delle masse popolari italiane nella prima metà del 1917." *Rivista storica del socialismo* (September–December 1963): 467–504.

De Maria, Luciano. Introduction to *Teoria e invenzione futurista*, by Filippo Tommaso Marinetti, xxix–c. 6th ed. Milan: Mondadori, 2005.

Del Puppo, Alessandro. *"Lacerba" 1913–1915*. Bergamo: Lubrina, 2000.

Della Terza, Dante. "F.T. Marinetti e i futuristi fiorentini: L'ipotesi politico-letterario di *Lacerba*." *Italica* 61, no. 2 (1984): 147–59.

D'Orsi, Angelo. *L'ideologia politica del futurismo*. Turin: Il Segnalibro, 1992.

Drucker, Johanna. *The Visible Word: Experimental Typography and Modernist Art (1909–1923)*. Chicago: University of Chicago Press, 1994.

Du Pont, Koenraad. "The 'Authenticity Effect': A Propaganda Tool in Trench Newspapers." In *The Great War in Italy: Representation and Interpretation*, edited by Patrizia Piredda, 3–12. Leicester, UK: Troubador, 2013.

Eruli, Brunella. *Dal futurismo alla patafisica: Percorsi dell'avanguardia*. Ospedaletto, Italy: Pacini, 1994.

Foot, John. *Italy's Divided Memory*. New York: Palgrave Macmillan, 2009.

Forgacs, David. *Italian Culture in the Industrial Era, 1880–1980: Cultural Industries, Politics and the Public*. Manchester: Manchester University Press, 1990.

Forti, Micol, Lucia Collarile, and Mariastella Margozzi, eds. *Armonie e diarmonie degli stati d'animo: Ginna futurista*. Exhibition catalogue, Rome, 12 March–10 May 2009; Florence, 23 June–20 September 2009. Rome: Gangemi, 2009.

Gatti, Gian Luigi. *Dopo Caporetto: Gli ufficiali P nella Grande Guerra; Propaganda, assistenza, vigilanza*. Gorizia, Italy: LEG, 2000.

Gentile, Emilio. "Il futurismo e la politica: Dal nazionalismo modernista al fascismo (1909–1920)." In *Futurismo, cultura e politica*, edited by Renzo De Felice, 105–60. Turin: Fondazione Giovanni Agnelli, 1988.

– *"La nostra sfida alle stelle": Futuristi in politica*. Rome: Laterza, 2009.

– *Le origini dell'ideologia fascista 1918–1925*. Bari: Laterza, 1978.

Gervasoni, Marco. "La nascita della retorica interventista: Dalla 'Plebe' alla 'Patria.'" In *Combattere a Milano 1915–1918: Il corpo e la guerra nella capitale del fronte interno*, edited by Barbara Bracco, 7–13. Milan: Il Ponte, 2005.

Gibelli, Antonio. *La grande guerra degli italiani*. Milan: Sansoni, 1998.

– *L'officina della guerra: La Grande Guerra e le trasformazioni del mondo mentale*. 3rd ed. Turin: Bollati Boringhieri, 2007.

Giocondi, Michele. *Lettori in camicia nera: Narrativa di successo nell'Italia fascista*. Messina: G. D'Anna, 1978.

Godoli, Ezio, ed. *Dizionario del futurismo*. 2 vols. Florence: Vallecchi, 2004.

Gooch, John. *The Italian Army and the First World War*. Cambridge: Cambridge University Press, 2014.

Greene, Vivien, ed. *Italian Futurism, 1909–1944: Reconstructing the Universe*. Exhibition catalogue, New York, 21 February–1 September 2014. New York: Guggenheim Museum Publications, 2014.

Habeck, Mary R. "Technology in the First World War: The View from Below." In *The Great War and the Twentieth Century*, edited by Jay Winter, Geoffrey Parker, and Mary R. Habeck, 99–131. New Haven, CT: Yale University Press, 2000.

Hanna, Martha. "A Republic of Letters: The Epistolary Tradition in France during World War 1." *American Historical Review* 108, no. 5 (2003): 1338–61.

Härmänmaa, Marja. "The Dark Side of Futurism: Marinetti and War." In *Back to the Futurists: The Avant-Garde and Its Legacy*, edited by Elza Adamowicz and Simona Storchi, 255–71. Manchester: Manchester University Press, 2013.

– "Futurism and Nature: The Death of the Great Pan?" In *Futurism and the Technological Imagination*, edited by Günter Berghaus, 337–60. Amsterdam: Rodopi, 2009.

Heyriès, Hubert. "I volontari italiani in Francia durante la Grande Guerra". In *Volontari italiani nella Grande Guerra*, edited by Fabrizio Rasera and Camillo Zadra, 81–96.

Horne, John. "Soldiers, Civilians, and the Warfare of Attrition: Representations of Combat in France, 1914–18." In *Authority, Identity, and the Social History of the Great War*, edited by Frans Coetzee and Marilyn Shevin-Coetzee, 223–49. Providence, RI: Berghahn, 1995.

Ialongo, Ernest. "Filippo Tommaso Marinetti: The Futurist as Fascist, 1929–37." *Journal of Modern Italian Studies* 18, no. 4 (2013): 393–418.

Innamorati, Isabella. "Un 'manifesto' fatto d'immagini." In *"L'Italia Futurista,"* edited by Luciano Caruso, 31–6.

Isnenghi, Mario. *Giornali di trincea (1915–1918)*. Turin: Einaudi, 1977.

– *L'Italia in piazza: I luoghi della vita pubblica dal 1848 ai giorni nostri*. Bologna: Il Mulino, 2004. First published 1994 by Mondadori.

– *Il mito della Grande Guerra da Marinetti a Malaparte*. 6th ed. Bologna: Il Mulino, 2007. First published 1969 by Laterza.

Isnenghi, Mario, and Daniele Ceschin, eds. *La Grande Guerra*. 2 vols. Turin: UTET, 2008.

Isnenghi, Mario, and Giorgio Rochat. *La Grande Guerra 1914–1918*. Bologna: Il Mulino, 2008.

Keller, Tait. "The Mountains Roar: The Alps during the Great War." *Environmental History* 14, no. 2 (2009): 252–74.

Kern, Stephen. *The Culture of Time and Space, 1880–1918*. 2nd ed. Cambridge, MA: Harvard University Press, 2003.

Kramer, Alan. *Dynamic of Destruction: Culture and Mass Killing in the First World War*. Oxford: Oxford University Press, 2007.

Labanca, Nicola. *Caporetto: Storia di una disfatta*. Florence: Giunti, 1997.

– "The Italian Front." In *The Cambridge History of the First World War*, edited by Jay Winter and Editorial Committee of the International Research Centre of the Historial de le Grande Guerre, vol. 1, 266–96. Cambridge: Cambridge University Press, 2014.

– "Trincea-trincee." In *La Grande Guerra*, vol. 2, edited by Mario Isnenghi and Daniele Ceschin, 620–9.

– "Zona di Guerra." In *La Grande Guerra*, vol. 2, edited by Isnenghi and Ceschin, 606–19.

Landis, Linda. "Futurists at War." In *The Futurist Imagination: Word and Image in Italian Futurist Painting, Drawing, Collage, and Free-Word Poetry*, edited by Ann Coffin Hanson, 60–75. Exhibition catalogue, New Haven, 13 April–26 June 1983. New Haven, CT: The Gallery, 1983.

Leed, Eric. *No Man's Land: Combat and Identity in World War 1*. Cambridge: Cambridge University Press, 1979.

Leoni, Diego. "Guerra di montagna / Gebirgskrieg." In *La prima guerra mondiale*, edited by Stéphane Audoin-Rouzeau and Jean-Jacques Becker, Italian edition edited by Antonio Gibelli, vol. 1, 237–46. Turin: Einaudi, 2007.

Leoni, Diego, and Camillo Zadra, eds. *La Grande Guerra: Esperienza, memoria, immagini*. Bologna: Il Mulino, 1986.

Libardi, Massimo, Fernando Orlandi, and Maurizio Scudicro. *Qualcosa di immane: L'arte e la Grande Guerra*. Scurelle, Italy: Silvy, 2012.

Lista, Giovanni. "Gli anni dieci: Il dinamismo plastico." In *Futurismo 1909–2009*, edited by Giovanni Lista and Ada Masoero, 83–180. Exhibition catalogue, Milan, 6 February–7 June 2009. Milan: Skira, 2009.

– *Arte e politica: Il futurismo di sinistra in Italia*. Milan: Multhipla, 1980.

– *Les futuristes*. Paris: H. Veyrier, 1988.

Luisetti, Federico, and Luca Somigli, eds. "A Century of Futurism, 1909–2009." Special issue, *Annali d'Italianistica* 27 (2009).

Lyons, Martin. "French Soldiers and Their Correspondence: Towards a History of Writing Practice in the First World War." *French History* 17, no. 1 (2003): 79–95.

Marchioni, Nadia. *La Grande Guerra degli artisti: Propaganda e iconografia bellica in Italia negli anni della prima guerra mondiale*. Florence: Pagliai Polistampa, 2005.

242   Bibliography

Martin, Marianne W. *Futurist Art and Theory, 1909–1915*. New York: Hacker Art Books, 1978. First published 1968 by Clarendon Press.

Martire, Anthony. "Il soggetto mutilato del futurismo: F.T. Marinetti e la costruzione dell'italiano futurista nel primo dopoguerra." *Memoria e Ricerca* 38 (2011): 99–110.

Melograni, Piero. *La storia politica della Grande Guerra 1915–1918*. Bari: Laterza, 1969.

Meyer, Jessica. *Men of War: Masculinity and the First World War in Britain*. Basingstoke, UK: Palgrave Macmillan, 2009.

Mondini, Marco. *Alpini: Parole e immagini di un mito guerriero*. Bari: Laterza, 2008.

– "The Construction of a Masculine Warrior Ideal in the Italian Narratives of the First World War, 1915–18." *Contemporary European History* 23, no. 3 (2014): 307–27.

– *La guerra italiana: Partire, raccontare, tornare 1914–18*. Bologna: Il Mulino, 2014.

Nazzaro, Gian Battista. *Futurismo e politica*. Naples: J.N. Editore, 1987.

Nelson, Robert. *German Soldier Newspapers of the First World War*. Cambridge: Cambridge University Press, 2011.

Nobili Vitelleschi, Giovanni. "The Representation of the Great War in Italian Cinema." In *The First World War and Popular Cinema: 1914 to the Present*, edited by Michael Paris, 162–71. New Brunswick, NJ: Rutgers University Press, 2000.

O'Brien, Paul. *Mussolini in the First World War: The Journalist, the Soldier, the Fascist*. Oxford: Berg, 2005.

Ortaggi, Simonetta. "Italian Women during the Great War." In *Evidence, History and the Great War*, edited by Gail Braybon, 216–38. New York: Berghahn, 2003.

Papini, Maria Carla. Introduction to *"L'Italia Futurista" (1916–1918)*, edited by Maria Carla Papini, 31–55. Rome: Edizioni dell'Ateneo e Bizzarri, 1977.

Paulicelli, Eugenia. "Fashion and Futurism: Performing Dress." In "A Century of Futurism," edited by Federico Luisetti and Luca Somigli, 187–207.

Pirocchi, Angelo L. *Italian Arditi: Elite Assault Troops, 1917–20*. Oxford: Osprey, 2004.

Poggi, Christine. "Folla/Follia: Futurism and the Crowd." *Critical Inquiry* 28, no. 3 (2002): 709–48.

– *In Defiance of Painting: Cubism, Futurism and the Invention of Collage*. New Haven, CT: Yale University Press, 1992.

– *Inventing Futurism: The Art and Politics of Artificial Optimism*. Princeton: Princeton University Press, 2009.

Procacci, Giovanna. *Soldati e prigionieri italiani nella grande guerra: Con una raccolta di lettere inedite*. Turin: Bollati Boringhieri, 2000. First published 1993 by Riuniti.

Quercioli, Alessio. "'Italiani fuori d'Italia': I volontari trentini nell'esercito italiano 1915–1918." In *Volontari italiani nella Grande Guerra*, edited by Fabrizio Rasera and Camillo Zadra, 201–14.

Ragazzi, Franco. *Marinetti: Futurismo in Liguria*. Genoa: De Ferrari, 2006.

Rainey, Lawrence. "Introduction: F.T. Marinetti and the Development of Futurism." In *Futurism: An Anthology*, edited by Lawrence Rainey, Christine Poggi, and Laura Wittman, 1–39. New Haven, CT: Yale University Press, 2009.

Rasera, Fabrizio, and Camillo Zadra, eds. *Volontari italiani nella Grande Guerra*. Rovereto: Museo della Guerra, 2008.

Re, Lucia. "Futurism, Seduction, and the Strange Sublimity of War." *Italian Studies* 59, no. 1 (2004): 83–111.

– "Maria Ginanni vs. F.T. Marinetti: Women, Speed, and War in Futurist Italy." In "A Century of Futurism," edited by Federico Luisetti and Luca Somigli, 103–24.

Roberts, David D. "Croce and Beyond: Italian Intellectuals and the First World War." *International History Review* 3, no. 2 (1981): 201–35.

Rochat, Giorgio. *Gli arditi della Grande Guerra: Origini, battaglie e miti*. Gorizia, Italy: LEG, 2006. First published 1981 by Feltrinelli.

– "The Italian Front, 1915–18." In *A Companion to World War 1*, edited by John Horne, translated by Paul O'Brien, 82–96. Chichester, UK: Wiley-Blackwell, 2012.

Salaris, Claudia. "Le donne futuriste nel periodo tra guerra e dopoguerra." In *La Grande Guerra*, edited by Diego Leoni and Camillo Zadra, 291–306.

– *Filippo Tommaso Marinetti*. Scandicci, Italy: La Nuova Italia, 1988.

– "The Invention of the Programmatic Avant Garde." In *Italian Futurism*, edited by Vivien Greene, 22–49.

– *Marinetti: Arte e vita futurista*. Rome: Editore Riuniti, 1997.

– *Marinetti editore*. Bologna: Il Mulino, 1990.

– *Storia del futurismo: Libri, giornali, manifesti*. Rome: Riuniti, 1985.

Sansone, Luigi, ed. *F.T. Marinetti = Futurismo*. Exhibition catalogue, Milan, 12 February–7 June 2009. Milan: Federico Motta, 2009.

– "F.T. Marinetti emblema del futurismo." In *F.T. Marinetti = Futurismo*, edited by Luigi Sansone, 19–51.

– *Futuristi a Dosso Casina*. Exhibition catalogue, Riva del Garda, 12 July–2 November 2008. Milan: Mazzotta, 2008.

Scarpellini, Emanuela. "Teatro e Guerra." In *Milano in guerra 1914–1918: Opinione pubblica e immagini delle nazioni nel primo conflitto mondiale*, edited by Alceo Riosa, 153–79. Milan: Unicopli, 1997.

Schiavo, Alberto. *Futurismo e Fascismo*. Rome: Giovanni Volpe, 1981.

Schnapp, Jeffrey T. "On *Zang Tumb Tuuum*." In *Italian Futurism*, edited by Vivien Greene, 156–8.

Scudiero, Maurizio. "Ennio Valentinelli." In *Dizionario del futurismo*, edited by Ezio Godoli, vol. 2, 1202. Florence: Vallecchi, 2004.

Scudiero, Maurizio, and Anna Maria Ruta, eds. *Futurismo e Futuristi a Firenze*. Exhibition catalogue, Florence, 15 April–15 May 2011. Messina: G. D'Anna, 2011.

Scudiero, Maurizio, Enrico Sturani, Enrico Crispolti, and Tullio Crali, eds. *Futurismi postali: Balla, Depero e la comunicazione postale futurista*. Exhibition catalogue, Rovereto, 11 April–18 May 1986; Grado, 31 May–31 August 1986. Rovereto: Longo, 1986.

Sica, Paola. "Regenerating Life and Art: Futurism, Florentine Women, Irma Valeria." In "A Century of Futurism," edited by Federico Luisetti and Luca Somigli, 175–85.

Somigli, Luca. "Past-Loving Florence and the Temptations of Futurism." In *The Oxford Critical and Cultural History of Modernist Magazines*, edited by Peter Brooker, Sascha Bru, Andrew Thacker, and Christian Weiskorp, vol. 3, *Europe, 1880–1940*, 469–90. Oxford: Oxford University Press, 2013.

Sorlin, Pierre. *Italian National Cinema, 1896–1996*. London: Routledge, 1996. Reprint 2005.

Tisdall, Caroline, and Angelo Bozzolla. *Futurism*. London: Thames & Hudson, 1977. Reprint 2003.

Todero, Fabio. "Alpini, guerra in montagna e letteratura: La nascita di un mito." In *Una trincea chiamata Dolomiti 1915–1917: Una guerra, due trinee / Ein Krieg zwei Schützengräben*, edited by Willibald Rosner and Emilio Franzina, 81–90. Udine: Paolo Gaspari, 2003.

Tournès, Ludovic. "The Landscape of Sound in the Nineteenth and Twentieth Centuries [review article]." *Contemporary European History* 13 (2004): 493–504.

Van Kalmthout, Ton. "Futurism in the Netherlands, 1909–1940." *International Yearbook of Futurism Studies* (2014): 165–201.

Various authors. *L'Arena: Il giornale di Verona; Centoventicinquesimo anniversario*. Verona: Athesis, 1991.

Verdone, Mario. *Il Futurismo*. Rome: Newton & Compton, 2003.

Vigezzi, Brunello. *Da Giolitti a Salandra*. Florence: Vallecchi, 1969.

Vinall, Shirley. "Marinetti, Soffici, and French Literature." In *International Futurism in Arts and Literature*, edited by Günter Berghaus, 15–38.

Watkins, Glenn. *Proof through the Night: Music and the Great War*. Berkeley: University of California Press, 2003.

Watson, Alexander. *Enduring the Great War: Combat, Morale, and Collapse in the German and British Armies, 1914–1918*. Cambridge: Cambridge University Press, 2008.

Wedekind, Michael, and Claudio Ambrosi, eds. *Alla conquista dell'immaginario: L'alpinismo come proiezione di modelli culturali e sociali borghesi tra Otto e Novecento*. Treviso: Edizioni Antilia, 2007.

White, John J. "Iconic and Indexical Elements in Italian Futurist Poetry: F.T. Marinetti's 'Words in Freedom.'" In *Signergy*, edited by Jac Conradie, Ronél Johl, Marthinus Beukes, Olga Fischer, and Christina Ljungberg, 129–56. Amsterdam: John Benjamins, 2010.

Wilcox, Vanda. "Encountering Italy: Military Service and National Identity during the First World War." *Bulletin of Italian Politics* 3, no. 2 (2011): 283–302.

– "'Weeping Tears of Blood': Exploring Italian Soldiers' Emotions in the First World War." *Modern Italy* 17, no. 2 (2012): 171–84.

Winter, Jay. "The Practice of Metropolitan Life in Wartime." In *Capital Cities at War: Paris, London, Berlin, 1914–1919*, edited by Jay Winter and Jean-Louis Robert, vol. 2, 1–19. Cambridge: Cambridge University Press, 2007.

Wohl, Richard. *The Generation of 1914*. Cambridge, MA: Harvard University Press, 1979.

Index

Page numbers with (f) indicate figures.